D0907137

THE
ISRAELI
SOLUTION

THE
ISRAELI
SOLUTION

A ONE-STATE PLAN FOR PEACE IN
THE MIDDLE EAST

CAROLINE B. GLICK

CROWN
FORUM
NEW YORK

Published in the United States by Crown Forum, an imprint of the
Crown Publishing Group, a division of Random House LLC,
a Penguin Random House Company, New York.
www.crownpublishing.com

CROWN FORUM with colophon is a registered trademark of
Random House LLC.

Library of Congress Cataloging-in-Publication Data
Glick, Caroline B.
The Israeli solution : a one-state plan for peace in the Middle East / by
Caroline Glick.—First Edition.
    pages cm
1. Arab-Israeli conflict—Peace. 2. Arab-Israeli conflict—Territorial questions.
3. Arab-Israeli conflict—Occupied territories. 4. West Bank—International
status. 5. Israel—Boundaries. I. Title.
DS119.7.G584 2014
956.05'3—dc23
2013032207

ISBN 978-0-385-34806-5
eBook ISBN 978-0-385-34807-2

Printed in the United States of America

Book design by Lauren Dong
Jacket design by Jessie Sayward Bright
Jacket photograph by Getty Images

10 9 8 7 6 5 4

First Edition

To my parents
Gerald (of blessed memory) and Sharon Glick (may she live to 120).
Thank you for my good life.

CONTENTS

Preface ix

PART I: THE MIDDLE EAST'S BELOVED CHIMERA

Chapter 1: A BIPARTISAN PIPE DREAM 3

Chapter 2:   CLINTON'S LEGACY OF BLIND FAITH 15

Chapter 3: HAJ AMIN EL-HUSSEINI AND THE FORGOTTEN LESSONS OF THE BRITISH MANDATE FOR PALESTINE, 1917–1948 24

Chapter 4: YASSIR ARAFAT: THE WORLD'S FAVORITE TERRORIST 49

Chapter 5: PHONY REFORMERS AND TOTALITARIAN DEMOCRATS 67

Chapter 6: DUMBING DOWN U.S. FOREIGN POLICY 85

PART II: THE ISRAELI ONE-STATE PLAN

Chapter 7: INTRODUCING THE PLAN 109

Chapter 8: THE DEMOGRAPHIC TIME BOMB IS A DUD 122

Chapter 9: A RECORD OF SUCCESS 136

Chapter 10: WELCOME TO PALESTINE 144

Chapter 11: WELCOME TO ISRAEL 155

Chapter 12: THE LEGITIMATE SOVEREIGN, NOT AN OCCUPYING POWER 164

Chapter 13: THE INDIGENOUS PEOPLE, NOT COLONIAL
USURPERS 179

PART III: PROBABLE FALLOUT

Chapter 14: LIKELY PALESTINIAN RESPONSES 195

Chapter 15: LIKELY REGIONAL RESPONSES 205

Chapter 16: LIKELY EUROPEAN RESPONSES 221

Chapter 17: DOES THE ISRAELI ONE-STATE PLAN
MAKE SENSE FOR ISRAEL? 235

Chapter 18: AMERICA, ISRAEL, AND THE ONE-STATE
PLAN 246

Acknowledgments 261
Bibliography 263
Notes 267
Index 313

PREFACE

Over the past generation, politics in America has become a zero-sum game, with conservatives and liberals moving farther and farther apart. On matters from the economy to social issues to national security and foreign policy, it has become harder, and sometimes impossible, to find common ground between their views.

In this polarized environment, one American policy stands out for its unique ability to attract supporters from both sides of the ideological divide. That policy relates to how the United States should deal with the Arab-Israeli conflict.

From left to right, among both Democrats and Republicans, the reigning consensus is that the United States must seek to resolve the Arab world's conflict with Israel generally—and the Palestinians' conflict with Israel in particular—by implementing the so-called two-state solution.

Establishing a Palestinian state, so the thinking goes, would be a panacea for all the region's ills. It would end the Arab world's conflict with Israel, because the reason the Arab world is anti-Israel is that there is no Palestinian state. It would also nearly erase the Arab world's anti-Americanism, because the reason the Arabs—and the larger Muslim world—are anti-American is that the United States supports Israel even though there is no Palestinian state. Based on this thought chain, most American policy makers across the ideological spectrum share the view that the establishment of a Palestinian state west of the Jordan River would remove the principal cause of the violent extremism that afflicts the Arab and the larger Islamic world.[1]

Ironically, the two-state solution is among the most irrational, unsuccessful policies the United States has ever adopted. For the past ninety years, the two-state solution has been tried more than a dozen times, and every time it has failed, abysmally. Between 1970 and 2013, the United States presented nine different peace plans for Israel and the Palestinians, all based on the two-state solution—and for the past twenty years, the two-state solution has been the centerpiece of U.S. Middle East policy. But despite this laser focus, American efforts to implement the two-state solution have all been dismal failures. Moreover, these abortive efforts have weakened the U.S. position in the Middle East: with each new attempt at achieving a two-state peace deal, the Middle East has become less stable, more violent, more radicalized, and more inimical to American values and interests.

There are two main reasons for this weakening effect. First, the repeated failures make the United States look impotent. Washington's failure to impose its will on far less powerful nations in the region makes it appear weak to the Muslim world and so decreases respect for American power among Muslim societies.

Second and more important, the mistaken assumptions that fuel U.S. policy makers' support for the two-state solution are the same ones that cloud their thinking and decision making about the Middle East at large. The two-state solution treats the Arabs and the broader Muslim world as objects to be acted upon rather than as actors whose actions, beliefs, and choices determine their fates. The policy assumes that only Israel and the United States are actors on the ground and that both are at fault for the conflict: Israel because it refuses to surrender to all the Palestinians' demands, and the United States because it has failed to force Israel to surrender to all the Palestinians' demands.

This overlooking of the rest of the Arab world, which stands at the heart of the two-state solution, is the core reason that U.S. policies in the region have been self-defeating ever since it began promoting that policy paradigm.

In Iraq and Afghanistan, for example, the Bush and Obama administrations failed to acknowledge or act on information that proved Iran was playing a leading role in fueling the insurgencies. Iran and Syria aided both Shi'ite and Sunni insurgents in Iraq by supplying weapons and manpower.[2] And in Afghanistan, Iran aided Al Qaeda and the Taliban in the same way. To a significant degree, America's refusal to respond to

Iran's aggression was caused by its fundamental assumption that Iran—like the rest of the Muslim world—was not motivated chiefly by internal impulses, such as ideology, nor by its perception of its own national interests, but from extraneous forces—specifically, Israeli and American actions. The United States doesn't need to act on Iranian direct aggression, or even against Iran's illicit nuclear weapons program, because once it succeeds in persuading Israel to give away the requisite lands to the Palestinians, and once it provides Iran with other concessions, much of the threat emanating from Iran will be neutralized.

Relatedly, both the Bush and Obama administrations engaged in negotiations with the Taliban, believing that the Taliban's jihadist worldview was not inherently hostile to American interests and values but was based on limited interests that could be appeased through negotiations. The Taliban openly hate America and all nonradical Islamic societies, and they reject democratic values like freedom for women and freedom of religion. Nonetheless U.S. leaders chose to believe that the Taliban's hatred of America was motivated more by U.S. actions than by their own inherently anti-American ideology. Washington has taken the same approach in its dealings with Syria, Hezbollah, Saudi Arabia, and the Muslim Brotherhood.

In all cases, America's embrace of the two-state solution as the centerpiece of its regional policy is the key reason that American policy makers insist that the actions, stated intentions, and ideologies of all regional actors aside from those of Israel are irrelevant. Regional peace can be established only after Israel surrenders to all the Palestinians' demands. Nothing anyone else—including the Taliban and Iran—does matters. All else can be set aside. All else can be explained away. All else can be appeased. Only America and Israel are responsible for creating and solving the problems of the region.

Despite the debilitating impact that the two-state solution has had on American strategic thinking and actions, any time a prominent policy maker or politician points out the policy's obvious futility, he is immediately castigated as a flame-throwing extremist.

Take the case of former Speaker of the House of Representatives

Newt Gingrich. During the 2011 Republican presidential primary debates, Gingrich mentioned the plain fact that the Palestinians are an "invented people" and that they indoctrinate their children to hate Jews, to perceive Jews as subhuman, and to seek their annihilation. For his statements, Gingrich was assaulted by Democrats and his fellow Republicans alike.[3]

Although conservative and liberal pundits piled criticism on him, all Gingrich had done was share readily available information.[4] Nearly every day a Palestinian leader announces that the Palestinians will not make peace with Israel under any circumstances. These statements are part of the public record, and all are published to great approval in the Arabic media.[5]

Palestinian children regularly appear on PA-controlled television children's programs, calling for the annihilation of Israel and demonizing Jews as subhuman. Summer camps are named after terrorists.[6] During her service as a U.S. senator, Hillary Clinton held multiple hearings on the Palestinian Authority's use of school textbooks to indoctrinate children to become terrorists and seek the destruction of Israel.[7]

In the face of such bad faith from the Palestinians, Gingrich didn't suggest abandoning the two-state formula—but he should have. Such a suggestion is well past due.

The two-state solution hasn't helped America win any friends, either in the region or in the world. No previously hostile Arab state has improved its relations with the United States due to its adoption of the two-state formula. In fact, America was better respected in the region before 1993, when Washington made the two-state paradigm the centerpiece of its Middle East policy. Even worse, America's embrace of the two-state solution has weakened its regional allies and empowered forces and regimes that are inimical to its interests.

The time has come for American policy makers to reconsider their devotion to the two-state formula and consider an alternative policy that makes sense both for the United States and for the Middle East.

This book lays out just such a policy. I call it "the Israeli one-state plan."

The Israeli one-state plan entails the application of Israeli law—and through it, Israeli sovereignty—over the west bank of the Jordan River:

the area that, from biblical times through the 1950s, was known to the world as Judea and Samaria. In Israel, Judea and Samaria remain the terms used to refer to the territory, and they are the names I use in the following pages.

Except during periods when they were physically barred from doing so—most recently during the Jordanian occupation of these areas from 1949 to 1967—Jews have lived in Judea and Samaria from time immemorial, just as they have lived in the rest of the historic Land of Israel for the better part of four thousand years. Based on this historic connection, in 1922 the League of Nations granted the Jewish people sovereign rights to Judea and Samaria and the rest of Israel.

On May 15, 1948, the day the Jewish state declared independence, Jordan joined Egypt, Syria, Lebanon, and Iraq in invading Israel with the intent of annihilating it. Jordan ended the war in possession of northern, southern, and eastern Jerusalem as well as Judea and Samaria. Under international law, this war was an illegal war of aggression. All Jews who had been living in the areas that the Jordanians conquered were expelled from their homes. Hundreds were massacred or taken captive in Jordan.[8]

The official position of the Israeli government is that Israel has a right to sovereignty over the areas. But in 2003 Prime Minister Ariel Sharon buckled under U.S. pressure and made the two-state solution the official position of his government and his political party. In 2009 Prime Minister Benjamin Netanyahu, who previously had also opposed Palestinian statehood, followed in Sharon's footsteps and announced his support for the two-state solution, contradicting the official policy of his government and his party.

U.S. pressure, however, has not managed to change the hearts and minds of Israel's citizenry. Polling data indicates that a wide majority of Israelis favor applying Israeli sovereignty over parts or all of Judea and Samaria.[9] Their attachment to the areas stems both from historic ties and from military necessity.

Israel's Arab neighbors have never accepted its right to exist as an independent entity. Even Egypt and Jordan, the two countries that have signed formal treaties of peace with Israel, have refused to implement the parts of their treaties that require them to normalize their relations with the Jewish state.[10] Polling data show that Jordanians and Egyptians—

and residents of Arab and Islamic states throughout the region and their world—are nearly unanimous in their hatred of Jews and in their rejection of Israel's right to exist.[11]

This hatred has been repeatedly translated into military aggression. And as a consequence, Israel, more than perhaps any other democratic nation in the world, needs defensible borders in order to survive.

Without Judea and Samaria, Israel is only nine miles wide from east to west. Particularly in the wake of the Islamic revolutionary wave that began in December 2010 and that has led to the overthrow, destabilization, or weakening of all the regimes in neighboring states, for Israel to withdraw from Judea and Samaria would be tantamount to inviting invasion and aggression.

Given the radicalism of the Palestinian leadership from the Palestine Liberation Organization (PLO) and Hamas alike, 83 percent of Israelis are convinced that an Israeli withdrawal to the 1949 armistice lines—that is, acquiescence to the Palestinian demand that Israel withdraw from all of Judea and Samaria and partition Jerusalem—would not end the Palestinian conflict against Israel.[12]

Beyond the military necessity for Israeli control of Judea and Samaria, most Israelis support the policy of applying Israeli laws there for other reasons as well. Israel was granted sovereign rights over the areas under the 1922 League of Nations Mandate for Palestine. Under international law, Israel has the strongest claim to sovereignty over the areas. And from a national historical perspective, Judea and Samaria—as well as Jerusalem—are the cradle of Jewish civilization. It was in these areas that the bulk of the history of ancient Israel took place. Following the destruction of Jerusalem in 70 CE, during the Jews' nearly two thousand years of homeless exile, it was for their return to Jerusalem, Hebron, Beit El, Susia, Elon Moreh, and Beitar that they prayed.

In 1993 Israel recognized the PLO, a terrorist organization bound by its charter to destroy the Jewish state, as the sole legitimate representative of the Palestinian people. In the framework of agreements that Israel signed with the PLO then and in 1994 and 1995, the terror group was empowered to establish a Palestinian governing authority to administer all the areas Israel transferred to PLO control. Since 1996 98 percent of the Palestinians have been governed by the Palestinian Authority. In Judea and Samaria the Palestinian Authority is controlled completely by the PLO. Even though they overlap in most cases, the PLO did not transform itself into the Palestinian Authority upon its establishment in 1994. Rather, it maintained sole responsibility for everything not explicitly controlled by the Palestinian Authority. This includes negotiating with Israel and handling foreign policy.

Under the PLO-controlled Palestinian Authority, the Palestinians in Judea and Samaria face a future of despotic rule by unelected corrupt politicians. Ever since Yassir Arafat's death in November 2004, PA chairman (and PLO chief) Mahmoud Abbas has governed with dictatorial powers. He was elected to his position for a four-year term in January 2005, having run virtually unopposed, but even though his term ended in January 2009, he remains in office.

Palestinian polling data indicate that a large and growing proportion of Palestinians—between two-thirds and three-quarters—admire Israeli democracy more than any other democracy in the world[13] and do not support an Israeli withdrawal from Judea and Samaria.[14]

The Israeli one-state plan will put an end to the subjection of Palestinians to despotic rule. It will grant the Palestinians who live in these areas automatic permanent residency status and render them eligible to apply for Israeli citizenship. As permanent residents, they will be accorded the same civil and legal rights as all Israeli citizens, and if they apply for and receive Israeli citizenship, they will have the right to vote in national elections. Gaza, from which Israel withdrew completely in 2005, will remain a self-governed Palestinian territory.

I have divided this book into three parts.

Part I provides a 360-degree analysis of the two-state solution and the reasons it has failed. It analyzes the causes of bipartisan support for the plan, and it surveys the policy's ninety years of continuous failure, beginning with the British Mandatory government that ruled the Land of Israel between 1919 and 1947.

Woven into the story of the British Mandate is the story of the father of Palestinian nationalism, the Nazi war criminal Haj Amin el-Husseini. A genocidal Jew hater, an Arab nationalist, and a jihadist, Husseini not only shaped Palestinian national consciousness, he shaped the politics that have directed the Arab world for more than ninety years. It was

Husseini's leadership that preordained the British failure to foster peace and moderation in the post-Ottoman Arab world.

Husseini's self-proclaimed successor was Yassir Arafat, and while Arafat may have exaggerated his ties to Husseini, his life's work as the architect of modern terrorism and political warfare, deployed with the aim of destroying Israel, made him a loyal successor to his role model.

Our story continues with a survey of the Palestinian leaders who have succeeded Arafat, as well as a discussion of Hamas. My discussion will show that their policies have never been geared toward the establishment of a Palestinian state. Rather, their principal goal has always been the destruction of Israel. For this reason, no amount of U.S. pressure and no Israeli concessions will suffice to bring peace. And still the United States is wedded to the two-state solution, despite its abject futility. As we shall see, to achieve it, Washington has willfully trampled its own most cherished values.

For example, in negotiations with Israel in recent years, the Palestinians have made a central issue of the Israeli communities that have been built in Jerusalem and in Judea and Samaria since Israel took control of these areas from Jordan in the 1967 Six Day War. They say that these so-called Israeli settlements are the main obstacle to peace. This assertion stems from the Palestinian leadership's insistence that it not only receive sovereignty over Judea and Samaria and Jerusalem but that it receive them Jew-free.[15]

The United States supports this position. And in so doing, it supports the establishment of a state that is so bigoted that it would require all Jews living in its claimed territory to be expelled from their homes just because they are Jewish.

If you have ever wondered why the U.S. government, under Democratic and Republican administrations alike, is so adamant about abrogating Jewish property rights in Judea, Samaria, and Jerusalem— insisting on a so-called settlement freeze or claiming not to recognize "the legitimacy of settlements"—this is the reason. The United States has adopted the Palestinians' anti-Semitic demand that all 575,000 Jews who live beyond the 1949 armistice lines in Jerusalem, Judea, and Samaria be expelled from their homes.

. . .

The two-state solution is just as antithetical to vital U.S. national security interests as it is to American values of tolerance and individual freedom. It requires Israel, America's closest Middle East ally, to transform itself from a powerful nation, capable of defending itself from infiltration and invasion, into a strategic basket case that survives at the pleasure of its enemies.[16] At the end of Part I, I will discuss how the United States came to embrace this destructive policy and transform it into the centerpiece of its Middle East strategy, as well as the deleterious impact the two-state solution has had on U.S. national security and U.S. policies in the Middle East at large.

Part II presents the Israeli one-state plan in a comprehensive manner.

In Chapter 7 I detail how it will be implemented on the ground, and what it will mean for the daily lives of Israelis and Palestinians living in Judea and Samaria.

In Chapter 8 I discuss the demographic ramifications of adding the Palestinians of Judea and Samaria to Israel's population rolls. Many of Israel's leaders and ardent supporters argue that if Israel exercises its sovereignty over Judea and Samaria, it will doom itself demographically, losing its Jewish majority and being forced to choose between its Jewish identity and its democratic form of government. Due to their demographic concerns, these supporters of Israel argue that as problematic as Palestinian statehood may be, Israel has no choice but to withdraw from Judea and Samaria and partition Jerusalem in order to make room for a Palestinian state.

But the fears about demography are based on demographic data that are completely fraudulent—namely, a 1997 census conducted by the Palestinian Authority that inflated the number of Palestinians by 50 percent. The census also lied about demographic trends in birthrates and immigration and so inflated the assessments of future growth.

Anti-Israel activists claim that the alternative to the two-state solution is a "one-state solution" under which Israel becomes absorbed into an Arab majority state and so loses its Jewish identity. Their claim rests solely on PA demographic data.

The basic difference between the Israeli one-state plan and the pro-Palestinian one-state solution, as represented by its supporters, is that the Israeli one-state plan is based on fact and the pro-Palestinian one-state solution is pure propaganda. What the real demographic data show is that even if all the Palestinians living in Judea and Samaria are granted Israeli citizenship, Jews would still remain a two-thirds majority of the citizens of Israel.[17]

As I previously mentioned, Gaza is not part of the plan, for several reasons. First, Israel withdrew its military forces and civilian population from Gaza in 2005, arguably renouncing its legal claim to the area. Second, there is no significant Israeli constituency for absorbing Gaza into Israel. Third, the strategic advantage that Israel would gain from dislodging Hamas from power in Gaza would be outweighed by the strategic price it would pay in terms of the likely need to fight an insurgency within Gaza.

The who's who of American foreign policy elites embrace the two-state solution despite its repeated failure, but the Israeli one-state plan remains orphaned despite its history of success. In 1967 Israel applied its sovereignty to eastern, northern, and southern Jerusalem, and in 1981 it enacted a de facto annexation of the Golan Heights. After both of these moves, the situation on the ground improved both for Israelis and for the local Arab population. In neither case did Israel's actions provoke a war from its neighbors. In neither case did conferring the right to apply for Israeli citizenship on the area's Arabs endanger Israel demographically. I provide a detailed examination of both precedents in Chapter 9.

The demographic argument put forward by pro-Palestinian one-staters and by champions of the two-state paradigm presents Israel with a false choice between its democracy and its Jewish character. The basic argument is that even if the Palestinians remain a minority in Israel—albeit a sizable one—after Israel applies its sovereignty to Judea and Samaria, Israel will not be able to morally assert its identity as a Jewish state. That is, it assumes there is a contradiction between Israel being a Jewish state and a state whose population is not almost entirely Jewish.

As I explain in Chapters 10 and 11, this view contradicts the basic tenets of democratic governance in liberal democracies. It ignores the fact that in liberal democracies like Israel and the United States, individual rights are not necessarily compromised by majority rule but thrive under checks and balances that prevent the majority from acting oppressively. Indeed, while Palestinians living under PA rule are denied basic freedoms of religion, property, and speech, Israeli Arab citizens enjoy the same civil rights and legal protections as Israel's Jewish citizens. If Israel asserts its sovereignty over Judea and Samaria, the rights of Palestinians living in those areas will be respected and protected to a far greater extent than they have been under the rule of the Palestinian Authority.

With demographic and democratic realities actually favoring Israel, the question becomes one of rights. Who has the best claim to sovereignty in Judea and Samaria?

Since 1967, and with increased intensity since Israel and the United States embraced the two-state paradigm in 1993, Israel's critics have argued that Israel has no legal right to Judea and Samaria. The very presence of Israeli military forces in the areas—not to mention Israeli civilians—represents, they claim, a breach of international law. This argument is heard so often, and it is made with such conviction, that many supporters of Israel have accepted it as fact. But as I show in Chapter 12, Israel's legal right to sovereignty over Judea and Samaria is far stronger than the Palestinian claims to sovereignty there.

Another way the Palestinians work to diminish international support for Israel is by presenting themselves as the indigenous population not only of Judea and Samaria but of all of the Land of Israel. In contrast, they portray the Jews as a group of European colonialists with no historical connection to the land. These efforts—like those that deny Israel's legal rights—involve nothing less than an attempt to deny and rewrite history. In Chapter 13 I show the baselessness of the Palestinian claims and also demonstrate the historical foundation for Israel's legal rights to these areas in light of the Jewish people's status as the indigenous people of the Land of Israel.

Another type of opposition to applying Israeli sovereignty over Judea and Samaria is concern for what will happen the day after Israel announced that it is applying Israeli law to the areas. Supporters of Israel envision a bleak future for Israel: regional war, international isolation, and economic strangulation, due to the levying of political and economic sanctions. Foreign forces, they warn, could be deployed to Judea, Samaria, and Jerusalem to compel Israel to withdraw. And Israel would face a Palestinian terror campaign, they intone, the likes of which it has never seen.

Part III considers the likely responses of all the relevant international actors to the implementation of the Israeli one-state plan. It concludes by analyzing the plan's risks and benefits for Israel and for the United States.

Chapter 14 considers likely Palestinian responses to such an Israeli announcement. It looks at the options for action open to the various Palestinian factions and discusses the opportunities and pitfalls these options present them.

As I demonstrate in detail in Chapter 15, Israel's neighbors in Egypt, Jordan, Syria, and Lebanon, like all other governments, will respond to the implementation of the Israeli one-state plan in a manner that they believe serves their interests. My discussion of their possible responses focuses on the impact of the political upheavals now engulfing Israel's neighbors and the economic realities they face going forward. I analyze Iran's role in the region, the rising power of Islamist forces from Cairo to Amman to Damascus and beyond, and the strategic consequences of Iran's nuclear weapons program for actors in the region.

My studies of both the Palestinians and the neighboring Arab states lead me to conclude that their responses to the application of Israeli law over Judea and Samaria will likely be far less dramatic and far more manageable than many observers warn. Although Israel's move will add a new dimension to the continuing Palestinian and pan-Islamic diplomatic and political campaign to dismantle the Jewish state, their responses are unlikely to be qualitatively different from what we have already seen in recent decades.

Ironically, the European Union would likely be the source of the angriest response to such an Israeli action. Since the Arab oil embargo in 1973, western Europe has served as the primary lobbyist for the two-state solution. America's embrace of the policy in 1993 would never have happened without years of prior open and subversive European diplomacy, both in Israel and in the United States. It is not a stretch to argue that with the Eurozone teetering on the brink of a financial abyss, support for Palestinian statehood may be the only EU policy that one could expect to remain consistent. Chapter 16 examines Europe's policy options and interests in responding to an Israeli announcement that it is applying its law to Judea and Samaria.

Given the obvious hazards, what would Israel gain from applying its law there and so risk bringing upon itself the wrath of the world? Why would Israel wish to do such a thing?

In Chapter 17 I analyze how asserting its sovereignty over Judea and Samaria will improve Israel's international position, its national security, and its ability to function as a democracy. I demonstrate that Israel's gains, on balance, will far outweigh its losses. Israel will secure its capacity to deter invasion and defend against aggression from the east. It will free its official representatives to speak candidly of Israel's rights and requirements without fear of angering the Palestinians. It will enhance Israeli democracy by securing the civil rights and property rights of Israelis and Palestinians alike. And by taking the most divisive issue in Israeli domestic politics off the table, it will strengthen Israeli society.

Finally, the question remains as to what implementation of the Israeli one-state plan would mean for America. How would Israel's exercise of sovereignty over Judea and Samaria affect U.S. interests in the region and in the world? Will those interests be harmed or advanced by such an Israeli move? What will such a policy require from America?

The answer to these questions is partially a function of how the United States responds to Israel's initiative, and is partially independent of that response. My book closes with a discussion of these issues.

I conclude that on balance, Israel's exercise of sovereignty over Judea and Samaria will enhance democratic values, as well as America's regional and global interests. Indeed, next to Israel and Jordan, the United States will be the greatest beneficiary of Israel's move. As for what America will have to do, the answer is: much less than what it is doing now.

In a time of fiscal austerity, and of domestic attempts to scale back America's foreign commitments, the Israeli one-state plan removes a financial burden from America's shoulders. The United States spends roughly a half billion dollars every year on aid to the Palestinians. It finances the terror-supporting PA budget, including the budget of the Hamas-led Palestinian government in Gaza. And it spends hundreds of millions of dollars each year training and maintaining the Palestinian armed forces, even though those forces are involved in terrorism and lead the terror campaigns against Israel.[18] Under the Israeli one-state plan, all these financial transfers and security projects would end.

I am moved to write this book because over the past twenty years, I have seen firsthand, and from multiple vantage points, the destructive impulse at the heart of Palestinian politics, and its egregious impact on Israel's security and national interests and on America's security and interests. In the 1990s, during my years of service as an officer in the Israel Defense Force (IDF) and a practitioner of the two-state solution, I saw up close how that policy is doomed to failure. From 1994 to 1996, I was a core member of Israel's negotiating team with the PLO. During those years, when the so-called peace process was at its height, I was involved in the negotiation of a half-dozen major agreements with the PLO.

From my position as the coordinator of negotiations on civil affairs, I saw how the same PLO leaders who negotiated with us were also negotiating with Hamas. The same PLO officials who broke bread with us proceeded, after negotiating sessions were adjourned, to oversee the Palestinian Authority's governing bureaucracies, breaching every word of the agreements they negotiated and signed with us. The same Palestinian negotiators who laughed and gossiped with their Israeli counterparts personally ordered murderous attacks against Israeli civilians and recruited terrorists to serve in their U.S.-trained security services.

I served with Israeli and American negotiators who embraced the two-state fantasy. Time after time these senior American and Israeli officials, when faced with overwhelming evidence of Palestinian bad faith, insisted that things would somehow magically change the moment a final peace was signed because the Palestinians were so friendly to their Israeli negotiating partners.

Throughout my tenure on the Israeli negotiating team, I took it upon myself to collate regular reports showing how the Palestinian leadership repeatedly breached the agreements it had signed. The reports were based on information gathered by field officers in the military government in Judea, Samaria, and Gaza. And they were devastating. They showed that the Palestinians were in material breach of all their commitments to Israel. My reports were distributed to all of Israel's senior military and political leaders. But they made no demonstrable impact on Israel's policies.

I completed my military service in the IDF at the end of 1996. In 1997 I began working in the Office of the Prime Minister of Israel as Benjamin Netanyahu's assistant foreign policy adviser. From that position, I saw how Israel's embrace of the two-state solution made it impossible for it to assert its rights, including the right of Jews to live in Jerusalem, Judea, and Samaria and to worship in Jerusalem. It also harmed Israel's ability to defend itself and its citizens from wanton terrorist attacks.

. . .

In July 2000, at the Camp David peace summit, the Palestinians re-jected peace and statehood; only two months later, in late September, they began a massive terror offensive against Israel. Early assaults in this campaign were carried out almost exclusively by U.S.- and EU-trained Palestinian security forces. On October 12, 2000, two IDF reservists who got lost and accidentally entered Ramallah were taken to a Pales-tinian police station. There they were lynched, literally torn apart by a mob, abetted by Palestinian security services. Between September 27 and October 30, twelve Israelis were murdered in six deadly attacks. Scores more were wounded as the Palestinian Authority organized and abetted stoning, firebomb, and shooting attacks throughout Judea and Samaria and Gaza. The next month saw the first two suicide bombings—the method that was to become the killing means of choice in the Palestinian terror war. On November 20 Palestinian security forces in Gaza carried out a roadside bombing of an Israeli school bus, killing two adults and maiming nine others, including five children.

As the PLO-led Palestinian Authority ended its phony embrace of peace and oversaw the political and terror aspects of its new round of war on Israel, I began working as a newspaper editor and columnist, first for *Makor Rishon*, a Hebrew-language newspaper, and then, beginning in 2002, for the *Jerusalem Post*. From these positions, I witnessed the dev-astating consequences of the American and Israeli embrace of a policy based on wishful thinking. And as time went on, as the bodies of the terror victims piled ever higher and as Israel's international position grew ever weaker, I watched in a mixture of shock, amazement, horror, and frustration as the United States and Israel expanded their devotion to the two-state solution.

One of the many casualties of America's continued fidelity to the two-state myth is the coherence of its counterterror strategy. The most obvi-ous aspect of this loss is the effective U.S. toleration of terrorism against Israel. To maintain its support for the two-state solution, the United States has turned a blind eye to the strategic nature of Palestinian terror-ism, even when the victims of that terrorism are Americans.

This might be reasonable if Palestinian terrorism were an occasional nuisance. But the sheer volume of attacks that the United States has countenanced has been of epic proportions. Between September 2000 and the end of 2009, Palestinians killed some 1,200 Israelis in terror attacks. More than 8,100 Israelis were wounded during that period. Over 70 percent of the Israeli casualties were civilians. A proportionate volume of attacks in America would leave 48,000 Americans dead—33,600 civilians—and 324,000 wounded. Since 2000 the Palestinians have carried out an average of ten attacks per day. These attacks run the gamut from rock throwing to stabbings to shootings to suicide bombings to missile launches.[19]

The two-state formula is based on the proposition that the root cause of the Palestinian conflict is Israel's unwillingness to surrender sufficient lands to the Palestinians, rather than the Palestinians' rejection of Israel's right to exist and their continued commitment to its destruction. Accordingly, the United States and the rest of the international community, maintaining allegiance to the two-state solution, have blamed Israel for the Palestinians' aggression.

Not only have successive U.S. administrations turned a blind eye to the Palestinian Authority's active leadership of the terror war against Israel—America's closest Middle East ally—they have actually rewarded it. The United States has overseen the building of a Palestinian army. And successive U.S. administrations have ignored requests of relatives of Americans killed by Palestinian terrorists to bring their relatives' murderers to justice.[20]

Even worse, the policy community's near-consensual blaming of Israel for the absence of peace and stability in the Middle East has severely impaired the ability of American policy makers, analysts, and elected officials to understand the region. To a significant degree, the U.S. embrace of the two-state policy has contributed to successive administrations' failure to adopt rational policies for dealing with the manifold and critical challenges that the Middle East poses for the United States.

As I discuss in Chapters 6 and 18, U.S. military commanders deployed in Middle Eastern theaters have repeatedly failed to consider the ramifications of Israel's experience for what awaited their forces because the U.S.

foreign policy elite refuses to consider Israel outside the "peace process" box and so to learn from Israel's experiences.

In Iraq, as a reporter covering a frontline battalion in the U.S. Army's Third Infantry Division, I saw the war firsthand—and at the outset, it was already clear to me that if U.S. policy makers had been less blinded by false ideological dichotomy that viewed Israelis as "occupiers" and U.S. forces as "liberators," they would have been better prepared for the insurgency that broke out in Iraq shortly after the U.S.-led invasion. Had they been willing to stop trying to be an "honest broker" between Israel and the Palestinians long enough to recognize that the Arab world views Israel and the United States as two sides of the same coin, they would have understood the nature of the war they were fighting and so been better prepared to fight it.

Massive, cumulative statistical data gathered over decades show conclusively that the American people as a whole are deeply supportive of Israel. They view Israel as a key ally, and they expect their government to implement a pro-Israel foreign policy.[21] And yet due to the U.S. embrace of the two-state formula, for the past twenty years U.S. Middle East policy has become more and more hostile to Israel and more and more supportive of the Palestinians, even as the Palestinians have become more and more open about their rejection of Israel and their desire to see it destroyed.

Something has to give.

An Israeli renunciation of the two-state solution and embrace of the Israeli one-state plan, which is based on actual Israeli rights rather than fictitious Israeli culpability, would liberate Israel to craft coherent strategies for contending with the rapidly evolving regional threat environment and the international assault on its right to exist. And at the more mundane level of the lives of individuals—Jews and Arabs alike—Israeli sovereignty in Judea and Samaria will increase the security of all. It will transform the region from one governed alternatively by a military government and a terrorist kleptocracy into one governed by a unified, liberal rule of law. Civil and property rights of Muslims, Christians, and Jews will be protected rather than neglected or denied outright.

Likewise, U.S. abandonment of the two-state paradigm in favor of the Israeli one-state plan will liberate American policy makers from the trap they crafted for themselves two decades ago. Unbound from the two-state solution's cognitive straitjacket, they will be free to base their assessments of Middle Eastern threats on reality, unvarnished by wishful thinking. It ought to go without saying that U.S. national interests and security will benefit from such a development.

I decided to write this book in the hope of empowering Israel's American supporters—Jews and non-Jews—to stand up to the intellectual tyranny of the two-state solution. The American people deserve the opportunity to consider critically the reasons for its continued failure. They deserve to know about the existence of a far better policy—one that has a record of repeated success, and one that is in line with U.S. interests and democratic values.

In writing this book, I do not purport to provide an exhaustive discussion of the Israeli one-state plan. Nor do I expect instant results. My objective is more modest: to provide a reasoned starting point for a conversation that can lead to a rational and relevant debate, in America and beyond, about the nature of the Arab-Israeli conflict and the best way to manage it. Such a debate holds the potential of making a real contribution to regional stability, and to eventual prospects for peace between Israel and its neighbors.

PART I

THE MIDDLE EAST'S BELOVED CHIMERA

CHAPTER I

A Bipartisan Pipe Dream

On May 23, 2002, Israel narrowly averted what would have been the most devastating terrorist attack in its history.

That morning an Israeli fuel tanker driver named Yitzhak Ginsburg drove to the Pi Gelilot liquefied petroleum gas depot to fill up his tank. The depot was located on the northern outskirts of Tel Aviv, adjacent to Ramat Hasharon, and Herzliya, which put it in the middle of the most densely populated area in the Western world.[1]

At seven a.m. Ginsburg passed through the security checkpoint, entered the depot, and began fueling. Suddenly the ground began to shake beneath him. "There was a massive boom," he later told reporters. "Everyone went flying in all directions, and the tanker, which weighs twenty tons, just exploded in the air. Everything was burning and going up in flames. Miraculously nothing happened to me. I thought it was an electrical malfunction. It never occurred to me that it was a terrorist attack."[2]

But it was. Palestinian terrorists had placed a bomb in Ginsburg's fuel tank. A cell member had followed Ginsburg to Pi Gelilot, waited for him to begin fueling, and remotely detonated the bomb.

The only reason Pi Gelilot is not remembered as the most deadly terror attack in history is because Ginsburg's tanker carried diesel fuel.[3] Had it been carrying gasoline, which is much more flammable than diesel, not only would the entire facility have been destroyed, but the fireball created by the explosion would have engulfed neighboring communities. Tel Aviv's tony Ramat Aviv neighborhood, home to 11,400 people, would likely have been reduced to a smoldering ruin. So would Ramat Hasharon and Herzliya, which have a combined population of 127,600.

And that wouldn't have been the end of it. Pi Gelilot is also located next to one of Israel's busiest traffic arteries, as well as the headquarters of the Mossad, Israel's foreign intelligence service, and of Israeli Military Intelligence. The Israel Security Agency, Israel's version of the FBI, is located nearby. Had the bomb worked as the Palestinian terrorists planned, the highway would have become a fireball at the height of rush hour, and Israel's intelligence nerve centers would have been leveled.

The attack at Pi Gelilot took place the morning after a suicide bombing at a pedestrian mall in downtown Rishon Lezion, a bustling coastal city due south of Tel Aviv. In the month that followed the attack, another sixty-five Israelis were murdered, including fifteen children, in Palestinian terrorist attacks of every sort carried out from one end of the country to the other. Adjusting for Israel's relatively small population, this would have been the equivalent of 2,600 Americans being killed.

More than 90 percent of the attacks that month were directed against civilian targets. Less than 10 percent of the dead and less than 5 percent of the wounded were Israeli military forces engaged in counterterror operations.[4] Teenage boys were gunned down at a basketball court. A grandmother and her infant granddaughter were blown up at an ice cream parlor. Another grandmother and her five-year-old granddaughter were blown up, along with five other people, at a bus stop. Two families were massacred in their homes, and a fourteen-year-old girl was murdered at a falafel stand.

The perpetrators of these attacks came from almost every active Palestinian terror group. Most were Fatah terrorists.

Fatah is the largest faction of the PLO. It was founded by Yassir Arafat in 1957 and the leaders of the PLO-controlled Palestinian Authority are overwhelmingly members of Fatah. The Fatah terror cells that perpetrated most of the terrorist operations were directed and funded by the Palestinian Authority.

Others attacks were carried out by Hamas and Islamic Jihad cells. Some of the terrorists served more than one master.

In perpetrating these attacks, terror groups openly collaborated with one another. Some of the attacks were carried out jointly by terrorists from different groups. For instance, a terror cell with members from Fatah and the Popular Front for the Liberation of Palestine massacred forty-year-old Rachel Shabo and her sons, sixteen-year-old Neria, twelve-year-old Zvika, and five-year-old Avishai in their home.[5]

This sort of mayhem is what passed for everyday life in Israel on June 24, 2002, when in a much-anticipated speech, President George W. Bush set out his position on the Palestinian conflict with Israel.[6]

Until that date, Bush had kept his position to himself. Warring factions within his administration competed over which narrative the president would advance. The establishmentarians, led by Secretary of State Colin Powell, wanted the United States to pressure Israel to make concessions to the Palestinians. The renegade hawks in the Defense Department and on Vice President Dick Cheney's staff wanted the United States to put pressure on the Palestinians and side openly with Israel in its war on the Palestinian terror wave that had engulfed the country. In the days leading up to President Bush's speech, the international community was abuzz with anticipation that America's commander in chief was finally ready to choose which side he was on.

To a certain degree, Bush lived up to those expectations. In that speech, he became the first U.S. leader since the onset of the peace process between Israel and the PLO in September 1993 to tell the Palestinians to get their house in order. Other American leaders had called for the Palestinians to fight terrorism, but Bush told them to stop sponsoring it. Moreover, he seemed to express that U.S. support for the Palestinians depended on a change in their behavior. "Today, Palestinian authorities are encouraging, not opposing, terrorism," he said. "This is unacceptable. And the United States will not support the establishment of a Palestinian state until its leaders engage in a sustained fight against the terrorists and dismantle their infrastructure."

Bush also spelled out what he meant by Palestinian political reform. In his words, "Reform must be more than cosmetic change, or a veiled attempt to preserve the status quo. True reform will require entirely new political and economic institutions, based on democracy, market economics, and action against terrorism."

Bush's words were like an adrenaline shot for the beleaguered Israeli citizenry. Not only had the president of the United States recognized that they were the victims of unrelenting terrorist assaults; he recognized that Israel's very right to exist was under attack. From the Arab world to Europe to U.S. university campuses, Israel was under the gun of hateful propaganda. Its army was being falsely and maliciously accused of committing the same very crimes that the Palestinians were carrying out against Israelis. Its leaders and generals were being targeted by scurrilous war-crimes allegations in European courts. And now here was Bush, the leader of the free world, pledging to put an end to this nonsense.

Unfortunately, a closer—and less emotional—reading of Bush's speech shows that there was less to the speech than met the eye. While the tone was indeed pro-Israel, Bush later acknowledged in his memoir that it was actually the most pro-Palestinian speech that any U.S. president had ever given.[7] It was the first time an American president openly embraced the cause of Palestinian statehood. Moreover, while Bush did call the Palestinians to account for their involvement in terrorism against Israel, he didn't give them an ultimatum. He didn't say, *Clean up your act or sacrifice U.S. support.* He said, *Clean up your act and get even more support.*

And he also blamed Israel for Palestinian misery. Indeed, every time Bush spoke of Israeli suffering, he matched that statement with one about Palestinian suffering. This pattern began at the outset of the address as he said, "It is untenable for Israeli citizens to live in terror. It is untenable for Palestinians to live in squalor and occupation."

Three months before Bush's speech, in April 2002, nearly a year and a half into the Palestinians' terror war, Israel's government had finally ordered the IDF to destroy the Palestinian terrorist infrastructure in Judea and Samaria. This involved reasserting Israeli security control of the Palestinian towns and villages that Israel, in the framework of the peace process, had ceded to the Palestinian Authority in 1994 and 1996.[8] Israel called its campaign Operation Defensive Shield. It came after a month in which the Palestinians carried out suicide bombings against Israeli civilians nearly every day. One hundred thirty people—nearly all civilians—were murdered. More than a thousand people were wounded, in a country of only 8 million people. In terms relative to Israel's overall population, the death toll in Israel was nearly as large as two September 11 terror attacks in the United States, but attacks in which the number of dead would be supplemented by more than 40,000 wounded.

Israel needed to reassert its security control of the Palestinian population centers because the Palestinian Authority had used its control of these areas to build not the institutions of a functional state but rather the most widespread and sophisticated terrorist infrastructure in the world.[9] After Israeli forces retook control, it required months for them to dismantle this architecture of terror.

From documents found in Yassir Arafat's headquarters in Ramallah, Israel discovered that Arafat had personally overseen the development of this terror machine. He had paid for attacks, and his lieutenants had played central roles in organizing and carrying them out.[10]

And yet despite everything that Israel—and the United States—had learned about the central role the Palestinian Authority played in Palestinian terrorism, Bush insisted in his June 24 speech that "as we make progress towards security, Israeli forces need to withdraw fully to the positions they held prior to September 28, 2000." In other words, he called for Israel to return control of these territories to the very PLO regime that had used its control of them to organize, plan, train, and finance the largest terror campaign against Israel that the Jewish state had ever experienced.

And that wasn't all. Bush also sided completely with the Palestinian narrative against Israel. That narrative claims that Israel has no rights to Judea and Samaria and that those areas belong to the Palestinians alone. Bush said, "Israeli settlement activity in the occupied territories must stop." That is, the U.S. president said that the property rights of Israeli citizens should not be respected in Judea and Samaria.

Less than a year later, on April 30, 2003, the Bush administration joined forces with the European Union, Russia, and the United Nations (a grouping that came to be known as the Middle East Quartet) and published a new "peace plan." The plan, officially called "A Performance-Based Roadmap to a Permanent Two-State Solution to the Israeli-Palestinian Conflict," effectively nullified Bush's call for Palestinian reform as a precursor to and condition for U.S. support for Palestinian statehood. The roadmap identified the principal goal of the U.S. government as the swift establishment of a Palestinian state, rather than the purging of terrorist elements from Palestinian society and governing structures. It reduced the requirement for Palestinian reform to mere declaratory phrases.

On the other hand, the roadmap required Israel to immediately renounce its rights to Judea and Samaria and take concrete measures to empower the same Palestinian Authority that was actively sponsoring the murder of Israel's citizens. The only aspects of Bush's June 24 speech that found their way into the roadmap were those involving Israeli concessions to the Palestinians.[11]

The inherent anti-Israel bias of the roadmap is nowhere more obvious than in its section on Palestinian incitement.

Since the inception of the Palestinian Authority in 1994, the PA-controlled media organs, school system, mosques, and governing ministries have carried out a massive, systematic campaign of incitement against Israelis. These institutions do not call for Israel's return to the 1949 armistice lines: they call for Israel's complete destruction. And they do not portray Israelis merely as citizens of an enemy state: they portray Israelis and Jews as satanic monsters, subhuman enemies of Allah. This campaign of incitement—which continues to this day—has encouraged Palestinians to make the destruction of Israel and the genocide of the Jewish people their highest goals in life.[12]

By the last year of Bush's second term in office, even his most enthusiastic Israeli supporters were unable to believe he was serious about his demand that the Palestinians reform their society and system of government or about making U.S. support for Palestinian statehood conditional on the implementation of such reform.

In 2005 Bush publicly credited Natan Sharansky—the former Soviet dissident, human rights activist, and political prisoner, turned Israeli politician, turned political theorist—with inspiring him to view the democratization of Palestinian and pan-Arab governance as the foundation for lasting peace and security in the Middle East.[13] For his part, Sharansky was one of Bush's most enthusiastic supporters and defenders in Israel and the United States.

But in early 2008 Sharansky broke publicly with Bush, accusing him of abandoning the freedom agenda. In an op-ed (coauthored with Palestinian human rights activist Bassam Eid) titled "Bush's Mideast U-Turn," he wrote:

> The real breakthrough of Mr. Bush's vision five-and-a-half years ago was not his call for a two-state solution or even the call for Palestinians to "choose leaders not compromised by terror." Rather, the breakthrough was in making peace *conditional* on a fundamental transformation of Palestinian society. . . .

But the past few years have shown that when it comes to dealing with Israelis and Palestinians, the vital link between freedom and peace is almost entirely ignored. . . .

Rather than begin the long and difficult process to transform Palestinian society and ultimately pave the road to peace, the administration has consistently supported quick and foolish solutions: from crafting a "road map" that only paid lip service to reform; to backing a unilateral disengagement [of Israel from the Gaza Strip] that by its nature ignored Palestinian society; to pressing for snap elections that preceded rather than followed reform and thereby brought Hamas to power.[14]

In truth, during his final two years in office, Bush's policy toward Israel and the Palestinians was notable mainly for its unconditional support for Palestinian statehood and its increasingly shrill demands for Israeli concessions to the Palestinians. For instance, in the run-up to the Annapolis peace conference in November 2007, Bush stopped even paying lip service to the need for the Palestinians to reform and cease supporting terrorism as a condition for U.S. support of Palestinian statehood. As Secretary of State Condoleezza Rice put it in a media briefing, there "could be no greater legacy for America" than to establish a Palestinian state. The U.S. goal was to lead "serious negotiations" that would establish a Palestinian state "as soon as possible."[15]

Rice pulled no punches in her treatment of Israel. She launched a libelous attack against Israel and its democratic system, saying that she could relate to the Palestinians because she grew up black in the segregated American South. "I know what it is like to hear to that you cannot go on a road or through a checkpoint because you are Palestinian," she said to participants at the Annapolis conference. "I understand the feeling of humiliation and powerlessness."[16]

The consistent erosion of Bush's demands for Palestinian political reform, and the consistent escalation of his demands for Israeli concessions to the Palestinians, demonstrate that his June 24, 2002, speech did not represent the significant shift in U.S. policy that it seemed at the time. Rather, it was just a temporary rhetorical deviation from a bipartisan consensus on the nature of the Arab-Israeli conflict and on the manner in which that conflict must be resolved.

The basic line of that consensus was clear enough. The goal—stated or unstated—of U.S. policy toward Israel is to establish a Palestinian state on all or most of the land that Israel took from Jordan and Egypt during the 1967 Six Day War. In a June 2001 interview, Ambassador Dennis Ross, who served as President Bill Clinton's chief mediator in the Palestinian-Israeli peace process, explained the basic rule of that consensus policy. The Americans neglected and politicized the prudential issues of Palestinian compliance, as he put it, in favor of keeping the peace process afloat. "Every time there was a behavior, or an incident, or an event that was inconsistent with what the peace process was about," Ross said, "the impulse was to rationalize it, finesse it, find a way around it, and not to allow it to break the process."[17]

The depth of this bipartisan consensus is reflected in President Barack Obama's policy toward Israel and the Palestinians, which, when broken down to its basic components, is indistinguishable from Bush's policy, which itself was indistinguishable from that of his predecessor, Bill Clinton. Whereas Bush was largely perceived as deeply supportive of Israel and cool toward the Palestinians, Obama has been widely perceived as hostile toward Israel and deeply sympathetic toward the Palestinians. But the two men's policies are identical. The distinction between Bush and Obama is rhetorical, not real.

This basic truth is made apparent by comparing the substance of Bush's June 24, 2002, speech with the speech on the Middle East that Obama made on May 19, 2011.[18] If Bush's June 24 address was seen as the most resounding statement of support for Israel made by a U.S. president in the past generation, Obama's May 19 speech was widely viewed as the most anti-Israel speech ever made by an American president.[19]

This assessment of Obama's speech was not unjustified. And just as the widespread perception that Bush's speech was pro-Israel owed to the circumstances in which he delivered it, so the perception that the hostility of Obama's speech was unprecedented was also due in large part to the circumstances in which he delivered it.

First there was the timing. Obama gave his speech while Israeli prime minister Benjamin Netanyahu was in the air flying to Washington, D.C., to meet him. There was a general sense that Obama had blindsided Netanyahu with his speech because Netanyahu was on record as opposing its basic positions.

Then there was the regional context. Less than a month before Obama's address, the U.S.-supported Fatah movement that runs Judea and Samaria signed a unity-government agreement with Hamas, the Iranian-sponsored Palestinian branch of the Muslim Brotherhood that runs Gaza.[20] Hamas is listed on the U.S. State Department's roster of specially designated foreign terrorist organizations;[21] it is dedicated to the eradication of Israel and the Jewish people as part of a global jihad.[22]

Hamas won the U.S.-supported Palestinian Legislative Council elections in 2006. In June 2007 Hamas, not content to share power with the U.S.-supported Fatah group, staged a bloody mini-coup against Fatah in the Gaza Strip. Hamas ousted all Fatah members from power and routed the U.S.-trained Fatah security forces in the area. For the most part, those U.S.-trained forces fled without a fight.[23]

After Hamas won the 2006 elections, the United States formally sided with Israel's demand that Fatah bar Hamas from any leadership position in the Palestinian Authority. In accordance with U.S. law, the Bush administration preconditioned U.S. support for the Palestinian Authority and for Palestinian statehood on the isolation of Hamas.[24]

In his May 2011 speech, in a striking departure from his predecessor's rhetorical position, Obama failed to condition U.S. support for Palestinian statehood on the revocation of the Fatah-Hamas unity deal and the denial of power to Hamas. Instead he offered a mere rhetorical flourish: "The recent announcement of an agreement between Fatah and Hamas raises profound and legitimate questions for Israel: How can one negotiate with a party that has shown itself unwilling to recognize your right to exist? And in the weeks and months to come, Palestinian leaders will have to provide credible answers to that question."

In his very next sentence, Obama signaled that this open-ended statement was not a condition for U.S. support of Palestinian territorial and political demands. "Meanwhile," he said, "the United States, our Quartet partners, and the Arab states will need to continue every effort to get beyond the current impasse."

Obama's message was obvious: regardless of what the Palestinians did, the United States would use its good offices to press for a Palestinian state, with or without Hamas, with or without Palestinian recognition of Israel's right to exist, and with or without a Palestinian rejection of terrorism.

These statements are but a sampling of the clear hostility toward Israel that is inherent to Obama's speech, and that so angered Israel's supporters in America. But when you filter out the adversarial tone and look only at the substantive policies that Obama put forward, the fact is that his positions are indistinguishable from those of his Republican and Democratic predecessors in the Oval Office. Like Bush, Obama claimed that the way to solve the Palestinian conflict with Israel was to aid in the establishment of a Palestinian state.

In Obama's words, "A lasting peace will involve two states for two peoples: Israel as a Jewish state and the homeland for the Jewish people, and the state of Palestine as the homeland for the Palestinian people, each state enjoying self-determination, mutual recognition, and peace." Bush had said, "My vision is two states, living side by side in peace and security." And in a town hall meeting with State Department personnel shortly after her appointment as secretary of state in January 2005, Condoleezza Rice had said, "I don't think any of us doubt that without a Palestinian state that is viable, that can represent the aspirations of the Palestinian people, that there really isn't going to be a peace for either the Palestinian people or for the Israelis."[25]

There is also no substantive difference between Bush's and Obama's views of the borders of a Palestinian state. Both expect Israel to recede to within boundaries that are indefensible.

Obama said, "The United States believes that negotiations should result in two states, with permanent Palestinian borders with Israel, Jordan, and Egypt, and permanent Israeli borders with Palestine. We believe the borders of Israel and Palestine should be based on the 1967 lines with mutually agreed swaps, so that secure and recognized borders are established for both states. The Palestinian people must have the right to govern themselves, and reach their full potential, in a sovereign and contiguous state."

In his June 24, 2002, speech Bush said, "The Israeli occupation that began in 1967 will be ended through a settlement negotiated between the parties, based on UN resolutions 242 and 338, with Israeli withdrawal to secure and recognized borders."

Bush's remarks and subsequent statements seem to indicate that he envisioned major revisions in the 1949 armistice lines that would work in Israel's favor. But in January 2005 Rice indicated that the contours

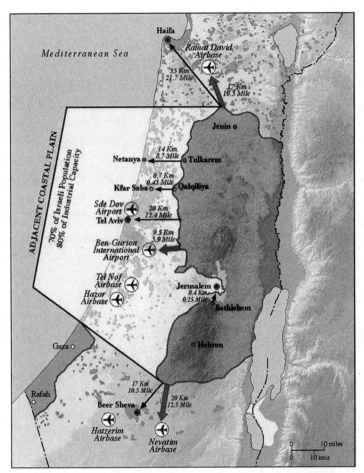

**Map of Israel's Strategic Vulnerabilities Within the 1949
Armistice Lines (pre-1967 Six Day War boundaries)**[26]

of the Palestinian state that the Bush administration envisioned would
be those laid out by Obama. She spoke of a "contiguous" Palestinian
state.[27]

In his address, Obama insinuated that the Palestinian conflict with
Israel was the root cause of instability throughout the Middle East. As he
put it, "This conflict has come with a larger cost to the Middle East, as
it impedes partnerships that could bring greater security and prosperity
and empowerment to ordinary people."

This statement probably goes farther in blaming Israel for the absence
of peace in the Middle East than statements by previous U.S. leaders

made during their tenures in office. But the difference is one of degree rather than kind. As we shall see, Obama's belief that the absence of a Palestinian state in Judea, Samaria, and Jerusalem as well as Gaza is the root cause of the Arab-Israel conflict is more or less consistent with positions adopted by every U.S. administration since Richard Nixon.

To sum up, then, Obama's May 19, 2011, speech set out a policy that was substantively indistinguishable from that of Bush's June 24, 2002, speech. In other words, the presidential address widely perceived as the most anti-Israel presidential speech in recent memory was substantively identical to the presidential speech that was widely perceived as the most pro-Israel speech in recent memory.

As I discuss in the following chapters, this bipartisan American policy, which in various forms has been in place since the early 1970s, is unsupported by reality. Successive U.S. administrations, and nearly the entire U.S. foreign policy elite, is of the opinion that if a Palestinian Arab state is established next to Israel and west of the Jordan River on land Israel has controlled since 1967, the Palestinians will resolve their conflict with Israel. So too the American policy establishment believes that after such a state is founded, the wider Arab world will also make its peace with the Jewish state.

But the Arabs—including the Palestinians—do not claim that this is the case. Aside from isolated statements given to the Western media, neither the Palestinians nor the wider Arab world has given the United States any reason to believe that they will settle their dispute with Israel if a Palestinian state is formed. To the contrary, all the major—and minor—Palestinian and pan-Arab leaders have made clear that they will not resolve their conflict with Israel even if a Palestinian state is founded.

To the minds of most Americans, and indeed of most observers around the world, the Obama and Bush administrations were as different as night and day. And yet on the issue of Israel and the Palestinians, they were of a piece, embracing a policy that has no basis whatsoever in reality and therefore has no chance of ever succeeding.

CHAPTER 2

Clinton's Legacy of Blind Faith

During Bill Clinton's presidency, PLO chief Yassir Arafat visited the White House more often than any other foreign leader.[1] Three days before Clinton left office, Arafat called him to say goodbye. "You are a great man," the Palestinian leader told him. Clinton responded, "To hell I am. I'm a colossal failure, and you made me one."[2]

To a degree, Clinton was right to blame Arafat for his failure. He had believed that Arafat was interested in achieving a peace agreement with Israel that would lead to the establishment of a Palestinian state. And Arafat had disappointed him. In the final months of Clinton's presidency, Arafat had spurned peace and opened a new round of terrorist war against Israel.

To another degree, however, Clinton's failure was his own fault. If he had paid attention to what Arafat and his PLO deputies had been saying and doing since the peace process between Israel and the PLO began in 1993, he would never have believed that they were interested in making peace with Israel. He would not have empowered Arafat and his minions to dictate whether his foreign policy would succeed or fail.

Clinton devoted his final two years in office in large part to foreign policy. The issue that most captivated his attention was not the war in the Balkans, nor Iraq's violations of UN Security Council resolutions, nor North Korea's nuclear program. It wasn't Russia's devolution from a superpower rival into a criminal state, or China's economic and military ascendance as a competitor to the United States.

Rather, Clinton's chief foreign policy interest was the peace process between Israel and the PLO. That process had begun in September 1993, when Israel and the PLO had exchanged letters of mutual recognition and signed the Declaration of Principles on the lawn of the White House. The Declaration was a framework agreement that set out a path, from the letters of mutual recognition, to the gradual establishment of peaceful relations and the eventual forging of a final peace treaty between Israel and the Palestinians.

In the seven years between that moment and Clinton's departure from office in January 2001, Israel and the PLO, in keeping with this declaration, had signed seven major agreements and another dozen or so minor ones. These deals had led to the establishment of PLO-controlled Palestinian Authority, which was empowered to govern the Palestinians living in Judea, Samaria, and the Gaza Strip. They set the terms for the Palestinian election in 1996. They determined the nature of security cooperation between the Israeli military and intelligence arms and the Palestinian forces that these agreements created. And they set a framework for relations between the Israeli government and the Palestinian Authority, and their respective peoples, on issues ranging from taxation policy to auto insurance policy to banning incitement to murder.

Accordingly, between June 1994 and February 1997, Israel transferred military and civilian control of all the major Palestinian population centers in Judea, Samaria, and Gaza to the Palestinian Authority. Since 1997, 98 percent of Palestinians living in these areas have been governed by the Palestinian Authority rather than by the Israeli military government.[3]

In 1999 Ehud Barak, the leader of Israel's dovish Labor Party, was elected prime minister. Taking office that July, he pledged to conclude a final peace with the Palestinians within sixteen months.[4]

To achieve a final deal, Israel and the Palestinians needed to reach an agreement on the most intractable issues of the Palestinian conflict with Israel. These issues—Jerusalem, Palestinian "refugees" from the 1948–49 pan-Arab invasion of Israel, final borders, security arrangements, and water—all dealt directly or indirectly with the issue of Israel's right to exist.

The issue of the so-called Palestinian refugees needs some explanation at the outset. On November 29, 1947, the UN General Assembly approved a resolution supporting the establishment of a Jewish state and an Arab state west of the Jordan River. The Palestinian response was to launch a massive terror war against the Jews of the Land of Israel—the day after the UN resolution passed. On May 15, 1948, Israel declared independence. At the urging of the Palestinians, five Arab armies invaded the nascent Jewish state with the stated intention of overrunning it and massacring all the Jews who lived there.[5]

But the Arabs lost the war. During the course of the war, several hundred thousand Palestinians had left the territory of Israel and relocated to neighboring Arab states. Since they left, the Arab states, aside from Jordan, have denied them and their descendants citizenship in the countries in which they reside and in which generations of descendants have been born and lived their entire lives.[6]

Today there are several million Arabs whom the United Nations classifies as Palestinian refugees who have lived for generations in the Arab states neighboring Israel. The Palestinian Central Bureau of Statistics claims that there are 5.1 million such refugees.[7] They demand that Israel allow these foreign Arabs to immigrate freely to Israel—not to the sought-for Palestinian state—in the framework of a peace deal.

This demand is without precedent in the history of warfare. There is no precedent of a civilian population, displaced by a war that their leadership started and lost, claiming a right to return to territory that they failed to conquer. There is similarly no precedent for the claim that not only those who left but their great-great grandchildren should be allowed to "return" as well.

In other words, the demand for a "right of return" for the "refugees" is a Palestinian—and pan-Arab, and UN—attempt to retroactively achieve the result they failed to achieve in a war of aggression instigated by their ancestors.[8]

Additionally, in order for a peace deal to be signed, even with the most forthcoming concessions from Israel's government, the Palestinians would have to recognize Israel's right to exist as a nation. If they did so, signing an agreement would be a relatively simple affair. If they refused, no deal could be signed, because any peace deal would be meaningless.

Ehud Barak was preceded in office by Benjamin Netanyahu, whose chief demand in the peace process was for reciprocity in fulfilling obligations between the Israelis and Palestinians. In return for Israeli transfers of land, Netanyahu demanded that the Palestinians abide by their commitments to Israel, which included ending their support for terrorism, ending classroom indoctrination of students to seek Israel's destruction, ending anti-Jewish incitement in official PA media organs, and cooperating in law enforcement to reduce the size of the Palestinian security forces to numbers agreed upon in previously signed agreements between Israel and the PLO.[9]

Netanyahu's demand for reciprocity stymied negotiations because the Palestinians refused to honor any of these requirements. They never amended the PLO charter, which calls for the destruction of Israel.[10] They added incendiary, anti-Jewish materials to the school curriculum. Children were taught to seek death in a violent jihad to annihilate the Jews, whom they were taught are subhuman evildoers who must be annihilated for Muslims to be free. For instance, the Palestinian Authority's eighth-grade textbook in Islamic education taught children that "Satan has, in the eyes of many people, made [one people's] evil actions appear beautiful until they thought that their race was the best of all, and their kind better than all others, and that other people are their slaves and do not reach their level. Such a people are the Jews."[11]

They propagated anti-Jewish programming on Palestinian television, and Arafat himself repeatedly called for the Palestinians to launch open war against Israel, saying, "It is important that we organize our homes and our movement so that we can more and more and more endure the coming battle, which we shall initiate. We must say these things because great battles lie before us. We are marching together to Jerusalem, Jerusalem, Jerusalem."[12]

And yet despite all this, Netanyahu bowed to U.S. pressure and agreed to move forward with Israeli concessions to the Palestinians. In 1997 he handed security control of the mixed Arab-Jewish city of Hebron to the Palestinians. In 1998 he signed the Wye Plantation Accords with Arafat, which set the conditions for the transfer of additional lands in Judea and Samaria. He retroactively approved the expansion of the Palestinian security services in breach of existing agreements.

Despite Netanyahu's willingness to make concessions, Clinton and his advisers felt that he was not committed enough to the peace process. As a consequence, Clinton sent his senior election advisers to Israel to run Ehud Barak's campaign.[13] The American contribution to Barak's election was so enormous that Israelis widely recognized that Barak owed his office to the Clinton administration.

Barak's sense of urgency regarding the need to sign a final peace deal with the Palestinians also stemmed from Clinton's impending departure from office in January 2001. Clinton and Barak both wanted to conclude a deal before Clinton left office.

And so in July 2000, Clinton brought Barak, Arafat, and their respective negotiating teams to Camp David. The goal of the summit was to achieve a final peace deal. During the course of the two-week summit, Barak made the Palestinians offers of peace that were unprecedented. He offered to share sovereignty over Jerusalem, something no Israeli leader—including Barak himself—had ever considered doing. He offered them all of Gaza, 92 percent of Judea and Samaria, and control of the Jordan Valley. The only area where Barak refused to compromise was on the so-called right of return, which as we previously noted, is an open demand for Israel's destruction.

And yet despite the expansiveness of Barak's offer, Arafat did not simply reject Barak's offer; he refused even to make a counteroffer, signaling that he and the Palestinians were not interested in making peace with Israel. They indicated instead that it would be impossible for Israel to satisfy their demands and still exist as a nation.

"Camp David failed," Shlomo Ben-Ami, Israel's foreign minister, said, "because Arafat refused to put forward proposals of his own and didn't succeed in conveying to us the feeling that at some point his demands would have an end.

> One of the important things we did at Camp David was to define our vital interests in the most concise way. We didn't expect to meet the Palestinians halfway, and not even two-thirds of the way. But we did expect to meet them at some point. The whole time we waited to see them make some sort of movement in the face of our far-reaching movement. But they didn't. The feeling was that they were constantly trying to drag us into some sort of black hole of more and more concessions without it being at all clear where all the concessions were leading, what the finish line was.[14]

For those who were still unconvinced of the PLO's bad intentions, the start of the Palestinian terror war two months later was evidence that the peace process with the PLO had been fraudulent. The PLO had no interest in ever living at peace with Israel. Similarly, it convinced the incoming

Bush administration that it made little sense for the U.S. government to devote its energies to resolving the Palestinian conflict with Israel.[15]

And yet, perhaps hoping to prove that the massive energy he had devoted to the issue had not been in vain, Clinton made one last effort to broker an agreement. On December 23, 2000, less than a month before he left office, he made a final offer to Israel and the Palestinians. He presented his proposal as "parameters" for a final peace. As he put it, "If they [the Israelis and Palestinians] accepted the parameters within four days, we would go forward. If not, we were through."

Clinton's parameters represented a wholesale U.S. adoption of the Palestinian negotiating positions on all but the most minor issues. Among other things, Clinton's parameters involved Palestinian sovereignty over the Temple Mount in Jerusalem.

The Temple Mount is the site of Solomon's Temple and the accepted site of Abraham's sacrifice of Isaac. In Jewish tradition, the Temple Mount is also the site where heaven and earth are joined. It is the place where the Messiah will appear. All the Jewish people's national and religious identity is tied to the Temple Mount. And in his parameters for peace, Clinton required Israel to cede sovereignty over the Temple Mount to the PLO.

The PLO's demand for Judaism's most sacred site is based on the Palestinians' post-1967 denial of Jewish history and cooptation of Jewish history to Islam. The Koran itself speaks of the Jewish Temple on the Temple Mount in Jerusalem. But beginning in 1950, the Palestinians began denying this history. This incipient trend became the official "truth" for Palestinians and, through them, for many Muslims worldwide following Israel's liberation of the Temple Mount from Jordanian occupation in 1967. That trend ignored Koranic texts and the historical record, and it denied the Jewish connection to Jerusalem, while claiming that the Temple Mount was sacred to the Muslims—and to a lesser degree the Christians.[16]

Beyond his transfer of sovereignty over Judaism's spiritual wellspring to the PLO, Clinton's plan generally called for Israel to agree to partition its capital city. The western part of Jerusalem would remain under Israeli sovereignty while eastern, southern, and northern neighborhoods would be transferred to the PLO.

Outside Jerusalem, Clinton's parameters called for Israel to relinquish control of between 94 and 96 percent of Judea and Samaria and to transfer sovereignty to the Palestinians over an additional 1 to 3 percent of sovereign Israel.

Clinton's parameters represented a radical departure from the U.S. position relating to the Palestinian conflict with Israel. Until he released these guidelines, the United States had never openly stated its support for the establishment of a Palestinian state. It had never asked Israel to give up Jewish control of the Temple Mount or to divide Jerusalem. The only Israeli positions that Clinton's parameters accepted were Israel's refusal to accept the Palestinian demand for a "right of return," and Barak's insistence that the agreement stipulate that the Palestinians recognize that with its signing, their conflict with Israel was over.

Despite the Clinton parameters' insistence that Israel surrender Jerusalem, and agree to shrink into indefensible borders, the Barak government accepted them.

But Arafat, who stood to get everything he said he wanted and in exchange was required only to accept Israel's right to exist in peace with a Palestinian state, rejected Clinton's parameters.[17]

As Ben-Ami explained, Arafat's rejection of the parameters, and his refusal to make a counteroffer, demonstrated that his stated peaceful intentions toward Israel were a bluff. Seven years after embarking on the peace process, Arafat was as unwilling to accept Israel's right to exist as he had been at the outset of his career as a terror leader in the late 1950s. His Palestinian brethren were similarly unwilling to make peace with Israel.

The peace process had been a hoax. In Ben-Ami's words, "Arafat's concession vis-à-vis Israel at [the outset of the peace process] ... was a formal concession. Morally and conceptually, he didn't recognize Israel's right to exist. He doesn't accept the idea of two states for two peoples. . . . Neither he nor the Palestinian national movement accept us."[18]

Ben-Ami concluded, "We are in a confrontation with a national movement in which there are serious pathological elements. It is a very sad movement, a very tragic movement, which at its core doesn't have the ability to set itself positive goals. . . . More than they want a state of their own, they want to spit out our state. In the deepest sense of the words, their ethos is a negative ethos."[19]

The peace process was and remains based on the assumption that the

PLO is interested in being appeased. It presumes that the Palestinians have aspirations for statehood that Israel can satisfy through a land-for-peace formula while still remaining a viable Jewish nation-state. Through their actions, every Israeli leader since the onset of the peace process with the PLO has shown a willingness to appease the PLO. Some leaders—like Shimon Peres, Barak, and Ehud Olmert—have stated their willingness to give the Palestinians almost everything they claim they want. Other leaders, like Netanyahu, who do not believe in the Palestinians' good intentions, nevertheless have bowed to U.S. pressure and continued on with the fraudulent peace process.

Given Israel's flexibility and the near-unanimous commitment of its political leaders to appeasement, if Clinton wanted peace between the Palestinians and Israel to be his crowning achievement as president, it would have made sense for him to concentrate his efforts on the Palestinians. That is, he would have better spent his time if he had focused his pressure and assessed the Palestinians' willingness to be appeased.

In this vein, Ben-Ami's point about the negative ethos of Palestinian nationalism is the key insight. An American president has a huge workload. In determining the priorities of his foreign policy, each president needs to consider where U.S. power and influence can have the most impact in terms of securing American national security and protecting the rights of the weakest members of the world community.

In his memoir, Clinton admitted that during his final months in office, he neglected other vital foreign policy challenges in order to devote his energies to the Palestinian-Israeli peace process. He postponed a trip to Japan, and he ignored North Korea—where millions are starved and enslaved by one of the most vicious and anti-American regimes in the world. The North Korean regime began developing its nuclear arsenal during Clinton's tenure in office.[20]

To chase the pipe dream of Middle East peace, Clinton neglected America's most important ally in Asia and ignored the most acute strategic threat to U.S. security in that region because he believed his time was better spent crafting a deal that Arafat—and the Palestinian people as a whole—had no intention of agreeing to.

Here it is important to recall the context in which Clinton made his proposal. His most pro-Palestinian proposal, the parameters that he communicated to the Israelis and the Palestinians on December 23,

2000, came two months into the Palestinian terror war against Israel. Nearly fifty Israelis had already been murdered. Most of the attacks had been carried out by forces controlled by Arafat, including members of his U.S.-funded and -trained security forces.[21]

The idea that, in the midst of an all-out Palestinian terror campaign that targeted Israeli civilians, the Palestinian leadership would be interested in setting violence aside and embracing Israel as its partner in peace is patently absurd. And yet that's when the United States made its most far-reaching offer of appeasement. Clinton put the full prestige of the White House behind a program that was not simply futile—it was counterproductive.

Perhaps the most unnerving aspect of Clinton's failure to recognize that the Palestinians were uninterested in being appeased in 2000 is that there was nothing new about this state of affairs. For the eighty years preceding the Camp David summit and Clinton's final weeks in office, all the Palestinian leaders, and the Palestinian people as a collective, had maintained the same intransigent position. Moreover, Israel's willingness to endanger its own existence in an attempt to persuade its neighbors to recognize its right to exist and to live at peace with it was also in keeping with eighty years of continuous Jewish willingness to pay almost any price for peace with the Arabs.

America's failure to recognize the implications of the Palestinians' position for their regional posture and interests is consistent with the failure of Great Britain—the world power the United States replaced as regional power broker. Rather than learn the lessons of Britain's failures, the United States has repeated those failures. In the next chapter, we shall study those lessons.

Haj Amin el-Husseini and the Forgotten Lessons of the British Mandate for Palestine, 1917–1948

Clinton's policy of appeasing the Palestinians at Israel's expense was of a piece with Britain's unfortunate forty-year history in the region in the first half of the twentieth century. As the successor of the British as a world superpower, U.S. policy makers should have studied the history of British involvement in the Land of Israel and learned from that experience. Had they done so, they surely would have recognized that the goal of the Palestinian national movement has far more to do with destroying the Jewish state than with establishing a Palestinian state.

From the end of World War I through 1948, Britain was in charge of the area that today comprises Israel, Judea, Samaria, and Gaza. From 1922 through 1946, present-day Jordan was also administered by Britain. British administration of the area was legally anchored in the 1922 League of Nations Mandate for Palestine.

The league set up the mandatory system as a means of administering the colonial possessions of the Ottoman Empire, which was defeated during World War I. The rationale of the mandate system was to place Allied powers in charge of the Ottoman Turks' former colonial possessions in order to prepare them for statehood.

WORLD WAR I AND THE BRITISH MANDATE FOR PALESTINE

The British experience in the Holy Land began with the best of intentions.

During World War I, Prime Minister David Lloyd George and Foreign Secretary Lord Arthur Balfour formed a core group of British statesmen who saw the approaching collapse of the Ottoman Empire as an opportunity to reshape the Middle East. The Jews, the only nation that ever had an independent state in the Land of Israel, would see a reconstitution of their commonwealth.

As for the Arabs, once freed of Ottoman imperial rule, they would be able to determine their destiny as an independent nation. As the British political leaders saw it, there was no contradiction between Zionism and Arab nationalism. They viewed the latter as a pan-Arab movement that could and would be satisfied outside the confines of the Palestine Mandate, the area that encompassed the historic Land of Israel on both sides of the Jordan River.

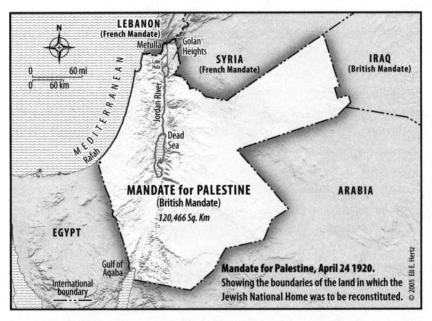

Original Territory Assigned to the Jewish National Home[1]

Whereas the Arabs would be given sovereignty over the rest of the Middle East, the Palestine Mandate was set aside for "close Jewish settlement," toward the reconstitution of the Jewish homeland after nearly two thousand years of forced exile.

To advance the goal of Jewish independence during World War I, the British government established two Jewish legions. First in 1915 the Zion Mule Corps fought at Gallipoli. Then in 1917 the Jewish Legion played an instrumental role in the British conquest of the Land of Israel.[2]

On November 2, 1917, Lloyd George's cabinet approved what became known as the Balfour Declaration. The declaration came in the form of a letter from Balfour to Lord Walter Rothschild, one of the heads of the British Jewish community. It represented a formal pledge of the British government to the Jewish people, represented by the Zionist movement.

Balfour declared: "His Majesty's Government view with favour the establishment in Palestine of a national home for the Jewish people, and will use their best endeavours to facilitate the achievement of the object, it being clearly understood that nothing shall be done which may prejudice the civil and religious rights of existing non-Jewish communities in Palestine, or the rights and political status enjoyed by Jews in any other country."[3]

The Balfour Declaration electrified world Jewry, and its pledge later was expanded and given the weight of binding international law. In 1922 the League of Nations gave Britain control of the Palestine Mandate—which included present-day Israel, Judea and Samaria, Gaza, and Jordan—to cultivate as the Jewish national home for the purpose of re-constituting a Jewish commonwealth over the entire area. The Mandate represents the anchor of Israel's sovereign rights to Judea and Samaria—and makes clear that Israel alone has a claim to legal sovereignty over those areas.

But as so often happens in democracies, the wishes of the political leadership were subverted by the bureaucracy. In the case of British support for Zionism, the political leadership's orders were subverted by the military authorities, first in Cairo and then, after the British conquest of Israel, in Jerusalem.[4]

Motivated in equal part by hatred of Jews and by a desire to build relations with the Arabs at the expense of the Jewish national project, the British military authorities, led by General Edmund Allenby, the high commissioner of Egypt, and General Louis Bols, the chief administrator of Palestine, colluded with the local Arabs to foment violence against the Jews, hoping that an early outbreak of violence would persuade the British government to withdraw the Balfour Declaration. During the Passover holiday in 1920, Arab rioters entered the Jewish quarter of Jerusalem and conducted a three-day assault on the defenseless Jewish population. Five were killed. Two women were raped. More than a hundred Jews were wounded.

The riots were directly incited by a local Muslim strongman from a prominent Jerusalem clan named Haj Amin el-Husseini. The following year British authorities appointed Husseini to lead the Palestinian Arabs.

Although Husseini's role was central to the attacks, they were not his brainchild. According to Colonel Richard Meinertzhagen, who served as the chief political officer for Palestine and Syria, the riots were conceived by Colonel Waters Taylor, an adviser of General Bols. A few days before Easter in 1920, Taylor met with Husseini and told him that "he had a great opportunity at Easter to show the world ... that Zionism was unpopular not only with the Palestine Administration but in Whitehall and if disturbances of sufficient violence occurred in Jerusalem at Easter, both General Bols and General Allenby would advocate the abandonment of the Jewish Home. Waters Taylor explained that freedom could only be attained through violence."[5]

In the aftermath of those riots, and in an attempt to hide their obviously anti-Jewish character, the British put out arrest warrants for the Arabs who had been involved in the violence and for the Jews involved in defending the Jews of Jerusalem from massacre. Haj Amin el-Husseini was indicted and tried in absentia (he had fled to Jordan) and sentenced to ten years in prison. Zev Jabotinsky, the Zionist leader who founded the Zion Mule Corps and the Jewish Legion, was tried and sentenced to fifteen years in prison for organizing the Jewish defense.[6]

The ensuing outcry from the local Jewish community and from Jabotinsky's supporters in Britain caused the British political authorities in London to end the military government in 1920. In its place, they set up a civilian-led Mandatory government headed by High Commissioner Herbert Samuel, a prominent British Jew with a history of support for Zionism.[7]

Whatever his initial intentions may have been, Samuel came under a barrage of insinuation and assault from the anti-Zionist military commanders in Jerusalem and Cairo. They claimed that his Zionist positions would inflame the passions of the Arab world against the British.

One of Samuel's first acts as high commissioner was to issue a full pardon for Jabotinsky. But under pressure from the military officials, he also issued a blanket pardon for all the Arabs and Jews who had been arrested and tried for their roles as assailants and defenders in the 1920 pogrom.[8]

Even worse, following the advice of his military advisers and colleagues, Samuel appointed Husseini the mufti of Jerusalem and elevated his status to that of grand mufti. No other another single action in the history of the British Mandate had a more devastating effect. From that moment on, British fortunes in the Palestine Mandate, and indeed throughout the Middle East, were tied to that decision. Husseini had already distinguished himself through his violent rejection of Jewish national rights to the Land of Israel; Samuel's elevation of him was the death knell for any prospect that the Arabs in the Palestine Mandate would live peacefully with the Jews in the Jewish national home.

WHO WAS HAJ AMIN EL-HUSSEINI?

Haj Amin el-Husseini was the founder of the Palestinian people. But he was more than that: arguably, he was the most important leader in the Arab world in the twentieth century.

Husseini played a major role in shaping the two major modern political streams in the Arab and Islamic world—National Socialism and Islamism. He was the most influential Muslim leader on the world stage during World War II. To a significant degree, he shaped the conditions that have governed the great powers' relations with the Palestinians and the Arab world as a whole ever since.

After appointing Husseini to serve as the mufti of Jerusalem, Samuel gave him the additional appointment of leader of the Supreme Muslim Council. The two offices gave Husseini absolute control of the Muslim community's religious and economic life: the office of the mufti was responsible for dictating the former, and the Supreme Muslim Council controlled the community's purse strings.

Samuel's appointment of Husseini as head of the Muslim Arab community had disastrous consequences for the British and the Jews alike. It initiated what became the pattern governing Britain's relations with the Palestinians: the Palestinians employed murder and terror to harm the Jews, and the British, hoping to appease them, rewarded them with more power.

When Husseini incited the 1920 pogrom, he was not acting out of Palestinian nationalist passion per se. He rejected the independent existence of a specifically Palestinian Arab land or people and saw the local Arabs as part of a larger pan-Arab or pan-Syrian nation, or Islamic *umma*. And so it is hardly surprising he had no interest in inculcating the Arabs of the Palestine Mandate with a positive, unique group identity, distinguishable from a larger pan-Arab or pan-Syrian identity.[9]

According to historians David Dalin and John Rothmann, Husseini forged his Islamic views as a young man in high school and university in Cairo. It was through those studies as well that he developed a genocidal, all-encompassing hatred of Jews as the enemies of God.[10]

When Husseini's rejection of the concept of a distinct Palestinian Arab people is combined with his belief in jihadist Islam and his genocidal anti-Semitism, it is hardly surprising that the identity he invented for the Arabs of Mandatory Palestine was based not on their positive aspirations but on their most destructive, negative urges. He forged a national pathos for the Arabs of Palestine shaped not around who they were but around whom they sought to destroy. Husseini's vision of the Palestinian Arab nation and national movement was based entirely on rejecting the Jewish national liberation movement—Zionism. His goal was not to build up his people; it was to destroy the Zionist movement and eradicate the Jewish presence from the Land of Israel.[11]

As the official leader of the Arabs of Mandatory Palestine, Husseini operated much as he had before he assumed his official roles. He employed a strategy based on terrorism, sabotage, and political agitation. His targets were the Jews and the British Mandatory government. His immediate goal was to end Jewish immigration.

Building on his success in leveraging his incitement of the 1920 pogrom into real political power, Husseini employed terrorism as a strategic weapon again and again. Between 1929 and 1933, he engineered successive waves of terror assaults against Jews and British throughout the country. In 1929 he incited a massive terror onslaught against the Jews. Jews living on the outskirts of Jerusalem, in Jerusalem, in Hebron, in the Gaza Strip, and in Safed were specifically targeted. By the end of the terror campaign, 135 Jews were killed, including entire families murdered in their homes, and 300 were wounded.

The British responded to the riots by persecuting the Jews. The ancient Jewish community of Hebron was their primary victim. Husseini's terrorists had massacred 67 Jews in Hebron; British authorities then forced the 435 survivors to evacuate their homes, surrendering them to their assailants.

In Gaza, Arab gangs attacked the Jews at Kibbutz Kfar Darom. There too the British evacuated the survivors, ceding their lands to their murderers.[12]

BRITAIN'S BETRAYAL OF THE MANDATE AND THE JEWS

Following the 1929 riots, successive British governments formed a series of commissions and published a series of reports, each one more hostile to Zionism than the last.

The March 1930 Shaw Commission report recommended placing limitations on Jewish immigration and sought to explain and so to justify the Arab assaults on defenseless Jews. The report claimed that the violence was due to "racial animosity on the part of the Arabs, consequent upon the disappointment of their political and national aspirations and fear for their economic future." The October 1930 Hope-Simpson report claimed that the Palestine Mandate—excluding Jordan, which had been removed from the Mandate in 1922—could not economically support more than twenty thousand additional families.[13]

Finally, the October 1930 Passfield White Paper, written by British colonial secretary Lord Passfield, attempted to renounce the Balfour Declaration. It claimed that the Mandate was discriminatory toward the Arabs of Palestine and that the policy should be revised. It called for restricting Jewish immigration and Jewish land purchases.[14]

The Passfield White Paper caused an uproar not only in the Jewish world but in the British House of Commons. There the remaining members of the government that had passed the Balfour Declaration arose in condemnation. Former prime minister David Lloyd George accused Prime Minister Ramsay MacDonald of "failing the trust he had inherited with office and breaking the word of England." The political backlash forced the MacDonald government to reverse course. On February 13, 1931, MacDonald penned a letter to Zionist leader Chaim Weitzmann repudiating the Passfield White Paper.[15]

In his book *Crossroads to Israel, 1917–1948*, British historian Christo-

pher Sykes considered the British practice of sending commissions of inquiry following massacres:

> The Shaw report is the starting point of a certain rhythm to be
> noticed from then on in the affairs of Palestine under the Man-
> date. A Royal Commission goes out to the troubled land; its rec-
> ommendations lead to the sending of a subsidiary commission to
> make definitive proposals on how to put the recommendations
> into effect; the proposals conflict with too much of settled con-
> viction and involve too much political risk to be acted on; both
> Commissions proved to have been a waste of talent and time. This
> frequent sending of abortive commissions to Palestine was part of
> that belief which continues at the present time, namely that if one
> can only get a clear statement of any problem, its solution must
> likewise become clear. The belief appears to be true of only a few
> areas of experience and was never to be true of Palestine.[16]

The practice of sending delegations continued in the 1930s. But as
the prospect of war with Germany increased, Britain's desire to appease
all opponents rose along with it. And as a consequence, "settled convictions" became less settled.

By the mid-1930s, the voices that had been powerful enough to scup-
per anti-Zionist proposals in 1931 were too weak to influence policy. As
the dangers to European Jewry intensified with the rise of the Nazis to
power in Germany, Britain betrayed its legal commitment to the Jewish
people under the Palestine Mandate. It sided with the Arabs, even as the
Arabs' sympathy and support for the genocidal goals of Nazi Germany
became more and more obvious.

The Nazis' ascent to power in Germany in 1933 and the increased
persecution of German Jewry had two related effects on the situation in
Mandatory Palestine. First, it demonstrated with ever increasing clarity
that European Jewry was endangered as never before. As a result, world
Jewry increasingly viewed Zionism as the best way to save the Jewish
people from physical annihilation and humiliating powerlessness.

On the other hand, the rise of the Nazis gave the Arab world, now
supportive of the jihadist movement in Palestine, a way of threatening

the British. With the United States deeply committed to isolationism as a foreign policy strategy, the Jews had no possible outside sponsor other than Great Britain. In contrast, the leaders of the Arab world repeatedly threatened the British with the prospect of forming an Arab-German alliance against them.

HUSSEINI AND THE 1936–39 ARAB TERROR WAR

From 1936 to 1939, the increasing peril of European Jewry and the expansion of Arab leverage against the British formed the backdrop of a renewed Arab terrorist onslaught. This terror war, popularly known as the Arab Revolt, actually began with anti-British violence in 1933.

In March 1933 Husseini made the case for an Arab revolt against the British. In his view, without British support, "Zionism was helpless and therefore the immediate need was to concentrate the attack not on the Jews but on their British supporters."[17]

In December 1935 the British high commissioner to Palestine, Sir Arthur Wauchope, presented a plan to establish a constitutional government in the Mandate. An elected council would govern the country; the proposed legislature would ensure a permanent majority for Arabs and so would end the British commitment to establishing a national homeland for the Jewish people.

Wauchope doubtless believed his proposal would alleviate Arab opposition to Britain. For the previous three years, Husseini and his followers had consistently demanded a representative governing council that would render the Jews a permanent minority in their homeland. But when Wauchope offered them precisely what they claimed they wanted, the Arabs refused to accept it. They argued that his proposal didn't go far enough because it didn't entail a complete cessation of Jewish immigration.[18]

In April 1936 the Arab terror war began officially, under Husseini's direction. In its initial stage, the Arabs confined their attacks to murdering defenseless Jews, including nurses and patients at a hospital, theatergoers, and bus passengers. In its later stages, they directed the terror against the British and against moderate Arabs who dissented from Husseini's policies. The terror war continued until 1939, during which time Husseini's henchmen murdered nearly an equal number of Arabs and Jews—547 Jews, and 494 Arabs.[19]

Husseini also used his position as grand mufti to impose sharia (Islamic law) as the law of the land for Arabs—Muslim and Christian alike. To this end, in August 1938 he issued an Islamic fatwa (religious decree) requiring all local Arabs—Muslim and Christian alike—to conform to an Islamic dress code. Although men in Mandatory Palestine traditionally wore the Turkish fez cap, Husseini required them to wear khaffiyehs, or Bedouin headdresses; those who refused were murdered. Women were required to hide their faces under veils; those who refused were harassed by Islamic goon squads.[20]

Significantly, by the end of 1936, the guerrilla forces involved in the terror war were commanded by foreign Arabs. Thus the Arab Revolt signaled the beginning of the pan-Arab commitment to the eradication of the Jewish national liberation movement—for the benefit not of the Palestinian Arabs but of the Islamic nation.[21] Husseini's decision three years earlier to frame his war against the Jews as a jihad in which the entire Islamic world held a stake "internationalized" the campaign against the Jews, as the surrounding Arab states assisted the Palestinian Arabs in their war to eradicate the Jews from the Land of Israel.

BRITAIN'S RESPONSE: THE PEEL COMMISSION REPORT

The British responded to the terror war by appealing to Arab leaders in Saudi Arabia, Transjordan, Yemen, and Iraq to call for an end to the violence. As payoff for their support, the British formed a new commission whose declared goals gave the Arabs reason to believe that the British would capitulate to their demands to completely betray their obligations to the Jews.

The royal commission led by Lord William Peel was formed in July 1936 and published its report and recommendations in July 1937. In his testimony before the commission, Husseini presented what had by then become his unyielding demands for the destruction of Zionism. He demanded that the British abandon their support for a Jewish national home; institute a complete cessation on Jewish immigration and Jewish land purchases; and abrogate the Mandate, replacing it with an Anglo-Arab treaty giving sovereign control of the country to the Arabs.

Lord Peel asked Husseini what he intended to do with the 400,000 Jews then living in the Palestine Mandate. Did he, for instance, intend to expel them "by a process kindly or painful as the case may be?" Husseini responded darkly, "We must leave all of this to the future."[22]

The Peel Commission determined that the two nationalist movements within the Palestine Mandate were incompatible. The commissioners further decided that the only way to solve the conflict was through partition—that is, the institution of a two-state solution. The Jewish state would be tiny, located along the coastal plain within indefensible borders.

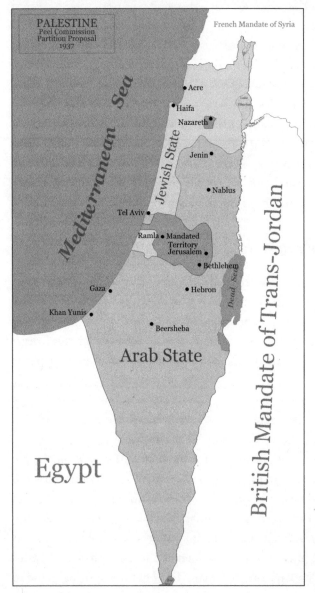

PALESTINE
Peel Commission
Partition Proposal
1937

French Mandate of Syria

Mediterranean Sea

Jewish State

• Acre
• Haifa
Nazareth •
Jenin •
• Nablus
Tel Aviv •
Ramla • Mandated
Territory
Jerusalem •
• Bethlehem
Gaza •
• Hebron
Khan Yunis •
• Beersheba

Arab State

Dead Sea

British Mandate of Trans-Jordan

Egypt

Peel Commission Partition Plan Proposed by the Peel Commission Report, 1937[23]

The rest of the territory would be transferred to Arab sovereignty and eventually absorbed into Transjordan, or, in the case of a corridor including Jerusalem and stretching to Jaffa port on the Mediterranean coast, remain under British mandatory control.

The boundaries of the proposed Jewish state were impossible for the Jews or their supporters to accept. But while the Zionist leadership rejected the proposed boundaries, most accepted the principle of partition.

On the other hand, the Arabs rejected the entire possibility of partition. This rejection was not merely a local Arab response. The Arab terror war, seeking the destruction of Zionism, became openly pan-Arab and pan-Islamic, as was made clear when British-allied Iraqi prime minister Nuri es Said told the Iraqi parliament, "Any person venturing to agree to act as head of such a state [meaning the Arab state in partitioned Palestine] would be regarded as an outcast throughout the Arab world."[24]

Following the publication of the Peel Commission report, the Arabs of the Palestine Mandate, led by foreign Arab commanders, escalated their terror war against the Jews and British alike. In the months after the Commssion's recommendations were made public, the leaders of the Arab states met twice, first in Syria and then in Cairo. At both conferences they threatened that if Britain failed to abandon its support for the Jewish national home, the Arabs would side with the Germans against the British.[25]

With the specter of war looming ever more menacingly, the British opted to appease the Arabs. They abandoned the last vestiges of their support for the Jewish national project. They took several preparatory steps to abandon the Peel Commission report,[26] and then on May 17, 1939, they published the White Paper.

BRITISH CAPITULATION TO ARAB TERROR: THE 1939 WHITE PAPER

The White Paper represented Britain's near-total acceptance of the Arab demands. It rejected the notion of a Jewish national home in Palestine and claimed that the British had never actually supported the establishment of any such thing. Instead, it claimed that the British, by allowing the Jewish population of Palestine to grow to 450,000, had met their obligations to the Jews, as set out in the Palestine Mandate. As the White Paper put it, "His Majesty's Government therefore now declares unequivocally that it is not part of their policy that Palestine should become a Jewish State."[27]

Rather than a Jewish state or partition, the White Paper stated, "the objective of His Majesty's Government is the establishment within 10 years of an independent Palestine State in such treaty relations with the United Kingdom as will provide satisfactorily for the commercial and strategic requirements of both countries in the future. . . . The independent State should be one in which Arabs and Jews share government in such a way as to ensure that the essential interests of each community are safeguarded."

While the White Paper was notably silent on how the Jews would be protected under such an arrangement, it was explicit about its intention to ensure that the Jews would be a minority in that state. It limited Jewish immigration to 75,000 over the next five years and said that any subsequent Jewish immigration would require the permission of the Arabs.

The White Paper also placed draconian limitations on Jewish land purchases. After the House of Lords passed the White Paper, the Mandatory government issued a series of edicts to implement its anti-Jewish policy. In March 1940, on the issue of land purchases, the British high commissioner divided Palestine into three zones. Zone A consisted of 63 percent of the land, including Judea and Samaria; there land transfers to Jews were prohibited. Zone B consisted of 32 percent of the land, where Jewish land purchases required the approval of the high commissioner. In the remaining 5 percent of the country, Jews were permitted to continue purchasing land.

The chairman of the League of Nations' Permanent Mandates Commission issued critical comments about the White Paper and the Land Transfer Regulations. Both were material breaches of Britain's obligations under international law. But the British were undeterred. Indeed, even the 5 percent of the Mandate that was supposed to be available for Jewish land purchase was an illusion, as Jews already owned half the land in that zone.[28]

For obvious reasons, the Jewish people—in the Land of Israel and throughout the world—condemned the White Paper and the Land Transfer Regulations as material breaches of Britain's international legal commitments under the 1922 League of Nations Mandate. By 1939 every major nation had blocked Jews from immigrating to their territory. On the eve of the Holocaust, as the gates of hell were closing in around European Jewry, the British opted to close their last remaining destination for escape.

MAP OF THE LAND TRANSFER REGULATIONS, FEBRUARY 1940[29]

The Prohibited Area: Zone A
Area in which consent is required: Zone B
The Free Zone
Jewish land holdings in the three Zones

Arguably more shocking than Britain's betrayal of the Jews was the Arab reaction to this betrayal. They objected to the White Paper's support for the immigration over five years of 75,000 additional Jews to Mandatory Palestine. When some Arab political activists indicated they would support the White Paper, terrorists controlled by Husseini murdered a member of the group. As for the Arab world, which the British sought to appease by abandoning Zionism, no Arab government agreed to accept the White Paper.[30]

Britain's belief that siding with the Arabs against the Jews would secure Arab support in World War II owed to its mistaken belief that the source of anti-British sentiment rampant in the Arab world was caused by earlier British support for Zionism and Jewish statehood. Underpinning this belief was a worldview that perceived the Arabs as objects, rather than actors; as people who responded to outside stimuli, rather than people guided by internal motivations and interests.

Despite the fact that he was appointed to his leadership roles by the British, Haj Amin el-Husseini became a Nazi agent. In Iraq, pro-Nazi allies of the mufti staged a coup in 1941 and overthrew the pro-British government. At Britain's moment of greatest peril, as Rommel's Afrika Corps was poised to take over Egypt and eject the British from the Middle East, London was forced to send massive reinforcements to Iraq to defeat the pro-Nazi coup and reinstall the previous government.[31]

Writing of the pro-Nazi sentiment rampant in the Arab world, in 1939 American journalist John Gunther noted, "The greatest contemporary Arab hero is probably Hitler."[32]

The main factor that motivated the Arabs to support the Nazis was not British actions in the Mandate. It was Jew hatred. The British recognized the potency of Islamic Jew hatred, and hoping to appease it, they betrayed the Jews. But their actions were doomed to failure. No matter how harshly they treated the hated Jews, the British could never match German anti-Semitism.

Since the British could never be more anti-Semitic than the Nazis, their treatment of the Jews in the Mandate would never be sufficiently genocidal to win over the hearts and minds of the Arabs. Given this depraved political culture, the only way the British could secure Arab support was by appealing to their other interests. Specifically, Britain needed to convince Arab leaders that their personal or national interests were best secured by siding with Britain against Germany. And, indeed, to the extent Arab leaders, including the kings of Saudi Arabia and Transjordan, supported Britain at all, they did so because they believed their personal—rather than pan-Arab or pan-Islamic—interests were best advanced by the British. In line with this, Arab support for Britain grew as the Allies' fortunes in the war became more positive. The bulk of Arab support for the British began after the 1943 Allied victories in Italy, because at that point many Arabs were convinced the Allies would win the war.

In short, power assessments and an affinity for the Germans' annihilationist anti-Semitism, rather than Arab dissatisfaction with any particular British policy toward the Jews in the Palestine Mandate, were what motivated Arab hostility toward Britain. And neither of these motivating factors was determined by British actions, except to the extent that by appeasing the Arabs, the British looked weak. All the steps to appease the Arabs that the British undertook from 1920 were for naught. Appeasement as a tool of statecraft was counterproductive toward the Arab world as it was toward Nazi Germany.

Counterintuitively, then, Britain's best move in managing the Mandate up to and during World War II would have been to support the Jews against the Arabs. By doing so the British would have demonstrated strength rather than weakness.

HUSSEINI AND THE SHAPING OF MODERN ARAB POLITICS

More than any other single individual, Haj Amin el-Husseini guaranteed that the British attempts to appease the Arabs had no chance of succeeding. For more than any other single individual, Husseini shaped the politics of the post–Ottoman Empire Arab world. Since it was the British who had empowered him, they were the authors of their failure in the Middle East.

In the 1920s, when the British appointed Husseini to lead the Arabs of the Palestine Mandate, the Arab world had been in a state of flux. The defeat of the Ottoman Empire, which had led the Arab world for hundreds of years, placed the Arabs on unfamiliar political terrain. Mustafa Kemal Atatürk, the founder of the post-Ottoman Turkish Republic, had abrogated the Ottoman caliphate in 1924, leaving a political and religious leadership vacuum that others sought to fill.

In Egypt, Islamist political activists and scholars led by Hassan al-Banna and Sayyid Qutb formed the Muslim Brotherhood in 1928. Their goal was to build a global Islamic network that would wage jihad to re-establish the caliphate as the ruler of the Islamic world and, once that succeeded, to wage jihad for world domination under the flag of Islam. Husseini became a partner to al-Banna and Qutb as he fashioned his local opposition to the Jews and the British into a pan-Islamic rallying cry for jihad.

In 1931, to advance his goal of establishing a pan-Islamic jihad against the Jews and the British, Husseini founded the World Islamic Congress. At its first conference in Jerusalem, the congress included representatives from every Islamic country. Husseini was elected to serve as its leader. He used the platform to call for the eradication of the Jews in the Land of Israel, and to call on Muslims to violently attack Jews and the British throughout the Islamic world.

One of Husseini's greatest contributions to Arab politics, both in the Palestine Mandate and throughout the Arab world, was his fusion of Islamic Jew hatred from the Koran with European racial anti-Semitism.[33] In one of his earliest and most significant forays into this field, he commissioned the translation, and oversaw the dissemination, of the anti-Semitic forgery *The Protocols of the Elders of Zion*. The *Protocols* were written in Russia by the czarist secret police and were first published in 1903. The forgery presents itself as an account of a Jewish conspiracy to dominate the world. The British historian Norman Cohn has argued that the *Protocols*, which were taught as fact in German schools during the Nazi period, were the ideological foundation of the Holocaust.[34]

Husseini had the *Protocols* translated and published in serialized form in the Arabic press in 1922. Since their first appearance, the *Protocols* have continuously served as the ideological basis for anti-Semitic politics throughout Europe, the United States, and beyond. By translating the work into Arabic, Husseini initiated the Islamic embrace of European-style genocidal Jew hatred that still dominates the Islamic discourse on Israel and the Jews today.[35]

HUSSEINI AND THE NAZIS

Husseini's enthusiastic fusion of Islamic Jew hatred from the Koran with European racial anti-Semitism made him an early and enthusiastic supporter of Adolf Hitler and the Nazis. Like much of the Arab world, he celebrated the Nazis' rise to power in Germany in 1933; he even sent a congratulatory letter to Hitler. From the outset, he sought to build an alliance between the Arabs and Berlin against the Jews and the British. Like his Nazi-supporting colleagues in Syria, Morocco, and Egypt, he was heartened by the passage of the 1935 Nuremberg Laws, which institutionalized the discrimination and dehumanization of Jews in Germany. And like them, he used the occasion of their enactment to redouble his efforts to forge an alliance with Nazi Germany.[36]

In the early years of the Nazi regime, Hitler felt constrained to maintain good relations with the British to facilitate his smooth consolidation of dictatorial powers in Germany and his remilitarization of German society and the Rhineland. The Nazis began responding positively to Husseini's attempts to forge a German-Arab alliance only in late 1937.

In that year, with his plans to annex Austria and take over Czechoslovakia finalized, Hitler saw that war with Britain was inevitable. Maintaining good relations with the British therefore slid to the bottom of his list of priorities. And supporting the Palestinian Arab terror war against the Jews and the British in Mandatory Palestine became an attractive proposition. By pinning the British down in the Middle East, Hitler could limit their ability to respond effectively to aggressive actions in Europe. And so in 1937, the Germans began arming and funding the Palestinian Arab terror war against the Jews and the British in the Palestine Mandate.[37] At the same time, they also began supporting the Muslim Brotherhood in Egypt.[38]

Husseini did not seek to hide his new alliance with Germany. He reveled in it. His followers in the Land of Israel greeted one another with the Nazi salute and wore swastika armbands. At celebrations of the Islamic prophet Muhammad's birthday, Arabs in Mandatory Palestine, as well as much of the rest of the Muslim world, flew Nazi and Italian fascist flags in the streets.[39]

Despite Britain's ardent desire to appease Husseini, his open ties with the Nazis and his instigation of the terror campaign against the British in Palestine finally forced its hand. In 1937 the British issued a warrant for Husseini's arrest. Husseini fled to Beirut. In 1939 he fled to Iraq.[40]

Outside Palestine, Husseini began agitating the wider Arab world to turn on Britain and side with the Nazis. During his two years in Iraq, he was in close contact with Fritz Grobba, the German ambassador in Baghdad. He also developed close ties with leading generals in the Iraqi military, who like him were ardent supporters of Germany.

Husseini assisted the Germans in writing and disseminating anti-Jewish and pro-Nazi propaganda. He incited the military leadership against Britain. In April 1941, under his guidance, four pro-Nazi Iraqi generals, led by General Rashid Ali al-Gaylani, overthrew the pro-British government of Regent Abdullah and Prime Minister Nuri as-Said.[41]

The ousted government had been in an alliance with Britain. Britain responded to its overthrow by invading Iraq. By late May, Britain had reinstated its control of the oil fields in Basra, and British victory was a foregone conclusion. Allied forces were poised to take over Baghdad. With hope for victory now nil, at Husseini's urging, the pro-Nazi junta used their residual power to carry out a massive assault on Baghdad's Jewish community.[42] One hundred twenty Jews were murdered, a thousand were wounded, and thousands more lost their homes as pro-Nazi mobs torched Jewish homes and businesses.[43]

Forced to flee the British forces descending on Baghdad, Husseini and al-Gaylani escaped to Tehran, which at the time was governed by the pro-Nazi shah Reza Pahlavi. Influenced by Husseini's pro-Nazi propaganda, and enthusiastically supporting the Nazi cause, the shah intended to bring Iran completely into the Axis, ending its oil exports to the Allies. In October 1941 the Allies forced the shah to abdicate in favor of his son, Mohammed Reza Pahlavi.[44]

Moving one step ahead of Allied forces, Husseini and al-Gaylani escaped again. Husseini was spirited out of the country on an Italian air force plane. Upon arriving in Rome, he met with Benito Mussolini and pledged that if the Axis powers recognized an Arab state under his leadership, encompassing Iraq, Syria, Lebanon, Transjordan, and the Palestine Mandate, he would galvanize Arab support for their war effort. He also secured Axis support for his proposal that the Axis would recognize the Arabs' right "to deal with Jewish elements in Palestine and in the other Arab countries according to their own interests."[45]

On November 7 he was flown to Berlin, and three weeks after his arrival, on November 28, 1941, he had a ninety-five-minute meeting with Adolf Hitler. There Hitler told Husseini of his plan to exterminate European Jewry. As the official Nazi report of the meeting says, after Hitler destroyed "the Judeo-communist empire in Europe," he would aid Husseini in the "destruction of the Jewish element residing in the Arab sphere."

Husseini, in his account of the meeting, wrote, "Our fundamental condition for cooperating with Germany was a free hand to eradicate every last Jew from Palestine and the Arab world. I asked Hitler for an explicit undertaking to allow us to solve the Jewish people in a manner befitting our national and racial aspirations and according to the scientific methods innovated by Germany in the handling of its Jews. The answer I got was: 'The Jews are yours.' "[46]

With Hitler's pledge to support his aim to annihilate the Jews and to elevate him to pan-Arab leadership in a German-controlled Middle East, Husseini eagerly used all his powers and resources to build pan-Arab and Islamic support for the Nazi war effort.

As we noted earlier, ahead of the German invasion of Poland, Hitler was keen to pin the British down in the Middle East by expanding the Arab war against them in Mandatory Palestine. To that end, on April 25, 1939, near Berlin, the Germans began around-the-clock Arabic-language broadcasts, with the most powerful shortwave transmitter in existence at the time. Shortly after his arrival in Berlin in late 1941, Husseini began daily broadcasts on the Nazi Arabic station. His programs were a refined synthesis of Islamic Jew hatred and European racial anti-Semitism that he had been developing for the past twenty years. He melded Koranic verses referring to Jews as the enemies of Allah and as descendent of apes and pigs with European conspiracy theories about Jewish plots to corrupt and dominate the world.[47]

Through his Nazi radio broadcasts, Husseini's became the most familiar voice in the Islamic world. Millions of ardent followers throughout the Middle East and North Africa listened to his calls for the Muslims to rise up against the British and the Jews.[48]

Husseini was also directly involved in expanding Germany's military capabilities by setting up Muslim military and SS units. His greatest contribution in this arena came in early 1943, when he helped establish the Handschar SS Division, comprised of Bosnian Muslims, which actively participated in the Holocaust. They murdered 90 percent—12,600—of Bosnia's Jewish community of 14,000.[49]

The founder of the Palestinian national movement was also instrumental in sealing the fates of at least ten thousand, and arguably more than a hundred thousand, Jews in Bulgaria, Hungary, and Romania. In the spring of 1943, the Nazis and the British were negotiating prisoner exchanges in which Jews would be ransomed for German prisoners of war. In one such negotiation, 4,500 Jewish children and 500 Jewish adults from Hungary, Romania, Slovakia, and Bulgaria were to be permitted to emigrate to the Palestine Mandate in exchange for 20,000 German war prisoners. After getting wind of the talks, Husseini intervened with SS chief Heinrich Himmler and other senior Nazis to end the negotiations and ensure that the Jews were sent to Auschwitz to be murdered instead.[50]

Adolf Eichmann, the SS officer responsible for planning and organizing the Holocaust of European Jewry, reportedly hosted Husseini in his offices and showed him plans for the eradication of every Jewish community in Europe. According to Eichmann's deputy Dieter Wisliceny, "The Mufti was one of the initiators of the systematic extermination of European Jewry and had been a collaborator and adviser of Eichmann and Himmler in the execution of this plan. . . . He was one of Eichmann's best friends and had constantly incited him to accelerate the extermination measures."[51]

After the war, Husseini's Nazi colleagues were arrested and tried for their war crimes, but Husseini was allowed to escape Europe and return to the Middle East. In 1946 King Farouk of Egypt received him as a war hero. Yugoslavia, France, and Britain had grounds to seek Husseini's indictment at the Nuremberg war crimes tribunal, but all preferred to leave him alone in the hopes of currying favor in the Arab world. The popularity of his outspoken hatred of and violence against the Jews in the Muslim world, which viewed him as a beloved leader due to his role in forming the Muslim Brotherhood and his radio broadcasts from Germany, rendered him immune from prosecution for his war crimes.[52]

THE BRITISH MANDATE IN THE POSTWAR PERIOD, 1945–1948

In the immediate aftermath of the Allied victory, the British might have been tempted to assume that their position in the Arab world would be stronger for their victory. But such an assumption would have been as misplaced as their earlier, prewar conviction that they could win Arab allegiance against the Nazis by appeasing their hatred of the Jews.

As we saw before, the degree to which various Arab leaders were willing to side with the British before and during the war was a function of their perception of British power relative to that of other world powers. As such, it was unrelated to the manner in which Britain administered the Palestine Mandate. So too, in the postwar years, British influence among the region's Arabs diminished as a consequence not of their policies toward the Jews in the Mandate, but of their dwindling power, which the Arabs correctly perceived.[53]

Britain emerged from World War II bankrupt and in desperate need of U.S. financial assistance. This hollowing-out of Britain's imperial capacity played a significant role in pan-Arab hostility toward Britain in the postwar years. So too Soviet competition for Arab support, abetted by the affinity between Arab nationalism and totalitarian governing systems, further contributed to Britain's inability to win Arab support. The Arab League, established in 1945, had "a distinct anti-British bias."[54]

After the war ended, the world was faced with the reality of the genocide that the Germans had committed against the Jews of Europe. Six million Jews, some 75 percent of European Jewry, had been murdered. For the most part, the survivors were unwilling and unable to return to their former homes and were living in displaced persons camps around Europe. The vast majority of them were interested in settling only in the Land of Israel.

On the other side, as Husseini's triumphant arrival in Cairo symbolized, the Arabs remained opposed to any peaceful coexistence with a Jewish state. They refused to budge from their total opposition to all Jewish land purchases in the Mandate and to all Jewish immigration there.

The British, rather than learn the lesson of Arab wartime treachery, adhered strictly to the policies set out in the White Paper. They denied entry to Holocaust survivors. They refused to allow Jews to buy land in most of the country. And by 1946 they turned their focus to destroying the Zionist leadership. The year after the liberation of the death camps, many of the senior leaders of pre-independence Israel were living in Europe in order to evade arrest by the British.[55]

The Holocaust caused a sea change in Jewish opinion worldwide. For the first time, the majority of world Jewry began supporting Zionism. Throughout the world, for Jews and non-Jews alike, the physical, political, and spiritual case for Jewish statehood became obvious.

Under President Harry Truman, the United States began playing a major role in the politics of the Palestine Mandate. It had emerged as a global superpower and as the clear heir to the British Empire; it desired to block the rise of Soviet influence in the region; and throughout the United States, concern for the plight of Jewish refugees in Europe was widespread. By 1945 U.S. lawmakers and the public alike were deeply supportive of the Zionist cause.

In its weakened position in 1946, Britain was unable to assert its sole authority over the Palestine Mandate, and by 1947 it was clear to Britain that its Mandate was as unsustainable as its rule of India. In April of that year, it turned the issue of the Palestine Mandate over to the United Nations, the successor of the League of Nations, which formed the UN's Special Commission on Palestine (UNSCOP) to study the issue. The commission determined that the British Mandate must come to an end. Most UNSCOP members recommended that Palestine be partitioned between a Jewish and an Arab state. Strategically and economically, neither of the states envisioned by UNSCOP was viable. Moreover, the two states would receive sovereignty only after ten years under UN trusteeship.

Despite the fact that the Jewish state on offer was indefensible and involved far less than the Jews' most limited demands for sovereign independence, the Jewish Agency accepted UNSCOP's majority report. Sykes referred to that acceptance as "the boldest essay in moderation . . . the Zionist ruling party ever made."[56]

But again the Arabs said no. The Arabs completely rejected the plan, and the Arab League issued threats of war and invasion of the nascent Jewish state.

Those threats were summarized by the Arab League secretary general Abdul Rahman Azzam on September 15, 1947. In his words, "any attempt to impose [UNSCOP's] recommendations, or any similar scheme would be implacably resisted by the Arabs. Let there be no doubt that the Arabs, if compelled, would fight for Palestine."[57]

In November 1947 the UN General Assembly voted to approve the partition plan, dividing the land under the British Mandate between an Arab and a Jewish state. The next day an all-out Arab assault against the Jews of the Land of Israel began.

At first this war was fought by local forces loyal to Husseini and was commanded by foreign Arabs. It was accompanied by Arab massacres of Jewish communities throughout the Arab world. By January 1948 foreign Arab forces were actively participating in increasingly organized assaults against Jewish villages throughout the country.[58]

On May 15, 1948, the British Mandate officially ended, as the last

UN GENERAL ASSEMBLY RECOMMENDED PARTITION PLAN, 1947[59]

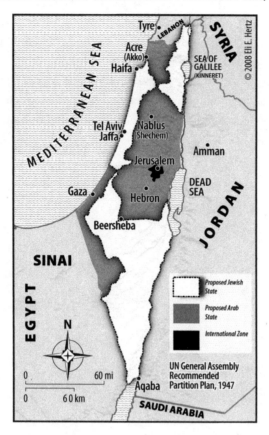

British forces left the country and the State of Israel declared independence. That same day, five Arab armies invaded Israel.

The British failure in governing the Palestine Mandate was bipartisan: the Labour and Conservative Parties both got it wrong, consistently. Both failed to understand that their efforts to appease the Arabs were futile. Both failed to appreciate the value of their alliance with the Jews and to recognize that the Jews were not the obstacle to peace. Both failed to recognize that factors outside their control determined regional realities and informed the decisions of local actors, particularly in the Arab world.

Eighty years later, had President Bill Clinton learned from Britain's

experience, and from the full history of the failure of the two-state solution, perhaps he would not have allowed Yassir Arafat to make him into
a failure as well. But not only did Clinton not learn from Britain's experience, he and his two successors embraced the same failed policy dream
that the British had chased for decades. Clinton, Bush, and Obama's
failure to recognize the impossibility of the two-state solution played a
significant, and arguably decisive, role in their difficulties in crafting successful policies not only toward Israel and the Palestinians but toward
the Middle East overall.

CHAPTER 4

Yassir Arafat: The World's Favorite Terrorist

"The bastard brought them in the trunk of his Mercedes."

That is what Yaakov Peri, the head of Israel's Security Agency, reported to Prime Minister Yitzhak Rabin on July 1, 1994. That day PLO chief Yassir Arafat entered the Gaza Strip in triumph as head of the PLO's newly created Palestinian Authority, responsible for governing the lands Israel transferred to PLO control in the framework of the peace process. In the trunk of his car, Arafat was smuggling in four hardened terrorists whose entry Israel had barred because its security forces believed they constituted a danger to the public.

Arafat's entry into Gaza followed the signing of the Gaza-Jericho Agreement in May 1994. That agreement set out the initial stage of implementation of what was supposed to be a five-year peace process between Israel and the PLO. Under the agreement, Israel transferred to the PLO control of most of the Gaza Strip and of the city of Jericho in Judea.

In order to administer these areas, the PLO set up the Palestinian Authority, which would serve as the interim government of the autonomous Palestinian areas. Arafat, as the head of the PLO, would lead the Palestinian Authority.

Ahead of his entrance into Gaza, Arafat asked Israel to allow his entourage to join him. In response, Israel approved the entry of thousands of PLO terrorists who were to serve in the Palestinian security services.

He also sent Israel a list of about a hundred "old friends" whom he wished to bring into Gaza with him. These "old friends" were all terrorist murderers and commanders who had the blood of hundreds of innocents on their hands. Still, in the atmosphere of peace and reconciliation that

Israel sought to foster, Rabin approved the entry of all but four of the men on Arafat's list.

So Arafat smuggled them in his car.[1]

Arafat's bad faith upon his entry into Gaza was brazen, but it was consistent with his record of action both prior to and following his entry into the peace process with Israel.

In 1994, a week after he signed the Gaza-Jericho Agreement, Arafat gave a speech at a mosque in Johannesburg before a closed audience of South African Muslims. The speech was surreptitiously taped by a South African Jew. In the speech, Arafat said that the agreements that the PLO had signed with Israel were a contemporary version of the Treaty of Hudaibiya, a peace treaty that the Islamic prophet Muhammad had signed with the Quraish tribe in Mecca in 628, only to renounce it two years later when the balance of power shifted in his favor.

"This agreement, I am not considering it more than the agreement which had been signed between our prophet Mohammed and Quraish. . . . Mohammed had accepted it, and we are accepting now this peace offer. But to continue our way to Jerusalem, to the first shrine together and not alone. We are in need of you as Muslims, as warriors of Jihad."[2]

When the transcript of his speech was reported, Israel's government responded with fury and demanded that Arafat retract his statement. Instead, he doubled down and repeated it, both publicly and in private, until his death in 2004.[3]

Like his predecessor, Haj Amin el-Husseini, Arafat was contemptuously confident that he could spell out openly his ill intentions toward Israel and the Jews and suffer no consequences.[4] Husseini had repeatedly told the British that if the Palestinian Arabs took control of the Palestine Mandate, they intended to annihilate the Jews living in the land.[5] And yet despite such statements, and despite Husseini's record of inciting and ordering the murder of Jews both in Israel and in Europe, and despite his direction of anti-British terrorism, and despite his pro-Nazi coups and governments, he continued to be treated as the legitimate leader of the Palestinian people and as a respected leader of the Arab and Islamic worlds generally.

Some historians claim that following his arrival in Egypt in the aftermath of World War II, Haj Amin el-Husseini became Yassir Arafat's mentor.[6] Others dispute this claim and merely allow that the two were distant relatives.[7]

Whatever the actual case may be, Arafat routinely praised Husseini and claimed to be his disciple and heir.[8] In a 2002 interview, for instance, he referred to Husseini as "our hero." He noted proudly that even though the West had known Husseini was a Nazi ally, the United States and Britain had been unable to get rid of him. Drawing a direct connection with himself, Arafat bragged that after the war Husseini "lived in Cairo, and participated in the 1948 war, and I was one of his troops."[9]

Whether Arafat was groomed for Palestinian leadership at Husseini's knee is less significant than the lessons he clearly took from Husseini's experience and beliefs. Husseini's most important legacy was his effort to unify the Islamic world with the Nazis around a shared hatred of Jews. Husseini's accomplishments in that regard transformed him into a figure of international importance. It also rendered him the father of the two most significant political forces in the Muslim world: the modern global jihadist movement, which today is followed by the likes of the Muslim Brotherhood and its terrorist spin-offs—from Al Qaeda to the Egyptian Islamic Jihad to Hamas; and secular pan-Arab fascism, followed by the likes of Egyptian president Gamal Abdel Nasser, the Assads of Syria, and Saddam Hussein of Iraq.

With regard to the Palestinian Arabs specifically, Husseini's fusion of Islamism with National Socialism gave both the secular and Islamic factions of the Palestinian movement the ability to claim they were the legitimate heirs of his legacy.[10]

Throughout his career Arafat, like Husseini, blended terrorism and political warfare. Like Husseini, he used superpower competition for influence in the Middle East to advance his interests at Israel's expense. In Arafat's case, the superpowers were not Britain and Germany but the United States and the Soviet Union. Just as Husseini had been a Nazi agent, so according to Lieutenant General Ion Pacepa, the former head of Romania's DIE (the Romanian version of the Soviet KGB) and the highest-ranking defector from the Soviet bloc to the West, Arafat was a Soviet agent.[11] And just as Husseini had used his alliance with the Nazis to leverage his position with the British, who were so desperate to secure Arab support for the Allied war effort that they adopted anti-Jewish policies in the Palestine Mandate just as the Holocaust was getting underway, so Arafat used his close ties to the Soviets to leverage his position with the United States, which sought to consolidate its power and influence in the Arab world at the Soviet Union's expense.

ISRAEL'S PLACE IN THE SOVIET POLITICAL WAR AGAINST THE WEST

A key part of the Soviet Union's Cold War strategy for fighting the West was to deny the United States and its allies the moral authority to lead the world in a struggle against Communism and tyranny. The Soviets recognized that by causing Western societies to doubt their morality and the justness of their cause, they would curtail the ability of Western leaders to confront Soviet aggression.

To this end, the Soviets sought to co-opt the postwar anticolonialist movement and transform the aspiration of colonial possessions to achieve national self-determination into an anti-Western prejudice. The Soviets believed that by subverting third-world independence movements in this way, they could convince the West, including the United States, that it lacked the moral authority to lead the world in international affairs.[12]

Rejecting Israel's right to exist, and castigating it as an imperialist, racist enclave was a key part of the Soviet strategy. Israel was an anticolonialist state par excellence. The Zionists had fought against both the Ottoman and British empires to secure an independent Jewish state. On the other hand, the Palestinians sided with the Nazis and their goal of global conquest, and they created the pan-Islamic and pan-Arab commitment to destroying the only non-Islamic and non-Arab state in the Middle East.

The combination of Soviet anti-Semitism, Israeli anti-Communism, and admiration for the United States meant that Israel's anticolonialist pedigree presented the Soviets with a serious problem.

So they set about delegitimizing the Jewish state.

The Soviets began their anti-Israel campaign in 1949, when they cut off relations with it.[13] They then began to develop a new political vocabulary for hating and seeking the defeat of Jews. The popular term for Jew hatred—anti-Semitism—had been discredited with the defeat of the Germans in World War II. So the Soviets developed a new term: *anti-Zionism*. In this manner they transformed Israel into the collective Jew, and denigrated Zionism—the Jewish national liberation movement—into a new repository for all the negative characteristics that haters of Jews had previously attributed to Jews as individuals.

In 1965—two years before Israel took control of Judea and Samaria—the Soviets brought their anti-Zionist pitch to the United Nations for the first time. They sponsored a draft resolution at the UN's Subcommission on the Prevention of Discrimination and the Protection of Minorities that lumped Zionism together with Nazism, castigating both as forms of racism. The motion failed, but the process of delegitimizing Israel on the world stage by equating it with Nazi Germany and so rehabilitating anti-Jewish political action as a legitimate policy tool was set in motion.

Eleven years later, the UN General Assembly passed Resolution 3379, which defined Zionism as a form of racism.[14]

YASSIR ARAFAT AND THE MODERN PALESTINIAN MOVEMENT

The Soviet political campaign against Israel, together with the Kremlin's subversion of the anticolonialist movement, is what enabled the Palestinians to gain political legitimacy in the postwar era. On the face of it, the geopolitical environment Husseini operated in during his heyday was much more favorable to the cause of eradicating the Jewish presence in the land of Israel than was the geopolitical environment in the late 1950s, when Arafat began to emerge as Husseini's successor. Husseini operated in a world where anti-Semitism and racism were acceptable political positions in the West. Being a Nazi was a status symbol. Calling for the destruction of Jewry won you influential and powerful friends and allies. And there was no independent State of Israel.

In the aftermath of the Holocaust, none of these positions could be voiced in polite company. Without the Soviet campaign to replace "anti-Semitism" with "anti-Zionism" and so delegitimize Israel and Zionism by linking both to the very forces of imperialism the Jews had fought in their struggle for independence, Arafat would have lacked the political cover to proceed in his open plan to continue Hitler's work.

Thanks to the Soviets, Arafat never even tried to hide that his goal was to destroy Israel, or that he and his followers were terrorists. To the contrary, Arafat declared these truths in the founding document of his Fatah terror group, written in 1957.[15]

Article 12 of Fatah's constitution called for the "complete liberation of Palestine, and eradication of Zionist economic, political, military and cultural existence."

Article 19 asserts, "Armed struggle [that is, terrorism] is a strategy and not a tactic, and the Palestinian Arab people's armed revolution is a decisive factor in the liberation fight and in uprooting the Zionist entity, and this struggle will not cease unless the Zionist state is demolished and Palestine is completely liberated."

That is to say, Arafat believed that terrorism could never be disavowed or abandoned. Palestine could be formed only on the ruins of Israel. And Israel could be destroyed only through violence. Diplomacy could never replace terrorism as a means of achieving Fatah's primary aim of destroying Israel.

Article 22 stipulates that it is Fatah's obligation to "oppos[e] any political solution offered as an alternative to demolishing the Zionist occupation in Palestine"—that is, any strategy that doesn't involve terrorism.

In keeping with the Soviet political warfare strategy against Israel and the West, while explicit in its strategic embrace of terrorism, Fatah's constitution carefully linked its violent, indeed genocidal cause to the politically popular anti-colonialist movement.

Article 4 declares, "The Palestinian struggle is part and parcel of the worldwide struggle against Zionism, colonialism, and international imperialism." Article 16 committed Fatah to "backing up oppressed people in their struggle for liberation and self-determination in order to build a just, international peace."

From the time he issued the Fatah constitution in 1957 until the day he died in 2004, all of Arafat's actions can be understood in the light of that document. It lays everything out. Depending on circumstances prevailing at various times, Arafat would give more prominence to certain aspects of Fatah's constitution, like terrorism, and minimize others, like the international struggle against imperialism. At other times he would reverse his emphasis. But all the aspects of his lifelong war against Israel are found in the pages of the Fatah constitution. And as we shall continue to see, the West's blindness to what he hid in plain sight owed to the success of Soviet propaganda, which convinced Westerners that to lead in international affairs, they needed the moral recognition of third world forces that were ideologically committed to denying the West's moral authority.

ARAFAT AND NASSER

Beyond its cynical use of the anticolonialist movement to justify its goal of annihilating a country established by an anti-imperialist national liberation movement, Fatah's constitution also positioned the terror group in relation to the rest of the Arab world. It stipulated that while the Palestinians are part of the larger Arab nation, they must serve as the advance guard in the Arab world's war to destroy Israel. Fatah was to be an independent organization, supported but not controlled by Arab governments.

During the 1950s and 1960s, Egyptian President Gamal Abdel Nasser was the unrivaled leader of the Arab world. Nasser was not interested in independent forces operating outside his direct control. In 1964 he founded the Palestine Liberation Organization as an umbrella group for Palestinian terrorist organizations. He placed Ahmed Shukeiri at the helm of the group to serve as his puppet. As initially construed by Nasser, the PLO was an Egyptian organization. Fatah's insistence on institutional independence made it impossible for Arafat to secure Nasser's support.

Israel's defeat of the Arab armies in the 1967 Six Day War caused Nasser to reconsider his strategy of destroying Israel through all-out war. He began to see an attractive alternative means in Arafat's strategy of terrorism. An independent Palestinian terror group would provide the plausible deniability that Nasser needed to continue to attack Israel, yet it would deny Israel the ability to claim that Egypt was breaching the ceasefire and thereby to gain a casus belli.

And so in July 1968, with Nasser's backing, Arafat's loyalists took over the PLO's legislative body, the Palestine National Council. Also in July 1968 Nasser took Arafat to the Soviet Union, where he met the Soviet leaders Leonid Brezhnev and Aleksei Kosygin in the Kremlin. During the visit, the Soviets agreed to arm the PLO under Arafat's leadership. In February 1969, with Nasser's approval, Arafat completed his takeover of the PLO and replaced Shukeiri as the chairman of the PLO's executive committee. He would hold that post until his death.[16]

The Bane of the Arabs, the Great Hope of the West

Arafat's strategy of independence involved playing all sides against one another to ensure that some would always be on his side. At various times, he was allied with every separate Arab regime and with Iran, and at other points, he was the enemy of them all. When he felt it necessary, he leveraged his pan-Arab influence to ensure Arab League backing for PLO initiatives. And when he felt it necessary, he pivoted toward the West to persuade it to save him from Arab governments that wished to destroy him and his PLO.

Beginning in 1968, Arafat based the PLO in Jordan. Pressured by Nasser, Jordan's King Hussein allowed him to establish a state within a state in the Palestinian-majority monarchy that the British had carved out of Mandatory Palestine. There the PLO operated military bases and autonomous governing structures from which it waged an unrelenting terrorist assault on Israel.

In 1970 Arafat decided to overthrow the Hashemite monarchy and transform Jordan into Palestine. King Hussein responded in September 1970, and with Israeli assistance, Jordanian forces crushed the PLO. Arafat and his militias were forced to flee the country.

They decamped to Lebanon, and in 1971 Arafat set up a PLO state within the Lebanese republic. The PLO used this base to develop a web of terrorist groups that operated worldwide, training Shi'ite militias as well as Communist terror operatives from Nicaragua's Sandinistas, Germany's Red Army Faction, the Irish Republican Army, and other terror groups.[17]

In the mid-1970s Arafat's PLO provided training for Iranian ayatollah Khomeini's Revolutionary Guards. These forces would make up the core of the revolutionary Islamic forces behind Khomeini's 1979 revolution.[18] Together with the PLO-trained Shi'ite militias, most notably Hezbollah, Khomeini's PLO-trained forces have since 1979 served as Iran's foreign legions of international terrorism.

Lebanon is a multiethnic, multiconfessional state. At the time of its establishment in 1943, Maronite Christians comprised the majority of its citizens, followed by Sunni Muslims. Shi'ite Muslims were the smallest major ethnic group. Lebanon's government was a fragile experiment in power sharing among its various populations. The PLO's operations de-stabilized this fragile balance of Lebanese government and society, pre-cipitating the Lebanese civil war, which began in 1974.

In 1982 the PLO escalated its terror assaults against Israel from Leba-non, forcing Israel to invade Lebanon with the aim of removing the PLO from the country. In November 1982 the Lebanese government expelled the PLO.[19]

With both the Jordanian and Lebanese experiences of hosting the PLO in mind, no Arab state agreed to host the PLO after it departed Lebanon. Having lost his second base of operations in twelve years, Ara-fat had never been more isolated.[20]

But then the United States stepped in to rescue him. The Reagan administration believed the PLO defeat in Lebanon created an oppor-tunity for Washington to transform Arafat from a terror leader into a peacemaker and to use him to prove American bona fides in the third world. According to this line of reasoning, Arafat would be so grateful for U.S. assistance that he would tell the developing nations of the world the United States was their friend.

And so in 1982 the United States pressured the Tunisian government to host Arafat and the PLO. As the PLO army fled Beirut for their new base of operations, U.S. Marines protected it from Israeli forces.[21]

Architect and Pioneer of International Terrorism

Arafat's ability to survive another day and continue his war to destroy Is-rael, despite his constant brinksmanship and continuous demonstrations of bad faith, were a product of his operational success in both terrorism and diplomacy.

Arafat and his supporters often likened him to leaders of so-called popular wars, like Che Guevara and Ho Chi Minh. But Arafat was quite different from them. The leaders of popular wars headed populist move-ments whose strategy was to take over a country by persuading the mass of people to side with them against the existing regime.

Arafat's strategy was different. He largely ignored the Arabs of Israel as well as the Arabs living in Judea, Samaria, and Gaza. He did not seek to persuade them to rise up against Israel. That strategy would not have worked since the overwhelming majority of Israel's citizens are Jews and oppose the eradication of the Jewish state. The Arabs of Israel had no chance of persuading the Jews to side with them in sufficient numbers to destroy Israel.

So Arafat's strategy was instead terrorism against Israeli civilians. As he saw it, the murder of Israeli civilians, at home and abroad, would foment the destabilization of Israeli society, end Jewish immigration to Israel, and persuade Israelis to emigrate. Once Israel was in internal disarray, "a quick blow by the regular armies [of the Arab states] at the right moment" would destroy it completely.[22]

Beyond demoralizing Israelis, terrorism would serve two other purposes. First, it would rally the Arab world, especially the Palestinians, to Arafat's side. And second, in the absence of a successful pan-Arab conventional war against the Jews, terrorism would keep the drums of war against Israel beating, and the cause of Israel's destruction front and center in Arab affairs.

To advance all these ends, beginning in 1968, Arafat began his campaign of international terrorism, with backing from the Soviets. It was in 1968 that the PLO conducted its first airline hijackings. By 1980 PLO member organizations and front groups had carried out forty-two acts of airline terrorism, including hijackings, bombings, ground assaults, and attempted surface-to-air missile attacks against jetliners.[23] Following Al Qaeda's September 11, 2001, attacks, Osama bin Laden's aide Abu Ubeid al-Qurashi said that Bin Laden saw the PLO's terror strikes as a model for the ones on September 11.[24]

Civilian air terrorism was just one part of Arafat's portfolio. From 1968 through the mid-1980s, he oversaw the kidnap and massacre of Israel's Olympic team at the 1972 Munich Olympics and the 1973 assassinations of the U.S. ambassador to Sudan, the deputy chief of the U.S. mission, and the Belgian chargé d'affaires. He oversaw repeated massacres of Israeli schoolchildren in raids on schools in northern Israel, as well as assaults on Jewish targets including synagogues and restaurants in Europe, bus bombings and hijackings, and train bombings.

According to Ariel Merari and Shlomo Elad, between 1969 and 1985 PLO groups committed more than eight thousand terrorist attacks. These attacks occurred mainly in Israel, but at least 435 were committed out-side the Jewish state. More than 650 Israelis were murdered, and more than three-quarters of the victims were civilians. Twenty-eight Ameri-cans were murdered, and dozens of nationals from other countries were also killed.[25]

Merari and Elad's numbers do not include attacks in which the PLO was not officially implicated. However, as Barry Rubin and Judith Colp Rubin note, a significant body of evidence directly implicates the PLO in the bombings of the U.S. embassy and Marine barracks in Lebanon in 1983.[26] Moreover, U.S. intelligence discovered that shortly after the November 1979 Iranian takeover of the U.S. embassy in Tehran, Arafat ordered Fatah to assist Iran in carrying out terrorist operations.[27] Arafat was the first foreign leader to visit Khomeini after the Iranian revolution.

As evidenced in the Reagan administration's decision in 1982 to res-cue the PLO following its expulsion from Lebanon, the United States and its allies believed that by appeasing Arafat politically, they could per-suade him to abandon terrorism. But as Arafat saw it—and rightly so—if it weren't for his deployment of terrorism, the West would never have sought to appease him.

That wasn't the only benefit he garnered from wantonly murdering innocents. To protect their own citizens from Arafat's terror machine, governments turned a blind eye or collaborated with his terror cells to secure Arafat's pledge not to target their citizens. According to Rubin and Rubin, in the aftermath of the PLO's assassination of U.S. ambas-sador Cleo Noel in Khartoum in 1973, President Richard Nixon autho-rized covert contacts between the CIA and the PLO; in return, the PLO promised not to attack Americans.[28] Also in the early 1970s, Italy agreed to allow the PLO to use Italy as a base of operations and a transit point for its weapons; in exchange, the PLO agreed not to target non-Jewish Italians.[29]

As subsequent events showed, the United States and Italy kept their parts of their agreements even after the PLO deliberately targeted their citizens (including their non-Jewish citizens).

Arafat's employment of terrorism empowered him politically in an-other way as well: it drew global media attention to the Palestinian war against Israel, popularizing and legitimizing it in the Western world.

The legitimizing effect of media coverage was not incidental. The Western media coverage of Palestinian terrorist attacks against Israel was
generally sympathetic. There were three reasons for this. First, most
journalists covering the PLO were from the Left and bought in to the
PLO's self-description as a member of the anticolonialist movement. Second, journalists covering the PLO were eager to gain access to its leadership, and this could be accomplished best by providing positive coverage
of the terror group. Third, reporters feared that if they accurately portrayed the PLO as a terrorist group dedicated to the destruction of Israel,
they would place their lives at risk.[30]

Arafat the World Statesman

Sympathetic attention from the global media certainly set the stage for
Arafat's subsequent diplomatic achievements. But there were other con-
tributing factors. First and foremost, in June 1974 the PLO's legislative
body adopted the "phased plan" for the liberation of Palestine. The plan
called for the Palestinians to set up an independent Palestinian National
Authority in any territory it liberated from Israel.[31] This territory would
serve as a launching base for further attacks against Israel, which would
then force it to concede still more territory. The phased plan aimed to
transform Israel into a weak, rump Jewish state, which in time could be
overrun by invading Arab armies.

The phased plan was meant to satisfy everyone. It allowed Arafat to
leverage his position in the West while retaining the support of more radical elements of the Arab and Islamic world. The latter would understand
the plan's purely tactical nature. As for the West, with its superficial
media coverage of Middle Eastern affairs and its appeasement-oriented
elites, it would blind itself to the rank duplicity of PLO statements inti-
mating a willingness to live at peace with Israel, and embrace the terrorist organization as a moderate partner for peace with Israel.

The diplomatic achievements that Arafat reaped from both his terrorism and the phased plan were dramatic. Months after the PNC approved the phased plan, Arafat was invited to address the UN General
Assembly. There, too, he made no attempt to hide his strategic devotion
to the murder of innocents. Arafat warned the international body that if
he didn't get his way, he would stop playing the diplomatic game along-

side committing acts of terrorism and would revert to only committing terrorism.

"Today I come bearing an olive branch in one hand, and the freedom fighter's gun in the other," he threatened. "Do not let the olive branch fall from my hand. I repeat, do not let the olive branch fall from my hand."

The next year the UN General Assembly passed Resolution 3379, which, recycling the Soviet language first introduced in 1965, labeled Zionism a form of racism. The PLO was granted observer status in the international body.

To understand how breathtaking these accomplishments were, it is necessary to place them in a historical context. Back when the 1967 Six Day War ended, the Palestinians were so marginal that they weren't even mentioned in UN Security Council Resolution 242, which set the terms for future peace between Israel and the Arabs; but by the end of the 1970s, eighty-six countries recognized the PLO. Only seventy-two recognized Israel.[32]

External factors also played a central role in facilitating the PLO's achievements. The 1973 Arab oil embargo, a reaction to Israel's defeat of the Egyptian and Syrian armies in the Yom Kippur War, played a significant role in causing the nations of western Europe to abandon their earlier support for Israel. [33]

The Soviets ensured that the PLO had the automatic support of all members of the Communist bloc and the Nonaligned Movement for their initiatives at the United Nations. Together with the Arab League member states, barring explicit U.S. threats to end funding for the UN, this support guaranteed Arafat an automatic majority in the General Assembly and in all UN bodies other than the Security Council for every initiative he wished to pass.

Riding the Tiger of the Intifada

During the mid-1980s, from his perch in faraway Tunis, Arafat struggled to remain relevant. His opportunity to return to the international center stage came with the outbreak of the Palestinian uprising, or intifada against Israel in Judea, Samaria, and Gaza in 1988. Until then, the Palestinians who lived in these areas—that is, in the homeland that the PLO claimed to be seeking to liberate—had received little attention from Arafat. They were kept in line through a combination of terror and patronage. Palestinians viewed as too supportive of Israel were murdered. Others were kept in line through cash payoffs. When in 1986 King Hussein sought to undermine the PLO by appointing pro-Jordanian mayors in the Palestinians cities in Judea and Samaria, Arafat ordered the assassination of the Jordanian-appointed mayor of Nablus, Zafir Masri.[34]

The Palestinian uprising against Israel was a largely local phenomenon and caught the PLO by surprise. It was an outgrowth of several factors. First local Palestinians felt ill-served by the PLO, which despite Arafat's bravado, had failed to deliver either peace or victory over Israel.

Second, Israel's strategy for governing Judea, Samaria, and Gaza was one of benign neglect. Israeli leaders believed that if left to their own devices, the Palestinians would live at peace with Israel. This laxity created the impression among the Palestinians that Israel was not committed to maintaining its control of the areas.

Third, after twenty years of Israeli rule, a generational change had taken place. Young Palestinians who were born and grew up under Israeli rule did not share their parents' sense of relief at not having to contend with the brutal Jordanian and Egyptian militaries that had controlled Judea, Samaria, and Gaza from 1949 to 1967.

Finally, Israel had encouraged the Palestinians to organize their own professional and social organizations, which Israel hoped could form the basis of a local governing nucleus that would replace the PLO in time. These organizations formed the grassroots networks that would transform the uprising from an unplanned outburst of violence against Israel into an organized popular insurrection.[35]

Arafat was quick to take advantage of the situation. He immediately began funneling large sums of money to the areas to ensure the continuation of the violence. His representatives co-opted the grassroots organizations and reassembled them into a hierarchy controlled by the PLO.[36]

To provide the local Palestinians with a sense that the PLO was bringing results, Arafat convened its legislative body, the Palestinian National Council (PNC), in August 1988. At the conference Arafat signaled readiness to renounce terrorism and recognize Israel's right to exist. In November 1988 he declared the independence of Palestine.

The West reacted with jubilation at Arafat's gestures. The UN held a special session of the General Assembly just to allow him to address the body. The United States opened a public dialogue with the PLO. More than eighty countries immediately recognized Palestine.

Nonetheless, under the leadership of Prime Minister Yitzhak Shamir, Israel remained impassive. By 1990 the uprising was a spent force as a popular movement and had devolved from a popular movement into an increasingly violent campaign carried out by terrorist cells.

Israelis were not the only targets of the gunmen's bullets. Much as Husseini had used the 1936–39 terror war as a means to liquidate his internal enemies, Arafat used the uprising as a means to eradicate voices that were willing to accept peaceful coexistence with Israel. Between December 1987 and January 1989, 21 Palestinians were killed by other Palestinians, but in 1989 that number rose to 138. In 1990 the number rose to 184. In the same year, only 119 Palestinians were killed by Israeli security forces.[37]

In what turned out to be the largest single blunder of his career, in August 1990, Arafat supported Saddam Hussein's invasion of Kuwait. Subsequently, in the 1991 Gulf War, he sided with Saddam and Iraq against the Arab League and the United States.

The PLO's decision to side with Saddam devastated the Palestinians' economic prospects. Beginning in late August 1990, more than 450,000 Palestinians were expelled from the Persian Gulf states. The monies these Palestinians had remitted to their families in Judea, Samaria, and Gaza disappeared, and the Gulf states ended their massive financial support for the Palestinians.[38]

Washington and Jerusalem to the Rescue

As a political organization, the PLO was essentially wiped out. Hamas, which had been formed in 1988 as an Islamic terror group, was gaining ground politically, socially, and militarily. In Judea and Samaria, calls for Arafat to resign were heard publicly for the first time.

But then President George H. W. Bush decided to leverage his success in the Gulf War to initiate a new Middle East peace process. In late 1991 the United States organized an international peace conference in

Madrid. The Palestinian delegation was officially not connected to the PLO, but due to Arafat's coercive power through threats of murder, it took its orders directly from Arafat, as did the delegations to subsequent negotiating sessions in Washington.[39]

Bush's decision to use his victory in the Gulf War to force Israel to negotiate with the Palestinians helped restore Arafat's position as the undisputed leader of the Palestinians. The Israeli far Left's Oslo gambit was sufficient to put him over the top.

Dissatisfied with the pace of negotiations in Washington, Israel's deputy foreign minister Yossi Beilin sent two of his friends in academia to begin "informal," secret negotiations with Arafat's deputy Mahmoud Abbas and other senior PLO officials in Oslo, Norway. The aim was to agree to a framework deal that would involve Israeli recognition of the PLO and the establishment of a Palestinian governing authority in Judea, Samaria, and Gaza.

On September 13, 1993, less than two years after his epitaph had been written in black paint on the walls of Ramallah and Gaza City, and as hundreds of thousands of Palestinians were ejected from their homes in Kuwait and Saudi Arabia, Arafat touched the sky. That day, Bill Clinton feted him at the White House for his willingness to sign the Declaration of Principles with Israel, which set the framework for the establishment of Palestinian control of Judea, Samaria, Gaza, and parts of Jerusalem. The next year Arafat received the Nobel Peace Prize.

In the seven years following the onset of the 1993 peace process between Israel and the PLO, Arafat built up his forces—consistent with the phased plan for the destruction of Israel. Based on his expressed commitment to fight terrorism, Israel provided his militias with guns. The United States and Europe provided them with military training. While he was building up the PLO's military capacity, Arafat was also enabling Hamas, and other terrorist groups not affiliated with the PLO, to massively expand their terrorist attacks on Israel. In November 1994 the PLO and Hamas reached an accord in which the PLO agreed to turn a blind eye to Hamas's terrorism.[40]

Just months after the era of the peace process between Israel and the PLO dawned, Israel suffered its first suicide bombing. In the seven years that followed the signing of the Declaration of Principles on the White House lawn, 269 Israelis were murdered in Palestinian terrorist attacks.

Between 1979 and 1993—that is, in fourteen years leading up to the onset of the peace process—232 Israelis had been killed by Palestinian terrorists.[41]

Throughout the active period of the peace process, from 1993 through September 2000, Arafat, when speaking to Western and Israeli audiences, maintained his innocence, blaming all the violence on Hamas. When the United States pressured him, he would enact mass arrests of Hamas members, only to release them in short order.[42] He also brought Hamas and other terrorists into the Palestinian Authority's security services.[43]

Just as devastatingly, Arafat built a Palestinian school system and media and appointed imams in mosques that fed Palestinian society a steady diet of jihadist and Nazi-style anti-Semitism.[44] Most of the suicide bombers in the Palestinian terror offensive that began in September 2000 were educated in the Palestinian Authority's school system.

In January 2002 the Palestinian Authority tried to smuggle fifty tons of sophisticated Iranian armaments into Gaza aboard an Iranian ship. But Israeli naval commandos seized the ship and its cargo. In 2006 Israeli security forces arrested Arafat's paymaster, Fuad Shubaki, for helping to organize the operation. During his interrogation, Shubaki divulged that after the onset of the peace process, Arafat had used international aid monies from the United States and Europe, as well as funds transferred from Israel, to purchase arms for Palestinian terror forces. He also confessed that senior commanders in the official PA security services had paid for terrorist attacks against Israel.[45]

Arafat died in November 2004. Since then many scholars, commentators and policy makers have claimed that he was a failure because he failed to establish a Palestinian state. But in truth, it is hard to see how Arafat failed at all. It was not he but the West, with its willful blindness to Arafat's unapologetic and consistent loyalty to his goal of destroying Israel, that failed. True, he never lived up to the West's expectation that he would abandon his highest goal—Israel's eradication—in favor of the establishment of a Palestinian state in Judea, Samaria, Jerusalem, and Gaza. But that doesn't make him a failure.

Judged by Arafat's own measuring rod, his career was clearly an extraordinary success. He rose to leadership when the Arab world was in a state of despair. The Palestinian nation, such as it was, had no unifying goal or sense of identity.[46]

Through his pioneering use of terrorism, he repeated Husseini's accomplishment of shaping a Palestinian national identity based on the rejection of Israel's right to exist. His savvy use of political warfare and manipulation of Cold War politics allowed him to win over the United States and the Israeli Left for the cause of Palestinian statehood, even as he maintained and expanded his terror war against Israel and made clear that his goal was not the establishment of a Palestinian state but the elimination of the Jewish state.

CHAPTER 5

Phony Reformers and Totalitarian Democrats

MAHMOUD ABBAS

On July 3, 2010, Mohammed Daoud Oudeh (aka Abu Daoud), the commander of the PLO terror squad that massacred the Israeli team at the 1972 Munich Olympics, died in Damascus, an unrepentant terrorist. Shortly before his death, he released a statement telling the Israeli people, "Today, I cannot fight you anymore, but my grandson will and his grandsons too."[1]

Given his unrepentant stance, a moderate leader who aspired to peace with Israel would at a minimum ignore Oudeh's passing and more likely condemn his life and legacy. But when word of Oudeh's death broke, PLO chairman and Palestinian Authority leader Mahmoud Abbas sent a telegram of condolence to Oudeh's family. The PA-controlled media published the text.

Abbas celebrated Oudeh's life, proclaiming him to have been "one of the prominent leaders of the Fatah movement." Abbas referred to Oudeh as "a wonderful brother, companion, tough, stubborn and relentless fighter."[2]

In an interview with *Sports Illustrated* in 2002, which marked the thirtieth anniversary of the Munich massacre, Oudeh revealed that Abbas had bankrolled the operation.[3]

Throughout his presidency, George W. Bush and his administration championed Abbas—Arafat's deputy of four decades—as a moderate leader. Unlike Arafat, they believed, Abbas would be willing to abjure terror and forge a peace with Israel.

Bush's position was contradictory. In the landmark 2002 speech that we discussed in Chapter 1, he said, "Today, Palestinian authorities are encouraging, not opposing, terrorism." But by elevating Abbas to serve as Arafat's replacement, Bush continued to empower and legitimize the very leadership that he acknowledged was acting in a manner antithetical to peace and Palestinian statehood.

The Bush administration's call for the Palestinians to choose new leaders was a leap of faith. It was based on the proposition that—despite the Palestinian rejection of peace and statehood and reversion to terror war against Israel—the guiding assumptions of the peace process were correct: that the Palestinian conflict with Israel (and the Arab world's conflict with Israel more generally) was caused by the absence of a Palestinian state in Judea, Samaria, Jerusalem, and Gaza; and that the way to resolve both the specific and the larger conflict was to establish such a state.

Bush's only departure from that paradigm was to hold Arafat personally responsible for the absence of peace, suggesting that, under different leadership, the Palestinians would finally begin to support a two-state peace plan. It wasn't that the patient was terminally ill, the Bush administration believed; the doctor was simply incompetent. If Arafat could be pushed aside, the two-state paradigm would succeed.

But was Arafat the problem, or did the issue run deeper? Let's assess Arafat's successors' record in power and decide whether anything has changed.

The Bush administration's decision to blame Arafat for the lack of peace was coupled with its decision to appoint his successors. The United States embraced Mahmoud Abbas and Salam Fayyad—the IMF representative to the Palestinian Authority—as moderate leaders who could replace Arafat and transform Palestinian society from one where the majority supported terrorism and sought Israel's destruction into a moderate, peaceable society. The reasonableness of Bush's embrace of the two-state solution came to depend entirely on these two men. If they failed to bring about the changes that the administration hoped for, then Bush's legacy would be the further empowerment of terrorists bent on the destruction of the closest U.S. ally in the Middle East.

Immediately after Bush's speech, Arafat bowed to U.S. pressure and appointed Fayyad to serve as the PA finance minister. He appointed Abbas to serve as prime minister in May 2003.

Three months later Abbas resigned his position because Arafat refused to cede power to him. But when Arafat died in November 2004, Abbas returned to power. He replaced Arafat first as PLO chief, then as interim chairman of the Palestinian Authority. Abbas was elected to the position for a four-year term in January 2005. He remains in the position now, even though his term ended in January 2009 and no new elections have been called.

As we shall see, the power-sharing arrangement between Fayyad and Abbas never produced a stable equilibrium. Like Arafat before him, Abbas has refused to share power with his prime ministers. Over strenuous objections from the Obama administration, Abbas forced Fayyad to resign his position as prime minister in April 2013 and replaced him two months later with Rami Hamdallah, a Fatah apparatchik with no independent power base.[4]

In the twelve years since Bush's speech set into motion the chain of events that brought Abbas and Fayyad into power, the only thing that has changed about the way the Palestinian Authority operates is that it no longer controls Gaza, due to the ascendancy of Hamas in the 2006 elections. But even with their political power diminished, Abbas and Fayyad did not use their remaining clout to draw a distinction between their presumed moderation and policy of peace and Hamas's extremism and policy of war. Certainly they made no attempt to distance themselves from Arafat's legacy.

Rather, since taking office, both men have used their power to wage and escalate political and economic warfare against Israel in the international community. The aim of that warfare is to delegitimize Israel's right to exist and to set the conditions for its demise and replacement with Palestine. Rather than fight Hamas on the level of ideas and values, they use the political tools at their disposal to prove that they are better than Hamas at fighting Israel. Moreover, both men continued Arafat's policy of supporting Palestinian terrorists and terrorism while telling the United States that they oppose them.

The Abbas No One Likes to Talk About

There was no reason anyone should have expected Abbas to behave differently than he has. His role in the Munich massacre, like his position at Arafat's side for forty years, sent the clear message that there was no substantive difference between Arafat's goals and his own. Then too, one glaring aspect of his career ought to have ended speculation that he could emerge as a Palestinian peacemaker: his Holocaust denial.

In 1982 Abbas matriculated in the doctoral program at the Patrice Lumumba University in Moscow. The title of his dissertation was *The Connection Between the Nazis and the Leaders of the Zionist Movement, 1933–1945.* In 1984 he published his thesis as a book in Arabic under the title *The Other Side: The Secret Relationship Between Nazism and Zionism.*

In both works, Abbas wrote that the Holocaust was a joint initiative of the Nazis and the Zionist movement. He alleged that the European Jews who were killed were actually the victims of the Jews from pre-state Israel who were in cahoots with the Germans.[5] In his words, "A partnership was established between Hitler's Nazis and the leadership of the Zionist movement. . . . [The Zionists gave] permission to every racist in the world, led by Hitler and the Nazis, to treat Jews as they wish, so long as it guarantees immigration to Palestine."

Abbas wrote that the Zionists wanted as many Jews as possible to be killed. "Having more victims," he wrote, "meant greater rights and stronger privilege to join the negotiation table for dividing the spoils of war once it was over. However, since Zionism was not a fighting partner— suffering victims in a battle—it had no escape but to offer up human beings, under any name, to raise the number of victims, which they could then boast of at the moment of accounting."

Abbas denied that six million Jews were killed in the Holocaust. This too was a Zionist plot. "The truth is that no one can either confirm or deny this figure," he wrote. "In other words, it is possible that the number of Jewish victims reached six million, but at the same time it is possible that the figure is much smaller—below one million.

"It seems that the interest of the Zionist movement, however, is to inflate this figure so that their gains will be greater," Abbas continued. "Many scholars have debated the figure of six million and reached stunning conclusions—fixing the number of Jewish victims at only a few hundred thousand."

When, in December 2006, Iranian president Mahmoud Ahmadinejad hosted a Holocaust denial conference in Tehran, most of the nations of the West condemned the event and rightly viewed it as proof that the

Iranian regime is fanatical and dangerous.[6] It is a testament to the West's desire to be misled by the Palestinians that no one in a position of power in the United States or Europe protested Mahmoud Abbas's elevation to power, even though he held the same twisted beliefs as Ahmadinejad. Moreover, Abbas's dissertation forms the basis of Holocaust studies in PA classrooms.[7]

Glorifier of Murderers, Partner to Terrorists

Abbas's inversion of history is not the only way his stewardship of the Palestinian Authority and the PLO represents an organic continuation of Arafat's tenure. He also uses his position to support, sponsor, and glorify terrorism.

First there is Abbas's relationship with Hamas. As previously noted, in January 2006, Hamas won the elections for the Palestinian Legislative Council, the lawmaking body set up under the peace accords signed between Israel and the PLO. Following the Hamas victory, Abbas signed agreements to set up a unity government with Hamas on three separate occasions, despite the terror group's refusal to accept the legitimacy of the agreements with Israel or pay lip service to abjuring terrorism against Israel.[8]

In addition to his persistent attempts to woo Hamas, Abbas also uses his position to glorify Palestinian terrorists as national heroes. In just one example, in October 2011, Israel agreed to release 1,027 terrorists jailed in Israeli prisons in exchange for Staff Sergeant Gilad Shalit, who had been kidnapped in June 2006 by a joint cell of terrorists from Fatah and Hamas. He was held hostage in Gaza for five and a half years by terrorists affiliated with Hamas.

After the deal went through, Abbas extolled the terrorists as heroes and role models for Palestinian children. In December 2011 Abbas traveled to Ankara where he met with twelve of the freed terrorists, including two convicted murderers who had been freed from prison and deported to Turkey as part of the Shalit ransom deal.[9]

It is often argued that Abbas has no choice but to embrace terrorists, given the popularity of terrorists, including Hamas, in Palestinian society. But if that is the case, then it simply proves that the Bush administration was wrong to contend that the only problem with the Palestinians was that they were ruled by Arafat. It is immaterial whether Abbas is a moderate with no choice other than to support terrorism, or a radical who supports terrorism because he believes in it. The whole rationale for U.S. support for Abbas is the belief that he is able and willing to bring peace.

Arafat's Disciple in Rejecting Statehood and Peace

But not only has Abbas not brought peace, like Arafat before him, Abbas has rejected peace with Israel.

On September 16, 2008, Israeli prime minister Ehud Olmert made Abbas a comprehensive offer of peace and Palestinian statehood. Olmert's offer was far more expansive than the offer Ehud Barak made to Arafat at Camp David in July 2000.

In exchange for peace and an agreement that the Palestinian conflict with Israel was over, Olmert offered Abbas 94 percent of Judea and Samaria, and an additional 327 square kilometers of land within sovereign Israel adjacent to the Gaza Strip and northern Samaria. He offered the Palestinians sovereignty over the Arab neighborhoods of Jerusalem, and offered to transfer sovereignty over the Temple Mount and other sacred areas of Jerusalem's Old City to an international body. He offered a limited right of immigration to a truncated Israel to descendants of Arabs who left Israel in 1948–49.[10]

Like Arafat at Camp David, Abbas failed to respond to Olmert's offer. And although Olmert remained in office for seven months after he made the offer, Abbas refused to see him again.[11]

After receiving Olmert's proposal, Abbas escalated the PLO's diplomatic war against Israel at the UN and internationally. The aim of this war is to gain international recognition for a sovereign Palestinian state, to be established outside the framework of peace with Israel. That is, in keeping with the PLO's phased plan for the destruction of Israel, Abbas's goal is to establish a Palestinian state that exists in a de facto state of war with Israel.

To this end, Abbas has undertaken two parallel policies. First, from 2008 through 2013 he refused to meet with Prime Minister Benjamin Netanyahu or to allow his representatives to meet with Israeli negotiators and renew negotiations toward the establishment of a Palestinian state at peace with Israel. And even after talks were started in August 2013, Abbas insisted that they be carried out in complete secrecy to avoid popular criticism. Under his leadership, the Palestinians have become more, rather than less opposed to peaceful coexistence with Israel.[12]

Second, he has waged an unrelenting and reasonably successful campaign at the United Nations to achieve recognition of a sovereign state of Palestine outside the framework of a peace treaty with Israel. In November 2012 he took a significant step toward this goal when the UN General Assembly approved Resolution A/67/L.28, upgrading the status of the PLO observer mission to the UN to the level of nonmember observer state. The General Assembly resolution has no international legal weight, but from a political perspective, Abbas and the Palestinian Authority have used this status upgrade to argue that Israel has no right to any presence in Judea and Samaria—even though the agreements the PLO signed with Israel recognize the inherent legitimacy of Israel's presence in the areas.

Just weeks after the General Assembly passed the resolution upgrading the PLO's status, Palestinian forces in Judea and Samaria began actively interfering with IDF counterterror operations, claiming that the operations represented unlawful trespass on sovereign Palestinian territory.[13]

In his statements to Israeli and Western audiences, Abbas claims that he is interested only in a Palestinian state in Judea, Samaria, Gaza, and Jerusalem.[14] And yet in his letter to UN secretary general Ban Ki-moon, which accompanied the PLO's application for an upgrade in its UN status, Abbas made no mention of those boundaries. Rather, he based his application on the lines of the UN's 1947 partition plan of the British Mandate for Palestine, which the Palestinians rejected when they were originally proposed.[15]

The 1947 boundaries were rejected at the time not only by the Palestinian Arabs but by the Arab world as a whole. Their rejection and subsequent war of conquest against the Jewish state rendered Resolution 181 null and void.[16] At any rate, even these borders weren't sufficient for Abbas.

In a post on his official Facebook page from October 11, 2012, Abbas referred to all of Israel as occupied Palestine, making clear that he rejected Israel's right to exist within any borders. When discussing the pending UN vote on upgrading the PLO's status as a state, Abbas wrote, "The [sought-for UN] recognition will not liberate the land the following day, but will prove that we are right that our land is occupied and not disputed territory, and this applies to all the territories that Israel occupied *before* June 1967" (emphasis added).[17]

Abbas has not hidden the PLO's rejection of Israel's right to exist from Western audiences. Ahead of the Annapolis Peace Summit, organized by Secretary of State Condoleezza Rice in November 2007, Abbas's chief negotiator Saeb Erekat stated outright that the Palestinian Authority does not accept Israel's right to exist as a Jewish state. Ignoring the fact that nearly every Arab state defines itself as "Islamic," Erekat told Israel Radio, "No state in the world connects its national identity to a religious identity," and therefore a specifically Jewish state has no right to exist.[18]

SALAM FAYYAD: AMERICA'S FAVORITE "REFORMER"

After Abbas forced Salam Fayyad to resign in April 2013, Western commentators and policy makers alike bemoaned the development as a blow to the peace process. But this was untrue on two counts. First, at no time in his tenure as PA prime minister did Fayyad have any role in PLO negotiations with Israel. Negotiations with Israel were always under the sole control of Abbas and the PLO, and Abbas never allowed Fayyad, who is not a member of the PLO, to participate in them. As a consequence, his presence or absence from Palestinian politics could have no possible impact on negotiations.

Second, and just as important, Fayyad never gave anyone reason to believe that he would be more accepting of Israel's right to exist or of its minimal demands than Abbas or Arafat.

Fayyad used his roles as PA prime minister and finance minister to advance the same goal that Abbas and Arafat sought: destroying Israel through terror and political delegitimization.

Since Bush elevated him to leadership of the Palestinian Authority in 2002, Fayyad was by all accounts America's favorite Palestinian. On both sides of the partisan aisle, Fayyad was upheld as a paragon of moderation and pragmatism.

The fact that Fayyad had no significant domestic constituency was never considered relevant. No mention was ever made of the fact that the paragon of Palestinian democratic governance was appointed rather than elected to his position, or of the fact that in the 2006 Palestinian elections he was barely elected to the Palestinian Legislative Council.

The United States has supported Fayyad ever since he began serving as the IMF's point man on the Palestinian Authority in 1996. One of the oddities surrounding this support was that during Fayyad's tenure as the IMF representative, Arafat built the Palestinian Authority into a kleptocracy where year in and year out, hundreds of millions of dollars in international aid money simply disappeared into mysterious bank accounts.[19] Fayyad did nothing to prevent or fight this rife corruption. He never distinguished himself as an anticorruption crusader.

Later, as PA finance minister, Fayyad had little impact on the fight for good governance in the Palestinian Authority. For instance, he was completely ineffective in contending with massive embezzlement at the PA's Petroleum Authority. When legislators in the Palestinian National Council asked for details about revenues from oil products, according to Issam Abu Issa, the founder of the Palestinian International Bank, "Fayyad shocked the lawmakers by declaring, 'Unfortunately, the documents related to the revenues from oil products—or how the money was used—cannot be found. They have disappeared from the ministry.'"[20]

Despite Fayyad's poor job performance at the IMF and at the reins of the Palestinian treasury, and despite the abysmal and continuous failure of the peace process since July 2000, George W. Bush and Barack Obama as well as their subordinates argued that the United States should underwrite the Palestinian Authority's budget with U.S. taxpayer dollars at ever increasing levels of funding. To justify this policy, U.S. leaders upheld Fayyad as an honest man at the helm who would ensure that these contributions would be used for legitimate purposes.

Since 2005 the United States has doubled its financial support for the Palestinian Authority. Since 2008, that assistance has averaged $600 million per year. Together with European and other international donors, the United States has made the Palestinians the largest international aid recipients in the world. Indeed, the Palestinians receive more aid per capita than any people has ever received.[21]

Yet in 2012, despite this massive foreign financial support, the IMF warned that the Palestinian Authority would face a $500 million funding gap.[22] Just as Fayyad's oversight of the Palestinian economy when he was at the IMF had been ineffective, so his vaunted reforms of the Palestinian economy since taking over as finance minister and prime minister had been ineffectual. The 2012 budget shortfall was further evidence that he failed to transform the Palestinian Authority into the credible, transparent, peaceful governing authority that U.S. leaders claim it became under his economic stewardship. Even worse, in October 2013, a report of the European Court of Auditors, the EU organ charged with auditing the EU's income and spending, determined that $27 billion in EU aid to the Palestinian Authority was unaccounted for between 2008 and 2012. Fayyad presided over the Palestinian treasury during these years.[23]

Regime corruption is not necessarily an indicator of violent intent; scores of corrupt governments worldwide are generally peaceful. From a purely strategic perspective, then, the question of mismanagement of the Palestinian treasury is of secondary importance.[24] On the other hand, the fact that in 2011 the Palestinian Authority allocated 31 percent of its budget to its security forces is an indication of violent intent.[25] This level of security spending is among the highest in the world, and the United States and its allies should view it with suspicion.

Fayyad, a Man of War

Corruption and security spending aside, the key question regarding Fayyad, like Abbas, is whether he used his power to advance the cause of establishing a Palestinian state that would live at peace with Israel. Did he use his positions to transform the Palestinian Authority into a peaceful governing apparatus that abjures terrorism? Did he invest international donor funds to develop a peaceful and moderate society and governing infrastructure that would live at peace with Israel and so contribute to the stability of the Middle East?

The answer to all these questions is, sadly, no. Regarding Fayyad's use of international funding, empirical data reveal a direct correlation between levels of international assistance to the Palestinian Authority and Palestinian terrorism.[26] The more aid the Palestinian Authority receives from the international community, the more terror attacks the Palestinians carry out against Israel. And Fayyad facilitated this situation.

Six percent of the annual PA budget went toward paying monthly salaries to Palestinian terrorists jailed in Israeli prisons, and to providing monthly stipends for families of Palestinian suicide bombers.[27] The terrorists who received these stipends hailed from all Palestinian terrorist groups—Hamas, Fatah, Islamic Jihad, and others. And the Palestinian Authority's equal-opportunity bankrolling of terrorists and their families didn't stop at the 1949 armistice lines: it paid salaries and stipends to the families of Israeli Arab terrorists as well.

This program was not a holdover from Arafat's period of PA control. This was Fayyad's project. In 2003 the Palestinian Legislative Council passed a law requiring payment of monthly salaries to jailed terrorists, and payment of monthly stipends to the families of suicide bombers and other dead Palestinian terrorists. In January 2011 Fayyad amended the law—he increased these salaries by up to 300 percent.

Economic Warrior

Throughout Fayyad's tenure as PA prime minister, the international Left waged a worldwide campaign to treat Israel like apartheid South Africa. The boycott, divestment, and sanctions (BDS) movement gained traction in European governments, trade unions, churches, and universities. In the United States it won victories in unions, college campuses, and mainline Protestant churches.

The "moderate" PA prime minister Fayyad was a major advocate and instigator of the BDS movement, and in 2009 and 2010 he began taking direct action against Palestinian trade with Israel. He promulgated a law outlawing all trade between Palestinians and Israeli businesses operating beyond the 1949 armistice lines. Two years later Fayyad abandoned his distinction based on those boundaries and called for a boycott of all Israeli goods.[28] He thereby signaled to his supporters throughout the world, particularly in the international Left in Europe and the United States, that the time had come to cut off Israel completely and end even paying lip service to Israel's right to exist.

In 2010 the Palestinian Authority began conducting house-to-house searches in which any Israeli products found in private homes were confiscated. On Fayyad's instructions, the Palestinian Authority also announced that 650 inspectors would force Palestinian businesses to comply with the boycott order.[29] In May 2010 a Palestinian merchant from Bethlehem was arrested for trying to sell wood products produced by Israelis.[30]

Fayyad's decision to drop even the veneer of moderation that he had given himself through his initial call for a limited economic boycott of Israel was consistent with Abbas's policies, and part and parcel of the Palestinian Authority's broader policy of not treating Israel as a legitimate political entity.

Throughout their entire tenures as Palestinian leaders, Abbas and Fayyad—Washington's cherished "moderates"—proved themselves to be the loyal successors of Haj Amin el-Husseini and Yassir Arafat. And they also showed themselves to be credible partners and precursors for a Hamas regime.

HAMAS

In Palestinian society, Hamas is the only political movement besides Fatah—Arafat's PLO faction—that has a significant constituency. Palestinian survey data generally give Fatah a healthy lead over Hamas in the polls, but the fact that Abbas has blocked new elections for PA chairman even though his term expired in January 2009 indicates that Fatah is not at all certain it would win such an election. The same is true of the Palestinian Legislative Council, control of which Hamas won in the last Legislative Council elections in 2006.[31]

Its name an acronym for the Islamic Resistance Movement, Hamas was founded at the start of the Palestinian uprising against Israel in 1988. Like Fatah and the PLO, Hamas set out its ideology and aspirations in a founding document that calls for Israel's destruction. But Hamas's covenant, published in January 1988, differs from those of Fatah and the PLO in several notable ways. Whereas the PLO and Fatah charters call for the destruction of Israel as part of a global anti-imperialist movement, Hamas calls for the eradication of Israel as part of a global Islamic imperialist movement whose aim is the restoration of the caliphate and the institution of global Islamic domination.[32]

Fatah and the PLO limit their goals to the eradication of Israel. They do not call for the annihilation of Jews outside Israel. But Hamas views

Islam as locked in a religious war against Israel due to the Jews' rejection of Muhammad and his revelations at the dawn of Islam in the seventh century. The opening paragraph of Hamas's covenant quotes the Koran saying that the Jews "are smitten with vileness wheresoever they are found."

Article 7 again quotes the Koran, making clear that Hamas's goal is the genocide of world Jewry: "The Day of Judgment will not come about until Muslims fight the Jews killing the Jews, when the Jew will hide behind stones and trees. The stones and trees will say O Muslims, O Abdullah, there is a Jew behind me, come and kill him."

Hamas defines itself as the Palestinian branch of the Muslim Brotherhood. It stipulates that its "program is Islam." The document explains that from the Muslim Brotherhood's perspective, Islam is a totalitarian creed and way of life.

In support of this belief, the covenant devotes great attention to the role of women in raising Muslim children devoted to jihad, to the role of art in inspiring Muslims to wage jihad, and to the role of journalists in glorifying, justifying, and defending jihad.

Just as Husseini had fused Nazi anti-Semitism with jihadist Islam, so Hamas's covenant merges European anti-Semitism with jihadist Islam. Article 22 blames alleged Jewish world domination for all the problems the world has suffered for hundreds of years, including the French Revolution, the Communist revolution, and World War II. "There is no war going on anywhere," it says, "without having [the Jews'] finger in it."

To galvanize pan-Islamic support for its jihad against the Jews, Article 32 of Hamas's covenant claims that Israel has plans for regional and even global domination. "The Zionist plan is limitless. After Palestine, the Zionists will aspire to expand from the Nile to the Euphrates. When they will have digested the region they overtook, they will aspire to further expansion, and so on. Their plan is embodied in *The Protocols of the Elders of Zion.*"

From Hamas's perspective, the only way for Christians, Jews, and Muslims to peacefully coexist is "under the wing of Islam." Hamas also makes common cause with all other jihadist groups worldwide.

As for the PLO, Article 27 of the Hamas covenant explains that although it respects the PLO's war against Israel, Hamas cannot join due to the PLO's secular ideology. Hamas believes Palestinian society will naturally progress from the PLO's secular nationalist war against Israel to Hamas's Islamic jihad against the Jews.

Programmatically, Hamas categorically rejects the PLO's moves toward peace processes with Israel in the international arena. Article 11 explains that Hamas "believes that the land of Palestine is an Islamic *wakf* [sacred trust] consecrated for future Muslim generations until Judgment Day. It, or any part of it, should not be squandered, it, or any part of it, should not be given up. . . . This *wakf* remains as long as earth and heaven remain. Any procedure in contradiction to Islamic Sharia, where Palestine is concerned, is null and void."

In a nutshell then, Hamas's founding document presents a totalitarian movement, dedicated to the genocide of Jewry and the obliteration of Israel in the name of Islam. No attempt to forge a compromise with Israel is permissible. Islam is the answer. Jihad is the only path to victory. And no Hamas leader has ever given any indication whatsoever that he is willing to reconsider the group's positions. Indeed, in a speech in Gaza on December 7, 2012, Hamas leader Khaled Mashaal spoke before a crowd of more than a hundred thousand supporters and, in essence, recited the main points of the covenant. Mashaal began by explaining that the goal of Hamas remains the violent destruction of Israel.

> Since Palestine belongs to us, and is the land of Arabism and Islam, we must never recognize the legitimacy of the Israeli occupation of it. The occupation is illegitimate, and therefore, Israel is illegitimate, and will remain so throughout the passage of time. Palestine belongs to us, not to the Zionists . . . .
>
> The liberation of Palestine—all of Palestine—is a duty, a right, a goal, and a purpose. It is the responsibility of the Palestinian people, as well as of the Arab and Islamic nation.[33]

The Roots of Hamas's Popularity

A notable aspect of Hamas's rise to power is how surprised the United States was by Hamas's victory in the 2006 elections. Secretary of State Condoleezza Rice said of it, "I don't know anyone who wasn't caught off guard by Hamas's strong showing."[34] The United States had been the primary party insisting that Hamas be allowed to participate in the elections, despite its refusal either to recognize Israel's right to exist or to put down its weapons.

But in the months preceding the elections, many voices had warned that Hamas would likely win, and Rice's ignorance of those warnings is a testament to the insular nature of U.S. foreign policy circles. The Bush administration insisted that the elections could be credible only if all sectors of Palestinian society were able to participate. To this end, the United States pressured the Sharon government to allow Hamas to field candidates, even in Jerusalem.[35]

The prevailing view within the Bush administration was that the Palestinians would reward Mahmoud Abbas for overseeing the August 2005 Israeli withdrawal from Gaza. To advance the electoral fortunes of Abbas's Fatah party, Rice coerced Israel into accepting an agreement on Palestinian control of international passages from Gaza to Israel and Egypt, which would later pave the way for massive weapons and terror personnel smuggling from Egypt into Gaza.[36] So too, ahead of the elections, the United States and the European Union lavished the Palestinian Authority with hundreds of millions of dollars in supplementary international assistance.[37]

The Bush administration's false assessment of Fatah's electoral strength was based on three fundamental misunderstandings of the Palestinian reality. First, it failed to realize that far from bolstering Fatah politically, Israel's unilateral withdrawal from Gaza the previous summer had augmented Hamas's popularity.[38] Prime Minister Ariel Sharon argued that by pulling out unilaterally from the Gaza Strip, Israel would be showing the Palestinians that it was willing to ignore them in order to advance its own national interests. But the message the Palestinians took from Israel's withdrawal was that if the Palestinians attacked the Jews enough, they would run away. In other words, Israel's pullout from Gaza signaled to the Palestinians that there was no reason to negotiate with Israel.

As the Palestinians saw it, what forced Israel's hand wasn't Fatah's embrace of diplomacy but Hamas's unrelenting terror war against the Jewish state. True, between 2000 and 2005, Fatah terrorists had conducted more terrorist attacks than Hamas;[39] but Hamas was still more popular because of its eschewal of diplomatic contacts with Israel.

The second cause of Hamas's rise in popularity was Arafat's death in November 2004. The Bush administration failed to recognize that the absence of the popular, charismatic leader in military fatigues would lead to a drop in public support for Fatah. Palestinian support for potential leaders has always been directly proportional to the leader's past or current terrorist activities. The bloodier a politician's record, the more popular he is. Abbas, the political warrior in a business suit, was no match for Hamas.[40]

Finally, the Americans failed to recognize that endemic Fatah corruption had soured the Palestinian public on the ruling party.

In the event, after Hamas won the Palestinian Legislative Council elections, Rice and the administration ignored the first two causes of Hamas's victory, limiting their comments and attention to the subject of official corruption.[41] By ignoring Palestinian society's love affair with terrorism and its commitment to the annihilation of Israel, Bush and his advisers signaled that their chief aim was not to achieve peace but to maintain their support for the two-state solution.

In the years that have passed since Hamas's electoral victory, its position in Palestinian society and in the wider Muslim world has been strengthened. In Palestinian society, Abbas has operated under two reasonable assumptions. First, he has clearly concluded that the United States is committed to keeping him in power. As a consequence, he felt comfortable forcing Fayyad to resign even though Secretary of State John Kerry implored him not to do so just a day before Fayyad announced his "resignation."[42] And Abbas has done nothing to address the issue of official corruption in the Palestinian Authority. To the contrary, numerous reports indicate that he and his family have increased their misuse of international donor funds for their personal enrichment.[43]

Second, Abbas's recognition of Palestinian society's pro-terror sympathies has caused him to radicalize his position on Israel and to try to entice Hamas to join a unity government with Fatah. To this end, Abbas has signed three unity governing deals with Hamas, and between March and June 2007, he ruled the Palestinian Authority as the head of a Fatah-Hamas unity government.

In the larger Arab arena, since Hamas's electoral victory, its Islamist brothers have been strengthened regionally. Ahead of the 2006 elections, Hamas forged a strategic alliance with Iran, which began massively supplying Hamas with weapons in late 2005.[44] Israel's failure to defeat Hezbollah in the 2006 war in Lebanon and northern Israel served to burnish the credibility of Islamist forces throughout the Middle East at the expense of pro-Western powers.

Since Barack Obama entered office in January 2009, the situation for Hamas has improved. Obama's withdrawal of U.S. forces in Iraq before a status of forces agreement was reached paved the way for Iraq's strategic realignment in the Iranian-led Shi'ite axis, of which Hamas became a de facto member in late 2005. Obama's support for the Muslim Brotherhood in Tunisia, Libya, and Egypt fomented the empowerment of the Muslim Brotherhood in all those countries. Although the July 2013 overthrow of the Muslim Brotherhood in Egypt was a setback for Hamas, Iran was quick to fill the vacuum: it strengthened its strategic ties with Hamas, which had been weakened due to the Muslim Brotherhood's opposition to Bashar Assad in the Syrian civil war.[45] Moreover, even with the setbacks that Muslim Brotherhood governments have suffered in Egypt and Tunisia, the movement is still far stronger than it was before the revolutionary wave began surging through the Arab world in 2010. Today, Hamas enjoys the full ideological backing of Arab states that used to be firmly in the PLO's corner.

As for the West, since Hamas's electoral victory in 2006, European governments, following the lead of Turkey's Islamist government, have begun a push to legitimize Hamas and have expanded their financial support for the Palestinian Authority.

The Fatah-led Palestinian Authority in Judea and Samaria rewarded its efforts by continuing to fund the Hamas regime in Gaza with international donor monies and Israeli tax revenues.[46] According to the latest figures, Fatah transfers $120 million each month to support the Hamas government.[47] It has continued to gain strength domestically and on the international stage while maintaining fierce allegiance to its platform of genocide of Jewry, brotherhood with fellow jihadist movements, the obliteration of Israel, and its replacement with an Islamic state.

Since Israel withdrew its military forces and civilians from Gaza in 2005, Palestinian forces there have shot more than eight thousand missiles, mortars, and rockets into Israel. After another major escalation in rocket and missile fire in early November 2012, Israel launched Operation Pillar of

Defense. During the operation, which ran for a week, Hamas forces shot more than fifteen hundred projectiles into Israel, including long-range missiles directed against Jerusalem and Tel Aviv. In all, 3.5 million Israelis found themselves within range and targeted by Hamas's projectiles.

At a rally in early December 2012 celebrating Hamas's "victory" over Israel, Hamas leader Khaled Mashaal made his first visit to Gaza and gave his speech restating dedication to Israel's annihilation.

In a sign of Hamas's rising international fortunes, EU members Portugal, Denmark, Ireland, and Finland tried to block the European Union from condemning Mashaal's call for the destruction of Israel.[48]

Europeans are not alone in their desire to accept Hamas as a legitimate force. In early 2009, ahead of President Obama's first inauguration, a bipartisan group of senior American foreign policy practitioners sent a letter to Obama calling for him to open an official U.S. dialogue with Hamas. The letter's signatories included Senator Chuck Hagel, who now serves as President Obama's secretary of defense.

Given the genocidal aims of Hamas, and the fact that the State Department has designated it a foreign terrorist organization, these officials' call for the United States to open contacts with the jihadist group represented a major diplomatic advance for Hamas.

Western leaders' increased willingness to accept Hamas is little different from their willingness to accept Arafat, Abbas, and Fayyad as legitimate leaders despite their support for terrorism and their actions to advance the cause of Israel's destruction.

This is because Western leaders refuse to recognize the true nature of the Palestinian people. Ever since Husseini invented the Palestinian people in the early 1920s, they have consistently defined themselves around the negative ethos of Israel's destruction and anti-Semitism. No significant Palestinian constituency or leadership has ever emerged that is based on a positive ethos of Palestinian nationalism, let alone on a willingness to peacefully coexist with the Jewish state. The Palestinians do not suffer from a leadership crisis per se. No "reformer," even one with the best of intentions, will ever convince the Palestinians to agree to a peace deal that doesn't involve, or greatly advance, Israel's destruction. The Palestinian leadership crisis stems not from bureaucratic misfortune but from the deformities and fanaticism inherent to the Palestinian national movement.

CHAPTER 6

Dumbing Down U.S. Foreign Policy

On the morning of October 15, 2003, a car containing U.S. embassy officials, en route to the Palestinian Authority's ministry of education, was torn apart by a remote-controlled roadside bomb. Three American security personnel were killed. A fourth was wounded.

According to eyewitness accounts, the bomb destroyed their armor-plated vehicle and gouged out a crater five feet deep and fifteen feet wide. Body parts of the victims were strewn in a thirty-meter radius of the blast. Based on the wreckage, experts assessed that the bomb was made of between 150 and 200 pounds of explosives.

The blast occurred within the sightline of a nearby manned Palestinian security checkpoint. Before detonating the device, the assailants first had to bury it—presumably in plain view of the security personnel at the checkpoint. As Matthew Levitt reported in the *Baltimore Sun,* "Immediately after the attack, journalists photographed Palestinian police officers standing by as onlookers cheered and roamed the crime scene, destroying critical evidence."[1]

President George W. Bush and Secretary of State Colin Powell condemned the attack on the diplomatic convoy. Bush seemingly placed the blame on PA chief Yassir Arafat's shoulders, saying, "Palestinian authorities should have acted long ago to fight terror in all its forms." Their "failure to undertake these reforms and dismantle the terrorist organizations constitutes the greatest obstacle to achieving the Palestinian people's dream of statehood."[2]

Arafat and his deputies condemned the attack and promised to bring the perpetrators to justice. But from the outset, they prevented U.S. officials from investigating what happened. The crime scene remained unsecured, and when FBI investigators arrived there later that day, dozens of Palestinian rioters shouting "Allah Akbar" attacked them with rocks. A crowd of several hundred Palestinians, who supported the rioters, surrounded the site.[3]

The Popular Resistance Committees, a consortium of terrorists from Fatah, Hamas, and Islamic Jihad—as well as members of the Palestinian Authority's security services—took responsibility for the attack.

In the years following the attack on the convoy, repeated congressional inquiries to the State Department regarding the status of the investigation have come up empty.[4] Journalists' requests to receive State Department communications related to the bombing and subsequent investigation have similarly been brushed off.[5] In early 2005 incoming secretary of state Condoleezza Rice announced her determination to ensure that the perpetrators were brought to justice. But by 2007 she seemed to drop the issue entirely. The bombing was no longer an agenda item in her meetings with Palestinian leaders.[6] In 2011, in response to an inquiry by one of the bombing victims' families, the FBI announced that the investigation had been closed, even though no arrests had been made.[7]

What explains the U.S. passivity in the face of the wanton murder of its embassy personnel? How could the United States, with its vast financial and political leverage over the Palestinian Authority, simply drop the issue?

The Palestinian Authority gave the United States every reason to believe that it was directly responsible for the attack on the embassy convoy and for the subsequent cover-up. It even appointed as lead investigator PA security chief Rashid Abu Shbak, who was known to have commanded a nearly identical roadside bombing of an Israeli school bus in Gaza three years earlier.[8]

And yet neither the Bush nor the Obama administration took any substantive steps to use American leverage to bring the killers to justice. Why did two administrations allow the Palestinian Authority to get away with murder?

The short and crass answer is that the United States cared about its relationship with the PLO more than it cared about bringing the murderers of U.S. embassy staff to justice.

The longer answer involves two overlapping policy trajectories: America's evolving relations with its western European allies toward the end of the Cold War, and the nature of U.S. relations with the Arab world. Both issues have contributed to the U.S. willingness to turn the other cheek when it comes to Palestinian terrorism against American citizens.

WESTERN EUROPE'S ROLE IN SHAPING U.S. POLICY TOWARD ISRAEL AND THE PALESTINIANS

Before the Cold War ended, the United States was willing to take positions in international affairs that were contrary to those of western European countries, especially if such a divergence would advance its position in relation to the Soviet Union. And for the final twenty years of the Cold War, Europe's policies diverged most sharply from Washington's in the Middle East. But when the Cold War ended, Washington became increasingly eager to align its position on the Middle East with its western European allies.

In the 1950s and 1960s western European nations were supporters and allies of the Jewish state. Indeed, in 1956 France and Britain allied with Israel in their war against Egypt.

The situation changed dramatically beginning in the early 1960s. Until 1962 France was Israel's closest ally. But after French president Charles de Gaulle pulled French military forces and civilians out of Algeria in 1962, he began to align his foreign policy toward the Arabs and away from Israel. By the end of the 1960s, Germany had followed France's lead. Both former allies instituted a total embargo on arms sales to Israel.[9]

Even as they ended their military support for the Jewish state, western European nations continued to lend political support to Israel, to varying degrees. But in the aftermath of the 1973 Yom Kippur War and the Arab oil embargo, western European governments abandoned their support for Israel and adopted the Soviet-Arab narrative of the Arab-Israeli conflict. That narrative deems Zionism inherently illegitimate and racist and claims that the Arab world's refusal to make peace with the Jewish state owes entirely to Israel's refusal to return the territory it took control of from Jordan, Egypt, and Syria during the 1967 Six Day War.[10]

By the mid-1970s, the Soviet-Arab narrative was updated, moving the focus away from the Arabs and toward the Palestinians. Before the shift, Israel had been blamed for the conflict because it refused to undo the

results of the Six Day War by surrendering the lands it had taken control of to the Arab aggressors who had attacked it. In the mid-1970s, the
previously ignored Palestinians became the focus of accusations of Israeli
land greed and bellicosity.

According to the rewritten "history," the root cause of the prolonged
conflict between Israel and the Arabs was not Israel's refusal to give land
to Jordan, Egypt, and Syria. Rather, it was the absence of a Palestinian state, and Israel was to be reviled because it refused to enable the
establishment of such a state in the lands it controlled. In light of Israel's
criminal culpability for the absence of peace, it necessarily followed that
"resistance" to Israel, in the form of terrorist massacres of its citizenry,
was legitimate.

A sign of how deeply the European anti-Israel narrative had pen-
etrated U.S. policy-making circles came in the immediate aftermath
of the September 11, 2001, attacks on the United States. In his speech
before a joint session of Congress nine days later, President George W.
Bush defined America's enemy in the war on terror as "a radical network
of terrorists and every government that supports them. Our war begins
with Al Qaeda, but does not end there. It will not end until every terrorist
group *of global reach* has been found, stopped, and defeated."[11]

By the time Al Qaeda terrorists attacked the United States on September 11, Israel had been under an all-out terrorist assault against its civilians for a year. Some 200 Israelis had been killed and 2,600 wounded
in Palestinian terrorist attacks; two-thirds of the dead and wounded
were civilians. As a proportion of its population, a comparable casualty
figure for the United States would amount to 8,600 dead and 111,800
wounded.[12]

By defining America's enemy as "every terrorist group of global
reach," Bush was clearly making a distinction between the localized Palestinian terror against Israelis and the global terror nexus against every
other nation in the world. The underlying message communicated by this
distinction was that Palestinian terror against Israel is acceptable, or at
least not punishable.[13]

The view that there is something basically acceptable about terrorism against Israelis and Jews originated with the Soviets and the Arabs;
the western Europeans adopted it in the aftermath of the 1973 Yom Kippur War and the OPEC oil embargo. There were four main reasons that

western Europe adopted this anti-Israel narrative. It is important to recount them in order to get a full picture of the ideological underpinning of the U.S. current policy regarding Israel, the Palestinians, and the Arab world.

The first reason was European anti-Semitism. Anti-Semitism as a political force in Europe had been dormant since the end of World War II. But on November 27, 1967, French president Charles de Gaulle gave a speech in which he castigated the Jews as "an elite people, self-assured and domineering." With this statement, as the French philosopher Raymond Aron noted in his 1968 book, *De Gaulle, Israel and the Jews*, "the anti-Semites . . . had received solemn authorization from the head of state to make themselves heard again and to employ the same language as before the Final Solution."[14]

The second reason western Europe broke with Israel was Soviet bloc subversion. In his 1987 memoir *Red Horizons*, Ion Mihai Pacepa, the former head of Communist Romania's KGB sister organization, the DIE, detailed how the KGB and the DIE had worked hand in glove with Arafat to transform socialist leaders of western European states into agents of political warfare against Israel. Pacepa defected to the United States in 1978, becoming the highest-ranking Soviet bloc official to ever defect to the West.

In *Red Horizons*, Pacepa described a 1978 conversation between Arafat and Romanian dictator Nicolae Ceauşescu. Ceauşescu suggested that Arafat pretend to abjure terrorism, in order to subvert the West's will to fight him and transform western Europeans into champions of his goal of destroying Israel. "How about pretending to break with terrorism?" he suggested. "The West would love it." The ruse would be effective, he explained, only if it was repeated continuously.

> "Political influence is built on the . . . basic tenet that quantitative accumulation [i.e., repeating a lie over and over again] generates qualitative transformation. . . .
>
> "[The lie] works like cocaine, let's say. If you sniff it once or twice, it may not change your life. If you use it day after day, though, it will make you into an addict, a different man. That's the qualitative transformation."
>
> "A snort of pacifist Arafat day after day . . . ?"

"Exactly, Brother Yassir. The West may even become addicted to you and your PLO."[15]

The third cause of western Europe's abandonment of Israel was Arab economic blackmail. In her groundbreaking history of European-Arab relations, *Eurabia: The Euro-Arab Axis,* Bat Ye'or explains that western Europe responded to the 1973 OPEC oil embargo by capitulating to the Arab demand to withdraw support from Israel.[16]

After Israel defeated the armies of Syria and Egypt in the Yom Kippur War, the Arab petroleum ministers in the OPEC oil cartel decided to quadruple the price of oil and reduce production by 5 percent. The Arabs imposed an embargo on oil exports to countries they viewed as being friendly to Israel—the United States, Denmark, and the Netherlands—and demanded that they withdraw their support for the Jewish state.[17]

The United States refused to give in, but the Europeans panicked. On November 6, 1973, the nine members of the European Economic Community (EEC) met in Brussels and put up the white flag. They issued a resolution declaring that "Israel must withdraw to the armistice lines of 1949; . . . [and] 'the legitimate rights of the Palestinians' must be included in any definition of peace for the Middle East."[18]

This position was unprecedented. Until the Brussels meeting, the Palestinians had never figured in European considerations. Hitherto, in line with the official Arab view, the Europeans had seen the Palestinians as being largely indistinguishable from the "Arab nation" or the Islamic *umma.* The notion of a distinct Palestinian nation was so outside the Arab narrative that even the 1968 PLO charter had denied its existence. The document said that Palestine "is an indivisible part of the Arab homeland, and the Palestinian people are an integral part of the Arab nation."

Not only did the EEC's resolution represent Europe's capitulation to the false Soviet-Arab narrative against Israel, it rendered hostility toward Israel the basis for a unified European foreign policy.

The final factor that contributed to western Europe's adoption of the Soviet-Arab anti-Israel narrative was European anti-Americanism.[19] Hostility toward Israel became a way to undercut American foreign policy and distinguish European foreign policy from that of the United States. In essence, from the Soviets and their satellites to the western Europeans, a major impetus for embracing the PLO and the cause of Israel's destruction has been a desire to cut America down to size.[20]

Until the end of the Cold War, to greater and lesser degrees, the United States rejected the Soviet-Arab anti-Israel narrative. By and large, it abided by the formulation of UN Security Council Resolution 242 from 1967, which in the aftermath of the 1967 Six Day War set the terms for an eventual peace between Israel and its neighbors.

Those terms included "withdrawal of Israel armed forces from territories occupied in the recent conflict," that is, an undefined Israeli withdrawal. They also involved a very specific requirement for the Arabs: "termination of all claims or states of belligerency and respect for and acknowledgment of the sovereignty, territorial integrity and political independence of every State in the area and their right to live in peace within secure and recognized boundaries free from threats or acts of force."

From 1967 through the end of the Cold War, the United States—like Israel—maintained that Israel could not be expected to surrender territory it took control of during the Six Day War until the Arab states recognized its right to exist and accepted its right to continue to exist, unmolested, within secure, defensible boundaries.

In other words, like Israel, the United States recognized that the root cause of the Arab-Israel conflict was not the absence of a Palestinian state and not the size of Israel. Rather it was the Arab world's unwillingness, in breach of the charter of the United Nations, to accept Israel's right to exist in peace. And until the Arabs changed their position, there could be no resolution of the conflict.

But under President Jimmy Carter in the mid-1970s, the United States began to incrementally align its policy with Europe's and away from Israel. In 1982, as we saw in Chapter 4, the United States rescued the PLO in Lebanon. It did so again in 1991 after the Persian Gulf War, when it prevented the Arab world from effectively burying Arafat and his terror group. And in 1989, as the Cold War wound down, the United States publicly opened a "dialogue" with the PLO.

In 1993 the United States gave its full sponsorship to the Israeli-PLO peace process. When President Bill Clinton accepted Arafat as the sole legitimate Palestinian leader and began pressuring Israel to make increasingly dangerous, always unreciprocated concessions to Arafat, he effectively aligned U.S. policy toward the Palestinians, erasing the most glaring discrepancy between America's Middle East policy and that of Europe.

Ironically, even though since 1993 the basic U.S. policy toward Israel and the Palestinians has been aligned with Europe's, this position has not won the United States support from Europe. And that makes sense. As previously noted, one of the reasons the EEC chose to embrace the false Soviet-Arab narrative against Israel was European anti-Americanism; America's adoption of the Soviet-Arab-European narrative simply made the Europeans radicalize their position still more.

Europe bears a significant share of the responsibility for shifting U.S. foreign policy toward the PLO. But that shift doesn't provide a complete explanation for American willingness in 2003 to let the PLO get away with murdering U.S. diplomats in Gaza.

MISUNDERSTANDING ARAB HATRED OF ISRAEL

The most reasonable explanation for this behavior is that whereas the United States was willing to part ways with western Europe on the Middle East, it was never willing to challenge two basic myths regarding the animating dynamics of the Arab world, myths that have long dominated U.S. thinking about the realities of the Middle East. The first is the myth of Arab unity.

Consecutive U.S. governments have claimed that "the Arabs" respond angrily to U.S. positions that are even marginally friendly to Israel or unfriendly to the PLO. But even though "the Arab street" *is* deeply hostile toward the Jewish people, "the Arab world" is no monolithic entity that responds to United States, Israel, and other nations as a bloc on all issues. It is also not true that the primary determining factor of the Arab world's positions toward any specific country, at all times, is that country's treatment of Israel.

As we saw in Chapter 3, during World War II, the overwhelming majority of Arab states sided with the Nazis and wished to see the Axis powers defeat the Allies. We also saw that the reason the Nazis were so popular there was that the Arabs shared their hatred of Jews and supported their plan to annihilate the Jews of Europe.

But despite the Arabs' ideological and programmatic affinity for the

Nazis, the Saudis and the Hashemites sided with the United States and Britain against Germany, Italy, and Japan. And the defeat of al-Gaylani's pro-Nazi coup d'état in Iraq and the overthrow of the pro-Nazi shah of Iran brought those states on board with the Allies, despite their publics' enthusiastic support for Hitler and the Nazi cause.

Moreover, in the sixty-six years that have passed since the establishment of the State of Israel, America's relations with the Arab world have developed and grown in parallel with the U.S. alliance with Israel. For instance, in the early 1970s, when Egyptian president Anwar Sadat determined to end Egypt's client state relationship with the Soviet Union and move under the American aegis, he did so not because he had become disenchanted with the Nazi anti-Semitism that brought him into the Muslim Brotherhood in the 1940s; no, Sadat remained the same anti-Semite he had been in 1953, when he wrote a hypothetical fan letter to Hitler.[21] Rather, Sadat the Jew hater expelled the Soviets from Egypt and forged an alliance with the United States because he had come to believe that it served his interests to do so. It was his perceived interests, not his deep-seated prejudices, that dictated his action.

At no point in the past sixty-six years has U.S. support for Israel kept it from achieving its goals vis-à-vis any specific Arab state. In the 1991 Gulf War, President George H. W. Bush rallied most members of the Arab League to his side in the U.S.-led coalition that ejected the Iraqi army from Kuwait. They did not join him because Bush had been less friendly to Israel than Reagan had been; they did so because their interests were advanced by the U.S. aim of removing Iraqi forces from Kuwait. Iraq's continued occupation of the oil sheikhdom harmed them.

Like other national governments, Arab governments are willing to put aside their anti-Semitic—and anti-American—ideology and act separately or in concert with the United States when they believe it serves their interests to do so, regardless of the U.S. policies toward Israel at any given time.

The second myth about Arab politics that has informed U.S. Middle East policy is that for the Arab world writ large, and for individual Arab governments, hatred of Israel—and conversely, support for the Palestinians—is the central issue around which Arab politics revolves.

Here too history tells a different tale. Although anti-Semitism and the desire to see Israel destroyed are certainly central, often ubiquitous themes in Arab life, it is not at all clear that this galloping hatred—or conversely, a deeply held affection for and loyalty to the Palestinians—has caused Arab governments to act in one way rather than another on the world stage. Israel has not been invaded since 1973. Syria's battles with the IDF in the 1982 Lebanon War marked the last time a national Arab army battled Israel. Every military conflict that Israel has been engaged in since then has been carried out either by remote control—i.e., Iraqi Scud missiles fired at Israel during the Gulf War—or by irregular terrorist paramilitaries from Lebanon, Egypt, and the Palestinian Authority.

As for the Palestinians, the fact is that if it hadn't been for the United States, the PLO would likely have disbanded or been marginalized as a terrorist organization and a nationalist force decades ago. The Arab states have at best a love-hate relationship with the PLO. In 1970, when Arafat sought to overthrow the Hashemite regime in Jordan, Jordan's King Hussein launched an all-out war against the PLO, killed thousands of PLO personnel, and expelled the rest from the kingdom; no Arab state interfered.

In 1982, when Israel's military forced Arafat and the PLO out of Lebanon, no Arab regime offered to host them. It took U.S. pressure to persuade Tunisian president Habib Bourguiba to permit them to transfer their base of operations to his country. The wider Arab world's assessment of Arafat was voiced by Jordan's King Hussein, who reportedly remarked, "Arafat never came to a bridge that he didn't double-cross."

In 1991 Arafat joined with Libyan leader Muammar Gaddafi and sided with Saddam Hussein in the Gulf War. The Persian Gulf states responded with fury. By the end of 1991, nearly 450,000 Palestinians had been expelled from their homes in Kuwait.[22]

The only reason the PLO—and with it the Palestinian nationalist movement—survived the Gulf War was that the United States resurrected it by organizing the Madrid Peace Conference in 1992 and coerced Israel to hold negotiations with a Jordanian-Palestinian delegation, even though the Palestinian delegates all received their orders from Arafat.[23]

Had it not been for the administration of George H. W. Bush, the PLO might well have been laid to rest as a political force with the collapse of the Soviet Union and the defeat of Iraq in 1991. Certainly it is hard to see why, after 1991, any Arab state—aside perhaps from Libya—

would condition its relations with the United States on U.S. pressure on Israel to establish a PLO state in its midst. Hatred for Israel is an overwhelming passion in the Arab world. But in practice, Arab regimes have not tethered their national interests either to the advancement of the PLO or to the destruction of Israel. Indeed, when they believed it served their interests, they have sided with Israel against what they perceived as common foes.

In 2006, for instance, the Sunni Arab world supported Israel's war against Iran's Hezbollah proxy in Lebanon.[24] And yet despite the Egyptian, Jordanian, and Saudi support for Israel, Condoleezza Rice persuaded George W. Bush to end U.S. support for Israel in its war against Hezbollah and to sue for a cease-fire. In his memoir, Bush related that Rice had said that if the United States supported an Israeli rout of Hezbollah, "America will be dead in the Middle East."[25]

Under the Obama administration, the situation has only become more acute. In June 2013 Secretary of State John Kerry made his fifth trip to Israel and the Palestinian Authority since taking office that February. He stayed for three days, shuttling between Jerusalem, Ramallah, and Amman in an effort to restart peace negotiations between Israel and the Palestinians. While he was engaged in these efforts, 22 million Egyptians signed a petition calling for the overthrow of the Muslim Brotherhood government; Turkey's Islamist leader Recep Tayyip Erdogan was engaged in a massive witch-hunt against his liberal opponents; and in Syria, with the support of Iran, Hezbollah, and Russia, the government of Bashar al-Assad was winning key battles against his U.S.-supported opponents in the Syrian civil war. Observers around the region and the world took Kerry's actions to mean that the United States was abdicating its leadership role in the Middle East. And indeed, that was the most charitable explanation for the administration's decision to devote itself to the most peaceful and stable area in the Middle East while key Arab states, as well as Turkey, were coming undone.[26]

The consistent U.S. policy of treating the PLO and Palestinian terrorism as distinct and more legitimate than non-Palestinian terrorism against non-Israeli and non-Jewish targets has not enhanced the U.S. position in the Arab world. Rather, it has damaged that position. America's consistent policy of accepting the narrative that the Palestinian conflict is the root cause of the Arab world's conflict with Israel, and a central determinant of the policies of Arab governments, has caused great harm to overall U.S. national interests.

THE MILITARY COST OF DENYING ISRAEL'S STRATEGIC IMPORTANCE

The decades-long U.S. support for the PLO has caused numerous unnecessary and counterproductive clashes with Israel, clashes that have had an adverse impact on Israel's strategic viability. But even more immediately important, Washington's willful misperception of the PLO has affected America's ability to assess Israel's strategic importance to U.S. national security; to understand the motivations and interests of Israel's Arab neighbors; and to comprehend how those motivations and interests affect those of the United States.

Lebanon, 1983

When Israel invaded Lebanon in 1982 to remove the PLO from the country, the United States viewed the war as illegitimate and joined the Soviets and the Europeans in reprimanding Israel at the UN Security Council and demanding an immediate cease-fire and withdrawal of Israeli forces.[27] During the course of the war, the United States placed a partial arms embargo on Israel.[28] And again, in 1982, it was the United States that stepped up and saved the PLO by forcing the Tunisian government to invite the PLO to resettle there.

The U.S. refusal to support Israel's war against the PLO and its Syrian and Shi'ite allies in Lebanon owed in large part to its diffident if not supportive position on the PLO. Again, that position was based on the view that the PLO's war against Israel was unconnected to the terror threat against the United States. By protecting the PLO from Israel, the United States believed it was strengthening its position in the wider Arab world.

The first casualties of the U.S. policy of preventing Israel from winning the war were the U.S. personnel in Beirut. On April 18, 1983, a suicide bomber blew up the U.S. embassy there, killing sixty-three people, seventeen of whom were Americans. On October 23, 1983, two suicide bombers drove trucks laden with explosives into the U.S. Marine barracks in Beirut, killing 241 Marines. Although not exhaustive, there is strong evidence that the PLO/Fatah played a key role in both bombings.[29]

Even if the PLO played no role in the bombings carried out by Arafat's Shi'ite protégé Imad Mughiyeh and his Iranian-run, PLO-trained and -organized Hezbollah force, the U.S. mission in Lebanon, in which U.S. forces were tasked with protecting Arafat from Israel, set the conditions for the attacks.

President Ronald Reagan had deployed the Marines to Beirut in April 1983 in order to prevent the IDF from completely routing the PLO. Their primary operational purpose was to force Israel to remove its military forces from Beirut. The United States assessed that if the IDF were gone, the Syrians would withdraw, and the violence would end.[30]

But ironically, as soon as Israel began drawing down its forces in Beirut in August 1983, the Shi'ite and Druze militias and the Syrian forces attacking the IDF began to attack the Marines instead. The Syrians not only refused to withdraw from Beirut, they began directly shelling American forces and aircraft. The Christian militias and the Lebanese armed forces (which had been allied with Israel) and the Syrians and the Druze and Shi'ite militias (which had been allied with the PLO) all escalated their fighting, in an attempt to fill the vacuum caused by the removal of Israeli forces from the city.

Much to their amazement, the U.S. forces in Beirut discovered that the IDF, far from being the cause of the violence, had been a restraining force. Once Israeli forces retreated from Beirut, the Marines found themselves filling the same role Israel had played. They were attacked by those who attacked Israel, and began actively supporting Israel's Christian allies.[31]

The Reagan administration had refused to recognize the nature of the war being fought against the Marines for good reason. Acknowledging reality would have required U.S. policy makers to discard the basic assumption of their Middle East policy: that supporting Israel was an altruistic act, not a strategic imperative. Avoiding this acknowledgment required the administration to also ignore the attacks on the U.S. peacekeepers in Beirut.

Michael Petit, a former Marine who survived the Marine barracks bombing, wrote a memoir of the attack and of his experiences in Lebanon.

He described in painstaking detail how the Marines' rules of engagement had denied the forces on the ground the ability to defend themselves or to deter attacks. Petit also explained that in the interest of winning over the local population (and so distinguishing U.S. forces from the Israelis), the Marines had not been allowed to construct the sort of barriers around their barracks that could have prevented the bombers from entering their compound with bomb-laden trucks. [32]

Iraq, 2003

The U.S. refusal to confront the strategic realities presented by Israel's war in Lebanon continued to haunt its military forces twenty years later, during the war in Iraq.

Perhaps the greatest failure of U.S. military planners and field commanders alike in Iraq was their failure to anticipate the terror campaign and insurgency that followed the U.S.-led invasion in 2003. They might have avoided this failure, had they considered Israel's experience in Lebanon as a relevant case study. In terms of demographic makeup, there is no Arab country more similar to Iraq than Lebanon. Israel's experience in Lebanon was a textbook case for how events would likely unfold for the United States and its British allies in Iraq.[33]

When Israel invaded Lebanon on June 6, 1982, the Christians and many Shi'ites who had been brutalized by the PLO greeted its forces with jubilation. Israel rapidly secured control over southern Lebanon. Eight days after the invasion began, the IDF, together with its Christian allies, was laying siege to Beirut. At that point, Israel stopped its advance, and its forces dug in to more or less static positions.

Over the months and years that followed, Syrian- and Iranian-backed terror forces, militias, and paramilitary groups began a slow-grinding terror war against them. This slow grind diminished domestic Israeli support for the war and harmed Israel's diplomatic standing in the world community. Ultimately, in May 2000, after eighteen years, Israeli prime minister Ehud Barak ordered IDF forces to evacuate Israel's security zone in southern Lebanon. Immediately after Israel withdrew, Hezbollah forces seized control of the area.

Rather than learn from Israel's experience in Lebanon, the United States rejected the relevance of that experience. The assumption guiding the U.S. military was that Israel had been "an occupier" in Lebanon, while the United States would be "a liberator" in Iraq.[34] Therefore the Iraqi and regional response to U.S. and allied forces in Iraq would be different from the response evoked by Israeli forces in Lebanon. In the event, the cheers that U.S. forces in Iraq received from the Shi'ites in southern Iraq, who had been violently oppressed by the Baathist regime, were identical to the cheers of Lebanon's Christians and Shi'ites in southern Lebanon in 1982. Iran and Syria played a nearly identical role in sponsoring terror groups and militias in both countries.

The prevailing perception of U.S. policy makers about the nature of the Middle East generally—and of Israel's war against the PLO in Lebanon specifically—had been based on the anti-Israel, pro-PLO narrative. Had it been otherwise, the U.S. campaign in Iraq would undoubtedly have been conceived and carried out very differently. At a minimum, U.S. military commanders and political leaders would not have been surprised by, and would therefore presumably have been better prepared for, the terror insurgency that began shortly after their forces entered Iraq.

THE WIDER COSTS OF ACCEPTING FALSE ASSUMPTIONS ABOUT THE MIDDLE EAST

Failure to Understand Developments in the Arab World

Willful American blindness, in the lead-up to and during its war in Iraq, to the relevance of Israel's military history in Lebanon points to the larger price that the United States pays for wedding its Middle East policy to the ungrounded view that the source of instability and violence in the Middle East is the absence of a Palestinian state.

To claim that the U.S. adoption of this view is entirely cynical would be unfair. U.S. officials would need to have a firm constitution in order not to begin to believe that Israel is the source of regional instability. As every U.S. policy maker who has dealt with Arab issues can attest, the first words out of most Arab leaders' mouths, upon meeting U.S. officials, is a complaint that the United States is not applying sufficient pressure on Israel to make concessions. Most U.S. leaders take such complaints at face value. Rare is the U.S. policy maker who is able to place them in the context of larger Arab political realities and social pathologies.

One policy maker who did understand the role of Israel bashing in Arab discourse was Defense Secretary Donald Rumsfeld. In his memoir of government service, Rumsfeld recalled that in a meeting with Egyptian president Hosni Mubarak in October 2001, just ahead of the U.S.-led invasion of Afghanistan, Mubarak "reflexively mentioned the Israeli-Palestinian issue as a root cause of terrorism but did not dwell on it. That was the standard line in the Middle East—everything was Israel's fault, although in truth, Arab nations had done little to help the Palestinians."[35]

But as Rumsfeld also noted, many U.S. officials believe that the Palestinian issue is the central issue in Arab politics, and this has had a destructive impact on their ability to realistically assess the conditions and dynamics of the Arab world.

As a consequence of its devotion to this irrelevant and inaccurate simplification of Arab world dynamics, the United States has consistently failed to anticipate or correctly interpret major events and trends in the rest of the Middle East. As we saw in Chapter 5, it blinded the Bush administration to the Palestinian public's disenchantment with Fatah (due to official PA corruption) and to the radicalization and Islamization of Palestinian society under Arafat. As a consequence, Hamas's victory in the Palestinian elections of January 2006 took the administration by surprise.

In the wider Arab context, the American fixation on Palestinian grievances against Israel has led the United States to underappreciate the impact of economic stagnation on social and cultural dynamics in the Arab world. Relatedly, the United States missed—and then misinterpreted—the social dynamics driving Muslim Brotherhood's popularity. As a consequence, U.S. policy makers on both sides of the partisan aisle cheered on the Arab Spring as the Muslim Brotherhood seized power in Egypt, Tunisia, and Libya. And they failed to understand the strategic implications of the rise of the Muslim Brotherhood for the future of U.S.-Arab and U.S.-pan-Islamic relations.

Perhaps most egregiously, the U.S. adoption of the anti-Israel narrative of Middle Eastern politics has blinded successive administrations to the value of the U.S. strategic alliance with Israel.

THE STRATEGIC IMPORTANCE OF THE U.S.-ISRAEL ALLIANCE

In his memoir, former vice president Dick Cheney related that during the official celebrations welcoming the victorious U.S. troops back from Iraq after Operation Desert Storm in June 1991, he called Major General David Ivry, the former commander of the Israeli air force. At the time, Cheney was serving as defense secretary.

Ivry, in Cheney's words, "had been commander of the Israeli Air Force on June 7, 1981, when the Israelis conducted a daring raid to take out Iraq's Osirak nuclear reactor. Although the Israelis had faced international condemnation for the attack, I believed they deserved our gratitude, and I wanted to thank Ivry. Without Israel's courageous action we may well have had to face a nuclear-armed Saddam Hussein in 1991."[36]

Cheney's statement is a reasonable place to begin considering Israel's strategic importance to the United States; to understanding why Israel is the most important U.S. ally in the Middle East; and to appreciating why the United States should seek to strengthen Israel as much as possible.

To that end, it is also necessary to dispassionately identify U.S. interests in the Middle East. The United States has three principal, permanent interests in that region:

1. Preventing radical regimes and radical substate and nonstate actors from acquiring the means to cause catastrophic harm;
2. Maintaining its own capacity to project its power in the region in order to protect its national security and defend its allies and interests in the region;
3. Preventing hostile regimes from artificially inflating the price of oil, through embargos (like the oil embargo of 1973) or through acts of war (like Iraq's invasion of Kuwait in 1990), and ensuring the smooth flow of maritime traffic through the Persian Gulf, the Gulf of Aden, and the Suez Canal.

As Cheney's statement about the importance of Israel's destruction of Iraq's nuclear reactor in 1981 made clear, in carrying out that raid—as well as the 2007 Israeli air force raid that destroyed Syria's illicit nuclear reactor—Israel secured all three of America's permanent interests in the region. And this makes sense: three permanent aspects of Israel's own strategic position ensure that it will always behave in a manner that advances these three permanent U.S. interests.

First, as the top target of the region's most radical regimes, substate actors, and nonstate actors, Israel has a permanent, existential interest in preventing these regimes and actors from acquiring the means to cause catastrophic harm. This is why Israel risked international condemnation and isolation and opted to destroy Iraq's nuclear reactor in 1981. This is why in September 2007 Israel acted against the direct wishes of Secretary of State Condoleezza Rice and destroyed Syria's North Korean-built nuclear reactor at al Kibar.[37] For its efforts in the 1981 case, the United States voted for a resolution condemning Israel in the UN Security Council, and delayed the shipment of aircraft to Israel that had already been authorized.[38]

The second aspect of Israel's strategic position that advances America's core regional interests is its nonexpansionist predisposition. Israel's neighbors know it has no appetite for territorial conquest. In Israel's sixty-six year history, it has controlled only land that it considered vital for its national security and land that was legally apportioned to it in the 1922 League of Nations Mandate. Israel's eschewal of territorial aggrandizement makes its military power inherently nonthreatening. In its sixty-six-year history, it has used force only in self-defense. Due to its desire to avoid war, the stronger Israel is, the greater its deterrent capacity, the smaller the probability that radical states and actors will opt for war, and the greater the chance that moderate regimes will survive.

Because they know that Israel is not aggressive, Israel's neighbors realize that its purported nuclear arsenal is intended only to guarantee its national survival and therefore is nonthreatening to moderate regimes. True, the Arab states consistently use Israel's presumptive nuclear arsenal to single it out at international forums. But for all their rhetorical bluster, their claimed concern about Israeli nuclear weapons has not caused any Arab state to enter a nuclear arms race.

In sharp contrast, of course, is the projected Arab response to Iran's nuclear weapons program. Iran's progress toward acquiring a nuclear arsenal has already caused Saudi Arabia and other Persian Gulf states to take steps to secure nuclear capabilities.[39] Egypt and Jordan have also begun to invest in nuclear reactors.[40] This tells us that while the Arabs view Israel's purported nuclear arsenal as nonthreatening, they perceive Iran's nuclear weapons program as inherently aggressive.

Finally, since the Jewish state is the regional bogeyman, no Arab state will agree to form a permanent alliance with it. As a consequence, Israel will never be in a position to join forces with another nation against a third nation. In contrast, the Egyptian-Syrian United Arab Republic of the 1960s was formed to attack Israel. Syria's alliance with Iran is inherently aggressive against Israel, the United States, and the nonradical Arab states and actors in the region.

In summary, Israel will always act to prevent the most radical actors from acquiring the means to cause catastrophic harm and so deny them the ability to destroy or deter other powers. Israel's inherently unaggressive nature makes its military force a stabilizing force in the region. And since Israel has no option other than to remain alone, its strategic posture is unlikely to ever change. That means that Israel's strategic value to the United States as the first line of defense of permanent U.S. interests in the region will never be diminished.

There are other, less sophisticated reasons that Israel is the most important U.S. ally in the region. First and foremost is the nature of the alliance. U.S. alliances with Arab states are made with regimes rather than peoples—and as a consequence, they have been subverted, ended, or rendered meaningless when the allied regimes are overthrown. But the U.S. alliance with Israel is with the people of Israel. Because the Israeli people support Israel's alliance with the United States, every Israeli government, regardless of its partisan affiliation, will strive to maintain and expand Israel's ties with the United States.

Furthermore, as a liberal democracy, Israel is not susceptible to revolutionary violence of the sort that has been gripping the Arab world since December 2010. When Israeli voters are tired of their leaders, they simply elect new ones.

Many have pointed out that Israel's entrepreneurial economy and pioneering spirit marks it as America's alter ego in the Middle East. Arab nations have always viewed Israel and the United States as two sides of the same coin.[41] And this makes sense. Values of freedom, equal opportunity, fairness, and individual responsibilities and rights have animated the American psyche since the first English colonists set foot in the New World; these are also the values that animate Israeli society, and they have informed the Jewish experience since biblical times.

Unfortunately, in recent years, owing in no small measure to their adoption of the false Soviet-Arab-European narrative of the Arab conflict with Israel, U.S. policy makers on both sides of the partisan divide have lost sight of America's actual strategic interests in the Middle East and have increasingly trivialized or even denied the importance of the cultural, moral, and spiritual affinity that Americans and Israelis share.

Successive U.S. leaders have placed achieving peace between Israel and its neighbors, or establishing a Palestinian state, at the top of their Middle East agenda. They have viewed it as the chief goal of U.S. policy, even though the achievement or nonachievement of formal peace treaties between Israel and its neighbors is immaterial to the three core U.S. interests in the region. It will similarly not advance, and indeed harm, America's ability to stay true to the principles that have guided it since before it was a nation.

As this chapter has demonstrated, the central position that the Palestinian conflict with Israel presently occupies in U.S. Middle East policy makes it difficult for most American policy makers to understand regional events, dynamics, and realities. It has caused the United States to disregard lessons of Israeli military campaigns that are relevant for U.S. forces. It has caused the United States to misread or miss major political, economic, and social developments in the Arab world. Misunderstandings of regional developments, and of the dynamics within individual Arab states, have caused the United States to find itself repeatedly unprepared and surprised by events, to the detriment of its national security and strategic position.

Finally, the incorrect U.S. belief that the major source of regional instability is the absence of a Palestinian state has caused the United States to embrace a policy that degrades Israel's ability to defend itself while ignoring the moral basis for its close ties to the Jewish state.

As we have seen in the preceding chapters, the two-state solution requires Israel to contract itself to the indefensible 1949 cease-fire lines and allow a hostile Palestinian state to take power in the areas it vacates. In other words, it is based on the belief that for peace to take hold in the Middle East, Israel must become weak and survive at the mercy of its neighbors.

In 1970 Israel was able to save the Hashemite regime in Jordan. In 1981 and 2007 it had the military capacity destroy the nuclear programs of radical neighboring regimes. But if Israel were to do what the U.S. wishes, it would become a rump state cowering inside indefensible boundaries while triumphant terrorists in Gaza, Jerusalem, Judea, and Samaria seek its destruction. Those terrorists, in turn, would be supported by radicalized regimes in surrounding Arab states as well as Iran. Such an Israel would be hard-pressed to repeat its previous accomplishments.

An Israel unable to secure its own interests would be an Israel unable to aid America in the region. Given the tremendous—generally unsolicited and rarely applauded—contributions that Israel has made to U.S. strategic interests over the past sixty-six years simply by being strong and defending itself, there can be no doubt that a severely weakened Israel would be antithetical to U.S. national interests and that a policy based on it should be discarded in favor of one that strengthens Israel.

In Part II, we will see how abandonment of the two-state paradigm, and the embrace of a one-state model in which Israel applies its laws to Judea and Samaria, will work. In Part III, we will also see how adopting this plan will advance America's regional and national security interests.

PART II

THE ISRAELI ONE-STATE PLAN

CHAPTER 7

Introducing the Plan

A week after the Six Day War ended, on June 18–19, 1967, the Israeli cabinet held a series of top-secret discussions to determine what to do with the territories over which the country had just taken control from Egypt, Jordan, and Syria.[1]

The easiest question was Jerusalem. The cabinet agreed unanimously that Israel should reunite its capital city and apply Israeli law to the areas it had liberated from Jordanian occupation, even if doing so meant offering Israeli citizenship to all the Arab residents of the newly incorporated neighborhoods.[2] On June 28, 1967, Jerusalem's municipal government extended the boundaries of its jurisdiction to include all these additional areas, thus reuniting the city under Israeli sovereignty.

Regarding the Sinai Peninsula (which Israel had taken over from Egypt) and the Golan Heights (which it had captured from Syria), the cabinet determined that while Israel had a better legal claim to sovereignty over these lands than did either Egypt or Syria (since Israel had won them in a war of self-defense, while Egypt and Syria had lost them in a war of aggression), Israel's interests would be best advanced by offering to give them back in exchange for full peace.[3]

As for Judea, Samaria, and Gaza, due to their inclusion in the lands slated for Israeli sovereignty in the 1922 League of Nations Mandate, and due as well to their historic and strategic importance to Israel, the government did not consider giving them up in return for peace. The cabinet decided that Israel should apply its laws to Gaza but postponed the move pending a decision about what to do with its Arab residents.[4]

Judea and Samaria, with their relatively large Arab populations, presented a greater challenge. Some ministers recommended applying Israeli law to the areas and waiting a few years before deciding what to do with the local population. Some called for applying Israeli sovereignty to the Jordan Valley and the Hebron area in the south while reaching a confederation deal with Jordan in which Jordan would have responsibility for governing the Arabs, and Israel would have security and diplomatic control of the areas. Others called for negotiating an autonomy agreement with the local population that would leave security and diplomatic responsibility for the areas in Israel's hands.[5]

In 1967 no one in the international community—not the UN, not the United States, and not the Arab League—supported the establishment of another Arab state in the areas, and few considered the local Arabs a distinct "Palestinian" nation. As a consequence, at no point in the Israeli government's discussions was the option of a two-state solution raised.

The government decided that, until the Arabs expressed willingness to negotiate with Israel, Israel would govern the areas—minus Jerusalem— through the IDF, which would set up a military government and a civil administration—an arm of the military government—to run the areas.

Israel communicated its positions to the United States and asked that the Americans communicate to the Arabs its extraordinarily conciliatory stand—which involved returning strategically vital areas from which it had just been attacked to the aggressors themselves.[6]

The Arabs were unmoved by Israel's largesse. On September 1, 1967, the members of the Arab League convened in Khartoum and issued what became known as the Khartoum Declaration of "Three No's: no peace with Israel, no recognition of Israel, and no negotiations with Israel."[7]

As a consequence, rule by the military government and its civil administration, which was supposed to be a short-term, stopgap measure until peace was achieved, became the status quo.

In practice, the civil administration became a means of enabling Palestinian autonomy. The vast majority of the civil administration's employees were Palestinians. They controlled their own governance. To the extent that Israeli authorities inserted themselves into the Palestinians' daily life, their primary purpose was to prohibit anti-Semitic materials from being taught in Palestinian schools, outlaw terrorist organizations, and improve public health and safety for the benefit of Israelis and Palestinians alike.

THE SEARCH FOR DEFENSIBLE BORDERS

In July 1967, shortly after the government completed its deliberations, Labor minister and retired Lieutenant General Yigal Allon presented the ideas he had put forward at the cabinet meetings on June 18–19 as a stand-alone plan. The Allon Plan, as it became known, called for incorporating into sovereign Israel the Gaza Strip and eastern Judea and Samaria, from the Jordan Valley up to the mountain range that spans the middle of the areas. Allon recommended transplanting the residents of Gaza to the western part of Judea and Samaria, where most of the Palestinian Arab population centers were located, and giving Jordan governing power over this area. The plan was made public in 1976.

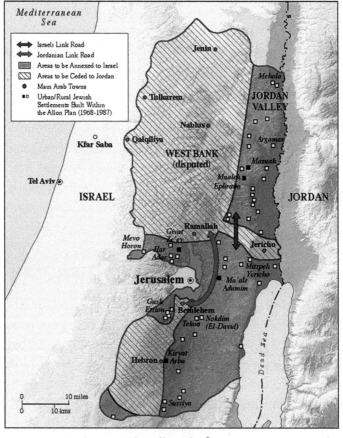

The Allon Plan[8]

Whereas Allon's plan considered the issue of how the Arabs of Judea, Samaria, and Gaza would be governed, most of the discussions carried out at the time and since limited their focus to the question of Israel's security requirements.

At no point during these deliberations was the possibility raised of Israel withdrawing from all the territories it took control over during the war. Everyone in Israel and the international community alike understood that the 1949 armistice lines were indefensible. As Israeli foreign minister Abba Eban evocatively summed up that consensus, the 1949 armistice lines were "Auschwitz borders."[9]

It was in recognition of the impossibility of defending the 1949 armistice lines (popularly, but wrongly referred to today as the "1967 borders" or "1967 lines") over the long term, that the UN Security Council stipulated in its Resolution 242, which set the terms of the peace that would eventually be wrought between the Arabs and Israel after the ceasefire was reached, that all states in the region had the "right to live in peace within secure and recognized boundaries."[10] In other words, Resolution 242 assumed that Israel could not return to the 1949 armistice lines.

Just weeks after the end of the war, President Lyndon B. Johnson instructed the U.S. Joint Chiefs of Staff to prepare a map of the territories that they believed Israel would require in perpetuity to ensure its ability to defend itself. A few weeks later, General Earl Wheeler, chairman of the Joint Chiefs, presented a map to Johnson that included most of Judea and Samaria, parts of the Golan Heights, the Gaza Strip, and the eastern Sinai, as well as Sharm el-Sheikh, along the Suez Canal at the southern tip of Sinai (see map opposite).

LIFE IN JUDEA AND SAMARIA UNDER ISRAELI RULE

For the Palestinian Arabs in Jerusalem, Judea, and Samaria, Israel's takeover of those areas was an economic and civil rights boon. Jerusalem's Arabs lined up to receive Israeli identification cards that granted them permanent residency status in Israel. In two censuses that Israel carried out in the months immediately following the war, Israeli authorities found a population of 65,000. By July 1968, they had issued 65,000 identification cards. Another 6,000 requests were outstanding, indicat-

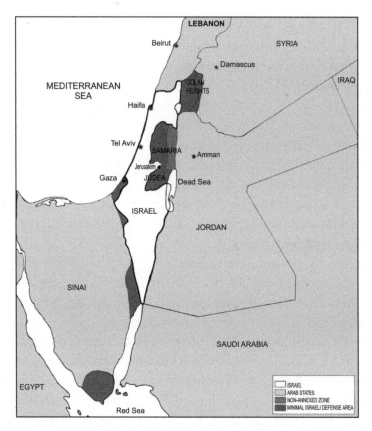

Joint Chiefs of Staff Map for Defensible Israeli Borders, June 29, 1967[11]

ing either that Israel had undercounted or that 6,000 additional Arabs had entered Israel from Judea and Samaria, or both.[12]

In Judea and Samaria, Israel's benign military rule brought positive results on the ground. By most recognized measures, the Palestinians' living standards rose steeply. From 1967 to 2000, Israeli investment in the local economy enabled the local GDP to grow 5.5 percent each year on average—nearly a full point more than Israel's own economy's average growth rate of 4.2 percent.[13] Literacy rates among the Palestinians rose from 52.5 percent in 1967 to 84.2 percent in 1995.[14] Israel opened six universities in Judea and Samaria and two in Gaza.[15] Levels of urbanization also rose steeply. Whereas in 1965 only 48.9 percent of Palestinians in Judea, Samaria, and Gaza lived in urban areas, by 1995 the figure was 70.4 percent.[16] Life expectancy increased sharply, from forty-eight in 1967 to seventy-two in 2000.[17] Infant mortality plummeted by three-quarters, from 60 per thousand live births to 15, as Israel built more than a hundred clinics, offered comprehensive health insurance,[18] and modernized and expanded sewage and electrical infrastructures.[19] Except in times of upsurges in terrorist attacks, Israel permitted Palestinians from the areas to commute to Israel for work. In 1986 some 109,000 Palestinians were regularly employed in Israel.[20]

Under Israeli rule, the Palestinians of Judea, Samaria, and Gaza exercised political freedoms that were nonexistent in the rest of the Arab world. These included freedom of association, freedom of the press, enfranchisement of women, and the ability to seek the protection of the Israeli court system.

In 1968 there was only one newspaper in Judea and Samaria. In 1994, when Israel transferred civilian authority to the Palestinian Authority, there were more than forty independent newspapers regularly published and distributed there.[21]

Israel had two principal reasons to exercise control of Judea and Samaria. First, militarily, Israeli control protected Israel from invasion from Jordan and blocked the development of powerful Arab terrorist networks and capabilities in the areas. Due to Israel's effective control, from 1967 through 1988, when the Palestinian uprising started, very few successful terrorist attacks were planned in or originated from Judea and Samaria.

Equally important, during this period, Israelis were able to reassert their national and property rights to Judea and Samaria. As we noted in Chapter 3, these rights—explicitly laid out in the League of Nations Mandate for Palestine—were first denied the Jews in February 1940 with Britain's publication of the Land Transfer Regulations. These regulations barred Jews from purchasing land in 63 percent of the Mandatory territories and restricted Jewish land purchases in another 32 percent. Jews were allowed to purchase land without restrictions on only 5 percent of the territory—and Jews already owned 50 percent of that land.[22]

During the Jordanian occupation of Judea, Samaria, and Jerusalem from 1949 to 1967, Jews were prohibited from purchasing land. And Jordan's war on Jewish property rights didn't end with its defeat in the Six Day War. In 1973 Jordan instituted the death penalty for any Arab caught selling land to Jews, and it applied the law to Judea and Samaria, even though those areas were controlled by Israel at the time.[23]

As Alex Safian reported in 1997, "According to the PA Attorney General Khalid al-Qidra, Jordan sentenced 172 people to death under the law. Amnesty International claimed that, as of 1988, many of the convictions were *in absentia,* and there had been no executions. However, PA Justice Minister Freih Abu Meddein claimed that Jordan had executed 10 violators."[24]

Moshe Zer, one of the largest Jewish land buyers in Samaria, made most of his purchases during the 1970s and 1980s. He has estimated that some 30 percent of the Arabs who sold land to him were murdered for their actions.[25]

Once Israel took control of Judea and Samaria, it sought to make amends for the historic injustice that Jews there had suffered under both the British and the Jordanian regimes. Partially as a means of compensating Jews for the legacy of bigoted laws that barred them from buying land, and in keeping with both domestic and international law and practice, Israel allocated state lands for the purpose of Jewish settlement in Judea and Samaria.

The majority of the land in Judea and Samaria is defined as State Lands. That is, they are owned by the sovereign power. Under Ottoman rule, State Lands were controlled by the sultan and his agents. Under the British Mandate, they were controlled by the British high commissioner, and under Jordanian rule, they were controlled by the king. Under Israeli rule, State Lands have been controlled by the civil administration of the military government. The use of State Lands for Jewish settlement was in keeping with the Mandate of the League of Nations, which called explicitly for the facilitation of "close settlement by Jews on the land, including State lands and waste lands not required for public purposes."[26]

From a national perspective, the policy permitted Jews to build communities in Judea and Samaria—the cradle of Jewish civilization. Historic Jewish communities in places like Hebron, Beit El, Susia, and Alon Moreh were reestablished, thus fulfilling Zionism's promise of returning the Jews to their historic lands. So too Jewish communities that had been overrun and ethnically cleansed by the Jordanian Legion during the 1948–49 Arab invasion of Israel (such as Kfar Etzion and Beit Haaravah) were rebuilt.

Since the Palestinian Authority was established in 1994, Judea and

Samaria have been ruled jointly by Israel's military government and the Palestinian Authority.

In 1996, following the implementation of the 1995 Israeli-Palestinian Interim Agreement on the West Bank and the Gaza Strip,[27] 98 percent of the Palestinians living in the areas came under the jurisdiction of the Palestinian Authority. The remaining 2 percent of Palestinians, as well as all the Israelis residing in the areas, continued to be governed by the Israeli military government. As we will see in Chapter 10, the Palestinian Authority, after taking power, ended the freedoms the Palestinians had enjoyed under Israeli rule and torpedoed their economy.

Everyday life under the Israeli military government undoubtedly provides more freedom and more economic opportunities, to Palestinians and Israelis alike. Israeli military control facilitates the terror-free environment that attracts investment and that enables Palestinians to move freely between Israeli population centers and their homes in Judea and Samaria for employment, marriage, and myriad other endeavors.

However, the military government also has clear drawbacks for both Palestinians and Israelis living in Judea and Samaria. As we shall discuss more fully in Chapter 10, the military government administers the areas through the Jordanian legal code and military orders promulgated since 1967, rather than through Israeli law. As a result, routine activities for the residents—from dealing with traffic accidents to criminal activities to agricultural and planning and zoning issues—are more wracked with bureaucratic hassles than they are for Jewish and Arab citizens living in sovereign Israel. Land registration, for instance, is nearly impossible.

Furthermore, Israel's inability to trust that the hostile Palestinian security forces will prevent terrorists from killing Jews requires Israel to set up roadblocks on roads. Roadblocks are a primary tool for fighting terrorism. But they make travel cumbersome and dangerous for Jews and Palestinians alike.

Both the Palestinian Authority and the Israeli military government were established as temporary measures that would end once peace was established between Israel and its neighbors. The initial peace accord, signed between Israel and the PLO in September 1993, envisioned that the Palestinian Authority would be replaced by a permanent Palestinian governing authority in five years. Instead the Palestinian Authority has now been governing the Palestinians for twenty years. Likewise, the military government was supposed to end when a permanent peace was reached between Israel and Jordan or the Palestinians, just as it was ended in the Sinai in 1981 following the implementation of Israel's peace treaty with Egypt. It is now forty-seven years old.

CLIMBING OVER A BRICK WALL

As events have demonstrated, the PLO was never interested in fulfilling its part of the bargain it signed with Israel. Whereas Israel ceded lands to the PLO, the group has refused peace and so has refused to establish a permanent governing authority. As we shall see in Chapter 10, the Palestinian Authority—the government that the PLO set up—rules as an authoritarian kleptocracy, whose leaders are less interested in building a coherent state and cementing peaceful relations with Israel than in stealing from the public trough, suppressing the Palestinians, and inciting hatred and violence against Jews. Fear, rather than trust, is the dominant feeling that Palestinians hold toward their PLO government. The two-state solution, it has become clear, is a recipe for war, repression, and poverty—not for peace, freedom, and prosperity.

Today there are no local Palestinians to whom Israel can safely transfer control of Judea and Samaria, or with whom Israel can exercise joint control of the areas. What constituency there may be for peaceful coexistence is a small minority that has no capacity either to sway the hearts and minds of their brethren or to implement any peace treaty that they could hypothetically sign with Israel.

The Jordanian option is also a dead end. Israel's initial hope for a confederation with Jordan that would involve Jordanian sovereignty over the Palestinians of Judea and Samaria has no chance of being implemented—and indeed it never had such a chance.

After Jordan took control of Judea, Samaria, and Jerusalem in 1949, the regime annexed the areas and gave Jordanian citizenship to all the Palestinian Arabs living there. During the PLO-controlled Palestinian uprising against Israel in 1988, Jordan's King Hussein, in a bid to mend fences with the PLO but also to weaken it, announced that Jordan was renouncing all its administrative and legal ties to the areas. Following his speech, the Jordanian government revoked the Jordanian citizenship held by all Arabs on the west bank of the Jordan.[28] Ever since, Jordanian legal scholars have claimed that Hussein's move was itself illegal, in breach of Jordan's constitution and international law.[29]

Despite this criticism, sometime around 2004 Hussein's son and successor, King Abdullah II, began arbitrarily revoking the Jordanian citizenship of ethnic Palestinians living in Jordan. His government also began removing ethnic Palestinians from the Jordanian armed forces and from positions in the government.[30]

Realistically, while the last word has not been spoken about the nature of the Palestinian-majority monarchy in Jordan, Jordan will be neither willing nor able to join a confederation with Israel at any time in the foreseeable future. Moreover, how long the minority Hashemite monarchy will survive, or who will replace it if it is overthrown, is unknowable. For all these reasons, the Hashemites cannot be considered viable partners with Israel for governing Judea and Samaria.

Lacking the option of forging a peaceful relationship with a Palestinian government, or of forming a confederation with the Jordanian government, Israel is left with three main options:

1. Reassert the military government as the sole governing body.
2. Maintain the current dual governance by the military government and the Palestinian Authority.
3. Incorporate Judea and Samaria into sovereign Israel.

The problem with option one, reasserting the military government as the sole governing body of the areas, is that it is not tenable over the long term. Certainly from economic and civil liberties perspectives, the Palestinians lived better under Israel's military government than they did under any prior government (or under the Palestinian Authority), but military government is not a reasonable long-term option. Both Arabs and Jews have the right to expect to be governed by a democratic, civilian government.

As for option two, maintaining the current dual system of governance: if joint rule with the PLO was a viable long-term option, the two-state paradigm would also be viable—and indeed, a Palestinian state would have been established fifteen years ago. Unfortunately, as we saw in Chapters 1 to 5, Palestinians from every part of the political spectrum have made clear through word and deed that they are uninterested in peacefully coexisting with the Jewish state under any conditions that would allow the Jewish state to survive. And so maintaining the joint rule that has been in effect for the past twenty years is no more viable than the two-state peace option.

This leaves us with option three: applying Israeli law to the areas, thereby incorporating them into sovereign Israel.

THE ISRAELI SOLUTION

Israel needs to control Judea and Samaria. It needs to be able to defend itself from the threats of Palestinian terrorism and external forces alike. Equally important, renouncing its rights to Judea and Samaria would mean denying Jewish history and heritage, and so emptying the Jewish state of meaning. Israel cannot do that.

For more than twenty-five years, due to successive Israeli governments' preference for the ideal over the good, Israeli leaders have pursued chimerical peace processes with the PLO and doomed confederations with Jordan instead of considering the viability and the desirability of applying Israeli law to Judea and Samaria, and incorporating the areas and their Palestinian residents into Israel.

Applying Israeli law to the areas would end the authoritarian repression that the Palestinians suffer under the rule of the Palestinian Authority. As permanent residents of Israel, with the option of applying for Israeli citizenship, the Palestinians would find themselves living in a liberal democracy where their individual rights are protected.

Contingent on security concerns—applied on an individual rather than on a communal basis—Palestinians will have the right to travel and live anywhere they wish within Israeli territory. Similarly, Israeli Jews will also be allowed to live anywhere they wish. All prohibitions on property and land sales to Jews will be abrogated.

From the outset, as permanent residents of Israel, Palestinians will have the right to elect their local governments. Those that receive Israeli citizenship in accordance with Israel's Citizenship Law will also be allowed to vote in national elections for the Knesset. The Israeli education system will be open to them. The Israeli economy will be open to them.

To be sure, there are many serious concerns about such a plan.

From an Israeli perspective, the principal concern remains the same as it was in 1967: the fear that the sudden influx of a large, unassimilated Arab population will destabilize the country and endanger the Jewish character of the state. This issue will be discussed in depth in Chapter 8.

From an American perspective, the incorporation of Judea and Samaria into Israel will require Washington to acknowledge that the two-state paradigm has been a disastrous failure, and to cease its funding of the Palestinian Authority and its armed forces. Chapter 18 will consider the ramifications of this acknowledgement for U.S. interests.

Finally, the application of Israeli law to the areas will block the possibility of a confederation between Israel, Jordan, and the Palestinians. But that prospect has been impossible since 1967.

In essence, then, the main thing that the Israeli one-state plan—that is, the application of Israeli law over Judea and Samaria—requires of both Israel and its closest ally is that they embrace reality, with all its opportunities and threats, and stop chasing fantasies of perfect resolutions.

The mechanics of the policy are fairly straightforward. Israel will apply its laws to Judea and Samaria and govern the areas as normal parts of Israel. The military government will be dissolved, as it was in the Golan Heights in 1981, when Israel applied Israeli law to that area.

The Palestinian Authority will be dissolved. Its security forces will be disbanded and disarmed, and the Israeli military and police will assume full security responsibility for the whole of the country. Israel will place reasonable limits on eligibility for citizenship. For instance, past or current membership in terrorist organizations, and past or current incitement to violence against Israel, should disqualify an individual from acquiring citizenship.

The PLO will no longer be the representative of the Palestinians in Judea and Samaria. Like their fellow Israeli Arabs and Jews, if they apply for and receive citizenship, the Palestinians in Judea and Samaria will be duly represented by legislators in the Knesset whom they elect. And all of them will be represented in their local governments by officials they will elect.

As I will discuss in detail in the coming chapters, implementing Israeli law in Judea and Samaria will doubtlessly cause a host of difficulties for Israel—not least, that such a move will burden its welfare services.

However, this policy has one key advantage that the two-state policy and the confederation-with-Jordan policy lack: it is a viable, realistic option, not a pipe dream. It also has an advantage over the option of prolonging the current dual governance by the Palestinian Authority and the Israeli military government: it is fair, liberal, and democratic.

CHAPTER 8

The Demographic Time Bomb Is a Dud

THE STATISTICAL TERROR WAR

In 1997 the Palestinian Authority carried out its first census of the Palestinian population in Judea, Samaria, and Gaza. In an interview with the *New York Times* while the census was being undertaken, Hasan Abu Libdeh, the founder and director of the Palestinian Central Bureau of Statistics (PCBS), said, "In my opinion, [the census data] is as important as the intifada. It is a civil intifada."[1]

On the face of it, Abu Libdeh's statement was confusing. Why would a census constitute the statistical equivalent of a terror war? What is aggressive about a population count? Israel had conducted a census of the populations of Gaza, Judea, and Samaria in 1967, and it had updated its data each year since then. It conducted its last updated survey in 1996.

But Abu Libdeh was right: the 1997 Palestinian census was an act of aggression against Israel. And his comparison of the census to a terror war was also apt. Terrorism is the use of violence to coerce a state to bend to the political will of the terrorists. The 1997 Palestinian census used statistics to coerce Israel to bend to the political will of the PLO.

Since the dawn of modern Zionism in the late nineteenth century, the demography of the Land of Israel has been a sensitive issue for the Jews. For more than five hundred years after the Second Commonwealth was destroyed by the Romans in 134 CE, the Jews constituted a majority or plurality of the population. Only with the Islamic conquest of the Land of Israel in the seventh century did Jews, beset by Islamic discrimination and terror, become a minority in their historic homeland.[2]

When the Jews began contemplating a return to the Land of Israel, the question of how to build a Jewish majority was always central in their minds. From 1948 on, due largely to mass Jewish immigration from around the world, Jews have constituted the overwhelming majority of the population of Israel, ranging from 75 to 90 percent. Muslims have constituted between 7 and 20 percent of the population. The rest of the population is made up of Christians and Druze.[3]

Despite the durability of Israel's Jewish majority, Israelis have a persistent fear of being overtaken demographically by Muslims. And this makes sense. Israel is the only non-Muslim-majority country in the Middle East, and the only non-Muslim-majority country between the eastern Mediterranean and India. To varying degrees, its neighbors, even those whose regimes have signed formal treaties of peace with the Jewish state, all remain implacably devoted to its destruction.

Playing on this insecurity, the PCBS, which conducted the Palestinian census in 1997, released findings that predicted Israel's demographic demise. If Israel did not quit Judea, Samaria, and Gaza, according to the census data, by 2015 the Palestinians could destroy the Jewish state simply by asking to be incorporated into Israel, by demanding citizenship and the right to vote. According to the data, by 2015, in the land west of the Jordan River (that is, in the land mass including Judea, Samaria, Gaza, and Israel within the 1949 armistice lines), Arabs would outnumber Jews.

The PCBS claimed that there were 2.86 million Palestinians living in Judea and Samaria in 1997 and forecast that by 2015 that number would grow to 5.81 million.[4] At the time, the Jewish population of Israel was 4.7 million,[5] and in 2012, it had grown to 5.9 million (6.1 million when ethnic Jews were included).[6] In 1997 Israel had one million Arab citizens,[7] and in 2012 that number had grown to 1.6 million.[8]

Neither the U.S. government nor the Israeli government conducted an independent assessment of the 1997 Palestinian census, despite its dire implications for Israel. Instead, everyone involved immediately accepted its numbers, as well as subsequent forecasts, as fact. Israeli politicians, demographers, military leaders, and the media all agreed that they spelled demographic peril for Israel.

This was a radical shift in elite opinion. Before the 1997 census, demographic fears had often been voiced, but they had never been the primary motivator for government policies. Certainly, they never motivated political leaders to contemplate making massive concessions to the PLO.

But following the 1997 Palestinian census, many prominent right-wing politicians, including Ariel Sharon, Ehud Olmert, and Tzipi Livni from Likud, abandoned their political and ideological camp for the Left, arguing that failure to transfer Judea, Samaria, and Gaza to the PLO would destroy Israel, which would have to choose between its Jewish identity and its democratic form of government.

The point was made most graphically by Olmert in 2007, during his tenure as prime minister. Echoing anti-Israel tropes that called Israel a racist, apartheid state, Olmert said, "If the day comes when the two-state solution collapses, and we face a South African–style struggle for equal voting rights [including the Palestinians in the territories], then, as soon as that happens, the State of Israel is finished."[9]

In other words, Olmert joined Israel's radical Left, and anti-Israel activists abroad, in arguing that if Israel refused to quit Judea and Samaria, it would share the moral and political fate of apartheid South Africa.

The demographic panic has led Israeli leaders like Olmert to argue that Israel needs a Palestinian state in Judea and Samaria (and Gaza) even more than the Palestinians do. As Olmert and his colleagues see it, the Palestinians can bide their time and wait for the day when Arabs outnumber Jews. Then they can destroy Israel simply by asking for what they refer to as the "one-state solution"—a unitary state west of the Jordan River in which Arabs will outnumber Jews.[10]

In 2005, largely as a consequence of their demographic fears, Sharon, Olmert, and Livni led the unilateral withdrawal of Israeli civilians and military forces from the Gaza Strip. After succeeding Sharon as head of their newly formed Kadima Party in January 2006, Olmert and Livni ran an electoral campaign centered around a plan of unilaterally withdrawing from much of Judea and Samaria. Fear of demographic collapse was what also drove Olmert to offer PA chairman Mahmoud Abbas Palestinian statehood in 2008, on terms even more generous than those Ehud Barak offered to Yassir Arafat at Camp David in 2000.

In much the same way, American leaders swallowed the PCBS's numbers whole and allowed them to dictate their positions on what peace in the region should look like. Politicians and policy makers from both major parties insisted that the only way for Israel to remain both a democracy and a Jewish state was to quit Judea, Samaria, and Gaza. So too, following the publication of the 1997 Palestinian census, almost every major

American Jewish organization, citing demographic concerns, began supporting Palestinian statehood.

In his speech before the American-Israel Public Affairs Committee (AIPAC) in May 2011, President Barack Obama channeled these fears, listing demography as the first reason that Israel had to agree to retreat from Judea and Samaria and to partition Jerusalem. "The number of Palestinians living west of the Jordan River," the president said, "is growing rapidly and fundamentally reshaping the demographic realities of both Israel and the Palestinian Territories. This will make it harder and harder—without a peace deal—to maintain Israel as both a Jewish state and a democratic state."[11]

THE PALESTINIAN DEMOGRAPHIC FRAUD IS EXPOSED

In 2004 an American tourist named Bennett Zimmerman came to Israel for vacation with a group of friends. Zimmerman, a businessman, had worked as a strategy consultant for Bain and Company and had conducted numerous due diligence audits on business and government organizations. In a drive along the Jordan Valley and through Judea and Samaria, he was struck by how few people he saw on the roads, and how small the Palestinian cities and towns were.

"Where are all the three point six million people hiding?" he asked his companions.

Recalling the trip a year later, Zimmerman explained, "That was when I decided I had to take a serious look at the Palestinian census data."[12]

He assembled a team of Israeli and American researchers, who included academics expert in forecasting models, demographics, and history; the former head of the civil administration in Judea and Samaria; and experts in mathematical modeling. Members of the team, which called itself the American-Israel Demographic Research Group (AIRDG), pored over the Palestinian census data and compared it to the Palestinian population data compiled by the Israeli civil administration in late 1996; to historic data compiled each year by the civil administrations from 1967 through 1996; to Palestinian Ministry of Health data; to data published by the Palestinian Central Elections Commission ahead of the 1996 and 2005 elections; and to immigration records compiled by the Israeli Ports Authority and border control.

The team presented its findings in January 2005 to the leading U.S. demographer Nicholas Eberstadt, from the American Enterprise Institute (AEI). Later that month, after receiving his support for their methodology and findings,[13] they went public with their report at a conference Eberstadt organized for them at AEI.

In a nutshell, the researchers discovered that the 1997 Palestinian census was a fraud. The PCBS had exaggerated the Palestinian population figures by nearly 50 percent, or 1.34 million people. It had accomplished this inflation, Zimmerman found, in two stages.[14]

First, it had inflated the existing Palestinian population base. In the 1997 census, the PCBS had included 325,000 Palestinians who lived abroad. It had also included 210,000 Arab residents in Jerusalem, who had already been accounted for in Israel's population count.[15]

The Palestinian census had included an additional 113,000 persons whose existence was not noted in the 1996 population survey undertaken by the Israeli civil administration. When the data was compared to the voter base published by the Palestinian Central Elections Commission (PCEC) in 1996 and 2005, the PCEC data substantiated the Israeli data. That is, the 113,000 people did not exist.[16]

Taken together, these three moves increased the Palestinian base population by 648,000 people or approximately 27 percent. Imagine if the U.S. Census Bureau had predicted that, in 2012, the United States would have a population base of 400 million, instead of its actual 2012 base size of 314 million.

The second stage of the population inflation involved exaggerating future growth.

First, it predicated the projections for future growth on a population base that—as we have seen—was massively inflated. Every annual growth assessment based on an inflated population model is necessarily false and inflated.

This fundamental problem was compounded by other factors. The PCBS inflated birthrates and massively inflated immigration rates. Moreover, it ignored the high numbers of Palestinians who immigrated to Israel by marrying Israeli citizens.[17] All told, the PCBS census claimed that the compound annual growth rate of the Palestinians in Judea, Samaria, and Gaza was 4.75 percent—the highest population growth rate in the world.[18]

Significantly, just as the Palestinians were claiming to be the fastest-growing population in the world, the Arab world, and the larger Muslim world, were entering a period of unprecedented demographic contraction, even collapse. In an analysis of Muslim-majority countries' population data compiled by the UN Population Division, Nicholas Eberstadt and Apoorvah Shah reported that over the past thirty years, fertility rates in the Muslim world have been dropping at an unprecedented rate. In their words:

> The estimated population-weighted average [growth] *for the Muslim-majority areas as a whole was −41 percent* [from 1975 to 2005] . . . by any historical benchmark, *an exceptionally rapid tempo* of sustained fertility decline. . . . In aggregate, the proportional decline in fertility for Muslim-majority areas was again *greater than for the world as a whole* over that same period (−33 percent) or for the less-developed regions as a whole (−34 percent). Fully 22 Muslim-majority countries and territories were estimated to have undergone *fertility declines of 50 percent or more* during those three decades—ten of them by 60 percent or more.[19]

Not only were the 1997 census data out of line with the wider Arab world, they were contradicted by other Palestinian Authority ministries. For instance, the PCBS's projected birthrates were higher than actual birthrates reported by the Palestinian Ministry of Health. When compounded with the problem of the exaggerated population base size, the PCBS forecasts for births were off by a third.

As the AIDRG found, the PCBS population forecast claimed that between 1997 and 2003, a total of 903,626 babies would be born in Judea, Samaria, and Gaza. In contrast, the Palestinian Ministry of Health recorded just 599,311 births during these years. That is a difference of 304,315.[20]

On the other hand, the inflated population base of the PCBS census also caused it to overstate death rates. The census forecast 98,280 deaths for the period between 1997 and 2003. The Ministry of Health reported only 65,767 deaths. In total then, the PCBS forecast for natural growth (number of births minus number of deaths) was inflated by 238,548 persons—more than 25 percent.[21]

The most serious flaw in the 1997 census projections, however, was not in the natural growth projections. It was in the projections for immigration. The PCBS census forecast that the Palestinian Authority would experience a wave of mass immigration, with 236,000 people immigrating to Judea, Samaria, and Gaza between 1997 and 2003. As it turned out, this forecast had no basis in reality.

Except for the year 1994, when the Palestinian Authority was established, and when Yassir Arfat entered the areas with thousands of PLO members in tow, the Palestinians experienced negative annual net migration numbers. The official emigration numbers tallied by Israeli border authorities was 74,000,[22] but anecdotal evidence indicates that the real number of emigrants reached hundreds of thousands by 2002.[23]

Based on official statistics, the Palestinian immigration figures were inflated by 310,000, when compared against the actual emigration figures.

Finally, the Palestinian census made no mention of the fact that each year thousands of residents of Judea and Samaria received Israeli citizenship by marrying Israeli citizens. This phenomenon became pronounced with the establishment of the Palestinian Authority in 1994.

To get a sense of the dimensions of the trend, from 1997 to 2003, fully 105,000 Palestinian Arabs received Israeli citizenship and were living within sovereign Israel. Those that preceded them from 1994 to 1997 were counted as residents of the Palestinian Authority even though Israel included them in its own population counts, just as the PCBS census counted the Arabs of Jerusalem as part of the Palestinian population, despite the fact that they already were included in Israel's population count. The actual number of Palestinian Arabs who immigrated to Israel during this period may be as high as 300,000.[24]

In all, the 1997 census predicted that between 1997 and 2003, the annual growth rate for Judea and Samaria would be 4.4 percent, and the overall annual growth rate for Gaza would be 5.2 percent. Actual data from those years showed real average annual population growth rates of 1.8 percent in Judea and Samaria and 2.9 percent in Gaza.[25] Those growth rates were in line with actual historic growth rates for the Palestinians of Judea, Samaria, and Gaza: 2.22 percent per year between 1967 and 1993.[26]

Based on official data from both Palestinian and Israeli sources, and working from a corrected data base, the researchers from Zimmerman's American-Israel Demographic Research Group found that, contrary to the PCBS forecast that the Palestinian population of Judea, Samaria, and Gaza would reach 3.8 million in 2004, the actual Palestinian population of the areas in 2004 was 2.47 million—1.4 million in Judea and Samaria and 1.07 million in Gaza, or 1.34 million less than the PCBS forecast.[27] Again, the magnitude of the error would be comparable to the U.S. Census Bureau suddenly increasing the population of the United States by 162 million people.

THE 1.34 MILLION PERSON GAP

Deaths	33K	**PCBS Model:**
PA Ministry of Health Births	238K	3.83 Million Total 2.42 Million West Bank
PCBS Birth Alterations	70K	1.41 Million Gaza
Immigration & Emigration Error	310K	
Migration to Israel	105K	
Inclusion of Jerusalem Arabs	210K	
Residents Living Abroad	325K	
Jump Over ICBS	113K	**Study Results:** 2.49 Million Total 1.41 Million West Bank 1.08 Million Gaza

Y-axis: Milions of People, scale from 2.0 to 4.0

Summary of AIRDG Findings [28]

As far as the Palestinians are concerned, it has all been downhill since then, with emigration rates rising precipitously as birthrates have plummeted in the years since the fraudulent census was issued, but you would never know it from the data their leadership presents. Those data, including another full-blown census conducted in 2007, continue to be based on the fraudulent 1997 census, with its exaggerated forecasts for population growth.[29]

Every year, a senior Palestinian official—generally the director of the PCBS—releases a statement saying that Arabs will outnumber Jews west of the Jordan River by 2010, or by 2015, or by 2020, depending how close to the end year the announcement is made. If nothing else, the utter fraudulence of the PCBS's Palestinian population data is exposed by its constantly changing timeline for the Palestinian demographic takeover of the Land of Israel.[30]

THE FERTILITY HYSTERIA

In an in-depth study of Arab and Jewish population growth trends published in August 2013, demographic researcher, mathematician, and computer engineer Yakov Faitelson assessed that the American-Israel Demographic Research Group, which he joined in 2005, may have overstated the size of the Palestinian population.[31]

Faitelson assessed the Palestinians' population growth and size based on an analysis of historical data compiled by Israel, the PCBS, the United States, the United Nations, and the Norwegian statistical nongovernmental organization FAFO. These data showed that from 1967 to 1990, the Palestinian populations in Judea, Samaria, and Gaza experienced an annual growth rate of 2.22 percent. Considering the decreasing fertility rates and increasing emigration rates from the Palestinian Authority, Faitelson saw no reason to assume that the Palestinian population under PA rule grew faster than historical averages. Moreover, the growth rates determined by the AIDRG from 1997 to 2004 seemed to reflect that historic trend.

At the outset, Faitelson extended the long-term population growth rate of 2.22 percent per year to 2010. This forecast brought him to an assessed 2010 Palestinian population in Judea, Samaria, and Gaza of approximately 2.57 million, or 1.53 million persons fewer than the PCBS claimed.

Starting from this number, Faitelson then considered actual Palestinian fertility rates and trends and compiled information about actual emigration rates from the PA-ruled areas.

According to data collected by the U.S. Census Bureau and the Israel Central Bureau of Statistics (ICBS), fertility rates among Palestinians in Judea, Samaria, and Gaza, as well as among Israeli Arabs, have dropped precipitously in recent years, in line with the general trend throughout the Muslim world. From 2001 to 2011, the total fertility rate of Palestinians in Judea and Samaria has dropped 25.2 percent, from 4.08 children per woman to 3.05 children per woman. In 2012 it dropped to 2.98 children per woman.

In Gaza, between 2001 and 2011, total fertility rates dropped 16.7 percent, from 5.69 children per woman to 4.74. In 2012 it dropped again, to 4.57 children per woman.

Among Israeli Arabs, fertility rates dropped 17.7 percent from 2001 to 2011, from 4.33 children per woman to 3.30. The rate dropped to 3.11 children per woman in 2012.

Compare this with the fertility rate for Israeli Jews, which between 2001 and 2011, climbed 18 percent—from 2.53 to 2.98 children per woman.[32]

The following table is a summary of the fertility data regarding Jews and Arabs west of the Jordan River.

TOTAL JEWISH AND ARAB FERTILITY RATES 2000-2012

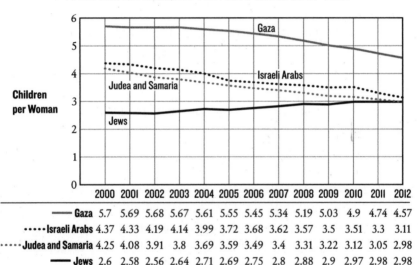

	2000	2001	2002	2003	2004	2005	2006	2007	2008	2009	2010	2011	2012
Gaza	5.7	5.69	5.68	5.67	5.61	5.55	5.45	5.34	5.19	5.03	4.9	4.74	4.57
Israeli Arabs	4.37	4.33	4.19	4.14	3.99	3.72	3.68	3.62	3.57	3.5	3.51	3.3	3.11
Judea and Samaria	4.25	4.08	3.91	3.8	3.69	3.59	3.49	3.4	3.31	3.22	3.12	3.05	2.98
Jews	2.6	2.58	2.56	2.64	2.71	2.69	2.75	2.8	2.88	2.9	2.97	2.98	2.98

A HEMORRHAGE OF EMIGRATION

According to historical data compiled by the ICBS, from 1967 to 1994 an average of 10,000 Palestinians emigrated each year from Judea, Samaria, and Gaza.

In 2004, as previously noted, Israeli border authorities told the

AIDRG that from 1997 to 2004 some 74,000 Palestinians had emigrated. However, the sense on the ground was that the real number was much larger. Fully 57 percent of Palestinian households in Judea, Samaria, and Gaza have a relative residing abroad.[33]

In December 2008, Yakov Faitelson and two other members of the AIDRG met with IDF Lieutenant Colonel Sharon Biton, the operations officer for the civil administration in Judea and Samaria.[34] At their request, Biton provided them with emigration data for Palestinians from Judea, Samaria, and Gaza for the years 1994–2008.

The civil administration data for 1994–2007 indicated that under the Palestinian Authority emigration levels more than doubled. During those years, the average emigration rate from Judea and Samaria alone was 23,000 per year, or 322,000 émigrés in total. Moreover, the numbers increased drastically beginning in 2005. The average (negative) net migration rate from 2005 to 2007 was 41,946 per year, with steep increases registered each year.

And the trend continued through 2008 and into the beginning of 2009. In 2008, a total of 63,386 Palestinians emigrated out of Judea and Samaria. In the first eight months of 2009, about 44,000 Palestinians left the areas.

Emigration rates from Gaza were similarly high and rising until 2005, when Gaza's border with Israel was sealed following Israel's complete withdrawal of all Israeli civilians and military personnel from the area. In 2005 nearly 25,000 Palestinians emigrated from Gaza. After the border with Israel was sealed, the number was reduced to a trickle, with 507 leaving in 2006 and 1,547 leaving in 2007.

In a 2007 interview with the pan-Arab *Asharq al Awsat* newspaper, Palestinian prime minister Salam Fayyad spoke of the hemorrhage of Palestinians exiting the Palestinian Authority. "How will we be able to deal with the problem of 40,000 to 50,000 Palestinians who have emigrated," he said, "and many more that are not emigrating just because they do not have the means? We are losing in this respect."[35]

Indeed, according to a 2006 study carried out by Bir Zeit University in Ramallah, 32 percent of all Palestinians and 44 percent of young Palestinians would emigrate if given the opportunity.[36]

In Gaza the numbers are even higher. After Hamas ousted Fatah from power in June 2007, 35 percent of Gaza youth expressed a desire to emigrate. More than 45,000 applications for visas poured into the foreign consulates operating in the area. Most of the applicants were unskilled laborers. According to news reports, the skilled laborers had already fled,[37] and according to a survey conducted in 2007 by the Ramallah-based Near East Consulting firm, 47 percent of Gazans would emigrate if they had the opportunity.[38] Taken together, this means that more than a million Palestinians in Judea, Samaria, and Gaza wish to emigrate.

Just as Jewish fertility rates are rising in the face of declining Muslim fertility rates, so Jewish immigration to Israel remains robust, even as Arab emigration rates are rising steeply. Following the mass wave of im-migrants from the former Soviet Union during the 1990s, according to ICBS data, Jewish immigration rates have declined, but in recent years they have remained positive. Between 2001 and 2011, a total of 241,673 Jews immigrated to Israel.[39]

Due to a surge of anti-Semitism worldwide,[40] economic recessions in Europe, and economic prosperity in Israel, levels of Jewish immigration to Israel may well rise significantly in the coming decade. Indeed, some anticipate that due almost entirely to Jewish immigration, Jews could comprise an 80 percent majority within the 1949 armistice lines and Judea and Samaria by 2035.[41]

Regardless of whether immigration rates to Israel rise or stay more or less at their current levels, Jews currently comprise 59 percent of the population west of the Jordan River, in sovereign Israel, Judea, Samaria, and the Gaza Strip. Jews make up two-thirds of the population of sov-ereign Israel and Judea and Samaria, and if current trends continue, the proportion of Jews west of the Jordan River will gradually rise, not pre-cipitously drop.

WHY GAZA IS NOT INCLUDED IN THE ISRAELI ONE-STATE PLAN

As we have seen, the Israeli one-state plan does not prescribe that the Gaza Strip be incorporated into sovereign Israel. The question will no doubt be raised, how can Israel incorporate Judea and Samaria but not Gaza?

There are several reasons that Gaza should remain outside sovereign Israel. First and most important, Israel relinquished all claims to Gaza in 2005, when it removed all its civilians and military personnel from the area and retreated back to the 1949 armistice lines. Once Israel quit Gaza, under international law, it had no residual responsibility toward the area or its residents.[42]

Beyond that, since 2007, Gaza has been governed by the Hamas terrorist organization and enjoys a close relationship with the Iranian regime. As the Palestinian branch of the Muslim Brotherhood movement, the Hamas-controlled government enjoyed a fraternal relationship with Egypt's Muslim Brotherhood government during its tenure in office in 2012–13.

Hamas played an active role in toppling Egyptian president Hosni Mubarak's regime during the mass protests that took place in Egypt between January 25 and February 8, 2011, in the service of the Muslim Brotherhood. It also assisted president Muhammad Morsi after he took over the Egyptian government. According to reports by the Muslim Brotherhood's political opponents, in early 2013, when Morsi expanded presidential powers far beyond those that Mubarak enjoyed, and opposition protesters rallied, Hamas deployed several thousand militiamen to Cairo to defend the Muslim Brotherhood regime against them.[43]

In 2012 Hamas sought to combine Gaza's electrical grid with Egypt's and to develop a free-trade zone between the two governments.[44] To this end, Hamas leader Ismail Haniyeh met with Egyptian president Mohamed Morsi in Cairo that August,[45] just days after Hamas gunmen allegedly murdered sixteen Egyptian policemen at a checkpoint on the Egypt-Israel border.[46] Morsi blamed the attack on Israel.[47]

In June 2013, during the mass demonstrations that led to the Egyptian military's seizure of power from the Muslim Brotherhood, the Egyptian army closed the land terminal linking Gaza to the Sinai and flooded the smuggling tunnels that traverse the border. The purpose of these actions was to prevent Hamas members from coming to the aid of the Muslim Brotherhood.[48]

To be sure, following the July 2013 overthrow of the Muslim Brotherhood regime, Hamas's hope to be absorbed within Egypt will not likely be borne out anytime soon. However, its aspiration to integrate with Egypt makes clear that Gaza's Palestinian government values its ties to Egypt—and to the Muslim Brotherhood—more than it values its ties to Israel or to Judea and Samaria.

And, indeed, the yearning for Egypt to come in and take charge of matters in Gaza is not unique to Hamas. In September 2013, Fatah leaders began speaking publicly of their hope that the Egyptian military would oust Hamas from Gaza and restore Fatah to power in the area. Fatah reportedly began collaborating with Egyptian intelligence services to train Palestinian agents who would destabilize Gaza and set the stage for such an Egyptian military action.[49]

While Fatah has not sought to merge Gaza into Egypt as Hamas has, the cultural affinity of its leaders in Gaza with Egypt is much higher than its leadership in Gaza's cultural affinity with Fatah leaders in Judea and Samaria.[50]

With Gaza removed from the demographic equation, the demographic argument in favor of Israel surrendering Judea and Samaria to the PLO becomes even weaker. Indeed, with Gaza removed, the Palestinians of Judea and Samaria have the option of moving to Gaza in the event that they prefer to live under Palestinian sovereignty. The fact is that since Israel removed its military forces and civilians from Gaza and gave up its control over Gaza's border with Egypt, Gaza has been an independent Palestinian state. True, the Palestinians claim that they continue to live under Israeli occupation because Israel controls the seacoast off of Gaza. But given that Gaza is a foreign entity governed by a terrorist organization that routinely engages in acts of war against Israel, under international law, Israel has the right to levy a maritime blockade of Gaza's coast. Moreover, the claim that Gaza remains under Israeli "occupation" lacks foundation in international law. It is made for the sole purpose of maintaining the fiction that Hamas-ruled Gaza and the PLO-ruled areas of Judea and Samaria are one territorial unit, when those living in both areas know that this is simply untrue.

At any rate, the actual population data—together with current population growth trends for Israel and the Palestinians—make clear that there is no Palestinian demographic time bomb. In fact, demography is one of Israel's greatest advantages.

CHAPTER 9

A Record of Success

On December 13, 1981, Israeli prime minister Menachem Begin was resting at home, convalescing from leg surgery. That evening as he was listening to a news update on the radio, he learned that Syrian president Hafez al-Assad had yet again pledged not to recognize Israel, even if the Palestinians did. Assad also said that the Arabs should delay any negotiations with Israel until they became powerful enough to impose their conditions on the peace proceedings.[1]

The news report reinforced a statement made on November 25, 1981, by Syrian foreign minister Abdul Halim Khaddam at a summit of Arab leaders in Fez, Morocco. "We must be willing to wait a hundred years and more until Israel's military prowess wanes," Khaddam declared, "and then we shall act."[2]

Upon hearing Assad's latest declaration, Begin had his chief of staff schedule a special cabinet meeting and a special legislative session for the next day. As Begin's adviser Yehuda Avner recalled in his memoir, Begin met with his cabinet members on the morning of December 14, 1981, and presented them with a draft of what became the Golan Heights Law. He had written it the night before with his attorney general. After receiving the unanimous approval of Begin's cabinet, the draft law was passed with a two-thirds majority vote at the Knesset that afternoon.[3]

The Golan Heights Law ended the Israeli military government and attendant civil administration under which the Golan Heights had been governed since Israel captured the strategic plateau from Syria during the 1967 Six Day War. In their place, Israeli law, jurisdiction, and administration were applied to the area, effectively rendering it sovereign Israeli territory. The Golan's non-Israeli residents, some 12,000 Syrian Druze who resided in four villages in the northern Golan Heights, were given permanent Israeli residency and the right to apply for Israeli citizenship.[4]

Israeli residents of the Golan, both then and now, have attested to close relations with the Druze, a religious and ethnic community whose faith is an offshoot of Shi'ite Islam.[5] Druze live in mountainous regions of Syria, Lebanon, Jordan, and Israel, and by tradition they are loyal to the governments of the countries in which they reside. As early as Israel's War of Independence in 1948, Druze began serving in the IDF. In 1956, in accordance with the wishes of the community's leaders, Israel imposed mandatory conscription on their young men.[6]

In the 1950s the Sunni-led government in Syria waged a violent campaign against the Druze of Syria, replete with the bombardment of Druze villages, but when the Alawites seized control of the country in 1964, the Druze received protection from the new regime. As a consequence, for nearly a half century, between the Alawite rise to power and the intensification of the Syrian civil war in late 2012, the Syrian Druze remained loyal to the regime.[7]

The fact that the Druze were loyal to Hafez al-Assad, and then to his son and successor Bashar al-Assad, did not deter the regime from terrorizing and blackmailing them. After Israel took control of the Golan Heights in 1967, the Druze living there received threats from the regime that their families in Syria would be targeted for revenge if they transferred their loyalties to Israel.

The situation became more complicated following Israel's peace treaty with Egypt. In exchange for concluding that peace, Israel agreed to return the Sinai Peninsula to Egypt. The Druze community leaders on the Golan Heights took the treaty as a sign that, regardless of what Israeli politicians might or might not say, Israel could one day decide to return the Golan Heights to Syria, thus forcing the Druze to return to life under the oppressive Syrian regime.[8]

Because of these concerns, the Golan Druze leadership responded to the passage of the Golan Heights Law by issuing an edict that prohibited community members from accepting Israeli identification cards or applying for citizenship. Any Druze who accepted Israeli documents, it declared, would be excommunicated. Acting on their leadership's instructions, those Druze who had already accepted Israeli IDs publicly burned them. In February 1982 the community began a general strike to register its opposition to the Israeli move. When the strike ended the following July, the Druze leaders agreed that their community members could accept Israeli ID cards and permanent residency but must refuse Israeli citizenship.[9]

In the three decades that have passed since the Druze ended their general strike, they have waged no further organized protests against Israeli rule, although most have continued to abstain from applying for Israeli citizenship.

This situation showed signs of change following the outbreak of the Syrian civil war in March 2011. In October 2012 the Israeli daily *Maariv* reported that Druze villagers in the Golan Heights were applying for Israeli citizenship at rates unlike anything ever seen.[10] As one local Druze told the paper,

> More and more people are recognizing that here [Israel] is a normal country where you can live and raise your children. In Syria there is mass murder, and if we lived under Syrian sovereignty, we would be liable to become victims of the atrocities. People see children being murdered and refugees fleeing to Jordan and Turkey with nothing, and are asking themselves, "Where do I want to raise my children?" The answer is clear, in Israel and not in Syria.[11]

Back in 1981–82, one of the impetuses for the Druze's anti-Israel campaign had been the international community's response to the Golan Heights Law. Three days after the law was passed, the UN Security Council had unanimously passed Resolution 497 condemning the law. Article 1 stated: "the Israeli decision to impose its laws, jurisdiction and administration in the occupied Syrian Golan Heights is null and void and without international legal effect." Article 2 called for Israel to rescind the law.[12]

For its part, the Reagan administration decided to punish Israel for passing the law by suspending implementation of the U.S.-Israel Strategic Cooperation Agreement. Defense Secretary Caspar Weinberger and his Israeli counterpart, Defense Minister Ariel Sharon, had just signed that agreement on November 30, 1981.

While these responses were a source of anxiety in Israel at the time, the condemnations—and the temporary suspension of the Strategic Cooperation Agreement—had no lasting impact on Israel's international position or on the viability of its jurisdiction over the Golan Heights.

On December 28, 1981, Egyptian president Hosni Mubarak told Israel's envoy to Cairo that the move would not affect relations between Egypt and Israel.[13] And a week after the United States announced the suspension of the Strategic Cooperation Agreement, U.S. officials assured Israel that they would veto any UN Security Council resolution calling for sanctions against Israel.[14]

In the absence of any real prospect for peace between Israel and Syria, the Israeli-Syrian border dispute has not been a pressing issue internationally. Additionally, since 1992, nearly every Israeli government has expressed varying degrees of willingness to cede the strategic plateau to Syria in exchange for peace, thus allaying U.S. concerns that the Golan Heights Law ruled out the possibility for peace based on Israeli surrender of territory.[15]

Israel applied its laws and administration to the Golan Heights for two main reasons. First, in light of Syria's refusal to end its state of war with the Jewish state, which has been in effect since 1948, Israel saw no reason to continue to treat the area differently from the rest of the country. Just as Jordanian law formed the basis for Israel's military government in Judea and Samaria, so Syrian law formed the basis of Israel's military government in the Golan Heights. But Syrian law was inadequate for dealing with civil and criminal disputes that arose in the Golan.[16]

Second and more important, without the Golan Heights, northern Israel is indefensible. Until Israel took control of the area, Syrian forces on the southern end of the plateau routinely fired on the Israeli communities situated just three to five miles below. Children in Galilee were known as the "children of shelters," since they spent much of their childhood racing for bomb shelters to hide from Syrian rockets and sniper fire.[17]

As Efraim Inbar explains, the Golan Heights controls the Galilee, the bay of Haifa, and the Jordan Valley. Without the Golan Heights, all of northern Israel would be at grave risk, particularly from Syria's sophisticated arsenal of ballistic missiles and chemical weapons.[18] Consequently, control of the Golan Heights is a strategic imperative for Israel.

Begin and his advisers went to great lengths to emphasize that the Golan Heights Law was an administrative move. And this was true. Begin never referred to the act as annexation. In his speech before the

UN Security Council, Israeli ambassador Yehuda Blum said, "The authorities on the Golan Heights, military and civilians, are Israelis. They certainly cannot wait a hundred years and more, as the Syrian Foreign Minister would wish, in order to register births, marriages and deaths."[19]

Begin's decision to minimize the political significance of the Golan Heights Law may well have been informed by his experience the year before, in passing the law that reunited Jerusalem under the Israeli government.

As we saw in Chapter 7, in the ministerial discussions following the 1967 Six Day War, the consensus view was that Israel should assert and retain full sovereignty over all parts of Jerusalem in perpetuity.[20] In line with this consensus, and in accordance with Israel's right to sovereignty over all Jerusalem by force of the 1922 League of Nations Mandate (which we shall discuss at length in Chapter 12), on June 28, 1967, the Knesset amended a standing law of administrative procedure, adding a clause that extended Jerusalem's municipal boundaries to include within Israel's capital city the areas of eastern, northern, and southern Jerusalem that had been liberated from Jordanian occupation during the war.[21]

Arab residents of the neighborhoods inside Jerusalem's new boundaries were given permanent residency status and were permitted to apply for Israeli citizenship. Unlike the Druze in the Golan Heights, the distribution of Israeli ID cards to the Arabs of Jerusalem was peaceful, uneventful, and oversubscribed. [22]

The international community's condemnation of Israel's move was harsh, but only in a nominal sense. Following the Knesset's actions, on July 4, 1967, the UN General Assembly passed Resolution 2253, which called on Israel to "rescind all measures already taken and to desist forthwith from taking any action which would alter the status of Jerusalem." Ten days later the General Assembly passed Resolution 2254, which reiterated 2253's call verbatim.[23] The following year the UN Security Council passed Resolution 252, which simply repeated what the General Assembly's resolution had said.

But none of the resolutions called for UN members to take any punitive action against Israel for applying its sovereignty to eastern, southern, and northern Jerusalem.

As for the United States, it was in the aftermath of the Six Day War that it began its strategic alliance with Israel. In January 1968 President

Johnson invited Israeli prime minister Levi Eshkol to visit him at his ranch in Texas. There, according to Yehuda Avner's first-person account, Secretary of State Dean Rusk said to Eshkol, "What we would like to hear from you today is, what kind of an Israel do you want the Arabs to live with? What kind of an Israel do you want the American people to support?"

Eshkol responded, "All I can say to you now is that our victory in the Six Day War blocked the Soviet Union from taking over the Middle East, and that, surely, is an American interest. As for the kind of Israel the Arabs can live with and which the American people can support, the only answer I can presently give you is an Israel whose map will be different from the one of the eve of the Six Day War."[24]

Eshkol had traveled to the United States to try to persuade Johnson to supply Israel with fifty F-4 Phantom aircraft. Until then, the United States had sold no aircraft to Israel, but at the end of their tense, three hour meeting, Johnson agreed to supply the fighter jets. Historians view this agreement as the beginning of the U.S.-Israel strategic alliance.[25]

Before the Six Day War, thirteen countries had located their embassies in Israel's capital city; the rest, including the U.S. embassy, were in Tel Aviv. Those thirteen countries maintained their diplomatic missions in Jerusalem after Israel unified the city under Israeli sovereignty following the war.

As for the Arabs, Egyptian president Gamal Abdel Nasser opened hostilities against Israel in the south almost immediately after the Six Day War ended. But Nasser's action was motivated by his continued desire to destroy Israel, not by anger over Israel's unification of Jerusalem.

In short, then, neither the Arabs of Jerusalem, nor the Arab world, nor the nations of the world took any concrete steps to punish Israel for applying its sovereignty over the Jerusalem neighborhoods taken from Jordan in the Six Day War.

This situation changed in 1980. In that year Begin decided that it was time to state outright that united Jerusalem was Israel's capital.[26] On July 30 the Knesset passed Basic Law—Jerusalem, Capital of Israel. The law declared "Jerusalem, complete and united, is the capital of Israel." But it changed nothing related to the legal status of the city—the situation remained as it had been since June 28, 1967.[27]

The same cannot be said, however, of the international status of the city. On August 20, 1980, the UN Security Council passed Resolution 478. Like Resolution 497, which followed Israel's application of its law and administration to the Golan Heights, Resolution 478 declared the Knesset law "null and void" and demanded that Israel "rescind" it. But unlike Resolution 497, Resolution 478 also enjoined the UN member states to take action against Israel following the passage of the law. Specifically, Resolution 478 called on "those states that have established diplomatic missions at Jerusalem to withdraw such missions from the Holy City."[28]

Within weeks, eleven of the thirteen governments with embassies in Jerusalem relocated their embassies.[29] Since 2006 no foreign government has located its embassy in Jerusalem.[30] Governments like the United States that maintain consulates in Jerusalem do not accredit their missions with the government of Israel. Their primary purpose is to maintain diplomatic relations with the Palestinians.[31]

The irony of the international community's rejection of Israeli sovereignty is that only under Israeli control have the rights of all religious groups in the Holy City been fully protected. Under Jordanian occupation, Jews both from Israel and from around the world were barred from entering the Old City, and Jewish holy sites and synagogues were desecrated and destroyed. Arab Israelis—both Muslim and Christian—were barred from entering the city. Non-Israeli Christian worship was also circumscribed.[32]

For its part, as we shall see, the PLO, whose claims to the city are preferred to Israel's by the U.S. government and by the international community as a whole, destroys Jewish holy sites, denies Jews entry into holy sites, persecutes Christians, and in 2002 took control of and desecrated the Church of the Nativity in Bethlehem.

Meanwhile since 1994 Jerusalem's Arabs have vastly expanded their attachment to Israel. Several thousand have applied for citizenship, and the trend toward full integration in Israeli society increases with each passing year.[33]

There are three major lessons to take away from Israel's three precedents in applying its sovereignty to areas beyond the 1949 armistice lines. First, the non-Jewish populations in the areas (Druze in the Golan, and Arabs in Jerusalem) prefer living under Israeli sovereignty to living under Syrian or Palestinian control.

Second, the international community is more apt to accept such an Israeli move when it is not accompanied by major declarations that foreign states may take as a challenge.

Third and perhaps most important, Israel's adoption of the "Israeli one-state plan" in Jerusalem in 1967 and in 1980, and in the Golan Heights in 1981, did not destabilize the region. Applying Israeli law to these areas did not increase the level of hostilities between Israel and its neighbors. It did not harm the national security interests of Israel's allies generally or of the United States in particular. To the contrary, by facilitating Israel's continued control, the application of Israeli laws and administration to Jerusalem and the Golan Heights contributed to the security of the country and the stability of the region.

CHAPTER 10

Welcome to Palestine

In April 2006 the body of Muhammad Abu al-Hawa, a forty-year-old father of eight from Jerusalem, was found in a burned-out car in Jericho.

Members of the Palestinian Authority's ruling Fatah party claimed responsibility for his murder. Al-Hawa, they explained, had been tortured and shot seven times in the head and chest for the crime of selling two apartment buildings in eastern Jerusalem to Jews.[1]

The Palestinian Authority was officially established in May 1994, when the PLO took over the Gaza Strip and the city of Jericho. The first official act that Yassir Arafat announced was the cancellation of all Israeli military orders that had been promulgated since June 1967.[2] This act constituted a material breach of the May 4, 1994, Gaza-Jericho Agreement, which Arafat had just signed with Israel. The Gaza-Jericho Agreement, which set the conditions for the establishment of the Palestinian Authority, called for legal continuity with the old regime.[3]

THE PALESTINIAN LEGAL JUNGLE

When the Palestinian Authority was established, the basic legislation governing the areas was Jordanian law. That law had been amended over the years by Israel to expand civil and individual rights of Palestinians, and to enable the areas to develop in line with prevailing conditions. Issues like road safety and public sanitation, as well as mandatory education laws that had gone unmentioned in the Jordanian legal code, had to be addressed. The understanding reached by Israel and the PLO required the Palestinian Authority to take the legal situation on the ground—that is, the mix of the Jordanian legal code and Israeli military orders—and amend it to make life better for the people living under the PA regime.

Aside from being a material breach of his agreement with Israel, Arafat's cancellation of all Israeli military orders promulgated over twenty-seven years threw the areas under PA control into legal chaos. This legal jungle facilitated Arafat's transformation of those areas into a corrupt, authoritarian kleptocracy.

In 1997, acting on Arafat's orders, PA justice minister Freih Abu Meddein reinstated the 1973 Jordanian law that made it a capital offense to sell land to Jews.[4] Later that year Palestinian lawmakers went even further, deeming land sales to Jews an act of treason punishable by death. The law applied to all areas of "Palestine" as defined by the League of Nations Mandate for Palestine. That is, it applied to sovereign Israeli territory as well as areas ruled by the Palestinian Authority.[5]

Shortly after the law was passed, the Palestinian Authority's supreme religious authority, Sheikh Ikremah Sabri, published a fatwa, an Islamic legal ruling, that transformed the PA's law into a religious writ. He decreed that any Muslim found selling land to non-Muslims would be denied burial in a Muslim cemetery.[6]

In accordance with Sabri's fatwa, Muhammad Abu Al-Hawa was buried in a makeshift grave on the side of the Jerusalem-Jericho highway.

Abu al-Hawa was just one of scores of Palestinians and Israeli Arabs who have been murdered for the "crime" of selling land to Jews since the Palestinian Authority was established. These killings usually are carried out extrajudicially and are perpetrated mainly by Fatah terror gangs but also by official PA security forces.[7]

The Palestinian Authority's determination that selling land to Jews is a capital offense, like the Jordanian law that preceded it, is a breach of international humanitarian law. Article 17 of the Universal Declaration of Human Rights stipulates, "Everyone has the right to own property." And Part III, Article 6 of the International Covenant on Civil and Political Rights states that "[in] countries which have not abolished the death penalty, sentences of death may be imposed only for the most serious of crimes. This penalty can only be carried out pursuant to a final judgment rendered by a competent court."[8]

Based on the laws promulgated by the Palestinian Authority and the

Jordanians before them, Palestinian leaders from Arafat to Mahmoud Abbas, to the last of their advisers and assistants, insist that Jews have no right to own or control land in Judea and Samaria. And their legal persecution of Jews and rejection of Jewish rights doesn't end with land sales. They insist that before they will accept sovereignty over Judea, Samaria, and the parts of Jerusalem that the Palestinian Authority demands, Israel must cleanse those areas of the Jews living there. In other words, racial purity is the sine qua non for Palestinian nationalism.[9]

FIRST THE JEWS, THEN THE CHRISTIANS

The Palestinian Authority's draconian land sale law is not directed against Jews alone. In his religious ruling that gave Islamic standing to the law, Sabri prohibited land sales to "infidels," a class that includes Christians as well as Jews.[10] Like Jews, Christians living under the Palestinian Authority are denied the right to buy property from their Muslim neighbors. Christians are also largely barred from selling their property to other Christians.[11]

Since the Palestinian Authority was established, there have been hundreds of cases in which Muslims have seized Christian homes and lands illegally. The official Palestinian security services, which are overwhelmingly Muslim, have done little to protect the property rights of Christians living under their jurisdiction.[12]

On Christmas Eve 2012, in keeping with a practice introduced by Arafat, Mahmoud Abbas traveled to Jesus's birthplace, Bethlehem, to participate in a Christian ceremony there. In the presence of the international media, Abbas extolled the local Christians as citizens of Palestine who enjoy the same rights as Palestinian Muslims and who suffer alongside their Muslim neighbors at the hands of the Israeli "occupation."[13]

But the truth is that under the rule of both Fatah and Hamas, Palestinian Christians are systematically oppressed and discriminated against.

Gaza's Christian community predates Islam by several hundred years. But the rise of Hamas in Gaza has made the lives of Christians there particularly unbearable. In 2007 the owner of the only Christian bookstore in Gaza was murdered.[14] Christians have reportedly been abducted and forced to convert to Islam under penalty of death.[15] At the end of the

Christmas holiday in 2012, dozens of the Gaza Christians who had traveled to Bethlehem asked Israel to grant them asylum.[16]

The Christians of Gaza are not alone in their suffering. In recent years, hundreds of Christian Arabs in Jerusalem have moved from Arab neighborhoods to Jewish ones because they feared persecution at the hands of their Muslim neighbors.

Since the establishment of the Palestinian Authority in 1994, thousands of Christians from Judea and Samaria have emigrated to other countries. Christians made up 85 percent of Bethlehem's population when the Jordanians took over in 1949[17], and 60 percent in 1990,[18] but by 2009 they made up a mere 12 percent.[19] Immediately after the Palestinian Authority took control of the city in 1996, Arafat seized the Greek Orthodox Monastery next to the Church of the Nativity and claimed it as his official residence.[20]

The Palestinian Authority refuses to publish statistics on Christian emigration, but it is known that between November 2000 and October 2001, a total of 2,766 Christians emigrated from Judea and Samaria.[21]

During that period, the Palestinian Authority took over private homes in Beit Jala, a Christian suburb of Bethlehem, and used them to fire at the neighboring Jewish neighborhoods of Gilo and Malcha in southern Jerusalem. The mass emigration of Christians from Bethlehem has created a situation where, in many cases, the Muslims who tormented the Christians into leaving now own their old homes and their shops along Manger Square.[22]

In May 2001 Fatah terrorists aided by the Palestinian Authority took over the Church of the Nativity in Bethlehem, holding the priests and nuns on the premises hostage for forty days. They desecrated and looted the sacred shrine, stealing icons, confiscating sacred gold and silver vessels, urinating against the walls, and defecating on prayer books.[23]

The PLO's persecution of Christians was nothing new. The chief victim of the PLO-instigated Lebanese civil war in the 1970s was Lebanon's Christian community. The epicenter of PLO mistreatment of Lebanese Christians was the Christian town of Damour, located along the Beirut-Sidon highway just north of the capital.

On January 20, 1976, PLO forces entered Damour and murdered 582 men, women, and children. Torture and abuse of the victims' corpses was widespread. Survivors were forced to flee the town of 25,000 people. Palestinians seized their homes.[24] Only after Israel's 1982 invasion of Lebanon, in which Israeli forces expelled PLO forces from the country, were Damour's Christian residents able to return to their homes.

Today Israel is the only state in the Middle East where Christians live without fear of persecution. While all known evidence indicates that, since 1994, masses of Christians have fled the Palestinian-ruled areas under Fatah and Hamas, the Christian community in Israel has grown steadily.[25]

THE PALESTINIAN AUTHORITY'S OVERARCHING TYRANNY

It may well be an iron law of political science that an authoritarian regime that treats minorities poorly doesn't treat the majority population well either. The absence of democratic norms in Palestinian society enables bigotry and prejudice to dictate the society's laws and practices, from the highest reaches of government all the way down to life on the street.

In 1994, when the PLO established the Palestinian Authority, Arafat and his men were not unique among Palestinians in their rejection of democratic governance. Survey data from the 1980s and 1990s indicated scant support for democracy and democratic norms in Palestinian society as a whole.[26]

In 1986, according to data compiled by Mehran Kamrava, only 20 percent of Palestinians supported democracy. In 1992 only 30 percent did. Writing in 1999, Kamrava expressed doubt that the Palestinians would likely increase their support for democratic norms of governance under the PLO-run Palestinian Authority. In his words, "Three social impediments prevent the emergence and consolidation of democratic values among Palestinians: the steady demise of civil society organizations since the institutionalization of the PA; the predominance of values inimical to democracy; and the activism of Islamist organizations."[27]

Kamrava's concerns are confirmed by recent history. The entrance of Arafat and his PLO colleagues to the areas did nothing to encourage the development of democratic habits among the people. To the contrary, the democratic institutions and habits that had been formed during the years of Israeli military rule were ruthlessly and summarily repressed.

During the 1980s, partly in opposition to Israeli rule and partially in conjunction with it, the number of civil society organizations in Judea and Samaria and Gaza skyrocketed. According to Kamrava, by 1995 there were 1,500 nongovernmental organizations operating in Judea and Samaria, and 700 in Gaza. They ranged from trade unions and student groups to medical and education organizations, to organizations that advocated for women's rights.

By the time the Palestinian Authority was established, NGOs handled "30 percent of all educational services for Palestinians, 50 percent of hospital care, nearly 60 percent of primary health care services, almost 100 percent of agricultural research and training programs, and 100 percent of disability care."[28]

The PLO viewed these NGOs as sources of independent political power that could challenge the new regime. So as soon as the Palestinian Authority was established, it began working to shut down the NGO sector. Arafat's associates dried up their funding by asking that all donor nations funnel their support for Palestinian NGOs through the Palestinian Authority. The impact of this policy was immediate and dramatic.

"Within one year," Kamrava reported, "sixty-six rural clinics located in remote areas of the West Bank closed down. Gaza was hit even harder. The Society for the Care of the Handicapped, once active throughout the Strip, was forced to dismiss 180 employees and cut services to 2,500 children after it lost $1.5 million of its donations to the PA. The Culture and Free Thought Association of Khan Yunis, also in Gaza, had to terminate thirty-nine positions after losing 60 percent of its budget."[29]

Like the NGO sector, the Palestinian media was another independent entity that the Palestinian Authority sought to crush upon entering Judea, Samaria, and Gaza. Before then the Palestinian media had been the freest in the Arab world. Although, like the Israeli media, the Palestinian media under Israeli military rule were subject to Israel's military censor, the censor rarely interfered in the operation of Palestinian media outlets, except when forced to remove anti-Semitic incitement.[30]

The situation changed drastically as soon as the Palestinian Authority was established. One of the first things Yassir Arafat did after taking over the areas was place all Palestinian media organizations under the direct control of the Palestinian Authority's Information Ministry, thus ending freedom of the press.[31]

Shortly after he arrived in Gaza, Arafat ordered the closure of the non-PLO *Al-Nahar* newspaper. He accused the newspaper of serving as a mouthpiece for King Hussein of Jordan.[32] Columnist Douad Kuttab organized a number of Palestinian journalists to sign a petition that protested Arafat's move, whereupon Arafat forced Kuttab's employer to fire him for his actions. After forty days of forced closure, *Al-Nahar*'s editor and publisher agreed to accept PA control of the paper's content, and Arafat allowed the paper to reopen.[33]

In early 1995 a number of Palestinian media outlets reported on the size of an anti-PA protest. All the editors of the publications were summoned to the PA Ministry of Information, which was headed by Arafat's loyal servant Yasser Abed Rabbo. The editors were ordered to publish only reports and statistics provided to them by Wafa, the Palestinian Authority's official news agency. When the *al-Ummah* opposition paper failed to comply, its press plates were confiscated, and its offices—although located in Jerusalem and therefore legally outside PA authority—were burned down.[34]

The Palestinian Broadcasting Corporation, which runs Palestinian radio and television and the Wafa news agency, are PA-controlled and serve as a mouthpiece for Fatah.[35] Most formerly independent newspapers are now owned by the Palestinian Authority. Between 1994 and 2004, thirty-eight Palestinian journalists were forced to leave their profession. Many were arrested by Palestinian security forces.[36]

Arafat's death in 2004 and his replacement by his longtime deputy Mahmoud Abbas did not lead to any liberalization of the repressive PA policy toward the media. To the contrary, the Palestinian Authority's control of the media has expanded to cover the Internet as well.

In the past decade, hundreds of bloggers have been imprisoned and beaten after writing about Palestinian corruption. For instance, in April 2012 Palestinian blogger Jamal Abu Rihan was arrested and held for thirty-six days after starting a Facebook page called "The People Want to End Corruption." In the same month, the Palestinian Authority ordered Internet service providers to block public access to Web sites critical of Abbas.[37]

According to a 2011 report by Human Rights Watch (HRW), PA security services in Judea and Samaria have arrested "scores of journalists" since 2009.[38] The group claimed that in several cases, the journalists were abused "during interrogation in a manner that amounted to torture."

HRW concluded the report by accusing the Palestinian Authority of abusing journalists in order to repress criticism of the regime: "HRW cannot point to instructions from PA leaders to the security services that they commit these violations, but the utter failure of the PA leadership to address the prevailing culture of impunity for such abuses suggests they reflect government policy."

Even as the Palestinian Authority implemented the repression of freedom of expression and independent social and political action, it established a Byzantine police state, through which it controls more than a dozen competing security forces. Until his death in 2004, all Palestinian security services were under Arafat's direct control. The security forces operate outside the control of any clear legal guidelines and are not subject to judicial oversight, due in large part to Palestinian courts' complete subservience to the PA leadership.[39]

Since Arafat's death, the various militias—which also boast their own detention centers—have been controlled by Abbas, except for the forces in Gaza, which since 2007 have been under Hamas's control. Under international pressure, the number of these militias has been reduced to six—but their force size has not been reduced. Estimates place that force size at 60,000 to 70,000 troops, or more than a third of the Palestinian Authority's 180,000-member workforce.[40]

Since Hamas seized power in Gaza in 2007, the Palestinian Authority has continued to pay the salaries of 30,000 security force members there.[41] In 2011, as we saw in Chapter 5, the Palestinian Authority allocated 31 percent of its budget to its security forces.[42]

The regime is also able to assert complete control of Palestinian society because of its control of the Palestinian economy. Shortly after it was formed, the Palestinian Authority became the largest employer in the areas by far.[43] Arafat developed a system of economic monopolies that his underlings controlled and that destroyed competition.[44] They forced independent banks out of business or compelled them to transfer their assets to the Palestinian Authority.[45] Arafat's cronies compelled businessmen to pay them protection money;[46] those who refused were subjected to arrest and torture.[47] And many Palestinian businessmen were—and continue to be—put out of business after being falsely accused of collaborating with Israel.[48]

The Massacre of "Collaborators"

The Palestinian Authority's persecution of those it accuses of collaborating with Israel is a deeply disturbing phenomenon in and of itself. During the years when Israel administered Judea, Samaria, and Gaza, some Palestinians had cooperated with Israeli authorities; concerned for their welfare, Israel insisted in 1994 that the PLO commit to protecting them as a condition for the establishment of the Palestinian Authority. Hence Article XVI, Paragraph 2 of the Interim Agreement from September 1995 (which defines the scope of PA powers in Judea, Samaria, and Gaza) states: "Palestinians who have maintained contact with the Israeli authorities will not be subjected to acts of harassment, violence, retribution or prosecution. Appropriate ongoing measures will be taken, in coordination with Israel, in order to ensure their protection."[49]

But as soon as the Palestinian Authority was established, its security forces began seeking out and murdering all Palestinians suspected of having cooperated with Israeli security forces since 1967. Even those who held Israeli citizenship were subject to assault and murder.[50] For instance, M. (whose full name has been redacted), who had cooperated with Israel's counterterror operations in the 1980s, was forced to flee to Israel when an informer exposed his role. During the Palestinian uprising against Israel from 1988 to 1991, Palestinians killed about a thousand Palestinians whom they accused of collaborating with Israel.[51]

M. was granted permanent residency in Israel. In March 2001 his sister contacted him and told him that his mother was in poor health and had asked to see him. As he entered his family's yard, eight members of the Palestinian security services approached him with drawn pistols and abducted him.

M. was interrogated and tortured for forty-six days. As Gershom Gorenberg reported in the *New York Times Magazine*, "They beat him. . . . They hung him for hours by his hands from the sprinkler pipes on the ceiling, took him down to give him 10 minutes to eat and hung him up again. [Although his career as an informer had ended years before,] they insisted he was still working . . . [for Israel] and had converted to Judaism."[52]

In 2002 Israel retook control of Palestinian towns and villages in Judea and Samaria during Operation Defensive Shield; troops found M. packed into a cell with thirty-three other inmates.[53]

The Palestinian Authority's Destruction of the Palestinian Economy

The Palestinian Authority's endemic corruption has led to wide-scale impoverishment in areas that, under Israeli military control, had sustained impressive levels of economic growth.[54] Between 1993 and 2006, Palestinian GDP plummeted by 68 percent in Judea and Samaria. Most of the decrease occurred before the start of the Palestinian terror war in September 2000 and was caused largely by the endemic corruption of the Palestinian Authority.[55]

Foreign donor governments, who pay for more than a third of the Palestinian Authority's operating budget,[56] have repeatedly requested that the Palestinian Authority take serious steps to remedy the situation, but it has not done so.[57] As the continued repression of freedom of the press since Arafat's death makes clear, the Palestinian Authority doesn't investigate allegations of corruption and authoritarianism to redress them—rather, it hides them by silencing its critics.

In 1997 Reyad Agha, a former president of the Islamic University of Gaza, described life under the Palestinian Authority to a *New York Times* reporter. "We don't have any kind of rules," he said, "in the government, in the ministries, in any of the institutions of our society. And when there are rules, Arafat can overrule them, and no one rejects his orders. We are living in a miserable situation, with a corrupt regime and a one-man show."[58]

At this writing in 2013, under Arafat's successor Mahmoud Abbas—whose four-year term of office legally expired in January 2009—little has changed. Speaking of the authoritarian practices of Abbas and his associates, Palestinian journalist Tariq Khamis told *Al Jazeera*, "The [PA] regime is very similar to other Arab regimes. If the PA had trust in themselves, they would let journalists get on with their work. But because of their mistakes and corruption, they fear the work of journalists."[59]

As we just saw, before the Palestinian Authority was established in

1994, most Palestinians had scant interest in democracy; but significantly, their suffering under the authoritarian PA kleptocracy has stoked their interest in representative forms of governance.

Their perception of Israeli democracy has also improved. In 2012 a joint poll asked Israelis and Palestinians how they would view an Israeli plan to unilaterally withdraw from Judea and Samaria, in a bid to advance the two-state solution. Forty-four percent of the Israelis supported the plan; 46 percent opposed it. Among the Palestinians, 35 percent supported the plan, while 59 percent opposed it. That is, the Palestinians were much more opposed to an Israeli withdrawal from Judea and Samaria than were the Israelis.[60]

This phenomenon is perhaps explained by survey data regarding Palestinians' assessment of the state of political freedom under PA rule, compared with the territories governed by Israel. In 2002 only 16 percent of Palestinians felt positively about the status of Palestinian democracy, and in 2010 only 27 percent of Palestinians in Judea and Samaria believed that a person could criticize the Palestinian Authority without fear. In sharp contrast, since the Palestinian Authority was established in 1994, Palestinian admiration for Israeli democracy and respect for human rights has remained high: between two-thirds and three-quarters of Palestinians express their appreciation for Israeli democracy and the status of civil rights in the Jewish state.[61]

Whereas, according to Kamrava, only 30 percent of Palestinians supported democratic rule in 1992, by 1995, under the Palestinian Authority, 79.6 percent of Palestinians said they believed in democracy.[62] Moreover, in 1996, while only 42.9 percent of Palestinians said they believed that the status of democracy and human rights was positive under the Palestinian Authority, 78 percent believed that the status of democracy and human rights was positive in Israel.

Year in and year out, Palestinians have ranked the status of democracy and human rights in Israel as being not only well above that in the Palestinian Authority but above that of the United States and every other country they were surveyed about.[63]

It is impossible to extrapolate from these data that Palestinians would prefer to live under Israeli law. But clearly the Palestinians think that Israel is an open society where human rights are respected, and that Palestinians would like to live in such a society.

CHAPTER 11

Welcome to Israel

In 2010, Corporal Eleanor Joseph became the first female Arab combat soldier in the Israel Defense Force.[1] Joseph, a Christian Arab, told Israel's daily *Maariv* that she carries around a drawing of the Star of David, with words from an Israeli pop song inscribed in it: "I have no other land, even when my ground is burning." The drawing, which she keeps as her good luck charm, was made for her by her commander.

"It is a phrase that strengthens me," Joseph explained. "Every time I experience hardship, I read it. Because I was born here. The people I love live here: my parents, my friends. This is a Jewish state? Yes, it is. But it's also my country. . . . What does it matter that I'm an Arab?"

Joseph is not alone in her Israeli patriotism and her desire to defend her country. Milad and Muhammad Atrash, two Israeli Arab Muslim brothers from the Galilee, volunteered to serve in the IDF's prestigious Golani Infantry Brigade.

Speaking to the IDF soldiers' newspaper *Bamahane*, Milad, the older brother, explained, "While still in high school, I asked my family, 'Why don't we Muslims enlist? Why do the Jews, the Druze, and the Bedouins enlist, while we don't?'"

His family explained to him, "Jews serve because it's their country . . . the Druze [have] signed agreements with the IDF and . . . we have a lot of Islamic movements that oppose military service in the IDF."

Milad responded, "I don't care about that. I want to join the army to protect my village, my country."

His brother Muhammad said he thought everyone should serve the country in whatever capacity they are assigned. "It doesn't matter where they serve—contribution is the most important thing. For me, it doesn't matter if I serve in Judea and Samaria, or on the Gaza border, and will have to confront Muslims from the other side of the fence. We are guarding our country, we have to protect it, and it doesn't matter who's on the other side—Arabs or not, Muslims or not. In the end, everyone protects his or her family."[2]

These young men and women—Christian and Muslim Arabs who embrace their Israeli identity—are signs of a small but growing trend among Israeli Arabs toward full integration into Israeli society. Other signs are the growing number of Arab families whose children study in Hebrew-language schools, and a rising interest in military and national service.[3]

Since 1949 Israel's Arab citizens have enjoyed the full rights and privileges of citizenship, contingent on security concerns. As citizens of Israel, they have the highest literacy rates and life expectancies in the Arab world. Indeed, the life expectancy of Israeli Arab men is even higher than that of their American counterparts.[4]

Israeli Arabs are represented at the highest levels of Israeli society. An Arab serves as a justice on Israel's Supreme Court. Arabs serve as senior diplomats in Israel's diplomatic corps. They are business leaders, popular culture icons, members of the Knesset, government ministers, and heads of regional councils that include both Jewish and Arab towns and villages. They serve as university professors, senior physicians, and police commanders.[5]

Israel is not a melting pot. It is a multicultural society. Arabic is an official state language along with Hebrew. Muslim and Christian holidays are recognized as national holidays by members of each religion, and Arab schoolchildren are taught in Arabic-language schools.

Although Israeli law mandates military conscription, Israel has not instituted compulsory military service for all its Arab citizens. Male members of the Druze and Circassian communities are subject to mandatory conscription, in accordance to the wishes of their communities. Male Bedouins also serve in significant numbers in the IDF.[6]

Although the number of Arab Christians and Muslims serving in the IDF remains small, it is rising. The number of Christian conscripts increased threefold between 2010 and 2012.[7] In October 2012 three hundred people, mainly high school students, participated in a conference on Christian Arab military service that took place in Upper Nazareth.[8]

The pro-integration sentiment expressed so strongly by these increases in military service is rising quickly. In a 2007 survey, Israeli Arabs between the ages of sixteen and twenty-two were asked whether they supported voluntary national service, which is an alternative to military service that generally involves a year or two of volunteer work in a hospital, school, or charitable organization. Many young, religiously observant Jewish women opt for national service instead of serving in the military. In the 2007 survey, 75 percent of the young Israeli Arabs supported voluntary national service (71.9 percent of men and 89 percent of women).[9]

Arafat's Incitement of Israeli Arabs

Until recently the integrationist bent of Israeli Arabs has been overlooked or belittled. It is counterintuitive and countercultural because since the 1970s—and at an escalating tempo since the establishment of the Palestinian Authority in 1994—the Israeli Arab community has undergone a process of radicalization and Islamization. This process has been engineered, funded, and directed by the PLO and the Palestinian Authority.

The very day the Palestinian Authority was established, Yassir Arafat began a program to incite Israeli Arabs to seek their state's destruction. In his first speech from Gaza, given on the day of his arrival in July 1994, he invoked the invidious *Protocols of the Elders of Zion* and pledged to "liberate" Israeli Arabs "from the Negev to the Galilee."[10]

His efforts brought stunning results. According to Efraim Karsh, "If in the mid-1970s, one in two Israeli Arabs repudiated Israel's right to exist, by 1999, four out of five were doing so."[11] By 2000 all of the Israeli Arab members of Knesset opposed Israel's right to exist. They rejected their Israeli identity and insisted upon being referred to as Palestinians. They directly incited the Israeli Arab community to take part in violent riots and other acts of terror and sabotage against Israel and Israeli Jews.[12] They broke Israeli laws and visited enemy states where they met with radical Arab leaders including the Libyan dictator Muammar Gaddafi, Syrian president Bashar Assad, and Lebanese leaders allied with Hezbollah.[13]

In 2007 Azmi Bishara, an Israeli Arab member of Knesset and the head of the irredentist Balad party, discovered that he was about to be indicted for treason for serving as a Hezbollah spy during the 2006 war between Israel and the Iranian-controlled Lebanese terror group. He fled Israel.[14]

This trend of galloping irredentism among the elected representatives of the Israeli Arab community, as well as the rise in influence of the Hamas- and Muslim Brotherhood–aligned Israeli Islamic Movement,[15] makes the integrationist trend that is now rising in the Arab communities of Israel remarkable. But Israel's Arab leaders have waged a campaign to discredit, excommunicate, and otherwise harm Israeli Arab citizens who support integrating into Israeli society and embracing their Israeli identity.

As a consequence of this concerted campaign, leaders of the Christian Arab community who participated in the pro-military service conference in October 2012 were barred from praying at the Church of the Annunciation in Nazareth. Their tires were slashed, and bloodstained rags were placed at their front doors. High school students who participated faced abuse and humiliation at the hands of their schoolmates and teachers, as their pictures were published in the Israeli Arab media and on Facebook.[16]

CAUSES OF THE INTEGRATIONIST IMPULSE

Despite this abuse, the integrationist countercurrent reverberates increasingly powerfully throughout Israeli Arab society.

As we saw in Chapter 9, in the aftermath of the 1967 Six Day War, when Israel unified Jerusalem, it granted permanent residency status to the city's new Arab residents and offered them the right to apply for citizenship. Permanent residency status provides its holders with rights and privileges identical to those enjoyed by Israeli citizens, the only difference being that, unlike citizens, permanent residents do not have the right to vote in Knesset elections.

Between 1967 and 1994, only a smattering of Arab Jerusalemites took up Israel's offer and applied for citizenship, deterred by the social stigma attached to such a move. Arab Jerusalemites who applied for Israeli citizenship were castigated by their community as traitors to the Arab nation, and the PLO openly threatened anyone who obtained it.[17]

But after Israel empowered the PLO to establish the Palestinian Authority, many of Jerusalem's Arabs feared being transferred to PLO control more than they feared enduring the social isolation and threats levied at those who supported Israel. Beginning in 1994, Arab Jerusalemites began applying for Israeli citizenship, first by the dozens, then by the hundreds and thousands. According to the Israel Central Bureau of Statistics, between 2002 and 2012, a total of 3,374 Arab Jerusalemites applied for and received Israeli citizenship.[18] Hatem Abdul Kader, a Fatah official who holds the "Jerusalem portfolio" for the Palestinian Authority in Judea and Samaria, says that in recent years more than ten thousand Jerusalem Arabs have received Israeli citizenship.[19]

In 2011 Dr. David Pollock, the former chief of Near East/South Asia/Africa research at the U.S. Information Agency, carried out an in-depth survey of Jerusalem's Arab residents. He found that 35 percent of them would choose to become Israelis rather than citizens of a Palestinian state, and only 30 percent would prefer to become citizens of a Palestinian state. Thirty-five percent refused to answer the question, but according to Pollock, their answers to the other survey questions were similar to those provided by the respondents who prefer Israeli citizenship.[20]

Most of the Arab Jerusalemites whom Pollock surveyed said they would not move to Palestine to avoid Israeli rule. And if their neighborhoods were transferred to Palestinian rule in the framework of a future peace deal, 40 percent said they would move in order to continue living under Israeli rule. Significantly, the survey found that most Jerusalem Arabs value their Israeli residency cards almost as much as they value their Palestinian and Muslim identities.

Pollock found a direct correlation between the importance that Jerusalem Arabs placed on politics and their desire to become Palestinian citizens. Desire to become an Israeli citizen corresponded with attaching importance to a high standard of living and good governance.

Israel's Attraction for Its Arab Citizens

Israel's economy is one of the most highly advanced, fastest-growing in the world, and for many Israeli Arabs who support their country, it is a powerful draw. Israel's workforce is among the most highly educated in the world. When Israel's modern, industrialized economy is compared with the Palestinian kleptocracy, it is little wonder that Israeli Arabs are uninterested in joining their fellow Arabs as they suffer under the economic and physical jackboot of the PLO and Hamas, which have dev-astated what was, under Israeli administration, a fast-growing, dynamic economy in Judea and Samaria. As we shall see in Chapter 16, Israel's high-tech sector has positioned it as a major, indeed vital player in the European economy, and it is also quickly expanding its economic ties to Asia. Everyone from Warren Buffett to the heads of China's largest cor-porations is eager to invest in Israel and develop joint ventures with the Jewish state. By any standard, Israel's marketplace is attractive. When compared to the Palestinian economy, there is no question that, for peo-ple whose main concerns are caring for their families and reaching their full personal potential, Israel is the place to be.

Then, too, there is the issue that Israel is a free country. One of the chief motivators in recent years for Arab integration into Israel has been the unraveling of the status quo in Arab states around the region.

Consider the story of Anet Haskia, an Israeli Arab Muslim and the proud mother of three Israeli soldiers. Haskia uses her personal Facebook page to defend Israel on Arabic websites and online forums.

Haskia has explained her position thus: "I was born in Israel, and it is my homeland. I thank God every day that I was born in the Jewish state because of everything that happens in the Arab states in general and Syria in particular. Not only do I support Israel, I am also willing to sacrifice my family for the existence of this state.

"You have to understand, Israel is my homeland. Just because I am an Arab Muslim does not mean I will support Arab countries against Israel or identify with a murderous organization like Hamas that wants to de-stroy my homeland."[21]

In the Knesset elections held in January 2013, Israeli Bedouin busi-nessman Attef Karinaoui formed a new pro-Israel, integrationist Arab party called El Amal Lat'gir or "Hope for Change." Interviewed by *The Times of Israel*, Karinaoui castigated the Israeli Arab political leadership for inciting Israeli Arabs against Israel and radicalizing their community. Extolling Israeli democracy, he said:

I'm a proud Arab and a proud Israeli too. I'm not Palestinian. . . . Look at Syria. Look at Egypt, look at Libya, look at Tunisia, and look at Bahrain: the problem is not Israel, it's the Arabs.

I have no problem with the Star of David on the flag or with the

national anthem—no problem at all. Israel is a democracy, and I respect every country that is a democracy. Israel did not expel me. I
kept my land. I have the right under the law to do whatever I want to
do, even to become prime minister. We Arabs need to thank God that
we live in this democratic country.

He concluded, "We need an Arab Spring here in Israel, against our own
Arab leaders."[22]

Shady Halul, a Greek Orthodox Arab who is active in the movement
to conscript Christian Arabs into the IDF, explained why he is willing to
stand up to criticism and threats from Israel's Arab leadership.

I would ask all of those who are inciting against us, including
those from the Christian community—what kind of security do
the Arabs and Muslims provide? Look at how they are slaughter-
ing each other in Syria and the other Arab countries. Why should
they care about us Christians? We need to fend for ourselves. In
the meantime, the only one that is giving us safety and security
is the state of Israel.[23]

Karinaoui's electoral bid was a failure, partly because financially, he was
no match for the anti-Israel Arab parties. His failure, and the Israeli Arab
politicians' continued sense that they can incite without consequence
against Israel and against their fellow Israeli Arabs who seek to integrate
into Israeli society, make clear that the trend toward integration has yet
to pass the critical threshold where it becomes inevitable.

Yet it is important to see how far the integrationist forces have come.
Less than a decade ago, stories like those of Corporal Joseph, the Atrash
brothers, Anet Haskia, and Aatef Karinaoui would have been unimaginable.

WHAT IF THE ANTI-ISRAEL FORCES WIN THE DAY?

Israel would certainly be better off with a fully integrated Arab minority than an irredentist Arab minority. But either way, Israel is better off
retaining sovereignty over its Arab communities.

Consider the following: according to Efraim Karsh's data, in 1999, on the eve of the Palestinian terror war against Israel, 80 percent of Israeli Arabs repudiated Israel's right to exist. Data regarding Palestinian views indicate similar sentiments.[24] At that time, there were 1.43 million Arabs living in Israel and an almost equal number living in Judea and Samaria. And yet between 2000 and 2004, only 236 Israeli Arabs were involved in terrorist attacks against Israeli Jews,[25] while thousands of Palestinians from Judea and Samaria were involved in such attacks.[26]

Given the proximity of the two populations, how can we account for the vast difference in their participation in terrorist activity? If Israeli Arabs share the Palestinians' goal of destroying Israel, why have comparatively so few of them participated in the terror war?

The simplest explanation is that they couldn't. Living under Israeli sovereignty, Israel's Arab community has far less ability to organize terror cells and to plan and carry out acts of terror than do their Palestinian brethren living under the terror-supporting Palestinian Authority. By governing the areas where Israeli Arabs live, Israeli authorities are more capable of thwarting terrorist attacks and preventing terrorist cells from carrying out their goals. This success in turn deters otherwise-hostile Israeli Arab citizens from joining terrorist groups, regardless of their sentiments.

THE CASE FOR JEWISH DEMOCRACY

In the increasingly shrill discourse on Israel and the Palestinians, the allegation is heard more and more often that Jewish self-determination is inherently at odds with democratic governance.[27] The assumption at the base of this claim is that Judaism and Jewish religious law are inherently antidemocratic, and therefore, the term "Jewish democracy" is an oxymoron.

The point should be moot, because Israel is among the freest countries in the world,[28] and because it is governed by the laws of the Knesset and not by Jewish religious law. But even if Jewish law were the source of Israeli law, it would not change Israel's position as a free, liberal democracy.

A scholarly examination of the roots of Western freedom undertaken over the past decade reveals that Western freedom is founded on Jewish law.[29] British political philosophers of the seventeenth century, such as

John Selden and Thomas Hobbes, who built the theoretical foundations of the modern state, based their understandings of what a modern republic should be on Jewish law and its rabbinic interpretations. As political theorist Fania Oz-Salzberger wrote in 2002, "According to Selden, the early Israelites created, with divine guidance, the first juridical state in history . . . which became the paradigm for the rule of law thereafter. The law given by God at Sinai was natural law itself, hence the Israelite laws deriving from it belong not in the realm of canon law, but in that of civil law in the proper sense."[30]

As political theorist Yoram Hazony has explained, Jewish law, which places God supreme and unknowable above man, is based on the assumption that no man can know God's true intentions; therefore Judaism can never endorse or accept a supreme human leader whose decrees are unchallengeable. And it cannot accept that any law is above interpretation and reinterpretation. As a consequence, "Jewish democracy" is not only not a contradiction in terms, but it can legitimately be asked whether a state can be a democracy if it is not based on—or at least inspired by—Jewish law.

In practice, and in keeping with Jewish tradition and legal history, as we have seen, life under Israeli rule is generally better than life under Palestinian rule. In both theory and practice, the Israeli government protects the rights of all Israel's citizens. And in both theory and practice, the Palestinian Authority has been a bigoted, authoritarian kleptocracy. It bars Jews from living in its territory and makes respect for Jewish property rights a capital crime. The Palestinian Authority systematically persecutes Christians and denies the basic civil rights of all of its citizens.

The trend toward the full integration of Israeli Arabs into Israeli society is incipient. But it is growing, and the ramifications of the strengthening integrationist pulse are strategically significant. If the government of Israel actively encouraged this trend, there is no reason to doubt that it would grow rapidly.

CHAPTER 12

The Legitimate Sovereign, Not an Occupying Power

On February 20, 2013, Israel's deputy ambassador to Great Britain, Alon Roth-Snir, was scheduled to speak at University of Essex in Colchester. Before he had a chance to say anything beyond "Good afternoon," anti-Israel protesters shouted him down. An attempt to move the speech to a smaller venue failed to stifle the assault. Roth-Snir was then evacuated by security officers and forced to flee the campus.[1]

Nathan Bolton, the president of Essex University's student union, praised the protesters. "I've made my position crystal clear," he said. "The Students' Union has a position, which reflects my own, that the state of Israel is a state which its very existance [sic] is a crime .... I'm proud to not give him [Roth-Snir] the attempt to justify his states [sic] oppression. I'm sure the hundreds of students were too. Freedom of expression isn't applicable here."[2]

At a debate the next day about Israel and the Palestinians at Oxford University, member of Parliament George Galloway stormed off the stage when he discovered that his debating opponent was an Israeli citizen. As he marched away, Galloway proclaimed, "I don't recognize Israel, and I don't debate Israelis."[3]

As these stories indicate, the last two chapters' description of the reality on the ground under Israeli rule and under that of the Palestinian Authority, and the perceptions of Arabs living in both places, is starkly at odds with the distorted depiction of events that the international media, academic discourse, and diplomatic parlance regularly present.

The utter absence of truth in popular, academic, and diplomatic discourses on Israel and the Palestinians is not limited to their misrepresentations of everyday reality as lived by actual people. Mendacity is the predominant theme across a wide array of issues and disciplines as they relate to the Palestinian conflict with Israel.

This chapter and the next will deal with two such disciplines. This chapter will consider the international legal basis for Israel's claim to sovereignty in Judea and Samaria. The next will consider Israel's national rights to sovereignty over Judea and Samaria. Legal rights are the rights to sovereignty that a state holds under international law. National rights are the basis for legal rights; they consist of a nation's historical and political ties to its sovereign land.

Israel's legal claim to sovereignty over Judea and Samaria is grounded in international law, through treaties and legal precedents, and is far stronger than the Palestinian claim to sovereignty over these areas. Yet this right has been systematically ignored, denied, and drowned in an ocean of lies and distortions about the nature of international law itself and about Israel's basic rights as a sovereign state.

This distortion and denial are not accidental developments. As we have already seen, Israel has been the target of a long-standing international campaign to delegitimize its right to exist. As we saw in Chapter 4, the campaign, now nearly fifty years old, was spearheaded by the Soviet Union in 1965.[4]

Two years before the Six Day War, the Soviet delegation to the United Nations began calling Zionism, the Jewish national liberation movement, a form of racism, calling into question Israel's very right to exist.[5]

Dr. Meir Rosenne, who served as Israel's consul to New York during these proceedings, said, "That forgotten episode ironically had a serious impact on the subsequent evolution of world opinion on international law regarding Israel and Zionism."[6] Rosenne explained that the Soviet maneuver paved the way for the November 10, 1975, passage of UN General Assembly Resolution 3379, which equated Zionism with racism.

This early initiative from the Soviets demonstrates that the campaign to demonize and delegitimize Israel is not primarily about seeking to reform or to end Israeli control of lands it took control of during the 1967 Six Day War. Rather its aim is to delegitimize the Jewish state, period.

The 1975 UN General Assembly resolution was repealed in 1991, but its influence did not wane thereafter. It set the precedent under which the Jewish state was subjected to a standard of behavior that was not applied to any other state, under which Israel—surrounded by enemies that sought its destruction and the massacre of its citizens—was always in the wrong.

A decade after Resolution 3379's official repeal, it became the basis for a renewed international campaign to demonize, criminalize, and dehumanize Israel in order to pave the way for its national destruction.

As we have seen, immediately after Yassir Arafat rejected Israel's offer of peace and Palestinian statehood at the Camp David summit in July 2000, he and his deputies began planning the Palestinian terror war against Israel, which began later that year.[7]

The Palestinians launched their terror war on September 28, 2000. The onslaught directed all manner of mass murder principally against Israeli civilians, who comprised more than 70 percent of the Israeli casualties. The Palestinian terrorist attacks ran the gamut from roadside bombs, to shooting ambushes along highways, to suicide bombings, to kidnap, torture, murder, and the mutilation of corpses. By September 2001, 170 Israelis had been killed and more than a thousand wounded in the attacks.[8]

And in that month, the Palestinians received the Good Housekeeping Seal of Approval from the UN and the international human rights community. The UN World Conference against Racism, Racial Discrimination, Xenophobia, and Related Intolerance was convened from August 31 to September 8 in Durban, South Africa. At the conference, the Palestinians took center stage as the greatest victims of racism and state terror in the world, and Israel—and Israel alone—was labeled as a racist and therefore criminal state.

The conference took place at two separate, parallel forums, one for state governments and one for nongovernmental organizations. And for both forums the foundational text was the repealed UN General Assembly Resolution 3379 that labeled Zionism as a form of racism.

In the weeks leading up to the conference, Palestinian terrorist attacks at a crowded restaurant in Jerusalem, at a junction near Netanya, at a train station in Nahariya, and near a hospital in Jerusalem had produced more than one hundred Jewish Israeli civilian casualties. But the NGO Forum's final resolution ignored Palestinian terrorist attacks on Israelis. Instead, it alleged falsely: "the targeted victims of Israel's brand of apartheid and ethnic cleansing methods have been in particular children, women and refugees." It defamed Israel as a "racist apartheid state" and guilty of "genocide," called for an end to its "racist crimes against Palestinians," and endorsed an international war crimes tribunal that would try Israeli citizens.[9]

The NGO Forum's final resolution also set out a "policy of complete and total isolation of Israel as an apartheid state," which included "the imposition of mandatory and comprehensive sanctions and embargoes, the full cessation of all links (diplomatic, economic, social, aid, military cooperation and training) between all states and Israel."[10]

"Thus," as Gerald Steinberg noted, "the Durban conference provided the strategy for the ensuing NGO-led political war against Israel, using the weapons derived from the rhetoric of human rights and international law, and conducted via the UN, the media, churches, and university campuses."[11]

The campaign to delegitimize Israel is not the subject of this book. However, it is important to note that since the Durban conference, political warfare has been waged against Israel to a massive degree. Every year Israel is condemned in hundreds of UN resolutions. Anti-Israel divestment campaigns have been carried out on university campuses in the United States, in Canada, and throughout Europe. Britain's University Teachers Union voted to boycott Israeli universities. Israeli students have been denied admission to British universities due to their nationality. Israeli stores have been picketed and forced to close. Performances by Israeli theater groups, dance troupes, and orchestras in Europe have been canceled, picketed, and interrupted.

The success of the movement to delegitimize the Jewish state tells us much about the temperament of the Western world today. But it tells us nothing about the merits of the arguments and claims that are being launched against Israel by the Palestinians and their Western supporters. Specifically, it tells us nothing about Israel's sovereign rights to Judea and Samaria under international law.

WHAT IS INTERNATIONAL LAW?

To understand the determinative nature of Israel's sovereign rights over Judea and Samaria under international law, it is first necessary to understand what international law is, and what it is not. International law is a set of rules that are generally accepted as binding in relations between states. But international law is unlike most other law. Usually when we think of law, we think of a lawmaker issuing instructions that citizens must follow. But international law is based on consent. There is no lawmaker, and there are no citizens. States follow the rules of international law to which they consent.[12]

International law has two chief components: treaties and custom. Treaties may be bilateral, such as the treaties of peace between Israel and Egypt and between Israel and Jordan. And treaties may be international conventions, like the 1949 Geneva Conventions, which codify parts of the laws of war; and the 1948 International Convention for the Prevention and Punishment of Genocide. Finally treaties may be multilateral, like the NATO Treaty.

Some treaties, like the UN Charter and the League of Nations Covenant, created international institutions. But while the treaties are binding under international law for the consenting parties, the institutions created by the treaties cannot make new law. The UN Charter does not grant legislative power to any UN body. The General Assembly is empowered only to pass resolutions that are recommendations. The Security Council has the power to pass binding resolutions, but exercise of that power is limited to situations that are considered threats to peace, breaches of peace, and acts of aggression against UN member states.[13] In the days before the United Nations, the League of Nations was a similar institution with similarly limited powers.[14]

Treaties, then, do not carry the same weight as legislation. States have to obey only the treaties to which they are parties. If a state is not a party to a treaty, it does not have to follow the treaty's rules. No consent, no law.

Custom, as a component of international law, is different. It "results from a general and consistent practice of states followed by them from a sense of legal obligation."[15] International law requires states to follow customary law even when the states have not explicitly consented to the custom.

However, customary law is also based on implied consent. A state that persistently objects to an international custom is not bound by that custom.

Identifying custom is not easy since by its nature, custom is not written down. Sometimes, however, treaties can be used to help figure out custom. Sometimes law develops as custom and is then summarized in treaties. This was the case with some of the rules of war codified in the Geneva Conventions. At other times law develops in treaties but spreads to become customary; for instance, many of the laws of war stated in the 1907 Hague Convention are now considered customary.[16]

The international laws of sovereignty are not set down in any treaty; they are solely a matter of customary law. It is by these ill-defined customary laws that we must judge Israeli and Palestinian claims on the Land of Israel.

INTERNATIONAL LAW AND THE MODERN MIDDLE EAST

For the first time in four centuries, determining sovereignty for Judea and Samaria, and indeed for the lands of the Levant in general, became a legal issue in 1917, when the Ottoman Empire was poised to disintegrate as a consequence of World War I.

The Ottoman Turks were arguably the biggest losers of World War I. The Allied victory in the war brought about the demise of the Ottoman Empire, which for the previous four hundred years had been the imperial sovereign of much of the Middle East. Its successor, the Republic of Turkey, surrendered all claims to the territories that had been controlled by the defunct empire. In the aftermath of the war, the new League of Nations was empowered to determine the fate of these lands, which included present-day Iraq, Syria, Lebanon, Israel, Jordan, Gaza, and Judea and Samaria.[17]

The spirit of the times eschewed colonies and championed national self-determination; accordingly, the victorious Allied powers agreed to allow the conquered territories eventually to become independent states. In the meantime, the Allied states created a new legal form of sovereignty, called a mandate, to be overseen by the League of Nations.[18] The Allied states agreed to let the League of Nations assign mandates and define their terms.

The league transferred control of present-day Iraq to the British, in what was called the British Mandate for Mesopotamia. It transferred control of present-day Syria and Lebanon to France, in what became known as the French Mandate for Syria and the Lebanon. And it transferred control of present-day Israel, Gaza, Judea, Samaria, and Jordan to the British, in what became known as the British Mandate for Palestine.

In order to ensure that these lands did not simply become additional colonial possessions of the victorious Allied powers, the terms of the mandates included explicit directions for how the territories had to be governed in order to empower them to emerge later as sovereign states.[19]

INTERNATIONAL LAW AND THE LAND OF ISRAEL

The British Mandate for Palestine was different from the other mandates because it accorded the political and eventually the sovereign rights to the mandate territory not to the local population but to the Jewish people, in accordance with the British government's Balfour Declaration of November 2, 1917.

As the Mandate's preamble explained, "The Principal Allied Powers have . . . agreed that the Mandatory should be responsible for putting into effect the declaration originally made on November 2nd, 1917, by the Government of His Britannic Majesty, and adopted by the said Powers, in favour of the establishment in Palestine of a national home for the Jewish people." The local population was to be accorded "civil and religious rights."[20]

Article 6 of the Mandate obligated the British Mandatory government to "facilitate Jewish immigration . . . and . . . encourage . . . close settlement by Jews on the land, including State lands and waste lands not required for public purposes."[21]

The reason the nations of the world decided to confer sovereign rights over the territories of the Palestine Mandate to the Jewish people is that they believed the land belonged to the Jews by historic right. As we will see at length in the next chapter, no nation other than the Jews had ever perceived the Land of Israel, or Palestine, as their national home. Not only had the nations of the world determined that the Jews had the best claim to national sovereignty over the land; the language of the Mandate indicates that they determined that the Jews had the only valid claim to national sovereignty there.

As the preamble put it, the Mandate was configured in "recognition . . . [of] the historical connection of the Jewish people with Palestine and to the grounds for reconstituting their national home in that country."[22]

MAP OF LEAGUE OF NATIONS MANDATE FOR PALESTINE [23]

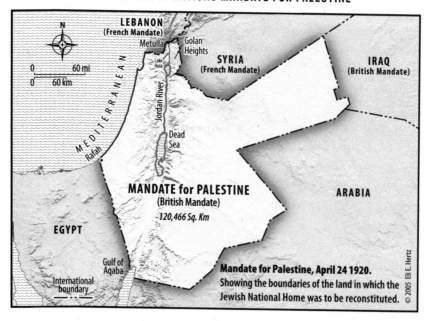

Mandate for Palestine, April 24 1920.
Showing the boundaries of the land in which the Jewish National Home was to be reconstituted.

REVISED MAP OF THE LEAGUE OF NATIONS MANDATE FOR PALESTINE AFTER REMOVAL OF TRANS-JORDAN [24]

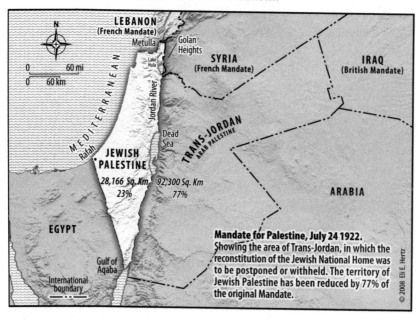

Mandate for Palestine, July 24 1922.
Showing the area of Trans-Jordan, in which the reconstitution of the Jewish National Home was to be postponed or withheld. The territory of Jewish Palestine has been reduced by 77% of the original Mandate.

The only "exit clause" within the Mandate regarded present-day Jordan—that is, the area east of the Jordan River. Article 25 of the Mandate permitted the British to separate "the territories lying between the Jordan and the eastern boundary of Palestine." There "the Mandatory shall be entitled, with the consent of the Council of the League of Nations, to postpone or withhold application of such provisions of this mandate as he may consider inapplicable to the existing local conditions."[25]

Armed with this exit clause, the British immediately separated and created Trans-Jordan out of this area, which comprised 77 percent of the territory of the Mandate. The British obligation to cultivate the remaining 23 percent of the land—present-day Israel, Gaza, Judea, and Samaria—as a Jewish commonwealth remained binding (see bottom map on page 171).

As we saw in Chapter 3, a lot happened between 1922, when the League of Nations approved the British Mandate for Palestine, and 1948, when Israel declared its independence and the Mandate ended. For instance, in 1937, in the midst of a Palestinian Arab terror war against the Jews, the British formed the Palestine Royal Commission (the Peel Commission) to come up with a means of appeasing the Arabs. The Peel Commission recommended partitioning what was left of the original Mandate between the Jews and the Arabs. Some 20 percent of the remaining land was to be granted to the Jews. The rest was to go to the Arabs and be incorporated into Trans-Jordan. The Jewish Agency, which served as the official representative of the Jewish population of the Mandate, accepted the partition with qualifications. The Arabs rejected it.[26]

At the end of World War II, the League of Nations ceased to exist. So in 1947, when the British felt unable to continue to govern the Mandate, they requested advice from the new United Nations on the future of the land. The United Nations recommended partitioning the land (not including Trans-Jordan) into a Jewish and an Arab state, with the Jewish state comprising 55 percent of the territory. The Arab state would comprise 45 percent of the territory but would have most of the arable land. The Jews accepted the partition plan, but the Arabs rejected it.[27]

The Palestinians and their supporters have claimed that the Jews' agreement to the UN's partition plan canceled the Jews' legal rights to the entire territory of the Mandate—minus Jordan—as established in the 1922 Mandate. In their telling, the legal basis for Israel's existence

MAP OF THE UN PARTITION PLAN [28]

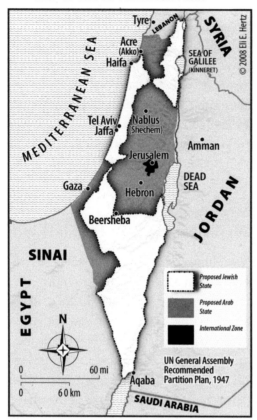

is now UN General Assembly Resolution 181, which approved the partition plan; Israel, they argue, has lost its sovereign rights to any territory beyond the borders of the state set out in the partition plan.[29]

As we briefly noted in Chapter 5, this claim lacks legal validity. In fact, the UN Charter addressed just such a contingency. When the United Nations was created in 1945, Article 80 of its charter explicitly preserved the rights of peoples in existing mandates of the League unless a new trusteeship agreement was reached and approved to replace the mandate.[30]

Elihu Lauterpacht, a judge on the International Court of Justice, has explained that because of Article 80, Resolution 181 could be valid only if it were accepted by all parties to the conflict. But the Arabs, including the Arabs of the Palestine Mandate, rejected it. In any event, Lauterpacht said, "the coming into existence of Israel does not depend legally upon the Resolution [181]. The right of a State to exist flows from its factual existence, especially when that existence is prolonged, shows every sign of continuance and is recognized by the generality of nations."[31]

Amplifying Lauterpacht's position, in 1981 the legal scholar Julius Stone wrote, "The State of Israel is . . . not legally derived from the partition plan, but rests (as do most other states in the world) on assertion of independence by its people and government, on the vindication of that independence by arms against assault by other states and on the establishment of orderly government within territory under its stable control."[32]

THE SOVEREIGN RIGHTS OF THE STATE OF ISRAEL

Because Israel's neighbors refused all agreements on borders, when Israel declared independence on May 15, 1948, its borders were determined by the doctrines of customary law that were in effect at that time. According to law professor Avi Bell, this meant that Israel's new borders were "based on the customary international legal principle of *uti possidetis juris*."[33] The literal meaning of that phrase is "as you lawfully hold."

The principle of *uti possidetis juris* asserts that when formerly non-self-governing territories—such as colonial or mandatory possessions—become sovereign states, their old administrative boundaries become their new national boundaries.[34] As Bell explains, "Under this international legal principle, when Israel declared its independence on May 15, 1948, the administrative boundaries of the British Mandate became Israel's national borders."[35]

This principle has been challenged and upheld in numerous border disputes between former colonies. For instance, the disputed border between Rwanda and Burundi, both former Belgian colonies, was settled on the basis of this principle.

In 1986 the International Court of Justice adjudicated the border dispute between Burkina Faso and Mali on the basis of their administrative borders. The court explained its decision on the grounds that *uti possidetis juris* was a binding principle of customary international law.[36] In the court's words:

[T]he Chamber cannot disregard the principle of *uti possidetis juris*. . . . [T]he principle is not a special rule which pertains solely to one specific system of international law. It is a general principle, which is logically connected with the phenomenon of the obtaining of independence, wherever it occurs. Its obvious purpose is to prevent the independence and stability of new States being endangered by fratricidal struggles provoked by the challenging of frontiers following the withdrawal of the administering power.[37]

According to Bell, nothing has happened since the Israeli Declaration of Independence to alter Israeli sovereignty over Judea and Samaria or the other areas of the British Mandate now under Israeli control.

Immediately after the UN General Assembly passed the partition recommendation on November 29, 1947, the Palestinian Arabs launched a guerrilla war against the Jews with the explicit aim of destroying the nascent Jewish state.[38] And after Israel declared independence on May 15, 1948, the armies of Jordan, Syria, Lebanon, Iraq, and Egypt invaded the new state with the same explicit aim.[39]

In 1949, after successfully fending off the invading Arab militaries, Israel signed a series of armistice agreements with all four bordering Arab states (Lebanon, Syria, Jordan, and Egypt). These agreements established cease-fire lines that the media and most of the international diplomatic community have misleadingly called "the 1967 borders."

Those cease-fire lines did not demarcate political borders. They were simply the points to which Israel had been able to beat back the pan-Arab invasion. Indeed, this distinction was explicitly stated in all the armistice agreements.

The end of the war found Jordan illegally occupying Judea, Samaria, and northern, southern, and eastern Jerusalem. Egypt was illegally occupying the Gaza Strip.[40] But even though the Hashemite Kingdom of Jordan had no legal claim to them, in 1950 it annexed Judea and Samaria, as well as the areas of Jerusalem that had fallen under its control in the war.

Jordan's illegal occupation and annexation of the areas as part of an illegal war of aggression had no impact whatsoever on the rights of Israel, the legitimate sovereign and the victim of aggression to sovereignty. In the event, Jordan's 1950 annexation of Judea and Samaria (which it renamed "the West Bank") and eastern Jerusalem was recognized only by Britain.[41]

As it happened, the Arab states' repeated aggressions against Israel have provided Israel with yet another legal basis for claiming sovereignty over Judea and Samaria. In 1967 Israel captured Judea and Samaria (together with east Jerusalem and other territories) in a defensive war. Judge Stephen Schwebel, who later became the president of the International Court of Justice, explained in a 1970 article in the *American Journal of International Law* that "where the prior holder of territory [in this case Jordan] had seized the territory unlawfully, the state which subsequently takes that territory in the lawful exercise of self-defense [that is, Israel in the 1967 Six Day War] has . . . better title."[42]

Schwebel maintained that, due to the explicitly aggressive aims of Egypt, Syria, and Jordan, Israel's acquisition of territories—including Judea and Samaria—was undertaken in the context of a lawful war.[43]

In 1968 the Israeli jurist Yehuda Blum made a related argument. In a much-cited article, published in *Israel Law Review*, Blum explained that disputes over sovereign claims do not occur in a vacuum. The question is not which of the disputing parties has the perfect claim to sovereignty, but which has the *better* claim for sovereignty. He ignored the question of Israel's sovereign rights to the areas under the Mandate and simply addressed the question of its legal rights in light of its takeover of the areas in the course of a defensive war.[44]

In light of Jordan's weak case for sovereignty, and the fact that there was never a Palestinian Arab state to claim sovereignty under international law, Blum concluded that Israel holds the most credible claim to sovereignty over Judea and Samaria. In his words, "The legal standing of Israel in the territories in question is thus that of a State which is lawfully in control of territory in respect of which no other States can show better title."[45]

Moreover, "since in the present view no State can make out a legal claim that is equal to that of Israel," Blum added, "this relative superiority of Israel may be sufficient, under international law, to make Israeli possession of Judea and Samaria virtually indistinguishable from absolute title."[46]

THE PALESTINIANS' DUBIOUS CLAIMS TO SOVEREIGN RIGHTS

The Palestinians base their claim to sovereignty on various arguments—aside from their repetitious and invalid claims based on nonbinding UN General Assembly resolutions and nonbinding legal opinions. Among these arguments is the assertion that Israel, through its peace offers to the Palestinians in 2000 and in 2008, effectively abrogated its right to sovereignty over Judea and Samaria.[47] Like their claim regarding the Peel partition plan and the UN partition plan, this claim would have weight if the Palestinians had accepted Israel's 2000 and 2008 offers. But since the Palestinians rejected the offers, these claims are rendered null and void.[48]

The Palestinians also argue that they are a people living in a non-self-governing territory, and as such, they have a right to self-determination. As Bell explains, this claim is disputable at best. First of all, the Palestinians have been exercising self-rule over these areas since 1994 through the Palestinian Authority. Second, the territory was already allocated by the 1922 Mandate for the self-determination of the Jewish people. Perhaps for these reasons, the United Nations does not recognize the Palestinians as living in a non-self-governing territory.[49]

Beyond all these factors, the major problem with this claim is that the right to self-determination does not equal a right to territorial sovereignty.[50]

International law permits self-determination claims to be satisfied by incorporation into the ruling state, by sovereign independence, or by anything in between. Israel, to abide by its obligation to respect the self-determination rights of the Palestinians, is required to undertake good-faith negotiations with the Palestinians in a bid to satisfy their self-determination rights.[51] It is an indisputable fact that Israel's attempts to reach a peace settlement with the Palestinians over the past twenty years constitute good-faith efforts to satisfy the Palestinians' self-determination rights, and so Israel has fulfilled its obligation in this sphere.[52]

As Bell notes, a legal precedent for recognizing that a right of self-determination does not necessitate a right to sovereignty was created by the Canadian Supreme Court. In its 1998 ruling on Quebec's right to secede from Canada, the court determined that under international law, the right of self-determination does not trump a state's right to sovereignty.[53]

By virtue of its sovereign rights since independence, its capture of the territory in a defensive war, and the limited nature of the right of self-determination (the Palestinians' strongest claim to sovereignty), Israel's legal claim to sovereign rights over Judea and Samaria is clearly stronger than that of the Palestinians.

Despite the propaganda claims of Israel's detractors, there is no international legal obstacle to the application of Israeli sovereignty to Judea and Samaria. Israel, far from being a foreign occupier of Palestinian lands, is the legitimate sovereign.

CHAPTER 13

The Indigenous People, Not Colonial Usurpers

In June 2012 the *New York Times* published an article about a Palestinian village south of Jerusalem called Battir, which hopes to be recognized as a World Heritage Site by UNESCO, the UN's Educational, Scientific and Cultural Organization. Battir bases its bid on its ancient irrigation system and terraced agriculture. According to the Palestinians and UNESCO, the system in question is "a Roman-era irrigation system."[1]

The *Times*'s account was right to describe the irrigation system as an ancient wonder. But from then on, the article was at best problematic. The Palestinian and UNESCO account, unquestioningly reported by the *Times,* attributes the irrigation system, the ancient agriculture, and the historic significance of the village to the wrong historical era and the wrong historical actors.

Battir is the Arabized name of the ancient Jewish town of Beitar. Beitar was the last stronghold held by the Jews in the Land of Israel during their final great revolt against the Roman conquerors, from 132 to 135. During those three years, Jewish warriors led by Simon Bar Kokhba destroyed two Roman legions. Bar Kokhba's fortress was located inside Beitar.

The historical significance of Beitar is not the advanced irrigation system that the Jews built there, or the advanced agricultural technique of terraced farming that they developed. That irrigation system, and the village's proximity to Jerusalem and to natural water sources generally, were among the reasons Bar Kokhba chose to locate his headquarters in Beitar. The village's historic significance is that it was the last place in the Land of Israel where the Jews would exercise sovereignty for the next 1,813 years—from its fall in 135 until the establishment of the State of Israel in 1948.[2]

Beitar is also popularly known as Khirbat al-Yahud, or "the Jewish ruin."[3] After finally defeating Bar Kokhba's forces, according to Josephus, the vengeful Roman forces killed 1.1 million Jews in the Land of Israel. An additional 97,000 were taken prisoner.[4]

In light of the Romans' genocide of Jewry, the Talmud claimed that the source of the village's fertility was not the irrigation system but something else. In the rabbis' telling, "For seven years [after the fall of Beitar] the gentiles fertilized their vineyards with the blood of Israel without using manure."[5]

It is not surprising that UNESCO would collude with the Palestinian Authority to expropriate Jewish history in the Land of Israel for the Palestinians. In October 2012, UNESCO condemned Israel for designating Rachel's Tomb in Bethlehem and the Patriarchs' Tomb in Hebron as National Heritage Sites. Instead, UNESCO declared that the tombs of the biblical Jewish patriarchs and matriarchs were mosques.

Israeli prime minister Benjamin Netanyahu harshly condemned the UN agency, saying, "The attempt to separate the nation of Israel from its cultural heritage is absurd." His office's formal condemnation read, "It is unfortunate that an organization that was established with the goal of promoting the cultural preservation of historical sites around the world is attempting due to political reasons to uproot the connection between the nation of Israel and its cultural heritage."[6]

UNESCO, the only UN agency that accepts "Palestine" as a member state even though no such state exists,[7] does not limit its cultural assault on Jews to Israel alone. It is active in a campaign to appropriate Jewish history as a whole to Islam. For instance, in a report issued in 2006, the agency said the greatest Jewish theologian in history, Rabbi Moses Maimonides (the Rambam), was a Muslim. And in 2009 the agency labeled Jerusalem as "a capital of Arab culture."[8]

UNESCO does not operate alone in this campaign.[9] In March 2011 Turkish prime minister Recep Tayyip Erdogan told a Saudi newspaper that the Temple Mount in Jerusalem, the Cave of the Patriarchs, and Rachel's Tomb "were not and never will be Jewish sites, but Islamic sites."[10] Erdogan's statement is no different from those made repeatedly by Palestinian leaders, who act in accordance with the PLO Charter's provision, which states, "Claims of historical or religious ties of Jews with Palestine are incompatible with the facts of history and the true conception of what constitutes statehood. Judaism, being a religion, is not an independent nationality. Nor do Jews constitute a single nation with an identity of its own; they are citizens of the states to which they belong."[11]

Palestinian Media Watch (PMW) is an Israeli NGO that reports on the official PA media; its reports have formed the basis of U.S. congressional and EU probes of Palestinian incitement against Israel. PMW has documented that the Palestinian Authority's denial of Jewish history and of the Jewish connection to the Land of Israel began with its establishment in 1994. So too PMW has documented how the Palestinians have systematically fabricated history in order to appropriate Jewish history to themselves. Among other things, they have claimed that Jesus was a Palestinian Muslim, and that the Jebusites, Canaanites, Philistines, and Jews of the Bible were Arabs, Palestinians, and Muslims—even though the final books of the Bible were written nearly a thousand years before the creation of Islam.

At a 1998 academic conference organized by the Palestinian Authority, PMW reports, Palestinian academics openly admitted that the goal of rewriting history is to deny all Jewish political rights to Israel, and to appropriate Jewish history to the Palestinians.[12] The official PA newspaper *Al-Ayaam* reported on December 4, 1998, that "Dr. Yussuf Alzamili [chairman of the history department at Khan Yunis Educational College] called on all universities and colleges to write the history of Palestine and to guard it, and not to enable the [foreign] implants and enemies to distort it or to legitimize the existence of Jews on this land." History lecturer Abu Amar "clarified that there is no connection between the ancient generation of Jews and the new generation."[13]

In keeping with this position, Yassir Arafat, Mahmoud Abbas, Salam Fayyad, and all major and minor PA officials and Palestinian religious leaders deny that the Jews have a national history in the Land of Israel. For example, at the July 2000 Camp David summit, Arafat told President Bill Clinton that there had never been a Jewish Temple in Jerusalem.[14] He insisted that had there ever been a Jewish Temple, it was in Nablus or in Yemen.[15]

In August 2012 Abbas issued a statement accusing Israel of seeking to destroy the Al Aksa Mosque, which the first Muslim conquerors of the Land of Israel, in the seventh century, built on the ruins of the Second Temple. He denied the existence of any historical Jewish settlement in

Jerusalem and referred to the Temple—in language typical of the Palestinians' historical discourse—as the "alleged Temple."

In the same statement, Abbas threated Israel with eternal war if it did not remove its Jewish citizens and surrender its sovereignty over Jerusalem. "There will be no peace or stability," he said, "before our beloved city and eternal capital is liberated from occupation and settlement." Abbas proclaimed that the city—which has served as the capital of the Jewish people for the past three thousand years and never has been the capital for any other people—"will forever be Arabic, Islamic and Christian."[16]

For his part, in April 2010, PA prime minister Salam Fayyad formally requested that Canada's prime minister cancel an exhibition of the Dead Sea Scrolls at Toronto's Royal Ontario Museum. The Dead Sea Scrolls were found between 1946 and 1956 in caves near the Dead Sea in Judea and contain the earliest known copies of the Bible. They date from the time of the Second Temple and include fragments from the books of Genesis, Psalms, and Deuteronomy, among others. Among other things, the Dead Sea Scrolls are further proof of the historic and religious ties that the Jewish people have to Israel.

Fayyad alleged that the scrolls had been stolen by Israel and were PA property. He asked that Canadian officials seize the scrolls and transfer them to the Palestinian Authority. He insisted that sovereignty over the Dead Sea belongs to the Palestinian Authority. The Jordanians also weighed in, insisting that Canadian authorities seize the scrolls and transfer them to Jordan.

As we saw in the previous chapter, neither the Palestinian Authority nor Jordan has ever legally exercised sovereignty over Judea and Samaria, including the Dead Sea region. Yet as scholar David Meir-Levi explains, from a political standpoint, the fact that Fayyad's claims had no basis in law or history made no difference whatsoever. What was supposed to be a cultural exhibition of early biblical texts from the land of their origins became a political event, in which Israel's very history was criminalized and demonized.[17]

On May 14, 2011, the eve of the sixty-third anniversary of Israel's declaration of independence, Abbas proclaimed, "We say to him [Netanyahu], when he claims that they [the Jews] have a historical right dating back to 3000 years BCE—we say that the nation of Palestine upon the land of Canaan had a 7000 year history BCE. This is the truth, which must be understood and we have to note it, in order to say: 'Netanyahu you are incidental in history. We are the people of history.'"[18]

Like his claim that Jerusalem is the "eternal capital" of the Palestinian people, Abbas's statement is a clear example of the Palestinians' shameless denial of historical fact. The Arabs never attributed religious or political significance to Jerusalem until the Jews reasserted sovereignty over the city in 1967.[19]

It is easy to understand why the Palestinians believe it is imperative that they deny Jewish history. If they acknowledge the validity of the region's Jewish roots, they will be forced to recognize that the Jews rather than the Palestinian Arabs are the indigenous people of the land. This state of affairs is so obvious that even the PLO has admitted it.

In January 2011 *Al Jazeera* and *The Guardian* published what they referred to as "the Palestine Papers." The papers, leaked to *Al Jazeera*, were in large part written by the Palestinian Negotiations Support Unit (NSU). The NSU is the PA department responsible for packaging and marketing the Palestinians' negotiating positions. The leaked papers included thousands of documents.

One of the leaked documents was titled, "Strategy and Talking Points for Responding to the Precondition of Recognizing Israel as a 'Jewish State.'" In the document, the NSU explained that Palestinian negotiators must never recognize Israel's *right* to exist as the Jewish state. It instructed Palestinian negotiators to limit their recognition to the *fact* of Israel's existence as a sovereign state. In an appendix, the NSU explained why the Palestinians must never extend any recognition to Israel's Jewish identity:

> Recognizing Israel as a "Jewish state," particularly in advance of agreeing to the final border between Israel and Palestine, could also strengthen Israel's claims of sovereignty over all of Historic Palestine, including the OPT [Occupied Palestinian Territory]. Recognizing the Jewish state implies recognition of a Jewish people and recognition of its right to self-determination. Those who assert this right also assert that the territory historically associated with this right of self-determination (*i.e.*, the self-determination

unit) is *all* of Historic Palestine. Therefore, recognition of the Jewish people and their right of self-determination may lend credence
to the Jewish people's claim to all of Historic Palestine.[20]

So for the Palestinians, even the most basic recognition of reality—that
Israel is a Jewish state—threatens their entire edifice of lies. One must
refuse to recognize the existence of the Jewish people, they say, for once
you recognize the Jewish people, you necessarily recognize their history,
which in turn requires you to recognize that the Jews are the only nation
that has ever claimed the Land of Israel as its homeland, and the only
people that has ever claimed Jerusalem as its capital.

Indeed, acknowledging the reality of Jewish existence and history
would require the Palestinians and their supporters to behave as the
framers of the League of Nations Mandate for Palestine did. That is, it
would force them to recognize that Jews are the indigenous people of
the Land of Israel, including Judea and Samaria, and that in the words
of the NSU, the Jews' "right of self-determination . . . is *all* of Historic
Palestine."

ISRAEL'S NATIONAL RIGHTS TO JUDEA AND SAMARIA

In truth, the Jewish people's rights to sovereignty over Judea and Samaria—as with their rights to the rest of the Land of Israel—are
overwhelming. From a historical and political perspective, during the
3,500-year political history of the Land of Israel, the Jews were the only
nation that viewed Israel as a single political unit, separate and distinct
from all other territory, and as territory that uniquely served as their national, political, religious, and territorial center.[21]

In an attempt to wipe out the Jewish identity of the Land of Israel, the
Romans renamed the area Palestina and incorporated it into the empire's
Syria-Palestina district. The name Palestina was chosen because it connected the identity of the land to the ancient Philistines, who had ceased
to exist hundreds of years before the Roman conquest.[22] The Romans
also changed the name of Jerusalem to Aeolina Capitalina and barred
Jews from entering the newly pagan city.

Until Jordan's illegal occupation and annexation of Judea and Samaria in 1949 and 1950, the areas had never been governed or viewed

as a geographical unit separate from the rest of the Land of Israel. They were known by their historic Jewish names: Judea and Samaria. The UN, for instance, referred to the area as "Samaria and Judea" in its 1947 partition resolution.[23]

Judea and Samaria came to be viewed as a distinct geographical unit only when the Jordanians instigated their occupation of the areas. They invented the term "West Bank" in order to ground their claim to sovereignty on an intuited but nonexistent political link between the west bank of the Jordan River and the east bank of the river, which was Jordan.

The Christians, who ruled the land under the Byzantines from 324 to 624, and again under the Crusaders from 1099 to 1291, did view the area as a stand-alone territory, rather than as a section of a larger territorial unit. But the Holy Land was never considered the political center of Christendom. The political centers of Christendom were in Rome and Constantinople. During the Crusader period, Jerusalem was but one administrative center, along with Antioch, Caesarea, and Damascus.[24]

Later the forces of Islam would rule the land under three separate regimes. The Arabs ruled the land from 624 to 1099. The Mamluks ruled from 1291 to 1517. And the Ottoman Turks ruled from 1517 to 1917. During the millennium of Islamic rule, the Land of Israel was never considered a unique geographical unit. Under all three regimes, the Land of Israel was ruled from Damascus and was seen as a part of a larger territorial unit that spanned the Levant.[25]

Although the League of Nations Mandate referred to the Land of Israel as "Palestine," the League was clear that the name held no political significance. Rather, its purpose was simply to define a geographical entity. "Palestine" was defined not by history but by geographical boundaries.[26]

The Palestinian attempts to convince the world that they are the descendants of the biblical Philistines, Canaanites, Jews, and Moabites, and to supplant the Jews and appropriate Jewish history, is contradicted by the historical record revealed by every square inch of Israeli territory. Jewish history pervades the land's geography.

Take Shilo, a Jewish community in Judea, for example. Modern Shilo was established in 1978. If one were to accept the Palestinian claim that Jews have no history in Israel generally, and specifically in Judea and Samaria, then it might be possible to accept the narrative that Shilo (and indeed all Jewish communities in Judea and Samaria) is a colonial outpost of Israel, that Israel is an occupying power born out of the destruction of the native Palestinians, and that the Palestinians are an indigenous people with a seven- or nine-thousand-year history in the Land of Israel, depending on how Mahmoud Abbas and his colleagues are counting on any particular day.

But like thousands of other places in Israel, especially those in Judea and Samaria, Shilo exposes the utter bankruptcy of the Palestinian campaign to rewrite history.

Shilo was the Jewish people's first capital in the Land of Israel. It is mentioned in the Bible thirty-one times: once in Genesis, then in the books of Joshua, Samuel, Judges, Kings, Psalms, and Jeremiah. Shilo is where Joshua divided the land among the Twelve Tribes of Israel.[27] It is where he apportioned the cities for the Levites[28] and where he mobilized the armies of Israel.[29] The Tabernacle was erected in Shilo.[30] For hundreds of years, before King David conquered Jerusalem and his son Solomon built the first Temple, Shilo was the home of the Ark of the Covenant. Jews made pilgrimages there three times a year, bringing their offerings to God.[31]

In 1983 the renowned archaeologist Israel Finkelstein excavated much of the ancient *tel* of Shilo. He found a storage area just a few dozen meters away from the presumed site of the Tabernacle. The storage area contained nearly undisturbed storage jugs filled with the remains of raisins and other organic materials that were apparently destined to serve as sacrificial offerings. Finkelstein conducted carbon-14 dating of organic materials, which dated the jugs to the time of Samuel.[32]

The storage jugs were so well preserved because they were buried under a layer of scorched earth. According to Finkelstein, carbon-14 dating of scorched grains found at the site indicated that the fire took place around the year 1050 BCE,[33] a time in which the Bible tells of the Jews' defeat in a war with the Philistines. During the war, the Philistines seized the Ark of the Covenant, which contained the Ten Commandments.[34]

In late 2012 archaeologists unearthed a pitcher in the level of ashes. The pitcher was also found to date from 1050 BCE, and so it strengthened the assessment that the biblical account of the battle, and the assumption that Shilo was destroyed in the war, are accurate.[35]

Both the archaeological remains and the Bible indicate that Jews resettled Shilo soon after the war with the Philistines. Although it lost its distinction as the seat of the Tabernacle, and of government, in 1050 BCE, Shilo remained a major Jewish town for the next eleven hundred years. It survived the destruction of the First Temple in 586 BCE[36] and also the Great Revolt against Rome in 66-70 CE, which ended in the destruction of Jerusalem. Shilo's residents participated in the Bar Kokhba Revolt in 132–35.[37]

The Jews of Shilo, like the Jews of the surrounding towns, were murdered by the Roman legions following Bar Kokhba's defeat.[38] Like its surrounding communities of Beit-El, Levona, Eli, and Ofra, among dozens of others, Shilo's reconstitution after the 1967 Six Day War was a fulfillment of the Mandate for Palestine.

PALESTINIAN THEFT OF JEWISH ARTIFACTS

The pitcher found in the layer of ashes at Tel Shilo was stolen a week after its discovery was made public.[39]

The identity of the thieves is unknown, but the theft, which removed additional proof of the accuracy of the biblical account of Shilo's history, is in keeping with what has become a routine Palestinian practice of destroying Jewish archaeological sites. For instance, on October 1, 2000, shortly after the launch of the Palestinian terror war, a Palestinian mob attacked Joseph's Tomb in Nablus, with the backing of Palestinian security forces. The rioters shot an Israeli border guard who was part of the security detail assigned to the holy site. Palestinian security commanders refused to allow his medical evacuation. As a consequence, nineteen-year-old Corporal Madhat Yusuf bled to death at Joseph's Tomb.[40]

Israeli forces abandoned the site, after receiving guarantees from Palestinian security commanders that they would protect it. But just two hours after the IDF withdrew, the Palestinians raided the site and burned the holy books and the yeshiva inside. Three days later the Palestinians repainted the domed roof of the tomb green as they prepared to transform it into a mosque.[41]

The site that has suffered the most from the Palestinian campaign of cultural and historic theft has been the Temple Mount. Following the

1967 Six Day War, in an act of unprecedented national self-abnegation, Israeli authorities allowed the Islamic religious trust or *waqf* to retain control of the Temple Mount, which the IDF had just liberated from Jordanian occupation forces.[42]

The Temple Mount is the most important archaeological site in Israel. It is also the holiest site in Judaism. According to Jewish tradition, the Temple Mount is where the world was created; it is also where Abraham bound Isaac. And, as the historical record proves, the Temple Mount is the site of the Jewish people's First and Second Temples.[43]

Since 1967, the *waqf* has repeatedly carried out unauthorized construction activities beneath the Temple Mount, in a bid to transform the cavernous area into a massive mosque. These unauthorized building activities have caused immense destruction of antiquities, including sacred articles as well as prosaic ones from the First and Second Temple periods and from the Byzantine period as well.[44]

According to Dr. Mordechai Kedar, an Arab studies expert from Bar-Ilan University, "These actions [by the *waqf*] are being carried out in the context of a practice known in Arabic as *Tams al-ma'alem,* an expression that means, 'erasing the signs' in the sense of destroying the relics of all cultures that preceded Islam."[45]

Beginning in 1995, the *waqf* embarked on what became a four-year undertaking, coordinated with the Hamas-aligned Israeli Islamic Movement, to destroy the archaeological remains of the Jewish temples. Over that period, the *waqf* removed some three hundred truckloads, or ten thousand tons of earth filled with priceless artifacts. It unloaded the earth at the municipal garbage dump in the Kidron Valley and in other locations outside the Old City.[46]

In December 2004 the private Ir David (City of David) Foundation funded an unprecedented archaeological endeavor. Led by archaeologists from Bar-Ilan University, volunteers began sifting through the ten thousand tons of debris from the Temple Mount. The debris was transferred from the city garbage dumps to the Tzurim Valley National Park at the foot of Mount Scopus, overlooking the Temple Mount.

By late 2006 the volunteers had discovered relics from the First and Second Temple periods; from prehistoric times, like ten-thousand-year-old flint tools; and from the times of the Jebusites and the Canaanite periods of the Iron Age.[47] Had it not been for the financial assistance of international donors and the labors of regular Israelis from all walks of life who volunteered to sift through the rubble by hand, these relics would have been lost forever.

The Palestinian campaign against Jerusalem is unquestionably the most offensive example of their ill intentions toward Israel and the Jewish people. The destruction of the Temple Mount is a cultural crime certainly no less damaging than the Taliban's destruction of the ancient Buddhist Bamiyan statues in Afghanistan in March 2001.[48] And yet while UNESCO, like much of the rest of the world, united in condemning the Taliban, UNESCO has joined the Palestinians and the wider Islamic world in their campaign to erase the Jewish history of Jerusalem.

But these efforts are doomed to fail. On an almost-daily basis, new historical evidence of the historical centrality of Jerusalem to the Jews, and of the Jews to Jerusalem, is uncovered.

For instance, in December 2010, archaeologists discovered a drainage canal beneath an ancient street linking the original city of Jerusalem—David's City—and the Temple Mount. The ancient street has been only partially excavated. By excavating the sewer, archaeologists were able to ascertain with certainty the path of the road above.

As Roni Reich from the Israel Antiquities Authority explained to Fox News, "The channel and the street reaffirm the existence of Jewish life of the Jewish city, of the Temple city of two thousand years ago." The archaeologists also found evidence that the sewer was used as an escape route for Jews fleeing the Roman army that overran the city in 70 CE.[49] Among other artifacts found at the site were the remains of food eaten by Jews hiding from the Romans in the sewage canal.[50]

THE HISTORY OF JEWISH SETTLEMENT IN ISRAEL

Just as thousands of Jews have volunteered their time to sift through the rubble of the Temple Mount to preserve what otherwise would have been destroyed by the *waqf*, so during the eighteen hundred years between the destruction of the Second Temple and the Second Jewish Commonwealth and the establishment of the State of Israel, Jews have tenaciously maintained a presence in Israel, often in the face of massive hardship and persecution. At no time have there been no Jews in the Land of Israel.[51] And whenever Jews had the opportunity to return to Israel in significant numbers, they did so.

According to Josephus, the Romans forcibly exiled some 75,000 Jews from the Land of Israel after the Bar Kokhba rebellion,[52] but for several centuries after the onset of the Roman rule, the Jews nonetheless remained a majority of the population of the Land of Israel. The centers of Jewish life during this period were in the Galilee, southern Judea, and the coastal plain. According to the historian Michael Avi-Yonah, after the defeat of the Bar Kokhba rebellion, Jews remained three-quarters of the population of the Galilee and a quarter of the population of the coastal plain and Judea.[53]

During the Byzantine period, Jews suffered from massive persecution. After Bar Kokhba and his army were defeated, the number of Jewish settlements in the Land of Israel stood at two hundred. By the end of the Byzantine period, only fifty remained. The Jewish population dwindled from 750,000–800,000 at the start of the Christian conquest to 150,000–200,000, or 10–15 percent of the population, when it ended.[54]

During the early Islamic conquest, with the institution of the Laws of Omar, which forced all non-Muslims into subservient status as dhimmis, the Jewish population of the Land of Israel dwindled still further. The prohibitive land taxes levied on non-Muslims during this period forced the Jews to abandon agriculture and settle in the cities. The main population centers for the Jews during these years were Jerusalem, Hebron, Rafah, Haifa, Acre, and Tyre.[55]

During the Crusader conquest of the Land of Israel, the Jews' position worsened even further. Due to the Crusaders' campaign of expulsion and massacre, the Jewish population of the Land of Israel had dwindled to fewer than two thousand by the late thirteenth century. The historian Moshe Gil has documented accounts by Jews who referred to the Crusader oppression and massacre of the Jews as nothing short of the "destruction of the Jewish population of Palestine."[56]

During the Mamluk period (1291–1517), the Land of Israel for the first time developed a large Muslim majority, as masses of Arabs fleeing from the Mongol invasion of Arabia settled there. The small Jewish population remained concentrated in the major cities of Jerusalem, Hebron, Gaza, Tiberias, Beit Shean, Ramle, and Safed.[57]

The Jews' position improved, and their numbers expanded, during the Ottoman period (1517–1917). The Ottoman Turks permitted Jews who had been expelled from Spain to settle in Israel. At the outset of the Ottoman reign, there were 6,000 Jews in Israel out of an overall population of 300,000, accounting for just 2 percent of the population.[58]

By 1907 the British consul in Jerusalem estimated that there were 100,000 Jews in the Land of Israel out of a total population of 400,000 or 450,000.[59] As a result, on the eve of World War I, Jews made up a higher percentage of the population of the Land of Israel than they did of any other country.[60] By the dawn of modern Zionism, Jews already comprised the majority of the population of Jerusalem, and there were large and growing Jewish communities in Hebron, Tiberias, and Safed.[61]

The people of Israel, and indeed the Jewish people worldwide, are a community of memory. The reconstitution of the Jewish state in the Land of Israel is an unprecedented historic accomplishment. No other indigenous people has preserved its national identity for so long and against such great odds, only to repatriate itself to its historic homeland—sometimes with the help of the nations of the world, sometimes in defiance of their collective will. The magnitude of the Jews' accomplishment in reestablishing their state is as remarkable as the Palestinians' obscene attempt to distort this accomplishment and destroy the historic record.

Through their collective memory, and their tenacious, stubborn attachment to the Land of Israel, the Jews preserved their national rights. And it was in recognition of this remarkable feat that in 1922, the nations of the world determined that the legal right to sovereignty over the Land of Israel belongs to the Jewish people alone.

PART III

PROBABLE FALLOUT

CHAPTER 14

Likely Palestinian Responses

In an interview with an Israeli newspaper a few weeks before the January 2013 Israeli elections, PA chairman and Fatah chief Mahmoud Abbas threatened to resign if the Israeli government wasn't forthcoming with major concessions. As he put it, "If there is no progress [in the peace process] even after the election I will take the phone and call [Prime Minister Benjamin] Netanyahu. . . . I'll tell him . . . 'Sit in the chair here instead of me, take the keys, and you will be responsible for the Palestinian Authority.'"[1]

Abbas's statement was nothing new. Since mid-2008, he has threatened to dismantle the Palestinian Authority on a dozen different occasions.[2] Moreover, one could be excused for dismissing these threats, considering that Abbas has held on to power even though his term of office expired in January 2009. Forget handing over the keys to Netanyahu—Abbas refuses to hand them over even to another Palestinian.[3]

As one senior Fatah member lamented in an op-ed published in the Palestinian media, Abbas has arrogated to himself absolute power over all facets of Palestinian society. With each passing day, Abbas displays less interest in sharing, much less abandoning, his hold on Palestinian affairs.[4]

Throughout his long career as a senior PLO operative, Abbas has employed political warfare as a means of demoralizing Israeli society and strengthening Israel's radical Left, with an end goal of compelling Israel to make unilateral concessions to the PLO. So too he has manipulated the diplomatic process to make the United States psychologically dependent on his continued role at the helm of the Palestinians.

In the Israeli context, by threatening to resign, Abbas seeks to intimidate Israeli voters into believing that if Israel's elected leaders are not forthcoming with concessions to the Palestinians, then demographic disaster awaits their country. As we saw in Chapter 9, the Israeli Left has accepted the Palestinian Authority's false population count, which has led them to insist that Israel's only salvation is the PLO—led by Mahmoud Abbas.

In the Western context, as we have seen, the U.S. bases its commitment to Palestinian statehood on its faith in Abbas and—before Abbas fired him—Salam Fayyad as "reformers" and "moderates." As the years have passed, and it has become increasingly apparent that there is no significant Palestinian constituency for peace with Israel, American dependence on the myth of Abbas's moderation has grown. In this light, Abbas's threats to resign constitute nothing less than a political version of putting a gun to the heads of Western policy makers. Every time Abbas threatens to resign, he is telling Washington—and Europe—that unless they expand their financial assistance to his government and widen their diplomatic support for his anti-Israel political warfare, he will abandon them.

In the weeks before Israel's 2013 elections, Abbas went on Israeli television and claimed that he would give up his demand that any final peace deal include unlimited immigration of foreign-born Arabs into Israel, and so he reinforced the Left's faith that he is Israel's irreplaceable savior. While Abbas's statement made headlines, the media failed to note that, just moments after his interview was broadcast, Abbas personally denied his own statement in a press release to the Palestinian media.[5] In other words, like his threat to resign, his words of peace were not fit for Palestinian consumption.

HOW WOULD THE PALESTINIAN PEOPLE RESPOND TO A ONE-STATE PLAN?

Since Abbas's behavior makes clear that he has no intention of abandoning power or dissolving the Palestinian Authority, the question of how he, and the people he will not stop leading, would respond to an Israeli decision to apply Israeli law to Judea and Samaria is necessarily the first question we must consider in analyzing possible fallout from such a move.

Here it is important to distinguish between Palestinian civilians and the Palestinian leadership in Fatah and Hamas. As we saw in Chapter 10, polling data show that Palestinians admire Israeli democracy and oppose an Israeli withdrawal from Judea and Samaria.[6] It is reasonable, then, to assume that shortly after Israel applies its laws to Judea and Samaria, the majority of Palestinians will register for Israeli permanent residency status.

The status of permanent resident will immediately and vastly improve the Palestinians' economic position. They will be provided with open access to the Israeli job market, and they will receive welfare and health benefits equal to those enjoyed by Israeli citizens. Today Palestinians need permits to work inside the 1949 armistice lines, and the health care they receive from the Palestinian system is inferior to that provided by Israeli hospitals and physicians.

In light of the precedent set by both Jerusalem Arabs and the Druze in the Golan Heights, it can be reasonably assumed that only a small number of Palestinians are likely to apply for full Israeli citizenship. Their unwillingness to become Israeli citizens will stem from two causes. First, the Palestinian Authority, as well as the various terrorist organizations operating in Judea and Samaria, will probably release statements branding any Palestinian who applies for Israeli citizenship a traitor.

The prospect that, contrary to expectations, the Palestinians will apply en masse for Israeli citizenship, and that as a consequence Israel's citizenship rolls will expand massively, is an important issue for policy makers to consider. But we need to keep our sense of proportion. As we saw in Chapter 9, were all the Palestinians of Judea and Samaria to apply for and receive Israeli citizenship, the Jews would still maintain a solid two-thirds majority of the population of the State of Israel. Abbas's demographic threat is empty.

As for the Palestinian leadership, Fatah and Hamas alike will likely respond to such an Israeli move as they have responded to every Israeli move. Since Hamas was established in 1988, and certainly since the Palestinian Authority was established in 1994, Hamas and Fatah have each tried to win the support of the Palestinian public at the other's expense. They have done so, among other things, by seeking to outdo one another in carrying out terror attacks against Israelis.

But their responses are limited by their organizational capacities. They can't do more than they can do, so to speak.

The Palestinians have two means of responding to an Israeli decision to apply Israeli law to Judea and Samaria: terrorism and diplomatic warfare. But these are, of course, the same means available to them today, when the Israeli government is not considering applying Israeli law to the areas—and the Palestinians are already operating at full capacity or near-full capacity in both spheres. As a result, it is difficult to imagine how the Palestinians could respond more forcefully to an Israeli one-state plan than they are already behaving on a daily basis.

The Terrorism Option

Ever since the Palestinian Authority was established in 1994, the United States has played an active role in training Palestinian security forces. In the 1990s the CIA was responsible for that training. And many of the security forces trained by the CIA played major roles in the terror war against Israel that began in September 2000.[7] Between 2005 and January 2013, the United States allocated $629 million to train a force of 6,700 Palestinian soldiers and officers, organized in eleven battalions, deployed throughout Judea and Samaria.[8]

In May 2010 IDF Major General Avi Mizrahi, commander of Israel's Central Command, which includes Judea and Samaria, described these U.S.-trained forces' latent capacities. "This is a well-trained force," he explained, "better equipped than its predecessors and trained by the U.S. The significance of this is that at the start of a new battle [with the Palestinians], the price that we will pay will be higher. A force like this one can shut down a built-up area with four snipers. This is deadly. . . . They have offensive capabilities and we aren't expecting them to give up."[9]

With these troops now fully trained—and capable of training others—Lieutenant General Michael Moeller, who commanded the U.S. training program until December 2012, told the House Foreign Affairs Subcommittee on the Middle East and South Asia that the next step for America was to help the Palestinian security forces "develop indigenous readiness, training, and logistics programs and the capability to maintain/sustain their force structure readiness and infrastructure."[10]

In other words, the United States was working to transform these disparate units into a self-sustaining, organized military.

U.S. commanders share Mizrahi's assessment that these U.S.-trained

Palestinian forces can be expected in the future to fight Israel. In a speech delivered in Washington in May 2009, Moeller's predecessor, Lieutenant General Keith Dayton, said that if the U.S.-trained Palestinian army did not see the establishment of a Palestinian state within a short period, it would likely turn its arms on Israel.[11]

There is nothing surprising about the nature of these forces. During the Palestinian terror war that followed Arafat's rejection of statehood and peace with Israel at Camp David, many of the more devastating Palestinian terror attacks were carried out by Palestinian security forces trained by the CIA. Israel had been asking the United States to curtail its training of Palestinian security forces since at least November 1999, reportedly warning U.S. officials that the Palestinian troops were liable to use the knowledge they gained from the U.S. training program to enhance terrorist capabilities against Israel. But these warnings made no impression.[12]

Beginning in 2012, reports began surfacing that shed light on intelligence-gathering operations that the Palestinians were running on Israeli communities in Judea and Samaria. PA intelligence operatives were repeatedly probing the communities' security systems. For Israeli security personnel on the ground, it is apparent that if terrorist groups decide to carry out a mass casualty attack against a Jewish community in Judea and Samaria, they have the capacity to do so.[13]

Such a massacre would be supported morally by Palestinian society. The abject refusal of all Palestinian leaders to condemn or disavow terrorism as evil; the Palestinian media's daily demonization and dehumanization of Israelis; and Palestinian society's continuous lionization of Palestinian terrorists would all provide the moral cover for such an act of mass slaughter of civilians.

From 1996 through 2002, Palestinian terrorists were able to carry out terrorist attacks against Israelis in Judea and Samaria and within the 1949 armistice lines almost at will. This capability owed to the PLO's security control of the major Palestinian towns and villages. With Arafat and his deputies in charge, terrorists could plan attacks, dispatch operatives from the safety of these population centers, and not worry that the IDF would respond by destroying their infrastructure.

But in April 2002, the IDF responded to the Palestinian terrorist war with Operation Defensive Shield. During the course of the operation,

Israeli forces took control of the Palestinian population centers in Judea and Samaria that had been transferred to PLO control in late 1995 and early 1996. Israel has largely preserved its security control of those areas ever since.

As General Mizrahi explained, largely through their American-trained security forces, over the decade since Operation Defensive Shield, the Palestinians have rebuilt their capacity to carry out mass attacks against Israeli targets that Israel destroyed from 2002 through 2004.

But despite their rebuilt capabilities, the Palestinians have largely opted not to carry out such attacks to date. Again, in light of the anti-Jewish indoctrination that permeates all layers of Palestinian society, their choice to stand down does not owe to some newfound love of Israel or desire for peace. It is about self-preservation. The Palestinians recognize that any mass terror attack they would conduct would cause Israel to take military action that would destroy their capacity to carry out further attacks in the future.

Indeed, Israel wouldn't just retaliate for a specific attack. If the Palestinians were to carry out a mass casualty attack against Israel, that aggression would provide Israel with an opportunity to dismantle the PA security forces completely.

True, this cost-benefit analysis may be discarded. Given Palestinian society's enthusiastic support for terrorism, the Palestinian leadership in Fatah and Hamas alike could throw caution and rationality to the wind and perpetrate a massacre anyway. But they would pay a price for their action.

Such an attack would likely be a one-time deal. With Israel in control of the security situation on the ground, the Palestinians' desire and capacity to commit terrorism is not matched by the capacity to carry out a sustained campaign of mass terrorism like the one that lasted from September 2000 to April 2002. Today Israel's military control of Judea and Samaria renders such a campaign impossible.

The Diplomatic Option

On the night of March 11, 2011, Palestinian terrorists entered the home of Ehud and Ruth Fogel and their six children in Itamar, an Israeli community in Samaria. The family was asleep. The terrorists butchered them.

They decapitated three-month-old Hadas Fogel. They mutilated Ehud and Ruth, eleven-year-old Yoav Fogel, and four-year-old Elad Fogel. The Fogels' bodies were found by twelve-year-old Tamar Fogel when she returned home from a friend's house. Left alive were two of her brothers, whom the terrorists had apparently not seen. When security forces arrived, they found two-year-old Yishai Fogel standing in a pool of blood at his parents' bedside trying to wake them up.

The international media largely ignored the story, focusing instead on Israel's response to the massacre.[14]

This episode illustrates an important fact: Palestinian terror has never been an end unto itself; rather, it has proven an extremely effective political tool. It has ensnared Israel in a trap in which it loses no matter what it does. When Israel opts not to respond to an act of Palestinian terrorism, Palestinian leaders can rally their people because Israel's nonresponse has made it look toothless and weak, while the Palestinians look strong and powerful. But when Israel does respond, the Palestinians utilize the international outcry to rally foreign sympathy.

More generally, since the establishment of the PLO in 1964, none of the dozens of UN Security Council resolutions concerning the Arab-Israeli conflict has focused on Palestinian terrorism. Instead, the basis for nearly all international condemnations of Israel—at the UN, in Europe, and in academic circles in the United States and throughout the Western world—has been Israel's defensive measures against Palestinian terrorism.

Due to this deformed international—and particularly Western—discourse on Israel, the Palestinians' most powerful weapon against the Jewish state is their ability to use the tools of diplomacy and political warfare to isolate Israel internationally. Their political war against Israel has brought about the situation in which Israel is far weaker diplomatically than the Palestinians are.

No doubt the Palestinian leadership—particularly Fatah—will respond to an Israeli decision to apply Israeli law to Judea and Samaria by seeking to provoke as strong an international backlash as possible. But although the Palestinians have reserve capacity to carry out acts of mass terrorism against Israel, it is far from clear that they have reserve diplomatic capacity. For years they have been operating in the diplomatic arena at full throttle.

As we saw in previous chapters, under international law Israel has a stronger legal claim to sovereignty over Judea and Samaria than do the Palestinians. Its national and historic rights to the areas are also stronger than those of the Palestinians. And yet in the international discourse, Israel is criminalized as a colonialist, illegitimate occupier of these lands, and the Palestinians are viewed as the sole legitimate, indigenous sovereign.

One area where the Palestinians seek to exploit their diplomatic strength against Israel is "lawfare," the use of the language of law to conduct political war against a state.[15] The chief venue where the Palestinians seek to escalate their lawfare operations against Israel is the International Criminal Court.

The International Criminal Court (ICC) was established in 2002, by the power of the 1998 Treaty of Rome, to investigate and prosecute genocide, crimes against humanity, war crimes, and the crime of aggression. The ICC can investigate alleged crimes that took place only in states that signed the Rome Treaty or in areas where the UN Security Council has empowered it to operate.[16]

In 2009 a minister in the Palestinian Authority, purporting to act on behalf of "Palestine," submitted a letter authorizing the ICC to prosecute crimes that had taken place on the soil of "Palestine." The Palestinians submitted their request in order to be able bring war crimes complaints against Israelis without UN Security Council authorization.[17] In the years since then, hundreds of complaints against Israelis have already been submitted to the ICC prosecutor.[18]

After three years of public deliberations, the ICC prosecutor explained that the court could not accept the Palestinian request due to the fact that "Palestine" is not a state. He hinted, however, that if the PLO were to win nonmember-observer-state status in the UN General Assembly, he would reverse his position and accept the request.[19]

In September 2011, the PLO formally requested that the UN Security Council accept Palestine as a UN member state. This initiative failed, but following the publication of the ICC prosecutor's statement, the PLO amended its UN agenda. In 2012 it asked the General Assembly for recognition as a nonmember observer state.

In November 2012 the UN General Assembly passed Resolution 67/19, which upgraded the PLO's status from UN observer to nonmember observer state. The General Assembly's determination could cause the ICC prosecutor to agree to accept ICC jurisdiction over crimes committed on the soil of the "state of Palestine."[20] That in turn could pave the way for the commencement of war crimes tribunals against Israelis. This still-unimplemented threat is what the Palestinians hold over Israel's head as a means of further constraining its diplomatic and military maneuver room.

The problem with the Palestinians' threat is that it is far from clear that the ICC is really a powerful weapon in their war on Israel. War crime complaints against Israel at the ICC might lead to trials of Israeli politicians, civilians, and military personnel for imagined crimes; but then again, they might not. More likely, Palestinian membership in the ICC will expose Palestinians to liability for charges of war crimes and crimes against humanity for their terrorist attacks against Israelis.[21] And certainly there are thousands of Israelis who would quickly submit such complaints to the ICC against the Palestinians.

Moreover, as the legal scholar Eugene Kontorovich has argued, even if the ICC accepts the PLO's request to accept them as a signatory on the Rome Treaty, it is doubtful that it would be willing to adjudicate any cases regarding alleged Israeli war crimes against Palestinians in "Palestine." One reason is that "Palestine has no set borders, and therefore determination of whether a crime occurred in its territory is beyond the power of the ICC."[22]

Moreover, if the PLO responds to an Israeli decision to apply Israeli law to Judea and Samaria by requesting ICC prosecutions of Israelis, such a move would actually not constitute a new campaign. The campaign is already an integral component of common Palestinian practice, and Israel will not require any new tools to cope with it.

Moreover, given the frivolousness of the Palestinian claims against Israel, once Israel adopts a policy predicated on defending its rights rather than appeasing Palestinians who seek its destruction, it will be far more capable of defending itself against such charges at the ICC and in any other diplomatic arena.

Beyond whatever else the Palestinians might do in response to Israel's move, they might also call for an international boycott of Israel. But the attractiveness of Israel's economy minimizes the capacity of political prejudices to dictate economic policy. In Britain, for instance, hatred for Israel is galloping, yet bilateral trade between Israel and Britain is booming and growing, with the trade balance in Israel's favor. It increased from $5.66 billion in 2011 to $5.77 billion in 2012. And between 2010 and 2011, it rose 34 percent. Israel is the United Kingdom's largest single trading partner in the Middle East and North Africa.[23]

Following an Israeli decision to apply Israeli law to Judea and Samaria, the Palestinians might expand their calls for international support. They might call for the Arab states to invade Israel on their behalf. They might call for the UN or NATO or the European Union to deploy forces to protect them from Israel. They might call for the EU to impose an economic boycott on Israel. We shall discuss the prospects of such calls being answered in the next two chapters. But what is clear is that the Palestinians can only call for such actions. They cannot determine whether their call will be answered.

Despite their diplomatic power and their terrorist aspirations and capacities, the Palestinians are not in a position to independently scuttle an Israeli decision to implement Israeli law in Judea and Samaria. Militarily, they lack the capability to sustain a terrorist offensive against Israel that could either defeat it or break its will politically. Diplomatically, while their political warfare campaign has severely weakened Israel's international position, they cannot escalate the war because they are already using their entire arsenal.

They can escalate their calls for international assistance, even calling for international invasions of Israel, either by Arab armies or by European forces. But they cannot compel either the Arabs or the Europeans to accede to their wishes.

CHAPTER 15

Likely Regional Responses

Israel declared its independence on May 15, 1948. Immediately thereafter it was invaded by the armies of Egypt, Jordan, Lebanon, Syria, and Iraq, with the full backing of the Arab League. The purpose of that pan-Arab invasion was to destroy the nascent Jewish state.[1] In 1979, Israel signed a formal peace treaty with Egypt. In 1994 it signed a peace treaty with Jordan. But even so, the people of Egypt and Jordan never made peace with Israel. Hatred of Jews in these and every other Arab state is endemic, reaching levels of between 98 and 100 percent.[2]

Since late 2010, the Arab world has been in a state of political ferment. Regimes throughout the region have been overthrown and threatened. Populist Islamist forces compete with traditional authoritarians for power. Secular forces are also making themselves heard. Yet all these opposing forces share one central position: they all hate Israel, and they all desire to see it destroyed—whether in the name of Islam or Arab nationalism or simple anti-Semitism.[3] None of them accept Israel's right to exist—in any borders. None of them recognize the legal, historic, or national rights of the Jews to any part of the Land of Israel, including Judea and Samaria. Indeed, throughout the Arab world, as among the Palestinians, revised versions of history that airbrush out the Jews are widely disseminated and accepted as fact.

And so even before we consider the likely responses of Israel's Arab neighbors to an Israeli announcement that it is applying its sovereignty to Judea and Samaria, we must take as a foregone conclusion that all of Israel's neighbors will condemn the move. The question then, is whether they will do anything beyond that.

EGYPT

Egypt is the most powerful Arab state and the most strategically significant actor in the Arab world. Long a coveted prize for superpowers due to its control of the Suez Canal, Egypt was the object of competition between the British, the Germans, the Russians, and the Americans. From an American perspective, Egypt's peace treaty with Israel is the most important strategic U.S. achievement in the region. The treaty formally blocked the prospect for a pan-Arab war against the Jewish state and so neutralized what was long seen as the greatest threat to regional stability. Moreover, through its sponsorship of the treaty, and through it the Egyptian military, the United States secured itself a privileged status for its naval craft along the Suez Canal, and effectively neutralized the Soviet threat to U.S. power in the Arab world.

Egypt's strategic value, as well as the long-term viability of the Egyptian-Israeli peace, was called into serious question with the advent of the so-called Arab Spring. The Arab revolutionary wave was unleashed in December 2010 when a Tunisian peddler, frustrated by state corruption, set himself on fire.[4] Since then the entire Arab world has been beset by violence, uncertainty, and competing radicalisms. This is nowhere more apparent than in Egypt, which, after enjoying fifty years of political stability, underwent two revolutions since January 2011.

The first Egyptian revolution began with protests in Cairo in January 2011 and led to the forced resignation of the long-serving Egyptian president Hosni Mubarak the following month. Mubarak was first replaced by a military junta, which in turn was replaced in June 2012 by Mohamed Morsi and the Muslim Brotherhood, which won Egypt's first open parliamentary elections and presidential elections.

In June 2013 massive anti–Muslim Brotherhood political demonstrations brought millions to the streets of Egypt's major cities.[5] The Egyptian military then forced Morsi and the parliament to resign and installed an interim government.

In both the January 2011 demonstrations that led to Mubarak's ouster, and the June 2013 demonstrations that led to Morsi and the Muslim Brotherhood's overthrow, the main issue for the protest movements was economic discontent. Egypt is backward, economically and socially.

Half its population is illiterate. Seventy percent of Egyptians work in agriculture, yet Egypt still has to import half its food. In 2006 Egypt's trade deficit stood at 10 percent of its GDP, but by 2010 a rise in global food prices had pushed that deficit to 25 percent.[6]

Morsi took a bad situation and made it worse. By the time he was ejected from office on July 3, 2013, Egypt's foreign reserves were depleted.[7] The country had a mere two-month supply of wheat,[8] and one in two Egyptians were subsisting on less than two dollars a day. Two-fifths of Egyptians were starving.[9] Fuel shortages caused miles-long gas lines and electricity outages for most of the day.[10]

As if this weren't enough to bring the Egyptians into the streets, Morsi's government also took steps to transform Egypt into an Islamist state governed by Islamic religious law, pushing many fence sitters over the edge.

The first major demonstrations against the Muslim Brotherhood government began on November 22, 2012. That day Morsi announced that he was assuming dictatorial powers. His decisions, he said, would no longer be subject to judicial oversight. His directive gave him absolute "power to take all necessary measures and procedures" against any threat to the revolution.[11]

Morsi used his new powers to push through an Islamist constitution that set the stage for Egypt's transformation into an Islamist state. The new constitution ended any semblance of press freedom and placed women and religious minorities in jeopardy.[12]

Following Morsi's ouster on July 3, the military government announced the abrogation of the constitution that Morsi and his Islamist partners had pushed through.

The military's ouster of the Muslim Brotherhood did not end Egypt's problems, however. The Brotherhood rejected the legitimacy of the military coup. As the Egypt expert Lee Smith explains, the military, by siding with the protesters against the Muslim Brotherhood, favored one half of Egyptians against the other half.[13] After playing by the ostensible rules of democracy and winning the 2012 elections, the Muslim Brotherhood saw its victory taken away. The path to civil war was clear.

By late July, two hundred people had been killed in clashes between security forces and Muslim Brotherhood supporters.[14] The Sinai Peninsula saw thirty attacks by Islamist militants on security forces in three weeks.[15] Fears increased that the insurgency swelling in the Sinai would spark a countrywide civil war.

The military responded to protests by the Brotherhood and attacks by its Islamist supporters by clamping down on the group and its allies. For instance, in early September 2013, the Egyptian military began destroying homes and sealing tunnels in Rafah, the border town linking Gaza and the northern Sinai. The move was seen as a prelude to the establishment of a buffer zone ten kilometers long and five hundred meters wide to prevent terrorist infiltration from Gaza into Sinai.[16] So, too, the interim government was considering outlawing the Muslim Brotherhood as a whole.[17]

These moves made tactical sense, as the Suez Canal was coming under increased terrorist attack,[18] and Egypt was increasingly destabilized through civil unrest and terror. But the moves also spoke of the inherent instability and desperation of the situation. The Muslim Brotherhood has tens of millions of members and supporters in Egypt. They will not disappear and they will not be appeased.

What Revolutionary Egypt Means for Israel

Hatred of Israel and of Jews has been a constant undercurrent of the revolutionary waves hitting Egypt. This is unsurprising; after all, 98 percent of Egyptians express hostile feelings toward Jews.[19]

In 2011 anti-Mubarak placards pictured him with a hooked nose and a Star of David.[20] In 2013 anti-Morsi protesters and media outlets claimed that the Muslim Brotherhood was in cahoots with Israel and the United States to suppress the Egyptian people.[21] In response to those protests, the Brotherhood and its supporters insisted that the protesters and the military were controlled by Jews. In fact, the Brotherhood alleged that Egypt's interim president, Adly Mansour, and its interim vice president, Muhammad El-Baradei, were Jewish.[22]

Since Mubarak's overthrow, Egyptian aggression against Israel has risen.

Under Mubarak Egypt provided Israel with half of its natural gas supply. Israel had agreed to let itself depend on Egyptian gas on the belief that making the Israeli economy codependent with Egypt's would effectively cement the peace between the two countries. Although Israel and Egypt had been in a formal state of peace since 1981, Egypt had refused—in material breach of its treaty obligations—to normalize its relations with Israel.

Between the start of the Egyptian revolution in January 2011 and April 2012, terrorists blew up the gas pipeline that runs between Israel and Egypt twelve times. That April Egypt's natural gas company informed Israel that it was abrogating its contract to supply the country with gas.[23] The East Mediterranean Gas Company, the jointly owned Israeli-Egyptian-U.S. company that operated the gas pipeline, responded that abrogating the contract was unlawful and constituted a material breach of the Egypt-Israel peace treaty. But it had no one to talk to.

By cutting the gas supply to Israel, Egypt put Israel's electricity grid at risk. The bombings of the pipeline and the military government's cancellation of the gas contract demonstrated that the peace treaty would never be more than a cease-fire agreement.

After Morsi was inaugurated president on June 30, 2012, Israel's relations with Egypt continued to deteriorate. Morsi is a virulent anti-Semite. In January 2013 the U.S. media reported on a series of interviews that Morsi had given in 2010 as a senior official in the Muslim Brotherhood. In them, he referred to Jews as "apes and pigs" and said that Egyptians must "nurse our children and our grandchildren on hatred" for Jews.[24]

The White House condemned Morsi's remarks after they were published in the *New York Times*. Morsi reacted to the burgeoning scandal by lamely muttering that his remarks had been "taken out of context." Then in a subsequent meeting with U.S. senators in Cairo, Morsi blamed the U.S. media—which, he intoned, is controlled by the Jews—for stirring up the controversy over his anti-Jewish remarks.[25]

But with 98 percent of Egyptians thinking ill of Jews, Morsi was clearly channeling the sentiments of virtually all of his countrymen. Calling Jews animals is a way for Egyptian leaders—secular and Islamist alike—to unify Egyptian society around themselves.

Egypt's Probable Response

After the Egyptian military overthrew Morsi, Lee Smith warned that in order to avert civil war, Egypt's military leadership would likely go to war against Israel. In his words, "A competent leader . . . will soon come to see that he has no choice but to make a virtue of necessity and export the one commodity that Egypt has in abundance—violence. So, why not bind the warring, immature, and grandiose Egyptian factions together in a pact against Israel, the country's sole transcendent object of loathing?"[26]

From an Israeli perspective, the prospect of war with Egypt is deeply problematic. Egypt, since signing its peace treaty with Israel, has received more than $50 billion in U.S. military aid. The power and range of the U.S.-trained and -armed Egyptian military makes it the most daunting conventional military threat that Israel has ever faced. The U.S.-platform-based Egyptian military of today is far more powerful than the Soviet-platform-based Egyptian military that Israel was hard-pressed to defeat in the 1973 Yom Kippur War. And in that war, the strategic depth of the Sinai Peninsula kept the main battles far away from Israel's population centers. A future war would be fought within range of all Israel's major metropolitan centers.

Yet for all Egypt's sophisticated hardware, it is far from clear that it has the logistical capacity to move its U.S.-made M1A1 Abrams tanks across the Sinai to engage Israeli forces, and to replenish its forces with spare parts, food, and reinforcements. Egypt is, in fact, impoverished. A war with Israel would likely be militarily futile and economically cataclysmic.

Moreover, following its ouster of the Muslim Brotherhood, the Egyptian military has displayed hostility rather than comity toward Hamas-controlled Gaza. It used the Muslim Brotherhood's fraternal relations with Hamas—the Palestinian Muslim Brotherhood—as a means to discredit it. Indeed, the military criminalized Morsi and the Brotherhood by accusing them of colluding with Hamas.[27] The two Brotherhood branches' initial steps toward incorporating Gaza into Egypt were used as a pretense for accusing them of implementing a nefarious Israeli-U.S. plot to undermine Egyptian sovereignty over the Sinai and pave the way for an Israeli conquest there.

With violence between Egyptian military forces and Islamist terror militias in Sinai allied with Hamas rising daily, by September 2013, leaders of Fatah began stating openly their hope that the Egyptian military would invade Gaza and reinstall them in power.[28] The concept of Egypt invading Gaza, or using Palestinian proxies to stage a coup, was not unfounded. Egyptian intelligence officers had reportedly become involved in training anti-Hamas operatives in Gaza.

But even in the unlikely event that Egypt decides to expand its battlefield to include Gaza and does in fact overthrow Hamas and install Fatah in power, such moves will not make Egypt more likely to go to war against Israel. Egypt would topple Hamas to protect its military regime from its jihadist enemies, not to help the Palestinians.

Furthermore, reinstating Fatah in power in Gaza would not expand the movement's options for attacking Israel following an Israeli decision to apply its law to Judea and Samaria. Fatah, which is not as powerful as the Egyptian military, would face the prospect of fighting its own civil war against Hamas and its supporters in Gaza, which could expand to Judea and Samaria. Such a scenario would leave Abbas and his colleagues with little opportunity to lash out at Israel.

Regardless of who will lead Gaza in the future, two aspects of the chaos in Egypt indicate that Israel needn't be overly concerned about its southern neighbor attacking it in response to the implementation of Israeli law in Judea and Samaria.

First, if Egypt decides it wishes to go to war with Israel, it can invent any pretext—from the sublime to the ridiculous—for doing so. During Mubarak's tenure in office, for instance, Egyptian officials accused Israel's Mossad spy agency of deploying sharks to Egypt's beaches to attack tourists. Subsequently, migratory birds fell prey to Egyptian security services who "arrested" them on suspicion of espionage.[29] But if Egypt decides that prudence is the better part of virtue and resists the temptation to wage war against Israel, then nothing Israel does will persuade it to alter that course either.

In other words, Egypt will go to war with Israel if its leaders determine that doing so will advance the interests of Egypt—and not out of solidarity with the Palestinians. A Palestinian call to war will have no impact on Egypt's decision making.

If war with Egypt comes, it will be due to internal developments within Egypt and not in response to any Israeli move. Therefore, Israel should feel free to advance its national interests without regard for Egypt's domestic pathologies.

JORDAN

Jordan's Obeidat Bedouin tribe is one of the largest in the kingdom. Until recently, the Obeidat were intimately tied to the Hashemite regime.

In October 2012 Jordan's King Abdullah II appointed a member of the tribe, Walid Obeidat, to serve as Jordan's ambassador to Israel. The tribe responded with a degree of fury that shocked regime watchers worldwide.

For most of Jordan's history, the Bedouins supported the kingdom's strategic ties to Israel. Those ties developed decades before Jordan and Israel signed their peace treaty in 1994. As we saw in Chapters 4 and 6, since 1970 Israel has acted as Jordan's protector, defending the monarchy of the Hashemite Bedouin tribe from Syria and the PLO. Israel's relationship with the Hashemites was an open secret, and as the principal supporters of the regime, Jordan's other Bedouin tribes knew about it and supported it.

But by late 2012, that support had all but disappeared. Rather than celebrate the appointment of one of their members to serve in the sensitive and key diplomatic posting, or let it pass by unremarked, tribal leaders responded by calling for the cancellation of Jordan's peace treaty with the Jewish state.[30]

As Assaf David, an expert on Jordanian society and politics told *The Times of Israel,* the Obeidat tribe's violent response to Walid Obeidat's posting to Tel Aviv was a telling indicator of how "relations between the tribes and the regime have drastically deteriorated," in recent years.[31]

Jordan is made up of three distinct population groups. Ethnic Palestinians constitute 80 percent of the population,[32] non-Hashemite Bedouins are the second-largest group, and members of the ruling Hashemite tribe comprise the smallest population group.

Due to the demographic challenges that the Palestinian majority presents to the ruling Hashemites, the regime has always depended on Western sponsors for its survival. The Hashemites were first installed in power and defended by the British. The British were eventually replaced by the Americans. And as we have seen, in 1970, when Israel intervened to prevent Syria from invading Jordan during its civil war, Israel emerged as the regime's primary protector.

The inherently precarious status of the Hashemite monarchy has made King Abdullah a bellwether of regional trends. In late 2004 he warned that Iran's rising role in Iraqi politics would form a "Shi'ite crescent" extending from Iran to Iraq, Syria, and Lebanon.[33] In 2013 he turned his attention to Sunni radicals, warning, "I see a Muslim Brotherhood crescent developing in Egypt and in Turkey."[34]

Abdullah occupies a unique position in the Arab world. He has no option but to remain a loyal ally to Israel and the United States; without their support, his regime would come crashing down. But his Hashemite tribe comprises only a small fraction of Jordan's population, and the two larger populations he rules—the Palestinians and the other Bedouins— are hostile to Israel and the United States. As a consequence, the Hashemite regime's likely, indeed all-but-certain response to an Israeli decision to apply its laws to Judea and Samaria will be to publicly condemn the move and privately celebrate it.

By applying Israeli law to Judea and Samaria, Israel will weaken both the PLO and Hamas, which would strengthen the Hashemites by limiting those groups' ability to undermine the stability of the Kingdom of Jordan.

Bedouin support for the Hashemite regime is unraveling today against the backdrop of the larger revolutionary atmosphere engulfing the wider Arab world. Given that Syria is in the midst of a bloody civil war, and the Egyptian military is now in open conflict with the popularly elected Muslim Brotherhood and their Islamist allies among the Bedouin tribes in the Sinai, the weakening of Bedouin support for the Hashemites is not in the least surprising. These regional upheavals make it impossible to assume that the Hashemites will long remain in power. As a consequence, when we are considering the likely Jordanian response to an Israeli decision to apply its laws to Judea and Samaria, it is not sufficient to determine how the Hashemite monarchy might greet the move. It is also important to consider the likely responses of the other populations in Jordan, specifically, the Palestinians and non-Hashemite Bedouins.

For the past several years, Abdullah has been limiting the civil rights of Palestinians in Jordan. He has arbitrarily stripped many Palestinians of their Jordanian citizenship,[35] removed Palestinians from the civil service and the Jordanian military,[36] and placed draconian limits on their parliamentary representation.[37]

But for their part, while Jordan's ethnic Palestinians certainly oppose the regime that treats them as second-class citizens, they are not interested in leaving the country and becoming citizens of a Palestinian state in Judea and Samaria or Gaza. A leaked 2008 cable from the U.S. embassy in Amman to the U.S. secretary of state exposed this basic reality. It demonstrated that, contrary to the Palestinian Authority and PLO's demand for the "right of return," most Jordanian Palestinians are uninterested in moving to Judea and Samaria. No less an authority than Mohammed Abu Bakr, the PLO representative in Amman, said, "If you tell me to go back to Jenin, I won't go."[38]

The Palestinian preference for remaining in Jordan will inform their response to an Israeli decision to apply Israeli law to Judea and Samaria. While they will no doubt loudly oppose the move, their operational response will be indistinguishable from that of the Iraqis or Saudis or Syrians. True, they are discriminated against for their Palestinian ethnic origins. But their Palestinian identity does not move them to action; it is at best symbolic and, in many cases, not a central component of their individual identity.

In a bid to obfuscate his abysmal treatment of the kingdom's Palestinian majority, Abdullah often singles out the Muslim Brotherhood as the primary threat to his regime. And there is certainly reason to give credence to his allegations. The Muslim Brotherhood is the only national political group in Jordan that has the organizational capacity to mount an independent challenge to the regime. It is the only non-Hashemite grouping that has both the national presence and the infrastructure to replace the Hashemites in power, in the event they are overthrown.

But even if the Muslim Brotherhood came to power in Jordan, it would lack the capacity to act on its aspiration to destroy Israel. Israeli control of Judea and Samaria effectively neutralizes the prospect of a major Jordanian military offensive against the Jewish state.

Moreover, like Egypt, Jordan depends on U.S. financial and military assistance to keep its economy afloat.[39] Even if the Jordanians felt they had a military option to attack Israel and wished to exercise it, they lack the financial capacity to finance such a war.[40] Indeed, such a military adventure would spell Jordan's economic ruin.

As for the Bedouin tribes, while they would no doubt oppose Israel's action (the leaked U.S. embassy memo noted that they believe they have the most to lose if the Palestinians of Jordan don't emigrate to Judea and Samaria), their capacity to strike out against Israel is also limited by Israel's control of the areas. With Israel exercising security control of the border with Jordan, the Bedouins will be hard-pressed to carry out a sustained or effective campaign against Israel.

SYRIA

The Arab world refers to May 15, 1948, the date Israel declared independence (and was invaded by five Arab states), as the Nakba, or "catastrophe." On May 15, 2011, several hundred ethnic Palestinians in Syria mustered on the Syrian side of the Golan Heights and marched toward the border with Israel under the banner of the so-called right of return, vowing to breach the border. The incident was the first time since Israel and Syria signed the disengagement of forces agreement on the Golan Heights in 1974 that Israel was attacked along its border with Syria.

The protesters took the Israelis by surprise, and the security forces lacked sufficient manpower at the border to stem the assault. Some two hundred marchers reportedly breached the border, although according to Israeli officials, many of them were only seeking asylum from the carnage in Syria. According to media reports, IDF forces killed thirteen after they attacked Israeli troops with rocks. [41]

In early June the Syrian governor of Quneitra, which borders Israel in southern Syria, leaked a government document showing that the regime of Syrian president Bashar Assad had planned, organized, and orchestrated the entire event. The document is worth considering at length for what it demonstrates about the regime's opportunistic use of conflict with Israel as a means of building public support.

The leaked report summarized a meeting that took place on May 14, 2011, between Quneitra's governor and the deputy chief of staff of the Syrian armed forces. As Michael Weiss, the reporter who broke the story at Britain's *Telegraph,* explained, the document set out "how the regime ordered the dispatching of 20 buses, each one with a passenger capacity of 47, to cross the border into Majdal Shams in the Golan Heights in order to precipitate a confrontation between Palestinian refugees and

Israeli soldiers and UN peacekeeping forces, thereby distracting international attention from the Syrian revolution." The memorandum instructed Quneitra's local officials:

> Permission is hereby granted allowing approaching crowds to cross the cease fire line (with Israel) towards the occupied Majdal-Shams, and to further allow them to engage physically with each other in front of United Nations agents and offices. Furthermore, there is no objection if a few shots are fired in the air.[42]

Ethnic Palestinians in Syria marched on the border for a second time on June 5, 2011, the anniversary of the start of the 1967 Six Day War. This time Israeli forces were ready. Twenty border breachers were killed. Some were killed when they refused Israeli forces' orders to stop their advance on the border. Others were killed when their fellow marchers threw incendiary devices at a marked minefield on the Syrian side, detonating two old land mines.[43]

As Weiss noted, Assad's intention in organizing the border assault was to deflect public attention away from the ongoing carnage in Syria. He clearly hoped that supporting the Palestinians in their war to destroy Israel would win him popularity points at home and perhaps in the wider Arab world.

The failure of Assad's ploy became clear later that month at the funerals for those killed in the second incident, held at Yarmouk refugee camp outside Damascus. Relatives of the dead attacked members of the regime-aligned terrorist group, the Popular Front for the Liberation of Palestine–General Command (PFLP-GC). They accused the PFLP-GC terrorists of sending their relatives to die for the regime. PFLP-GC gunmen responded by opening fire at the protesters, killing twenty.[44]

A PLO official at the camp blamed the regime for their deaths, saying, "They are bargaining with the blood of Palestinians to suit the Syrian regime."[45] In other words, by seeking to exploit popular hatred for Israel to garner support for his regime, Assad lost the support of Palestinians who didn't appreciate being used as cannon fodder.

Six months later Assad revealed the cynicism of his "support" for the Palestinians when he decided to exact a price for Palestinian abandonment of support for his dictatorship. On December 16, 2012, Syrian air force jets bombed the Yarmouk refugee camp, killing twenty-five.[46] The bombing caused a mass exodus of camp residents. On July 21, 2013, Syria allegedly attacked the Yarmouk camp with chemical weapons, killing twenty-two.[47]

Some 500,000 ethnic Palestinians live in Syria, mainly in UN refugee camps around Damascus. In early March 2013, Palestinian human rights activists in Syria reported that since the Syrian civil war began, more than a thousand Palestinians had been killed.[48] Thousands more had fled to Lebanon and Jordan.[49]

While Assad is just as likely to kill Palestinians as he is Israelis, opposition forces are no more civilized in their approach to the Palestinians and Israel.

By November 2012, much of the Syrian-Israeli border had fallen under the control of rebel forces, who in March 2013 took twenty-one Philippine soldiers from the UN observer mission on the Syrian side of the border hostage for several days.[50] Around the same time, rebels in control of a strip of land along the Syrian-Israeli border filmed themselves taking potshots at the UN signpost and threatening to begin attacking Israel. One of the rebels turned to the camera and declared, "We are now in front of the occupied Golan, the blessed land sold by Hafez Assad. For 40 years, not a single gunshot has been fired on this land. . . . We will free the Golan and it will return to the free Syrian people, with the help of Allah."[51]

Rebel forces associated with Al Qaeda took control of sections of Israel's border with Syria in the Golan in November 2012.[52] Since then, Israel experienced sporadic attacks on its military positions and civilian towns from Syria. Units associated with Al Qaeda have boasted that they are following Israeli troop movements along the border and learning Israel's modes of operation.[53] Meanwhile Assad has threatened to permit Hezbollah terrorists to occupy the border region along the Golan Heights and use it as a launching ground for missile and terrorist attacks, thus replicating the Hezbollah model for attacking Israel from southern Lebanon.

Israeli defense officials have claimed that while the rebels certainly wish to attack Israel, they are constrained by their need to concentrate their efforts on fighting the regime.[54] Israeli political and military leaders, far less sanguine about the threat from Hezbollah, made clear that

Israel would not stand by and allow Hezbollah to set up bases of operations in the Golan.[55]

To prepare for all possible contingencies, Israel set about building a fence along the border with Syria. It has warned Western leaders that they must not be deceived into believing that the Syrian opposition is any better than the regime. Other regional leaders, from King Abdullah II in Jordan to Prime Minister Nouri al-Maliki in Iraq, have warned the United States and other world powers that a clear-cut victory for either side in the Syrian civil war would bring peace neither to the country nor the region as a whole.[56]

The situation in Syria is deeply dangerous for Israel and for the wider region. But the danger lies in developments within Syria, not in what happens within Israel. As demonstrated by Assad's failed attempts to play the Israel card to win domestic support for his regime, he would certainly like to attack Israel, but with his army and regime under assault, he has more urgent issues on his agenda. He simply cannot devote the resources necessary to launch a serious attack on Israel. Moreover, in all likelihood, he would not want to pick a fight with Israel. Not only would he lose the fight, he would lose his regime.

As a consequence, if Israel were to apply its laws to Judea and Samaria, Assad would have little capacity to respond.

As for the rebels, the Al Qaeda forces fighting in Syria neither need nor seek an excuse to attack Israel. Just as Al Qaeda has attacked the U.S. mainland and U.S. targets abroad whenever it has had the opportunity, without connection to any specific U.S. policy, so Israel can expect Al Qaeda forces in Syria to attack it without connection to anything it does.

If Israel applies its laws to Judea and Samaria, the move in and of itself would have no bearing on the probability of war with Syria or the potential for escalated violence along the border. The prospect of war or cross-border assaults is wholly a function of the capacity of the warring factions in Syria.

LEBANON-HEZBOLLAH

Hezbollah, Iran's proxy force in Lebanon, has a consistent policy of opportunistically attacking Israel. From its perspective, this policy is eminently logical. Hezbollah operates independently from Lebanese government authority, and its forces are more powerful than the Lebanese military. To justify its independence, Hezbollah feels constant pressure to attack Israel. Only by demonstrating that it is at the forefront of the war against Israel can Hezbollah justify its refusal to subordinate its military to the sovereign authority of the Lebanese government.

As a consequence, Hezbollah would be more likely than any other regional military force to respond to an Israeli decision to apply its sovereignty over Judea and Samaria by launching a war against the Jewish state.

Yet despite its independence from Lebanese governmental authority, Hezbollah is not an independent entity: it is controlled by the Iranian Revolutionary Guards Corps. Tehran, not the group's leadership in Lebanon, sets Hezbollah's military priorities.[57]

From the outset of the Syrian civil war in March 2011, Hezbollah forces, acting on orders from Tehran, have actively fought on behalf of Assad, who is himself a vassal of the Iranian regime. Together with Iran's Revolutionary Guards, Hezbollah forces have trained a pro-Iranian militia of 50,000 men in Syria that, should Assad be deposed, would secure enclaves to maintain supply lines from Syria to Lebanon. Hezbollah fighters have actively engaged Syrian rebel forces, and while they were transferring advanced weapons from Syria to Lebanon, Israel has bombed them.[58]

Hezbollah's actions on behalf of Assad have diminished the group's credibility in Lebanon. In February 2013 Syrian opposition forces attacked Lebanese targets in what they claimed was retaliation for Hezbollah attacks in Syria. Former Lebanese prime minister Saad Hariri harshly questioned Hezbollah's legitimacy in light of its participation in the Syrian war. "What is Hezbollah doing on the Syrian front?" he said. "We were not far from the truth when we declared that Hezbollah's main aim is not resistance [against Israel], but rather that its weapons are used for other purposes."[59]

Other voices in Lebanon that are more sympathetic to the Iranian proxy have expressed concern that the demise of the Assad regime could weaken Hezbollah to the point that Israel would be able to destroy it completely. At a symposium in Beirut organized by the Carnegie Middle East Center, in the presence of senior European diplomats, the center's director Paul Salem raised the prospect that the demise of the Assad regime could render Hezbollah impotent and invite a crippling Israeli military operation against it.[60]

Hezbollah's military strength is indeed a product of Syrian and Iranian will and power. If Syria's regime is toppled, then Iran's power to maintain Hezbollah will be vastly diminished.

But if Hezbollah and Iran manage to secure safe havens for their flow of arms and for Iranian loyalists in a post-Assad Syria, then Iran may be able to maintain Hezbollah's strength. Moreover, if Iran emerges as a nuclear power, then Hezbollah will be far freer to commit acts of aggression against Israel, operating under Iran's nuclear umbrella.

In light of this fluid and unknowable state of affairs, it would be better, from Israel's perspective, to apply its laws to Judea and Samaria while Hezbollah remains tied down in Syria and consequently weakened at home. So too Israel would be well advised to make such a move before Iran emerges as a nuclear power.

A move by Israel to apply Israeli law to Judea and Samaria would not likely spur any serious response from either Egypt or Jordan, due in large part to both countries' dire financial straits, political instability, and economic dependence on the United States (and in Jordan's case, on Israel as well). Syria's component parts would not be likely to attack Israel, due to their need to concentrate their forces in their domestic battles. Finally, Hezbollah, while it is tied down in Syria, and before Iran acquires nuclear capabilities, would likely not have the capacity to strike Israel—if only because Iran would not permit it to do so. However, in the event that Iran acquires nuclear weapons, or Assad successfully defeats his opponents, Hezbollah would be likely to respond to an Israeli decision to apply Israeli law to Judea and Samaria by attacking the Jewish state. At the same time, it is important to recognize that, as we saw in 2006 when it went to war against Israel, Hezbollah does not need Israel to do anything in order to go to war against it. It is just as happy to invent pretexts, or even attack Israel with no pretext at all, if it believes that doing so advances its interests, and those of its Iranian superiors.

CHAPTER 16

Likely European Responses

In 2013 Israel was the only country in the Middle East that was stable. Israeli farmers and ranchers in the Golan Heights worked their lands in peace, while across the border in Syria, just miles and sometimes yards away, a bloodbath was taking place.

As tourists flocked to Israel's vacation capital Eilat, along the Red Sea, just across the border in the Egyptian Sinai, Al Qaeda forces joined with Hamas and Bedouin militia to wage an insurgency against Egyptian security forces. Country after country in the Arab world saw its regime destabilized, overthrown, and threatened by the revolutionary ferment that pitted radicals against radicals, regimes against jihadists, and jihadists from one type of mosque against jihadists from another type of mosque.

While all this was going on, in January 2013, Israel held a regularly scheduled national election. Like all previous national elections, the 2013 election took place without incident. Two major parties in Israel's lively multiparty parliamentary system were wiped out, while two others rose to prominence. Prime Minister Benjamin Netanyahu was reelected as his ruling Likud Party won the largest number of seats in the Knesset.

On the day of Israel's national election, British foreign minister William Hague gave a speech in the British Parliament regarding Israel. He did not congratulate Israel for being an island of stability in the midst of the Arab political tsunami. He did not congratulate Britain for its wisdom in maintaining a close alliance with the only liberal democracy in the Middle East. He declared that the most pressing foreign policy concern for Britain was the establishment of a Palestinian state.

Seven months after Hague delivered his speech, Egypt experienced its second revolution in two years. The death toll in the Syrian civil war reached 100,000,[1] and the rebels there had come under the leadership of Al Qaeda and the Muslim Brotherhood.[2] The regime was making widespread use of chemical weapons.[3] Lebanon was being dragged in,[4] and the Syrian conflict was looking more and more like the first front in an all-out war for Islamic primacy between Sunni jihadists and Shi'ite jihadists.[5]

Meanwhile the European Union's foreign policy commissioner, Catherine Ashton, led the West's multiparty negotiations with Iran over its illicit nuclear weapons program. By July, the consensus was that the talks had failed. Iran was but a stone's throw—if that—from emerging as a nuclear power.[6]

In July 2013 the European Union's response to all these developments was to announce the implementation of economic sanctions against Israel. From 2014, no EU funds would be dispersed to any Israeli entity that was either located or operating beyond the 1949 armistice lines.[7]

Additionally, Ashton announced that by the end of 2013, the European Union would issue mandatory guidelines for attaching special labels to Israeli goods produced by Jews beyond the 1949 armistice lines.[8] In an interview with the *Jerusalem Post* in May 2013, Lithuanian foreign minister Linas Linkevicius warned Israel that the labeling of Jewish-made products manufactured beyond the 1949 armistice lines was a first step toward a complete boycott of Israeli goods.[9]

Even without Linkevicius's warning, the purpose of the labeling program was clear enough. By placing special labels on Israeli goods, the European Union seeks to condition European consumers to view Israeli products as being morally inferior to other products, thus leading to a consumer boycott of all Israeli goods.

THE ROOTS OF EUROPE'S POLICIES TOWARD ISRAEL

The Europeans argue that they have opened a trade war with Israel in order to uphold international law and to advance the peace process between Israel and the PLO. But neither of these claims is supported by facts.

After the European Union published its ban on transferring EU funds to Israeli entities operating beyond the 1949 armistice lines, Ambassador Alan Baker, the former legal adviser to Israel's Foreign Ministry, wrote that the EU actions are unsupported by international law. The EU claim that Israel's presence beyond the 1949 armistice lines is unlawful is not supported by any treaty or custom.

As we saw in Chapter 12, Israel's legal rights to sovereignty over Judea, Samaria, and Jerusalem are recognized under the law of nations through the 1922 League of Nations Mandate for Palestine, which also called for "close Jewish settlement" of these areas. The Mandate's allocation of sovereign rights over these areas to the Jewish people, and its recognition of the Jews as the indigenous people of the areas, have been abrogated by no subsequent treaty. To the contrary, they were reinforced by Article 80 of the UN Charter.

Moreover, as Baker noted, the European Union wrongly claims that Jewish communities beyond the 1949 armistice lines are illegal under Article 49 of the Fourth Geneva Convention, from 1949. Authoritative interpretations of Article 49 make clear that it does not apply to such communities.

The lines that the European Union points to as Israel's legal borders were never borders and were never legal. The 1949 armistice lines, which the European Union falsely refers to as the 1967 borders, represent nothing more than the lines at which Israeli forces halted the invading armies of Arab states that illegally assaulted the nascent Jewish state on May 15, 1948.

The armistice agreements explicitly stated that the armistice lines lack all legal significance in terms of claims of parties to lands beyond the lines.

Finally, as Baker noted, the European Union itself has repeatedly supported UN resolutions and international agreements that recognize the legality of Israel's continued control and civilian presence in the areas. As a consequence, the European Union's own actions contradict its claim that Israel's presence and the presence of Israeli civilian communities beyond the 1949 armistice lines are illegal.

Beyond that, Ashton's directive on labeling Jewish-made products produced beyond the 1949 lines itself constitutes a breach of international law because it contradicts binding rules of international trade that the European Union committed to observe as a member to the World Trade Organization.[10]

The European Union's claim that it is levying trade sanctions on Israel in order to advance the peace process is similarly without foundation. The EU announced its ban on funding Israeli entities the very day Secretary of State John Kerry announced that peace talks between Israel and the Palestinians would be relaunched after a five-year hiatus. The confluence of these events could not demonstrate more clearly that the EU's diplomatic onslaught against Israel has nothing to do with the conduct of negotiations with the PLO. If the EU's chief interest were bringing Israel and the PLO to the negotiating table, then Brussels would be sanctioning the Palestinians, who had refused to negotiate with Israel since 2008.

If the European Union's obsessive hostility toward Israel has nothing to do with peace, and nothing to do with international law, what explains its behavior? How can the EU seemingly focus only on attacking the Jewish state, even as the Arab world is imploding? How does coercing Israel to renounce its legal and national rights to Judea, Samaria, and Jerusalem trump preventing the rise of anti-Western jihadists to power from one end of the Middle East to the other in Europe's foreign policy priorities?

The short answer is that Europe is obsessed with hating Israel. Indeed, opposing Israel and seeking to cut the Jewish state down to size is the only coherent foreign policy that the European Union has consistently held.

While this statement may on its face seem absurd, public opinion polling data of European citizenry shows that while harsh, it is an accurate description of European priorities.

In November 2003, a Eurobarometer poll conducted by the European Union found that 59 percent of Europeans viewed Israel as the greatest threat to world peace. In Holland, 74 percent of people believed that Israel was the greatest threat to world peace. In contrast, in a poll of Americans carried out in December 2003 by the Anti-Defamation League of B'nai B'rith, Israel placed tenth on the list of threats to world peace—just ahead of the United States itself.[11]

In a 2011 poll of 8,000 Europeans in eight representative countries, carried out by the German Bielefeld University, 40 percent of respondents said that Israel is carrying out a war of extermination against the Palestinians. As Dr. Beate Kupper, one of the authors of the study, told the *Jerusalem Post*, the study showed a strong presence of "anti-Semitism that is linked with Israel and hidden behind criticism of Israel, and is not neutral."[12]

Europe's decision to sanction Israel, then, springs from a wider pathology that guides European politics and culture. That pathology views the only liberal, human-rights-and-international-law-respecting democracy in the Middle East as the greatest threat to world peace, indeed as a demonic society actively engaged in committing a genocide of Palestinians.[13]

IMPLICATIONS OF EUROPE'S OBSESSION WITH THE JEWISH STATE

From a pure policy perspective, Europe's obsession-driven position on Israel has three notable aspects. First, the goal of European policy toward Israel is to force Israel to surrender its legitimate claims to sovereignty over Judea, Samaria, and Jerusalem, which, as we saw in Chapter 13, are the historic and religious heartland of Jewish history and heritage. They are also the guarantors of Israel's physical survival, for without them— and particularly without the Jordan Valley, the Samarian Mountains, and the Hebron Hills—Israel would be unable to defend itself from foreign invasion or defend its remaining territory from infiltration and missile attacks. And so at its core, the European fixation on coercing Israel to surrender all claims to and control of these areas is an impulse to force the Jewish state to renounce Jewish history and rights and to reduce itself to an indefensible statelet, which, like the Jewish communities in the Diaspora until the founding of the Jewish state, would be dependent on the goodwill of outsiders for its very survival.

The second notable aspect of the European position is that in their rejection of the legitimacy of all Israeli presence in Judea, Samaria, and Jerusalem, the Europeans have adopted a stance that is more extreme than the PLO's, at least as expressed in its agreements with Israel. All the agreements that the Palestinians signed with Israel are based on the PLO's acceptance of the legitimacy of Israeli sovereignty over Jerusalem and its authority in Judea and Samaria pending the signing of a permanent peace between the sides. The PLO has agreed to continued Israeli sovereignty over Jerusalem, and the sharing of powers and authorities between Israel and the Palestinian Authority in Judea and Samaria. But the European Union's position is to reject all such powers and authorities and work to foment Israel's surrender of them outside the framework of a negotiated settlement between Israel and the PLO.

The third notable aspect of the European position on Israel is that despite the European Union's stated support for democracy and democratic government, it works avidly to subvert Israel from within by using domestic Israeli agents to undermine not only Israeli control of Judea, Samaria, and Jerusalem but also sovereign Israeli authority in general.

In July 2013 the European Union made one exception to its ban on transferring EU funds to Israeli entities located or operating beyond the 1949 armistice lines. As Paragraph 15 of the sanctions directive stipulated, "The requirements [banning the transfer of EU funds to Israeli entities operating beyond the 1949 armistice lines] ... do not apply to activities which, although carried out in the territories ... aim at benefiting protected persons under the terms of international humanitarian law who live in these territories [i.e., the Palestinians] and/or at promoting the Middle East peace process in line with EU policy."[14]

In other words, Israeli-registered NGOs that work to undermine Israeli control of these areas are exempt from EU sanctions, since their work advances European goals.

Over the years, the European Union has massively funded political groups inside Israel that seek to undermine the Israeli government's ability to defend the country from aggression and to assert Israeli sovereignty over its non-Jewish citizens. One such political organization is B'Tselem, which uses the language of human rights to criminalize Israel's presence in Judea and Samaria, delegitimize IDF operations, and delegitimize Israel's existence as a Jewish state.[15]

In 2009 the UN Human Rights Committee published the so-called Goldstone Report, which falsely accused Israel of committing crimes against humanity against the Palestinians in Gaza during Operation Cast Lead, between December 2008 and January 2009. The purpose of Cast Lead was to end the Palestinian rocket, missile, and mortar campaign against Israel, during which thousands of projectiles were launched against Israeli civilian targets.

B'Tselem played an instrumental role in the production of the Goldstone Report.[16] Ninety-two percent of the negative citations from Israeli sources used in the report came from sixteen Israeli NGOs, many of which receive massive funding from the European Union.[17] B'Tselem was the most-cited source.[18]

In April 2011 Judge Richard Goldstone, chair of the commission that published the report, publicly distanced himself from its accusations against Israel. In an op-ed in the *Washington Post,* he wrote, "If I had known then what I know now, the Goldstone Report would have been a different document." Goldstone also admitted that Israel had not "intentionally targeted civilians," contrary to what his eponymous report alleged.[19]

In January 2010 B'Tselem's executive director Jessica Montell met with Michael Posner, assistant secretary of state for democracy, human rights, and labor at the U.S. embassy in Tel Aviv. The embassy's report on their meeting was published by WikiLeaks.[20] Montell told Posner that the aim of B'Tselem's involvement with the Goldstone Commission "was to make Israel weigh world opinion and consider whether it could 'afford another operation like this.'"

Following the publication of the Goldstone Report, in light of the massive involvement of foreign-government-funded Israeli-registered political NGOs in the campaign to undermine the ability of Israel's government to function, Israel's Knesset began deliberating on a series of bills aimed at regulating the operations of such groups.

In February 2010 Montell had another meeting at the U.S. embassy in Tel Aviv to discuss those deliberations. The embassy report of this meeting was also published by WikiLeaks. Montell told U.S. officials that 95 percent of her $2.4 million budget was funded by foreign money, mainly from European governments.[21]

To undermine Israel's sovereignty throughout the country, the European Union uses its funding activities to encourage Arab Israelis to reject the government's sovereign prerogative to apply its laws without prejudice on all the country's citizens, including its Arab citizens. An internal document from late 2011, composed by European ambassadors in Tel Aviv, called on the European Union to work to undermine Israel's rights to enforce its laws on its Arab citizens. The report said the issue of Israel's Arab community should be considered a "core issue, not second tier to the Israeli-Palestinian conflict."[22]

The European Union's main interest in this area has traditionally been planning and zoning laws: specifically, it objects to Israeli application of planning and zoning laws against illegal Arab building. Whereas illegal Jewish building is destroyed as a matter of course,[23] due in part to pressure exerted by EU-funded Israeli groups, illegal Arab building in

Israel goes largely unaddressed. By 2012 there were more than 100,000 illegally constructed Arab buildings in southern Israel alone.[24] These illegal building activities are organized largely by radical Arab politicians and the Israeli Islamic movement.[25] Whenever the Israeli government seeks to take action to end this phenomenon, it comes under massive pressure from these EU-funded organizations and official EU institutions, which claim that action against these structures is proof of Israel's inherent racism.[26]

POSSIBLE EUROPEAN RESPONSES

In light of Europe's deep-seated hostility toward Israel, in the event that Israel applies its laws to Judea and Samaria, Europe's responses will not be wholly motivated by rational policy considerations. Consequently, the potential damage that Israel could incur from a spectrum of potential European actions—from economic sanctions to diplomatic assaults to military incursions—must be considered seriously.

First, the Europeans could enact intensified economic sanctions. The European Union is Israel's second-largest trading partner after the United States. Israel is the European Union's twenty-fifth largest.[27] In 2011 bilateral EU-Israel trade stood at 29.4 billion euros, or approximately $40 billion. In 2011 the trade balance was about $6.5 billion in Europe's favor. Also in 2011 European exports made up 34.5 percent of Israel's total imports. Exports to Europe constituted 26.1 percent of Israel's total.

Even before it announced it was enacting actual sanctions against Israel in July 2013, the European Union used its economic leverage over Israel to push its anti-Israel foreign policy. Brussels linked upgrading its economic relations with Israel to making "progress" in the peace process—that is, unreciprocated Israeli concessions to the Palestinians.[28]

Europe's options for levying intensified economic sanctions against Israel range from officially downgrading its economic relations with Israel, to abrogating the free-trade agreement between the EU and Israel, to outlawing military sales between Europe and Israel. Europe could also downgrade its technological ties with Israel. Other than Israel's government, the EU is the largest funder of Israeli public research.[29]

THE LIMITATIONS OF EUROPEAN LEVERAGE OVER ISRAEL

Levying such sanctions, however, would not be a cost-free undertaking for Europe. European weapons developers would lose a paying customer, and even worse, European governments would lose a business partner, ending highly beneficial cooperative relationships with their Israeli counterparts. Moreover Israel sells European countries billions of dollars in arms and has been instrumental in developing local arms industries in Poland and other EU member states. Presumably, Israeli arms exports to Europe would suffer the same fate as European military exports to Israel.[30]

In the sphere of technological cooperation, European governments recognize Israel's comparative advantage in high-tech. EU member state governments aggressively compete with each other in courting Israeli Internet, biomedical, agri-tech, and other high-tech companies to partner with their countries. Speaking to *The Times of Israel* at an Israel-Europe business conference in Tel Aviv, Xavier Buck, the CEO of EuroDNS, which is responsible for Internet domain names in Europe, explained that European businesses are frantic to partner with Israeli firms, and European governments are aggressively recruiting Israeli firms to collaborate with European businesses. "Europe's old industries are failing," Buck said, "and EU countries are desperately looking for something else to replace them. Governments see what Israel has accomplished, and they want Israel to help them become a tech power as well."[31] And according to Edouard Cukierman, the head of a firm that builds Israeli-European business partnerships, "What is invested here [in Israel] in venture capital today represents half of what is invested in all the European countries put together."[32] Clearly Europe would pay an economic price for limiting its trade with Israel.

For Israel's part, Europe is not as irreplaceable as it once was. In recent years, Asian partners—particularly China and India—have been rapidly expanding their bilateral trade with Israel, thus diminishing the importance Israel places on expanding its ties with Europe.

CHINA AND INDIA RISING

In 2011, according to the Israel chamber of commerce in Beijing, bilateral trade between Israel and China stood at $8.17 billion. Israeli exports to China were valued at $2.72 billion, and Chinese exports to Israel totaled $5.45 billion. That level of trade represented an annual increase of 17 percent. In the first six months of 2012, bilateral trade increased 6.3 percent over the same period in 2011 and almost doubled the same period in 2010.[33]

China appears not to share Europe's delusion that the Palestinian conflict with Israel is the most pressing conflict in the Middle East. Following the first Egyptian revolution that toppled Hosni Mubarak, China, fearing the impact of Egypt's domestic chaos on shipping through the Suez Canal, began looking for alternatives. Within a year, it had determined that Israel was the best alternative to the Suez Canal.

In July 2012 China signed two agreements with Israel to link Israel's Red Sea port in Eilat to its two Mediterranean ports at Ashdod and Haifa.[34] China agreed to pay some $5.5 billion to build a 110-mile freight railway link with Eilat. It also agreed to build an inland canal port north of Eilat to expand the capacity of Israel's existing port. As the Israel Ministry of Transportation explained, "The idea is to offer an Israeli rail landbridge alternative to the Suez Canal."[35] The agreements will massively expand Israel's strategic importance to the global economy as it becomes a major transport bridge between Asia and Europe.

Then there is India. India is the largest purchaser of arms on the international market. Israel is its second-largest supplier, after Russia. In late 2012 Indian Defense Ministry officials assessed that Israel was likely to surpass Russia in arms sales to the world's largest democracy within one or two years.[36]

In 2011–2012, Israel's bilateral trade with India stood at $5.1 billion, with Israel enjoying a trade surplus of $844 million.[37] It topped $6 billion in 2012–13.[38] By mid-2013 India and Israel were in advanced stages of negotiations toward signing a free-trade agreement.[39] Such an agreement is expected to double or even triple bilateral trade within a decade.[40]

ISRAEL: AN EMERGING ENERGY EXPORTER

Israel's importance to the world economy may surpass expectations, due to the fact that the country is on the verge of an energy boom. In January 2009 natural gas was discovered off Israel's Mediterranean shores by a team led by Texas-based Noble Energy. The Tamar field is estimated to contain 275 billion cubic meters (9.7 trillion cubic feet) of natural gas.[41] In March 2013 the Tamar field went online, and gas sufficient to satisfy Israel's domestic demand for two decades began flowing to Israel's mainland.[42]

In June 2010 the Noble team found a far larger gas field adjacent to Tamar. Called Leviathan, it has at least 19 trillion cubic feet of natural gas.[43] The massive field is expected to turn Israel into a major exporter of natural gas when it comes online in 2016.[44]

David Wurmser, the founder of Delphi Global Analysis Group, has done extensive assessments of the geopolitical implications of Israel's gas fields. He wrote in April 2013 that Israel's newfound natural gas resources provide the Jewish state with another opportunity to emerge as a major strategic bridge between Europe and Asia.[45]

Israel already signed an agreement with Australia's Woodside firm, awarding it a third of the rights for Leviathan. Woodside's business activities are focused in Asia. Its partnership with Israel at Leviathan signals that Israel is looking to Asia rather than Europe as its primary natural gas market. [46]

In order to transport the gas, Israel is leaning toward building liquefied natural gas (LNG) terminals in Israel, probably at Ashkelon on the Mediterranean and adjacent to the Red Sea port at Eilat. Like the Chinese-built rail link between Eilat and the Mediterranean ports in Haifa and Ashdod, the LNG terminals would make Israel a major infrastructural link between Europe and East Asia, thus augmenting its critical importance to both markets.[47]

Gas shipments to Europe could directly raise Israel's strategic importance there. But as Wurmser argues, "Europe is already increasingly dependent on Israel's high-tech in critical sectors of its economy. Yet such dependence has done little to alter what Israel views [as] a continued European drift towards greater antagonism towards Israel."[48]

Then there is oil. In 2009 Israel discovered massive deposits of shale oil in a field south of Jerusalem. Scientists assess the size of the field at 150 billion barrels—or 60 percent of Saudi Arabia's reserve capacity. Court intervention on behalf of environmentalist movements delayed for five years a pilot project to determine the viability of extraction technology, but it was expected to go online by the end of 2013. In the event that the technologies enable cost-effective extraction of the oil, Israel would become a major player in the international oil market within a decade.[49]

POSSIBLE EUROPEAN RESPONSES TO A ONE-STATE PLAN

Should Israel decide to apply its laws to Judea and Samaria, it is possible that cooler heads will prevail in Europe, and that EU member states will take only minimal steps to punish it. However, since Europe's economic policies toward Israel reflect European peoples' unhealthy obsession with the Jewish state, it is impossible to predict with any certainty that rationality will prevail.

The European Union can very well impose economic sanctions against Israel. Since Europe is still Israel's second-largest trading partner, those sanctions could damage Israel's economic strength in the short term. But thanks to Israel's rapidly expanding economic ties with Asian economies, and its emerging energy independence, its economy will not collapse as a result. In the medium term, Israel will be able to contain the damage. Its versatile, knowledge-based economy, strategically buffeted by its newfound natural gas fields and export capacity, will continue to grow regardless of European actions.

In the diplomatic arena, the European states could downgrade their relations with Israel. Britain considered downgrading its ties simply because Israel sought to retaliate—rather weakly and completely lawfully—against the PLO's illegitimate decision to ask the UN to upgrade its status to nonmember observer state.[50]

Europe's consistently extreme diplomatic opposition to Israel places it in a position not unlike that of the PLO. Europeans are already using the tools of diplomacy to weaken Israel. True, unlike the Palestinians, they could escalate their diplomatic campaign, but such escalation could backfire due to Israel's rapidly increasing importance in the global economy. At any rate, diplomatic warfare against the Jewish state will have only marginal results unless it is joined by Israel's only diplomatic supporter: the United States. We will discuss that prospect in the next two chapters.

Although remote, there is a slight possibility that the European Union might consider deploying military forces to the region to force Israel to cancel its move.

In 2002 Samantha Power (who would serve on President Obama's National Security Council during his first term in office, and as U.S. ambassador to the UN in Obama's second term) gave an interview in which she suggested deploying a "mammoth protection force" to Judea and Samaria, at the cost of "literally billions of dollars," to protect the Palestinians from Israel.[51] Power's remark shocked many observers because it clashed with the general sentiments of the American public. According to a 2012 survey of U.S. opinion, 64 percent of Americans said that their sympathies are more with the Israelis than with the Palestinians. Only 12 percent said their sympathies were more with the Palestinians, while 23 percent did not express a preference.[52] Given this political reality, it is extremely unlikely that Congress would authorize the president to deploy, or to support the deployment of foreign forces, to Judea and Samaria to protect the Palestinians from Israel.

EUROPE'S NONEXISTENT MILITARY OPTION

For their part, the Europeans would much more likely jump at the opportunity to serve in such a force. European nations have routinely participated in multinational forces deployed to Palestinian-controlled areas and along Israel's borders with Syria and Lebanon. The question, then, is whether Europe actually has the capacity to deploy a "mammoth protection force" to fight Israel on behalf of the Palestinians.

Given the European militaries' performances in Afghanistan, Libya, and Mali, the answer appears to be no. In a farewell address at NATO in June 2011, the outgoing U.S. defense secretary Robert Gates blasted the Europeans for not having sufficient forces to project power and serve effectively. Gates said that Europe's performance in both Libya and Afghanistan had been totally ineffective because "the military capabilities simply aren't there."[53]

Then too, France's intervention in Mali, aimed at blocking an Al

Qaeda affiliate from taking over its former colony, was possible only due to U.S. assistance. The U.S. Defense Department dispatched surveillance, refueling, and transport aircraft to assist the French military.[54]

EUROPE IN A NUTSHELL

In summary, due to the centrality of the Palestinian-Israeli conflict to European foreign policy, Europe will likely react more dramatically to an Israeli decision to apply Israeli law in Judea and Samaria than either the Palestinians or Israel's Arab neighbors. On the economic front, the European Union will likely respond with various sanctions, and since Europe is Israel's second-largest trading partner, those sanctions will harm Israel's economy. However, Israel's burgeoning economic relations with Asia, and its emergence as a net exporter of natural gas and, down the line, perhaps of oil as well, rule out the possibility that the damage incurred will be sufficient to collapse or paralyze the Israeli economy.

Moreover, Israel is emerging as a vital artery for international economic activity and as a result is rapidly becoming the most strategically vital state in the Levant. Consequently, if the European Union were to pursue an economic war against Israel, it would likely find itself under severe international constraints.

And absent U.S. support for diplomatic war against Israel, a European diplomatic offensive against Israel will harm Israel only at the margins.

As for European military intervention, although EU member states collectively field armed forces in excess of two million men,[55] the European Union lacks the power-projection capabilities to deploy its forces to the region without U.S. assistance. Therefore the likelihood that European powers will consider such deployment, in response to an Israeli decision to apply its laws to Judea and Samaria, is effectively nonexistent.

CHAPTER 17

Does the Israeli One-State Plan Make Sense for Israel?

WHY ISRAELIS SUPPORT THE ISRAELI ONE-STATE PLAN

In April 2013 Israel's Ariel University polled Israeli Jews on their views about the prospect of applying Israeli law to all or parts of Judea and Samaria. The results were stunning, mainly for what they demonstrated about the independent-mindedness of the Israeli public.

Ever since the inauguration of the peace process between Israel and the PLO on September 13, 1993, the public discourse within Israel on the Palestinian conflict has been frozen in time. The persistence of Palestinian terrorism after repeated promises of peace, together with the repeated Palestinian rejection of Israeli peace offers, have convinced most Israelis that Israel has no chance of reaching an accord with the Palestinians.[1] Yet there has been no serious discussion of policy options other than the two-state paradigm due to the leftist ideological uniformity of Israel's mass media.

But even in the absence of public discussion of the issue, and even in the face of the Israeli media's outright rejection of the possibility, the Israeli public supports the idea that Israel should apply its laws to the areas. According to the Ariel University survey, 59 percent of Israeli Jews believe that Israel should apply its law to all or parts of Judea and Samaria. Only 12 percent of Israeli Jews believe that it should not do so. And 20 percent think Israel should apply its laws to Judea and Samaria only in the framework of a peace treaty with the Palestinians.[2]

The public's rejection of the failed two-state paradigm, and its readiness to implement unilateral programs, are brought home by the fact that a mere 20 percent of Israelis think their government should apply Israel's laws only in the context of a peace treaty with the Palestinians. The vast majority of Israelis find unrealistic and unacceptable the prospect of continuing to condition Israel's sovereign rights and national interest on Palestinian approval of those rights and acceptance of those interests.

And this makes sense. For two decades, bound by the two-state paradigm, Israelis have watched in disbelief as government after government has endangered Israel's national security and humiliated the country in endless efforts to appease the patently unappeasable Palestinians.

For instance, in July 2013 the Palestinians agreed to meet with Israeli negotiators in Washington, but in exchange for the meeting, they insisted that Israel first agree to release more than one hundred convicted terrorists from prison.[3] All of the terrorists had committed acts of murder or attempted murder. All had been sentenced to life in prison for crimes that collectively involved the murder of seventy-six Israelis and the wounding of hundreds.[4]

The very fact that a consistent Palestinian demand is for Israel to release terrorists from its prisons is proof of their ill intentions toward Israel. If the PLO had truly turned over a new leaf and accepted the necessity—or dare we say it, desirability—of living at peace with Israel, it would not be asking for Israel to free mass murderers.

Eighty-four percent of Israelis opposed the Palestinian demand.[5] And yet like all his predecessors since Israel embraced the two-state solution in 1993, Prime Minister Benjamin Netanyahu bowed to U.S. pressure to release them. He forced a decision along these lines through his cabinet, with no public debate or defense of his patently indefensible action. All Netanyahu could say was that "sometimes prime ministers are forced to make decisions that go against public opinion—when the issue is important for the country."[6]

Such releases defile the memory of the Israelis murdered by these terrorists, and cause those who were wounded and those whose loved ones were murdered to relive their trauma. Moreover, Israel's history of terrorist releases proves that they are dangerous for all Israelis. According to the Almagor Terror Victims Association, between 2000 and 2005, 180 Israelis were murdered by Palestinian terrorists who had been freed in previous releases.[7]

For their part, the Palestinians didn't even try to hide their contempt for this self-abasing Israeli gesture. Shortly after Secretary of State John

Kerry announced he had received their agreement to restart peace talks with Israel, the Palestinians began denying they had agreed to negotiate.[8] And indeed, the first round of "peace talks" was limited to technical issues.[9]

In other words, in exchange for its agreement to release 104 Palestinian murderers from prison, Israel was given the right to talk about the shape of the table around which the Palestinians would speak with them. Three months later, PLO officials told reporters they were planning to announce that the talks had failed and blame the failure on Israel.[10]

Over twenty years of the so-called peace process, Israelis have experienced terrorism on a scale unmatched in post–World War II history. Fifteen hundred Israelis have been murdered, in every imaginable—and unimaginable—way. The good name of their country has been dragged through the mud, as the nations of the world, eager to embrace the PLO and present the architects of modern terrorism as a legitimate party to talks, whitewashed or simply ignored their radicalism, their commitment to Israel's destruction, their anti-Semitism, and their active involvement in terrorist attacks against Israelis.

Moreover, even as the Palestinians have proven on a daily basis their utter contempt for Israel and the phoniness of the so-called peace process, Israelis have seen successive governments come under ever-escalating pressure from the United States and Europe to make deeper and more dangerous concessions to the Palestinians. Indeed, the U.S. decision to back the Palestinian demand that Israel release terrorist murderers from prison as a precondition for Palestinians to meet with Israeli negotiators was unprecedented.[11]

It is little wonder that Israelis have soured on the two-state solution.[12] And it is little wonder that despite the blanket discouragement of Israel's media and intellectual elites, the majority of Israelis want to be done with this humiliating, dangerous nightmare. They want to assert Israel's legitimate rights to Judea and Samaria and secure the country. They want their leaders to stop begging the Palestinians to stop the terrorist onslaughts they initiate. In other words, it is not the least surprising that, after this prolonged twenty-year nightmare of fake peace with terrorists committed to their destruction, Israelis want justice and security, and they have come to understand that the only way to achieve these aims is to secure the sovereign rights of the Jewish people to Judea and Samaria.

THE DANGERS OF IMPLEMENTING THE ISRAELI ONE-STATE PLAN

In the previous three chapters, we discussed the likely consequences of an Israeli decision to apply its sovereignty over Judea and Samaria.

While the picture is mixed, it is not rosy. The Palestinians will try, and might well succeed, in retaliating by carrying out a massive terrorist attack against Israel. If Hezbollah is not bogged down in Syria—or another theater of the rapidly expanding war between Sunni jihadists and Shi'ite jihadists—under the Iranian aegis, it would be likely to renew its war against the Jewish state. And the European Union and its member nations will very likely impose various types of economic sanctions against Israel.

Then there are the demographics. As we saw in Chapter 8, adding the Palestinians of Judea and Samaria—who number 1.66 million[13]—to Israel's population rolls will not endanger Israel's solid Jewish majority. Jews will still comprise two-thirds of the population. But adding them to Israel's population rolls—and particularly its welfare rolls—will pose an economic burden to the country.

The precedents set by the Arab population of Jerusalem and the Druze population of the Golan Heights show that the Palestinians of Judea and Samaria will not likely apply for Israeli citizenship in large numbers; but suddenly reducing the Jewish majority from 75 percent to 66 percent will undoubtedly have unforeseeable consequences on Israeli politics.

Expanding Israeli sovereignty to include Judea and Samaria will thus involve direct costs for Israel. And on many levels Israel is doing well today without them under its sovereign control.

In April 2013 Israel turned sixty-five years old. Except for its international diplomatic weakness, it has been a massive success by every possible measure. During the 2009–12 global economic downturn, Israel's economy grew 14.7 percent. In comparison, the U.S. economy grew just 3.2 percent over the same period, and the economies of the Eurozone contracted 1.5 percent. Per capita income in Israel grew 5.2 percent, while it grew a bare 0.1 percent in the United States and contracted 2.7 percent in the Eurozone.[14]

Israel's life expectancy of 81.6 years is among the highest in the world and ranks fifth in the OECD.[15] Israelis are among the happiest in the club of economically developed nations in the OECD.[16] A poll of Israeli Jews taken for Israel's sixty-fifth independence day showed that 92 percent are proud of being Israelis and 74 percent believe Israel is a good place to live.[17]

Given Israel's prosperity and the general contentment of its citizens, why would it want to rock the boat? Why would it want to add the headache of hundreds of thousands of new welfare recipients? Why would it want the burden of governing a hostile population that does not accept its right to exist and has been indoctrinated to work toward its destruction? How would applying Israeli law to Judea and Samaria actually advance Israel's national interests?

Before definitively answering, we must note that all the external blows that Israel will likely suffer following a decision by its government to apply Israeli law to Judea and Samaria are blows it is already suffering or will likely suffer even if it does not apply its law to Judea and Samaria. As we have seen, the Palestinians are already engaged in terrorism against Israel. By late 2012, terrorist attacks had risen more than 400 percent above their level the previous year.[18] These attacks were organized by the Palestinian Authority and, in most cases, carried out by Fatah terrorists, with support from the U.S.-trained and -financed PA security forces.[19] The Palestinians' diplomatic war against Israel has been moving ahead at full throttle for years.

The implosion of the wider Arab world increases the danger that Egypt and Syria will opt to go to war against Israel. But as we have seen, if they do decide to launch hostilities, their decisions will be a function of domestic considerations. Israeli actions will have little to no impact on their decision making.

As for Europe, as we saw in the last chapter, the Europeans decided to place sanctions on Israel the day the United States announced the reinstatement of peace talks between Israel and the Palestinians. This in itself shows that Israel's actions have no impact on Europe's treatment of the Jewish state. When Israel does what the Europeans claim they want it to do, the EU attacks Israel; and when against the stated wishes of Europe, Israel defends itself from outside aggression and internal subversion, the EU also attacks Israel. Like the surrounding Arab nations, Europe's treatment of Israel tells us far more about Europe than about Israel.

THE ADVANTAGES OF THE ISRAELI ONE-STATE PLAN

All the actions that would likely be undertaken against Israel, then, are already being undertaken, even as Israel maintains good faith with the two-state paradigm. The main price Israel will pay for applying its laws to Judea and Samaria, it is clear, will be the demographic burden of increasing its potentially hostile Arab minority by 1.66 million people.

Facing this cost, it is time to ask, what advantages will Israel gain by applying its laws to Judea and Samaria?

From a military perspective, Israel will be far better off, for four reasons.

First, at present, Israel is sharing control of the areas with a hostile political entity that possesses a massive military force.[20]

As we have seen in previous chapters, Palestinian forces have repeatedly deployed against Israeli military forces and civilians. This hostile deployment began in earnest in September 1996 when, at Arafat's direction, Palestinian security forces took a lead role in PA-incited and -organized riots against Israel and Israeli Jews. Arafat claimed that the riots were a response to Israel's decision to open an entrance to a tunnel that abuts the surviving wall of the Second Jewish Temple in Jerusalem, which was destroyed by the Romans in 70 CE. In the weeks of violence that ensued, 17 Israeli soldiers were killed, mainly by Palestinian security forces. Seventy Palestinian rioters were also killed.[21]

By 2002, all the Palestinian security forces from all official Palestinian security services had either directly participated in terrorist attacks against Israel or had provided material support for Fatah's Al Aksa Martyrs Brigades, Hamas, Islamic Jihad, or Hezbollah in carrying them out.[22]

The danger that Palestinian military forces would attack Israelis has not disappeared. As we saw in Chapter 14, in May 2009, Lieutenant General Keith Dayton, the U.S. security coordinator for Israel and the Palestinian Authority, warned that these U.S.-trained forces could be expected to turn their guns on Israel if they did not receive a state within two years. In his words, "With big expectations come big risks. There is perhaps a two-year shelf life on being told that you're creating a state, when you're not."[23]

Given Dayton's assessment, which aligns with that of Israeli military commanders, and given the impossibility of reaching a stable partition agreement with the PLO, it is clear that Israel will eventually face the U.S.-trained Palestinian army, as well as the rest of the Palestinian Authority militias. Israel would be far better off doing so on a battlefield it initiates than on one the Palestinians initiate. Certainly, Israel will be better off facing these forces while the IDF controls Judea and Samaria.

We have discussed the spillover effect of the Arab Spring on Israel's regional stature. In remarks to the Israeli media, Colonel Yani Alaluf, a brigade commander in Judea, noted that the Palestinian Authority has been even more profoundly affected by this Islamic wave than has Israel.

The probability of a factional battle among warring Palestinian groups grows larger every day.[24] At a minimum, regional events are pushing the Palestinian areas of Judea and Samaria into a period of severe political turbulence. The fact that the Palestinian Authority permits armed militias to operate semiautonomously in its areas of responsibility exacerbates the dangers associated with this turbulence.

Many pundits assumed that the fall of the Muslim Brotherhood in Egypt would weaken Hamas. But just weeks after the overthrow of the Morsi government, Hamas reinstated its strategic collaboration with Iran.[25]

With instability and chaos increasingly endemic to the region, Israel is better off controlling as much of its environment as it can. That is, Israel is better off minimizing uncertainty in all areas where it has the capacity to do so. By asserting sole sovereign rights over Judea and Samaria, Israel will be in a better position to break up terror cells as they form and to prevent them from operating.

To be sure, Israel already has the ability to deploy militarily throughout Judea and Samaria and to act against terrorists. However, in the current environment, Palestinian security forces can shelter terrorists from Israel (as they have many times in the past).

True, by asserting its power, Israel might unify the warring Palestinian factions to war against it. But by the same token, it will be easier to fight them if they operate in tandem, because their lines of communication will be longer and hence more vulnerable than those of isolated cells and groups. Moreover an Israeli assertion of central authority over the areas will likely have a significant moderating impact. Once the population feels there is a central governing authority in place, that sense of order will likely neutralize a significant amount of opposition momentum spurred by anti-Israel animus.

Another military advantage of implementing the Israeli one-state plan is the long-term strategic impact it will have on Israel's deterrent posture toward outside forces. As we noted in Chapter 15, securing permanent control of the Jordan Valley and the Samaria and Hebron mountain ranges will enable Israel to maintain in perpetuity its capacity to prevent invasion and terrorist infiltration along its eastern border. This will become all the more necessary in light of the political instability in neighboring Jordan, Syria, and Iraq.

From a diplomatic perspective, Israel will take a hit in the short term from its decision to apply Israeli law to Judea and Samaria. But in the long term, its diplomatic position will be enhanced. As we noted in Chapter 6, until Israel embraced the PLO as its peace partner and adopted the two-state paradigm, Israel's position was based on the understanding that the cause of the Arab world's conflict with Israel was Israel's existence, not its size. Israel understood that the only way peace could be achieved was for the Arab world to abide by the dictates of the UN Charter and live peacefully alongside the Jewish state. Israel was able to easily communicate that it stood on the side of justice and could not be held responsible for the bad behavior of its neighbors.

By accepting the PLO and the two-state paradigm, Israel embraced a policy-making framework that defined Israel as the guilty party in the Arab world's war on Israel. The two-state paradigm is based on the assumption that that conflict is due to the absence of a Palestinian state, and that a Palestinian state does not exist because Israel refuses to surrender sufficient land to the PLO.

Once Israel accepted this basic narrative, it lost the ability to launch a coherent defense of its actions. If Judea and Samaria were supposed to be part of the Palestinian state, then why were Jews building homes and communities there?

Israel justified its continued presence in the areas by attaching them to its security requirements. But if the land doesn't belong to Israel, then why should its security requirements trump the Palestinians' national rights? The Palestinian claim assumed even greater gravity as more and more Western policy makers adopted the position that the root cause of the instability and jihadist violence emanating from the Islamic world is the absence of a Palestinian state. After all, if the main thing sustaining jihadist forces from Saudi Arabia to Chechnya to Boston is the absence of a Palestinian state in Gaza, Judea, Samaria, and Jerusalem, then Israel's provincial security concerns are selfish and insupportable.

Israel attests that the issue of sovereignty in Judea and Samaria is disputed. But due to its acceptance of the validity of the two-state model—and by inference, the anti-Israel narrative that sustains it—Israel rarely defends or advances its own right to sovereignty. It ignores its own legal right to sovereignty under international law and rarely asserts its national rights. Trying to defend Israel's actions under these circumstances is like trying to drive with both hands tied behind your back. It is impossible.

By asserting its sovereign rights and applying its law to Judea and Samaria, Israel will finally bring clarity to its diplomatic position. It will be able to present a coherent case for Israel's strategic posture and its military actions. It will be able to present a clear model for democracy and civil rights in a multicultural society with a Jewish majority. And it will be able to tell the truth about the PLO's involvement in terrorism and incitement against Israel without worrying that its words will discredit the central plank of Israel's foreign policy—the two-state solution—which requires it to ignore and cover up Palestinian bad faith.

Applying Israel's laws to Judea and Samaria will also be beneficial for the cause of civil rights—for Israelis and Palestinians alike. As we have seen, the current situation of shared control, in which Palestinian residents are governed by Palestinian law and the Israeli residents are governed by military orders, has diminished the civil rights of both. Once Israel applies its laws to Judea and Samaria, Israelis will have the same rights in Judea and Samaria, including access to state lands and the ability to purchase land, as they have in the rest of Israel. By the same token, Palestinians will have the same legal and civil rights as the rest of the residents and citizens of Israel.

THE REAL DEMOGRAPHIC THREAT

The real demographic threat that Israel faces is not that Palestinians will become the majority west of the Jordan River. The real demographic threat is that if a Palestinian state is created, vast numbers of Palestinians will flee to Israel (as they began to do immediately after Israel undertook its "peace process" with the PLO in 1993), and a sufficient number will emigrate to Judea and Samaria from surrounding Arab countries to overwhelm Israel.

At the end of the day, the issue of demography is not about population count—it is about the capacity of one demographic group to harm its neighbors. If the increasingly radicalized, militarized Palestinian Authority is permitted to remain in power in even a limited area of Judea and Samaria, over time its capacity to demonize Israel internationally and so enable the immigration of large numbers of foreign-born Arabs will mount. And under PLO or Hamas control, the capacity of this growing population to cause Israel strategic harm—whether by overwhelming national infrastructures or through terrorism—will only grow.

The Palestinians whom the PLO wishes to bring into a Palestinian state—and Israel—have been living in UN refugee camps in surrounding countries since 1948. For sixty-six years the United Nations, the PLO, Hamas, Al Qaeda, Hezbollah, and governing regimes have fed them a steady diet of pure hatred toward Israel. With such populations immigrating to the Palestinian state, pressure for Israeli concessions within the 1949 armistice lines will only grow, along with the Palestinians' ability to threaten Israel within those lines.

Given this prospect, it is clear that, demographically, Israel will be far better off taking sole responsibility for the Palestinian population of Judea and Samaria. And again, this is true despite the obvious demographic price Israel will have to pay.

THE DANGER TO ISRAEL'S SOVEREIGN RIGHTS

Finally, Israel will gain from applying its sovereignty to Judea and Samaria in the realm of its international legal rights. As we have seen, Israel, in order to maintain its allegiance to the two-state formula, maintains that the issue of sovereignty over Judea and Samaria is disputed. But Israel has abstained from either asserting or defending its own rights to sovereignty over the areas under international law. At the same time, it has also done nothing to abandon its legal rights to sovereignty over the areas. This position, however, is not without danger.

According to law professor Avi Bell, there are two ways a state can give up its sovereignty over territory without any formal agreement. One is abandonment, when a state gives up control of territory with the intent to relinquish sovereign claims. The other is acquiescence, when a state remains unjustifiably silent while a rival claimant to sovereignty presents claims to the territory and exercises rights over it. Israel, for instance, may very well have abandoned its claim to sovereignty over the Gaza Strip when it removed its military forces and civilian population in 2005. And the longer Israel waits to assert its rights in Judea and Samaria, the greater the risk that it will do something that will rightly be interpreted as acquiescence.[26]

For asserting its legal and national rights to the Jewish people's historic heartland and the cradle of Jewish civilization, Israel will pay a significant short-term diplomatic price. But the alternative—remaining attached to the failed two-state paradigm—will be worse. Over the long term, a decision to apply Israeli law to Judea and Samaria will significantly strengthen Israel's strategic, diplomatic, democratic, demographic, and legal positions.

CHAPTER 18

America, Israel, and the One-State Plan

JOHN KERRY IN FANTASYLAND

In May 2013 Secretary of State John Kerry visited Israel and the Palestinian Authority, his fourth visit since he was sworn in three months earlier. The goal of the trip—like the previous three—was to persuade PLO chief and PA chairman Mahmoud Abbas to agree to restart the peace talks with Israel that he had cut off in December 2008.

In the course of the visit, Kerry addressed regional and world leaders in Jordan at the annual World Economic Forum summit. There Kerry unveiled a new U.S. initiative to bring $4 billion in investment funds to the Palestinian Authority. "The plan for the Palestinian economy," he boasted, "is bigger and bolder and more ambitious than anything proposed since [the initiation of the peace process at] Oslo more than twenty years ago." The plan, if fully implemented, he said, could increase the Palestinian GDP by 50 percent over three years and cut unemployment by two-thirds, from 21 percent down to 8 percent.[1]

The U.S. secretary of state assured his audience that there was no hidden agenda behind the extraordinary plan. The United States expected nothing in return.

The initiative was not a ploy to buy Palestinian flexibility on the core issues that were seemingly preventing the signing of a final peace accord. The massive influx of U.S. investment funds was not even meant to "build peace" through Palestinian prosperity and so reduce the need for America to pressure Israel to concede to the PLO's other demands. In Kerry's words, "The political approach [i.e., pressure for Israeli concessions] is central and it is our top priority."[2]

Rather than thank the United States for its largesse, PA leaders—controlled by Abbas—reacted with indignation and contempt and rejected Kerry's proposal. Addressing the forum after Kerry, Abbas insisted that peace talks could start only after Israel agreed to withdraw to the 1949 armistice lines, released all Palestinian terrorists imprisoned in Israel, and agreed to the unlimited immigration of millions of foreign-born Arabs who claim to be descended from Arabs who left Israel during the pan-Arab invasion in 1948–49, under the invented "right of return."[3]

After the conference, senior PA and Fatah officials castigated Kerry for trying to "bribe" the Palestinians into making concessions. "I don't think there is anything called economic peace or security peace or political peace," senior PA negotiator Saeb Erekat said. "These are intertwined elements and the key to peace and stability lies in Israeli acceptance of the two-state solution on the 1967 borders, ending settlement construction, and releasing prisoners."[4]

Senior Fatah official Abdullah Abdullah similarly excoriated Kerry, saying, "We have to be clear that we don't want this economic peace. We are not animals that only want food. We are a people struggling for freedom."

Not only did the Palestinian Authority reject Kerry's overture; Fatah officials ratcheted up an "anti-normalization" campaign that Fatah initiated before the World Economic Forum meeting. The campaign called for an economic boycott of the Palestinian businessmen who accompanied Abbas to Amman and of Palestinian businessmen who visited Haifa and met there with Israeli business leaders at the invitation of Haifa's chamber of commerce. Participants in the campaign included Fatah activists, politicians, writers' unions, and labor unions.[5]

Immediately after Kerry finished unveiling his economic plan and returned to Washington, Abbas, as if to eliminate any doubt, announced that he was appointing Fatah apparatchik Rami Hamdallah to succeed U.S.-supported Salam Fayyad as PA prime minister. Hamdallah, an English professor from An-Najah University in Nablus, had no political experience, no independent power base, and no economic training. According to Palestinian journalist Khaled Abu Toameh, Abbas chose Hamdallah for two reasons: he would obediently fulfill all of Fatah's demands for siphoning donor funds earmarked for the Palestinian Authority and development projects; and his perfect English would enable him to present a friendly face to international donors as he absconded with their hundreds of millions of dollars in aid funds.[6]

In other words, Kerry came to the region and presented an enormous aid plan for the Palestinians in a bid to build goodwill and strengthen the PLO's commitment to peace. The Palestinians responded by condemning his plan as an attempted bribe; castigating Palestinian businessmen who dared to meet with Israelis (thus diminishing the chance that international businesses will agree to invest in the Palestinian economy); and appointing as prime minister a man whose only qualification for the job was his ability to ensure that donor funds would continue to be misappropriated.

The Palestinians' contemptuous response to Kerry's plan was not well reported—but that was par for the course. It didn't fit into the narrative that informs most Americans' thinking about the Palestinian conflict with Israel. As we saw in Part I, that narrative—the two-state narrative—assumes that the cause of the Palestinian conflict with Israel is the absence of a Palestinian state.

Given the proper mix of concessions, goodwill gestures, and territorial acquisitions in Judea, Samaria, and Jerusalem (together with the territory they already control in Gaza), the Palestinians will embrace Israel as a neighbor and accept statehood and international norms of behavior. Moreover, the situation in the region as a whole will stabilize as the principal cause of pan-Islamic anger at the United States and the West—the absence of a Palestinian state—amid its recognition and support for Israel, will dissipate.

But as we have seen, that narrative is without foundation. The Palestinians are not interested in a state of their own at Israel's side and never have been. Ever since the establishment of the British Mandate in Palestine, the goal of the Palestinian national movement has been the destruction of the Jewish state in the Land of Israel. What will replace that state is not the issue. The goal of destroying Israel unifies Fatah with Hamas, and it unifies them both with Iran, the Muslim Brotherhood, and Saudi Arabia. This is the goal that has informed and animated the actions of Fatah and the PLO since they were established, years before the 1967 Six Day War.

Indeed, in a 2013 speech at an event marking the forty-ninth anniversary of the founding of the PLO, Abbas made clear that the original goal of the movement—the destruction of Israel—remains the goal of the movement today.[7]

The Palestinians could not be any clearer about their goals and intentions. They have never hidden them behind anything but the flimsiest, most temporary veneers. So why does Kerry get it wrong? Why does he insist on living in fantasyland?

Kerry is not unique in his failure to accept or contend with reality, as it relates to the Palestinians, and neither is the Obama administration as a whole. As we have seen, this reality rejection syndrome has been a bipartisan failing. George W. Bush and his secretaries of state were no less afflicted with it than President Barack Obama and his secretaries of state have been.

CLINTON'S MISUNDERSTOOD LEGACY

The failure of both the Bush and Obama administrations to accept the truth about the Palestinians and their intentions owes in large part to the misunderstood legacy of Bill Clinton's Middle East policy.

Most Americans think that Clinton's policy was a success, and they accept as fact three basic assumptions. First, they believe that at the Camp David peace summit in July 2000, Clinton very nearly achieved a peace deal between the Palestinians and Israel. (He was *this* close!") Second, they believe that if that deal had been reached, peace would have prevailed, and the agreement, unlike all the earlier Israel-PLO peace agreements, would have been honored. Third, they believe what Clinton, his advisers, and his successors have all claimed: that "everyone knows" the broad contours of an agreement.[8] Those contours, as all the experts would have it, involve the establishment of an independent Palestinian state in Judea, Samaria, Gaza, and parts of Jerusalem, including the Temple Mount.

Based on their acceptance of these three assumptions, Bush and Obama both believed that to succeed in bringing peace to Israel and the Palestinians—and consequently, to bring stability and moderation to the entire Middle East—all they needed to do was to build on the firm foundation that Clinton had established.

But in fact, Clinton's Middle East policy was not a reliable blueprint for future policy in the region. On the contrary, it was a catastrophic failure. And the only reason it wasn't widely understood to have been a failure is that most of its horrific consequences emerged after Clinton left office.

When Clinton left office in January 2001, the Palestinian terror war was in its opening stage; the U.S. policy community had yet to grasp its dimensions and strategic implications. Only in the months that followed Clinton's departure did it become clear the terror campaign was a full-blown war. Only in 2002 was evidence of the Palestinian Authority's central role in organizing the terror exposed. And when the Palestinians, undaunted by their proven culpability, escalated their diplomatic campaign to delegitimize Israel, they proved the mendaciousness of their alleged wish to make peace.

By the time all this became clear, it was possible to blame the deterioration of conditions on Bush. In other words, Clinton's false legacy of near-success remained intact despite the dire consequences of his policies, because those consequences were blamed on his successor.

THE BUSH AND OBAMA COROLLARIES TO CLINTON'S LEGACY

With Clinton's false assumptions guiding them, it is not surprising that Bush's and Obama's Middle East policies failed utterly. The tragedy of their embrace of the PLO was that not only did they fail to recognize the error at the root of the policy, which guaranteed that it would never succeed; they built their entire Middle East policies atop their incorrect understanding of the Palestinian conflict with Israel.

Both Bush and Obama believed that all that was required to make Clinton's two-state, PLO-centric paradigm a success was an ideological vision for how it would work. Both men's visions for bringing it across the finishing line also served as the foundation for their wider policies toward the Islamic world.

Bush believed that the way to reach the peace that had just barely eluded Clinton was through the promotion of democracy. His signature policy in the Arab world was to promote democracy, whether in the Palestinian Authority or Egypt, in Afghanistan or Iraq. He first introduced this policy in a systematic way in his June 24, 2002, speech where he called for new Palestinian leadership, which we discussed in Chapter 1.

The means Bush chose to promote this aim was to encourage—and where possible insist—on the conduct of free and open elections. He believed that if people were given the opportunity to determine their own destiny by choosing their leaders, they would choose leaders who would transform their societies into peaceful, liberal democracies.

Bush's faith in elections as a panacea for the social and political pathologies of the Islamic world, although well intentioned, was deeply deluded. Like his misconstruing of the events at the July 2000 Camp David summit, it was based on the false belief that the Palestinians and the wider Islamic world were by their nature moderate and peaceful, just like the Americans and Israelis, and that even Islamists like Hamas and the Muslim Brotherhood would govern responsibly if elected.

Bush spelled out this naïve belief in 2005: "There's a positive effect when you run for office. Maybe some will run for office and say, 'Vote for me, I look forward to blowing up America.' . . . I don't think so. I think people who generally run for office say, 'Vote for me, I'm looking forward to fixing your potholes, or making sure you got bread on the table.'"[9] But as repeated polling data and electoral results have borne out, this is simply not the case.

When Islamists are permitted to run for office, they generally win. The most popular ideology in the Islamic world is not liberalism but Islamism. This totalitarian ideology teaches that Israel must be obliterated, that women must be subjugated, and that non-Muslims and non-Islamist Muslims must be persecuted. It is inherently and necessarily anti-American.[10] And the Islamists do not run for office to fix potholes. They run for office and win to implement this ideological platform. And their voters understand this. In time, Bush's democratization-through-elections policy became the vehicle through which Hamas was empowered in the Palestinian Authority and the Muslim Brotherhood won free elections in Egypt and Tunisia. The result of these victories has been violence, instability, and chaos.

Rather than learn the lessons of Bush's mistakes, Obama has aggravated them. His vision for peace, stability, and moderation in the Middle East is built on "mutual respect and mutual interests" with the Muslim world.[11] Obama explained this expression in his speech at the University in Cairo on June 4, 2009. There, he made clear his belief that the core of the difficulties in U.S.-Islamic relations, including America's failure to bring peace between Israel and the Palestinians, is not Bush's naïve belief that once in power Islamists will become liberal democrats. Rather, the core of America's difficulties in U.S.-Islamic relations is the perceived U.S. disrespect for Islamists.

In a telling string of events, Obama bowed before the Islamist King Abdullah of Saudi Arabia on April 2, 2009, and four days later placed the United States on the same moral plane as its foes in a speech before the Islamist-dominated Turkish parliament. [12] "All of us have to change," he said, "And sometimes change is hard. . . . The United States is still working through some of our own darker periods in our history."[13]

In mid-2009 Egypt was the most stalwart U.S. ally in the Arab world, and the Arab anchor of the U.S. war against Islamist terrorism. But Obama didn't call his June 4 speech in Cairo an address to "the Egyptian people." Rather, he referred to it as a speech to "the Muslim world." In doing so, he adopted the language of Egyptian president Hosni Mubarak's greatest domestic foes: the Muslim Brotherhood. It was Mubarak's rejection of the Brotherhood's pan-Islamic, totalitarian message that made him a stalwart ally of the United States in its war on terror.

To be clear, "the Muslim world" is an Islamist concept. By addressing "the Muslim world," Obama signaled an acceptance of the Islamist view that all Muslims are motivated to act by the same totalitarian religious and political impulses that inform the actions of Islamists from the Muslim Brotherhood and the Iranian regime.

In the face of Mubarak's open objections, Obama invited members of the Muslim Brotherhood to attend his speech. This invitation communicated unmistakably that Obama viewed their movement as legitimate and sympathized with their rejection of the Egyptian nation-state and their goal of reestablishing a global caliphate.

As for the content of his hour-long address, from the outset, Obama drew moral equivalence between the United States and its democratic allies and the Islamic world. "The relationship between Islam and the West includes centuries of co-existence and cooperation," he said, "but also conflict and religious wars. More recently, tension has been fed by colonialism that denied rights and opportunities to many Muslims, and a Cold War in which Muslim-majority countries were too often treated as proxies without regard to their own aspirations. Moreover, the sweeping change brought by modernity and globalization led many Muslims to view the West as hostile to the traditions of Islam."

Obama chastised the United States for invading Iraq. "Unlike Afghanistan," he said, "Iraq was a war of choice that provoked strong differences in my country and around the world. Although I believe that the Iraqi people are ultimately better off without the tyranny of Saddam Hussein, I also believe that events in Iraq have reminded America of the need to use diplomacy and build international consensus to resolve our problems whenever possible."

Obama drew moral equivalence between the United States and Iran. He placed the CIA-sponsored 1953 coup against the pro-Soviet Iranian prime minister Mohammed Mossadegh on the same plane as the war Iran has waged against the United States ever since the 1979 Islamic revolution. "In the middle of the Cold War," he said, "the United States played a role in the overthrow of a democratically elected Iranian government. Since the Islamic Revolution, Iran has played a role in acts of hostage-taking and violence against U.S. troops and civilians."

While he put the United States on equal moral footing with the Muslim world, Obama placed Israel in a morally inferior position to that of the Muslims—and of the Palestinians in particular. Like jihadist leaders, including Iranian president Mahmoud Ahmadinejad, Obama rooted Israel's existence not in the Jewish people's four-thousand-year history in the Land of Israel, nor in their legal right to sovereignty over the land in accordance with the League of Nations Mandate for Palestine, but in the Holocaust, saying, "The aspiration for a Jewish homeland is rooted in a tragic history." He then discussed his plans to visit Buchenwald death camp.[14]

Obama drew moral equivalence between the genocide of European Jewry and the "suffering" of the Palestinians under Israeli rule. "The situation for the Palestinian people is intolerable," he intoned, then compared Israel's control of Judea and Samaria to the pre-civil rights movement American South and to apartheid South Africa. He attacked Israeli communities in Judea and Samaria, falsely claiming that Jewish construction in Judea, Samaria, and Jerusalem "violates previous agreements and undermines efforts to achieve peace."

Obama's efforts to degrade the moral legitimacy of both the United States and Israel by drawing a moral equivalence between the United States and its Islamist foes, and by demoting Israel to a moral standing inferior to Islamic totalitarians who seek its annihilation, backfired. As we saw at the outset of this chapter, it empowered the Palestinian Authority to treat the United States with unvarnished contempt and reject all of Obama's efforts to establish a Palestinian state through a negotiated settlement with Israel.[15]

In the wider Islamic world, countries following Iran's leadership have rebuffed Obama's repeated efforts to appease them. Syria, both before and after the outbreak of its civil war, rejected his attempts to appease Damascus into moderation. Following his withdrawal of all U.S. forces from Iraq, the Iraqi government effectively allied itself with Iran, allowing Iran to transport weapons to Syria through its territory, among other things.[16] As for Iran, it has used all his efforts to reach a "grand bargain" on its nuclear weapons program as a means to complete its nuclear weapons program.

Whereas Obama was indispensable for the Egyptian Muslim Brotherhood's ascent to power, the Muslim Brotherhood government similarly treated Obama with contempt. President Mohamed Morsi allowed Islamists to attack the U.S. embassy on September 11, 2012. He publicly called for the United States to free the mastermind of the 1993 World Trade Center bombing, Sheik Omar Abdel-Rahman, from prison.[17] He stood behind the arrest and indictment of American citizens who worked in Egypt for American NGOs to promote democracy. The only U.S. national who failed to flee the country after the indictments were filed was sentenced to two years in prison for his work.[18]

FANTASY-BASED POLICIES AND BLINDNESS TO REALITY

In July 2013, during the massive anti–Muslim Brotherhood demonstrations in Egypt that precipitated the military overthrow, protesters held placards condemning Obama for supporting terrorism through his support for the Brotherhood.[19]

As Obama made clear in his 2009 speech in Cairo, his administration believed that the way to build good relations with the "Muslim world" was by supporting the totalitarian Islamists. Like Bush's Pollyannaish belief in open elections as a panacea for all political pathologies, Obama's belief that empowering Islamists was the answer to the region's ills blinded him and his advisers to the dangers the Muslim Brotherhood posed to Egypt, and to the mounting opposition to Morsi's open moves to transform Egypt into an Islamist state.[20]

Because of the Obama administration's commitment to supporting Islamists, the president and his advisers were taken by surprise by the size and force of the anti–Muslim Brotherhood demonstrations. Failing to see the writing on the wall ahead of the demonstrations, Anne Patterson, the U.S. ambassador in Egypt, told Egyptians not to protest the government and so placed the United States on the side of the now-hated Muslim Brotherhood regime.[21]

After the military ousted the government, the United States was paralyzed. Obama and his advisers were incapable of understanding the harsh judgment of the Egyptian protesters or the military's refusal to share power with the totalitarian Brotherhood. "None of us can quite figure this out," a senior administration official told *The Wall Street Journal*. "It seems so self-defeating."[22]

The inability of successive U.S. administrations to foresee or even understand the significance of events in the Arab world and the wider Islamic world is deeply rooted in their core assumption that the Palestinian conflict with Israel is the central conflict in the region and is the cause of all other conflicts. This misapprehension of reality has two direct consequences for U.S. policy makers.

First, they feel free to trivialize the pathologies of the Arab world. After all, if the region's problems all stem from the absence of a Palestinian state, then illiberalism, misogyny, anti-Americanism, anti-Semitism, religious bigotry, intolerance, and totalitarian sensibilities are either beside the point or mere affectations that are easily abandoned given the right set of inducements from the U.S.

The Bush administration felt comfortable downplaying or ignoring the popularity of totalitarian movements, while attributing the loftiest liberal democratic impulses to societies where they were utterly absent— because at the end of the day, whether the Iraqis, Afghans, Palestinians, or Egyptians were liberal democrats or totalitarians didn't matter. All their pathologies would magically disappear—or at least cease to threaten America—the minute Israel surrendered enough land to make the Palestinians happy.

With Obama, the problem is even deeper. Bush's acceptance of Israeli culpability for the absence of peace in the Middle East caused him to believe the best about the Arabs—who were, in his mind, no different from Americans or Israelis.

In Obama's case, his acceptance of the assumption that Israel's refusal to surrender to all the PLO's demands is responsible for the absence of peace and stability in the Middle East causes him to believe the worst about Israel—and by extension, about the United States, which supports Israel. Obama's repeated apologies for purported American bad behavior, and his condemnations of Israel in front of rabidly anti-Semitic audiences in Cairo, Ankara, and Riyadh, were grounded in his foundational belief that the United States and Israel are to blame for the violence that engulfs the region and emanates from it.

Obama's embrace of totalitarian Islamists, and his administration's admitted incomprehension of Islamic and Arab opposition to the Muslim Brotherhood, is the corollary of his rejection of American and Israeli moral authority. If the United States and Israel are rogue actors in the Middle East, it follows that the most extremist actors in Arab and Muslim societies are morally acceptable. Only by first rejecting the basic justness of America and Israel—the greatest liberal democracy on earth and the only liberal democracy in the Middle East—could Obama embrace the totalitarian Muslim Brotherhood and insistently refuse to take any effective action to prevent Iran from acquiring nuclear weapons. Obama could not have embraced the Muslim Brotherhood without first holding the view that Israel is guilty for the absence of regional peace and stability, and that Israel's guilt renders it morally inferior to its neighbors.

Bush's and Obama's decisions to base their Middle Eastern policies on Clinton's failed two-state paradigm, coupled with their attachment to their own ideological models for implementing that paradigm, brought about a situation where by mid-2012, when Morsi succeeded Mubarak as president of Egypt, the United States had lost all but one of its allies in the Middle East.

ISRAEL: AMERICA'S INDISPENSABLE ALLY

In the wake of the collapse of the two-state paradigm, America's failed drive toward democratization, and the disastrous U.S. embrace of Islamism, Israel emerged as America's only stable, unwavering ally in the Middle East.

And yet rather than embrace Israel and strengthen it, in July 2013, John Kerry remained so fixated on "solving" the Palestinian conflict with Israel that he pressured Prime Minister Netanyahu into agreeing to release 104 Palestinian and Israeli Arab murderers from Israeli prisons, just to induce the Palestinians to sit down at a table with Israeli negotiators.[23]

Israelis and pro-Israel commentators often raise the question, "How would the United States respond?" if U.S. leaders were pressured to do what they pressure Israel to do.[24] And that is a reasonable question.

But at this point, with the Arab world embroiled in a maelstrom of radicalism, war, and revolution, and with Israel as the only stable U.S. ally in the Middle East, its only trusted friend there, and the only party in the region that shares its core values, the question ought to be: how much longer does the United States intend to maintain its allegiance to a policy that weakens, demoralizes, and humiliates Israel? How much longer will the United States embrace a policy based on falsehoods that blinds it to the realities of the region and so renders it incapable of understanding them or competently dealing with the manifold and dangerous challenges that the Middle East poses for U.S. national security?

No U.S. interest or value is advanced by pressuring Israel to free men like Mahmoud Salam Saliman Abu Harabish and Adam Ibrahim Juma'a-Juma'a from prison. In 1988 they firebombed an Israeli bus and incinerated five people: a twenty-six-year-old teacher named Rachel Weiss, her three children, who ranged in age from three years to nine months, and an Israeli soldier who tried to rescue them.[25]

No American interest or value is advanced by spending hundreds of millions of dollars to fund and train a Palestinian military whose forces participate in terrorist attacks against Israel and who remain dedicated to the destruction of America's only stalwart ally in the Middle East.[26]

Nor is any American interest advanced by spending billions of dollars to promote a Palestinian economy controlled by kleptomaniacal terror supporters, who steal donor money to finance terrorism, to incite anti-Semitism, and to line their pockets.[27]

The time has come for the United States to put this two-decades-long foreign policy debacle behind it. The time has come for the United States to adopt a Middle East policy that reflects its values and its interests. And at the core of such a policy must be the recognition that Israel—the only human-rights-respecting liberal democracy in the region, and the only regional military power capable of defending itself by itself—is its greatest ally and strategic asset in the Middle East.

Additional fundamental moral and strategic truths flow from this core factual premise. As we have seen, under international law, Israel is the lawful sovereign of Judea and Samaria. History proves that the Jewish people are the indigenous people of the Land of Israel. Israel's Arab and Muslim neighbors' refusal to accept these truths has nothing to do with Israel or its actions but owes to their internal pathologies. And those pathologies are far from trivial. They are the causes of the instability, violence, and radicalism that engulf their societies and render the Middle East so dangerous.

Conversely, the PLO, like the Palestinian Authority it controls, today remains what it has always been: a terrorist organization, and the architect and perpetuator of modern terrorism. The Palestinian people as well remain what they have been since Haj Amin el-Husseini invented them in 1920: a people that has never built a national identity based on anything other than the rejection of the Jewish people's national identity and rights.

A strong Israel defends and advances U.S. national security interests in the Middle East because Israel is inherently nonaggressive, and its enemies are also enemies of America. A weak Israel empowers and emboldens the most radical forces in the Arab and Islamic world.

The Palestinian conflict with Israel is a function of the larger Arab and Islamic world's refusal to accept that Israel has a right to exist. Arab states do not organize their politics or their foreign policies around the Palestinian issue; rather, they exploit it as a means to coerce the Americans—and before them the British—into taking actions to appease them. The Palestinian conflict with Israel is the core of nothing but the ongoing and ever-deepening radicalization of Palestinian society. And the Palestinians' radicalism always rises proportionately with the intensity of the West's commitment to pressuring Israel to make concessions to them.

As U.S. policy makers stare in utter confusion at the morass that is the Arab world, they should recognize that the first step toward building a new network of allies in the Middle East is to strengthen—not endanger—Israel. As America's only remaining ally there, the United States has a paramount national security interest in ensuring the military strength and social cohesion of the Jewish state. The stronger and more internally stable Israel is, the more secure American regional interests are.

EMBRACING THE ISRAELI ONE-STATE PLAN

Israel already has the most powerful military force in the region. No doubt, the United States could offer to sell Israel certain weapons systems that would diminish its vulnerabilities in various areas and make it stronger. But by far the lowest-risk way the United States could empower Israel and secure its own interests would be to abandon the two-state solution model and adopt the Israeli one-state plan as its policy paradigm for dealing with the Palestinian conflict with Israel.

The Israeli one-state plan provides an equitable, democratic means of resolving the conflict, and by safeguarding Israel's national and legal rights, it secures Israel's strategic posture. It neutralizes the Palestinians' capacity to destabilize Israel domestically and delegitimize it internationally, and it strengthens Israel militarily, both from foreign invasion and from terror assaults.

For the United States, adopting the Israeli one-state plan is a win-win proposition. It will defuse a major issue that is used to criticize the United States. Indeed, the United States can stifle much of the international criticism it receives for supporting Israel simply by ending its attempts to appease the Arabs and by ceasing to placate their cynical criticism of that support.

Moreover, at a time when fiscal considerations are becoming more and more crucial for U.S. policy makers, the Israeli one-state plan stands out for its frugality. Since 1993, the United States has spent some $7 billion on direct and indirect aid to the Palestinian Authority. In fiscal year 2013 alone, the United States committed $440 million in taxpayer dollars to direct financial support for the Palestinian Authority.[28]

As we have seen, this money has consistently gone to financing a corrupt kleptocracy and to funding and training a Palestinian military force that is dedicated to destroying Israel, and whose members have participated in attacks against Israeli civilian and military targets in the past. Moreover, both American and Israeli generals who work with this force have warned that it can be expected to play a major role in future Palestinian warfare against Israel.[29] So aside from the massive savings that would be involved in cutting off U.S. support for the Palestinians, doing so would right the wrong of having played a major role in financing and training a military organization that is inherently hostile toward the chief U.S. ally in the Middle East.

Israel will likely not require any U.S. assistance in financing the implementation of the one-state plan—beyond, perhaps, loan guarantees to facilitate Israeli borrowing on the international markets to finance the initial shock that its economy will likely absorb following the sudden, steep rise in the number of applications for its welfare rolls after it grants permanent residency to the Palestinians in Judea and Samaria.

Backing the one-state plan is a low-risk strategy. The United States will not need to deploy military forces to advance it. All it will have to do is what it has been doing for the past fifty years: block anti-Israel measures from passing at the UN Security Council and oppose EU sanctions against the Jewish state.

Finally and most important, the Israeli one-state plan will liberate Americans from the stranglehold of the two-state solution's mythology. For the first time in a generation, American foreign policy hands, politicians, and regular citizens will be able to see the Arab and Islamic worlds for what they are, and not view them through the distorting, mendacious lens of a policy paradigm that falsely places the blame for all their failings and problems on Israel.

The misperceptions that fed the Middle East policies of Clinton, Bush, and Obama can finally be discarded in favor of the facts. And equipped with a fact-based assessment of regional events, for the first time in twenty years, American policy makers will be less likely to be surprised by the tumultuous developments in the Middle East that so affect American national security and challenge American values.

In other words, by supporting the Israeli one-state plan, the United States will regain the main resource that it has lost in its two decades of pursuing the chimera of the two-state solution: the truth.

ACKNOWLEDGMENTS

Many people played important roles in helping me to write this book. None has made a larger contribution than my agent Mel Berger, from William Morris Endeavor. Without Mel's enthusiasm and support, I never would have written it. And for his able assistance, he has earned my undying gratitude.

My editor at Crown, Derek Reed, was brought in late in the game, but he hit the ground running. His edits were thoughtful and on target. They forced me to clarify my arguments and in general made this a better book.

My research assistant Neta Dror was vital in preparing the manuscript. Neta worked at all hours to find the sources I needed and to collate information for me quickly and competently, saving me literally hundreds of hours of research work.

My friend and colleague Avi Bell, from Bar Ilan University Faculty of Law and the University of San Diego Law School, was a constant sounding board for this book. Aside from serving as my own personal international law professor, Avi read over early drafts and provided helpful suggestions for improvements.

Steve Linde, editor in chief of the *Jerusalem Post*, was supportive of this book from the outset. Steve graciously enabled me to take a prolonged leave of absence from the paper so that I could devote myself to this project.

David Horowitz and Michael Finch, from the David Horowitz Freedom Center in Los Angeles, have also shown extraordinary forbearance as I essentially slid down the rabbit hole for several months in order to write this book.

Marc and Suri Provisor from Shilo, Israel, gave me constant moral support through the long grind of book writing. Their home was always open to me and my children, when I needed a break; and the view from their living room, of the ancient road—now Highway 60—that Jews have traveled since biblical times was a source of inspiration.

Similarly, Kerem and Adam Perlman kept up my morale during the writing process, helping me through bouts of writer's block just by being there for me.

My friend and colleague Major General Gershon Hacohen was always ready to help me piece together my arguments. Gershon taught me a great deal about the development of Israel's relations with the Druze in the Golan Heights, where he built his home.

Finally and most important, my family is the source of my strength. My children give meaning to my life. They renew my hope for the future each and every day. I pray that this book will play some role in securing that future for them.

This book is dedicated to my parents, Gerald (of blessed memory) and Sharon Glick. My father became ill while I was writing the manuscript and passed away while I was editing it. Throughout his heroic battle with a horrible disease, he remained the spirit behind this book, always pushing me to complete chapter after chapter. I read him early texts as I sat by his bed in the hospital. Just as he provided feedback for all my writings, going back to my schoolgirl days, lying in his hospital bed, my father continued to be my greatest writing coach.

My father and mother have been my greatest friends and my anchor in stormy seas. Without their stalwart support, both during the writing of this book and throughout my life, I would never have completed this project, or anything else of note.

BIBLIOGRAPHY

Amit-Cohn, Uzi, et. al., *Israel, the "Intifada" and the Rule of Law*, Tel Aviv: Israel Ministry of Defense Publications, 1993.

Andrew, Christopher and Vasili Mitrokhin, *The World Was Going Our Way: The KGB and the Battle for the Third World*, New York: Basic Books, 2005.

Aron, Raymond, *De Gaulle, Israel and the Jews*, Piscataway, N.J.: Transaction Publishers, 2004.

Atashe, Zeidan, *Druze and Jews in Israel: A Shared Destiny?* Brighton, U.K.: Cambridge University Press, 1992.

Auerbach, Jerold S., *Hebron Jews: Memory and Conflict in the Land of Israel*, Lanthan, Md.: Rowman and Littlefield, 2009.

Avi-Yonah, Michael, *The Jews of Palestine: A Political History from Bar Kokhba to the Arab Conquest*, Oxford: Basil Blackwell, 1976.

Avner, Yehuda, *The Prime Ministers: An Intimate Narrative of Israeli Leadership*, Jerusalem: Toby Press, 2010.

Black, Edwin, *The Farhud: Roots of the Arab-Nazi Alliance in the Holocaust*, New York: Dialog Press, 2010.

Brian, Denis, *The Seven Lives of Colonel Patterson: How an Irish Lion Fighter Led the Jewish Legion to Victory*, Syracuse, N.Y.: Syracuse University Press, 2008.

Bush, George W., *Decision Points*, New York: Crown, 2010.

Chafets, Ze'ev, *Double Vision: How the Press Distorts America's View of the Middle East*, New York: William Morrow, 1985.

Cheney, Dick with Liz Cheney, *In My Time: A Personal and Political Memoir*, New York: Threshold, 2011.

Clinton, Bill, *My Life*, New York: Vintage, 2005.

Cohn, Norman, *Warrant for Genocide: The Myth of the Jewish World Conspiracy and the Protocols of the Elders of Zion*, London: Serif, 2006.

Dalin, David G. and Rothmann, John F., *Icon of Evil: Hitler's Mufti and the Rise of Radical Islam*, New York: Random House, 2008.

Esco Foundation for Palestine, *Palestine: A Study of Jewish, Arab and British Policies*, New Haven, Conn: Yale University Press, 1947.

Feith, Douglas, *War and Decision: Inside the Pentagon at the Dawn of the War on Terrorism*, New York: HarperCollins, 2008.

Gil Moshe, *A History of Palestine, 634–1099*, Cambridge, U.K.: Cambridge University Press, 1992.

Gilbert, Lela, *Saturday People, Sunday People: Israel through the Eyes of a Christian Sojourner*, New York: Encounter Books, 2012.

Gilder, George, *The Israel Test*, Minneapolis, Minn.: Richard Vigilante Books, 2009.

Gold, Dore, *Hatred's Kingdom: How Saudi Arabia Supports the New Global Terrorism*, Washington, D.C.: Regnery, 2003.

Harel, Menashe, *Historical Geography of the Land of Israel* (Hebrew), Tel Aviv: Zmorra Bitan, 1997.

Josephus, *The Jewish War*, New York: Penguin Books, 1981.

Karsh, Efraim, *Arafat's War: The Man and His Battle for Israeli Conquest*, New York: Grove Press, 2003.

Killebrew, Ann, *Biblical People and Ethnicity: An Archaeological Study of Egyptians, Canaanites, Philistines and Early Israel 1300–1100 BCE*, Atlanta, Ga.: Society of Biblical Literature, 2005.

Kozodoy, Neal, ed. *The Mideast Peace Process: An Autopsy*, New York: Encounter Books, 2002.

Kuntzel, Matthias, *Jihad and Jew Hatred: Islamism, Nazism and the Roots of 9/11*, New York: Telos Press, 2007.

Lauterpacht, Elihu, *Jerusalem and the Holy Places*, London: Anglo-Israel Association, 1968.

Ledeen, Michael, *Accomplice to Evil: Iran and the War Against the West*, New York: St. Martin's Press, 2009.

Mallmann, Klaus-Michael, and Martin Cuppers, *Nazi Palestine: The Plans for the Extermination of the Jews in Palestine*, New York: Enigma Books, 2005.

Ma'oz, Moshe, *Studies on Palestine During the Ottoman Period*, Jerusalem: Magnes Press, 1975.

Marcus, Itamar and Nan Jacques Zilberdik, *Deception: Betraying the Peace Process*, Israel: Palestinian Media Watch, 2011

McCarthy, Andrew C., *The Grand Jihad: How Islam and the Left Sabotage America*, New York: Encounter, 2010.

Morris, Benny, *Righteous Victims: A History of the Zionist-Arab Conflict 1881–1999*, New York: Alfred A. Knopf, 2000.

Oppenheim, Lassa, *International Law: A Treatise, Volume 1, Peace*, London: Longmans, Green, 1905.

Pacepa, Ion Mihai, *Red Horizons: The True Story of Nicolae and Elena Ceauşescus' Crimes, Lifestyle, and Corruption*, Washington, D.C.: Regnery Gateway, 1987.

Patterson, J. H., *With the Judaeans in the Palestine Campaign*, London: Hutchinson & Co., 1922.

Petit, Michael, *Peacekeepers at War: A Marine's Account of the Beirut Catastrophe*, Boston: Faber and Faber, 1986.

Prawer, Joshua, ed., *The History of the Land of Israel: Volume 6, The Islamic and Crusader Periods, (634–1291)* (Hebrew), Jerusalem: Yad Ben Zvi, 1981.

Rubin, Barry and Judith Colp Rubin, *Yasir Arafat: A Political Biography*, Oxford: Oxford University Press, 2003.

Rumsfeld, Donald, *Known and Unknown: A Memoir*, New York: Sentinel, 2011.

Stav, Arieh, ed., *Israel and a Palestinian State: Zero Sum Game?* Tel Aviv: Zmorra-Bitan Publishers, 2001.

Sterling, C. *The Terror Network*, New York: Holt Rinehart & Winston, 1981.

Stone, Julius, *Israel and Palestine, Assault on the Law of Nations*, Baltimore, Md.: Johns Hopkins University Press, 1981.

Sykes, Christopher, *Crossroads to Israel: 1917–1948*, Bloomington, Ind.: Indiana University Press, 1965.

Ya'alon, Moshe, et.al., *Israel's Critical Security Requirements for Defensible Borders*, Jerusalem: Jerusalem Center for Public Affairs, 2011.

Yadin, Yigal, *Bar-Kochba: The Rediscovery of the Legendary Hero of the Last Jewish Revolt Against Imperial Rome*, London: Littlehampton Book Services, 1971.

Ye'or, Bat, *Eurabia: The Euro-Arab Axis*, Madison and Teaneck, N.J.: Fairleigh Dickinson University Press, 2005.

NOTES

PREFACE

1. Dore Gold, *Hatred's Kingdom: How Saudi Arabia Supports the New Global Terrorism* (Washington, D.C.: Regnery, 2003), pp. 9–10. In a speech on the Middle East in 2010, Bill Clinton claimed that the creation of a Palestinian state, would "take about half the impetus in the whole world—not just the region, the whole world—for terror away. It would have more impact than anything else that could be done." See Peter Huessy, "Are We Willing to Defend Ourselves," Gatestone Institute International Policy Council, August 29, 2013, http://bit.ly/141EXlQ.

2. See, for instance, Brian Ross, "Iran Caught Red-handed Shipping Arms to the Taliban," *ABC News*, June 6, 2007, http://abcn.ws/17cJnHh; and Michael Ledeen, "The Fears of the Terror Masters: If We Want a Peaceful Iraq, We Will Have to Confront the Mullahs," *National Review*, June 29, 2004.

3. Thomas Beaumont and Daniel Estrin, "Gingrich: Palestinians 'Invented' People Is Truth," *Boston Globe*, December 10, 2011.

4. Daniel Pipes, "The Year the Arabs Discovered Palestine," *Middle East Review*, Summer 1989, http://bit.ly/aqERsz.

5. These statements are made at every possible opportunity. For instance, in an interview on Qatar's Al-Kass sports network on June 2, 2013, the former PA security chief and current chairman of the PA's Olympic Committee Jibril Rajoub said that Palestine includes all of Israel, "from the river to the sea." See Itamar Marcus and Jacques Nan Zilberdik, "Jibril Rajoub: 'All of Palestine—From the River to the Sea—It's All Occupied,'" *PMW Bulletins*, Palestinian Media Watch, June 10, 2013, http://bit.ly/11aCTB2. To get a sense of the scale of these statements, look generally at the Palestinian Media Watch website, www.palwatch.org.

6. See, for instance, "Girl Recites Poem: Jews Are 'Allah's Enemies, the Sons of Pigs,'" from PA-controlled Palestinian TV, March 22, 2013, and "Fatah Summer Camp Named After Terrorist Dalal Mughrabi," from the official

PA mouthpiece Ah-Hayat Al-Jadida, July 16, 2012, both at Palestinian Media Watch, http://bit.ly/wKpHxo.

7. Yaakov Lappin, "Clinton Slams PA Indoctrination: U.S. presidential candidate—PA textbooks Incite Hatred, Fail to Educate," *Ynet News*, August 2, 2007, http://bit.ly/142DKc0.

8. The Jordan Arab Legion massacred some 130 Jews after they had surrendered Kfar Etzion on May 13, 1948. The four survivors, and 320 other Jews from surrounding communities that were overrun, were taken prisoner and held under subhuman conditions in Jordan until March 1949. See Yair Sheleg, "The Death and Rebirth of Kfar Etzion," *Haaretz*, May 3, 2007.

9. In an April 2013 poll, 79 percent of Israelis supported applying Israeli sovereignty to all or part of Judea and Samaria. Fifty-nine percent supported doing so regardless of the status of peace talks with the Palestinians. These results indicated a steep rise in this support over the previous year, when the poll was first carried out. "Positions Regarding Application of Israeli Sovereignty to Judea and Samaria," Geocartographia polling firm for University of Ariel, April 2013.

10. See Herb Keinon, "Anti-normalization Forces Gaining Strength in Jordan," *Jerusalem Post*, August 9, 2011; and Dan Eldar, "Egypt and Israel: A Reversible Peace," *Middle East Quarterly* 10, no. 4 (Fall 2003), pp. 57–65, http://bit.ly/bf2g8h.

11. See, for instance, "Arab Media Review: Anti-Semitism and Other Trends," Anti-Defamation League, January–June 2012, http://bit.ly/186Ax93.

12. Ariel Ben Solomon, "Majority of Israeli Jews Pessimistic About Peace," *Jerusalem Post*, January 1, 2013.

13. Palestinian Center for Policy and Survey Research, "While Demand for Holding Local Elections Increases . . ." Public Opinion Poll No. 38, December 29, 2010, http://bit.ly/18xUCXO.

14. Palestinian Center for Policy and Survey Research, Joint Israeli-Palestinian Poll, June 17–23, 2012, http://bit.ly/LJUJCi.

15. Khaled Abu Toameh, "Abbas Vows: No Room for Israelis in Palestinian State," *Jerusalem Post*, December 25, 2010.

16. Mark Landler and Steven Lee Myers, "Obama Sees '67 Borders as Starting Point for Peace Deal," *New York Times*, May 19, 2011; Moshe Ya'alon et al., *Israel's Critical Security Requirements for Defensible Borders: The Foundation for a Viable Peace*, Jerusalem Center for Public Affairs, 2011, http://bit.ly/16jnHTf.

17. Bennett Zimmerman, Roberta Seid, and Michael L. Wise, "The Million Person Gap: The Arab Population in the West Bank and Gaza," Begin-Sadat Center for Strategic Studies, Bar-Ilan University, February 2006, http://bit.ly/14Ie6Wy.

18. In June 2013 the IDF's commander in Judea and Samaria, Major General

Nitzan Alon, stated that the PA funds and commands the mob violence against Israelis in Judea and Samaria. These assaults include stoning, fire-bombing, and shooting attacks at Israeli motorists as well as attempted infiltrations of Israeli communities in the areas. Dan Williams, "Israel General Says Palestinians Quietly Aiding U.S. Peace Drive," Reuters, June 18, 2013.

19. "Analysis of Attacks in Last Decade, 2000–2010," Israel Security Agency, undated, http://bit.ly/15JV2Xd.

20. Erick Stakelbeck, "American Victims of Palestinian Terror Seek Justice," CBN News, February 2, 2012, http://bit.ly/xemXGG.

21. See McLaughlin and Associates and Caddell Associates, "National Survey," August 10, 2011, http://bit.ly/LbrI5W. These data also indicate that most Americans do not believe that a Palestinian state would secure Israel or enhance either U.S. security or its position in the Middle East.

CHAPTER I: A BIPARTISAN PIPE DREAM

1. Israel is the most densely populated country in the Western world, with 860 people per square kilometer. Pi Gelilot is located in one of the most densely populated areas in the country, with 7,000 people per square kilometer. See Evgenia Bystrov and Arnon Soffer, "Israel: Demography 2012–2030: On the Way to a Religious State," University of Haifa, May 2012, http://bit.ly/11vpnIT; and Israel Central Bureau of Statistics, "Localities, Population and Density Per Sq. Km. by Metropolitan Area and Selected Localities," 2009, http://bit.ly/16S79rS.

2. Atilla Somfavli, "Thousands of People Saved from Death at Pi Gelilot" (Hebrew), Ynet, May 24, 2002, http://bit.ly/16AL9yW.

3. John Kifner, "Bomb Explodes at Israeli Fuel Depot, But Disaster Is Averted," New York Times, May 24, 2002.

4. "Victims of Palestinian Terrorism Since September 2000," Israel Ministry of Foreign Affairs, undated, http://bit.ly/13u79a8.

5. Ibid.

6. "President Bush Calls for New Palestinian Leadership," White House, June 24, 2002, http://1.usa.gov/jKNkZ8.

7. George W. Bush, Decision Points (New York: Crown, 2010), p. 404.

8. Gabi Siboni, "Defeating Suicide Terrorism in Judea and Samaria, 2002–2005," Military and Strategic Affairs 2, no. 2 (October 2010), pp. 113–24, http://bit.ly/16OsRdF.

9. "Suicide Bombing Terrorism During the Current Israeli-Palestinian Confrontation (September 2000–December 2005)," Intelligence and Terrorism Information Center at the Center for Special Studies, January 1, 2006, http://bit.ly/17NTxtW; and "The Nature and Extent of Palestinian Terrorism, 2006," Israel Ministry of Foreign Affairs, http://bit.ly/19vNyiU.

10. "The Involvement of Arafat, PA Senior Officials and Apparatuses in Terrorism Against Israel: Corruption and Crime," Israel Ministry of Foreign Affairs, May 6, 2002, http://bit.ly/11NMQ6s; and "Yasser Arafat's Mukata Compound in Ramallah—A Center for Controlling and Supporting Terrorism," Israel Ministry of Foreign Affairs, April 2, 2002, http://bit.ly/17sosMe.

11. "A Performance-Based Roadmap to a Permanent Two-State Solution to the Israeli-Palestinian Conflict," April 30, 2003, press statement, http://bit.ly/1dxfQZG.

12. "Recent Examples of Palestinian Authority Incitement," Israel Ministry of Foreign Affairs, March 13, 2011, http://bit.ly/14NOkGn; "Glorifying Terrorists and Terror," at Palestinian Media Watch, http://bit.ly/ePPp4a; and Justus Weiner, "The Recruitment of Children in the Current Palestinian Strategy," Jerusalem Issue Brief (Jerusalem Center for Public Affairs) 2, no. 8 (October 1, 2002), http://bit.ly/15OGxhH.

13. Yoav Stern, "Want to Know What Bush Thinks? Read Sharansky," Haaretz, February 22, 2005.

14. Bassem Eid and Natan Sharansky, "Bush's Mideast U-Turn," Wall Street Journal, February 11, 2008.

15. Rick Richman, "Rice's Road Map," New York Sun, October 10, 2007.

16. Glenn Kessler, "Rice, Israeli Official Share Perspectives," Washington Post, November 29, 2007.

17. Daniel Mandel, "The Peace Battler: Dennis Ross—the Man in the Middle," Review (Australian/Israel and Jewish Affairs Council), June 2001, http://bit.ly/15JUtfY.

18. The White House, "Remarks by the President on the Middle East and North Africa," May 19, 2011, http://1.usa.gov/13UuSS8.

19. Bret Stephens, "An Anti-Israel President: The President's Peace Proposal Is a Formula for War," Wall Street Journal, May 24, 2011.

20. "Fatah and Hamas Sign Reconciliation Deal," Al Jazeera, April 27, 2011.

21. "Foreign Terrorist Organizations," U.S. Department of State, Bureau of Counterterrorism, September 28, 2012, http://1.usa.gov/zSr040.

22. "Hamas Covenant 1988: The Covenant of the Islamic Resistance Movement," August 18, 1988, at http://bit.ly/Vyfc.

23. Reprinted with permission from the Jerusalem Center for Public Affairs.

24. David Rose, "The Gaza Bombshell," Vanity Fair, April 2008.

25. Although this is the formal U.S. position, the Bush and Obama administrations both maintained financial support for the Palestinian Authority, despite its consistent diversion of funds to the Hamas-controlled Palestinian Authority in the Gaza Strip and so used U.S. taxpayer dollars to fund an illegal terrorist organization. It has done so despite heavy congressional pressure to end the practice. See "Rep. Wants Hamas Payment Explained,"

Jewish Telegraphic Agency, August 13, 2007, http://bit.ly/16eC3aT; and "Ros-Lehtinen Reiterates Call for U.S., Foreign Governments to Cut Off Funds to Palestinian Authority, Block U.N. Recognition of Palestinian State," May 5, 2011.

26. "Condoleezza Rice Remarks at Town Hall Meeting," Washington, D.C., January 31, 2005, at http://bit.ly/16AOHBk.

27. "Condoleeza Rice Remarks at Town Hall Meeting."

CHAPTER 2: CLINTON'S LEGACY OF BLIND FAITH

1. Tony Karon, "Clinton Saves Last Dance for Arafat," *Time*, January 2, 2001.

2. Michael Hirsh, "Clinton to Arafat: It's All Your Fault," *Newsweek*, June 26, 2001.

3. "Freedom in the World—West Bank, 2012," Freedom House, undated, http://bit.ly/16jvuAo.

4. Ilene Prusher, "Barak Meets Arafat to Rekindle Peace," *Guardian*, July 27, 1999.

5. Netanel Lorch, "Israel's War of Independence 1947–1949," Israel Ministry of Foreign Affairs, http://bit.ly/1cQfgaM.

6. See Khaled Abu Toameh, "Lebanon's Apartheid Laws," Gatestone Institute International Policy Council, June 21, 2013, http://bit.ly/124QJID.

7. Elliott Abrams, "How Many Refugees?" Council on Foreign Relations, June 20, 2012, http://on.cfr.org/M6iGGZ.

8. For an in-depth study of the Palestinian refugee issue, see Arlene Kushner, "The UN's Palestinian Refugee Problem," *Azure* 22 (Autumn 5766/2005), pp. 57–77.

9. "Statement to the Knesset by Prime Minister Benjamin Netanyahu on the Protocol Concerning Redeployment in Hebron," Israel Ministry of Foreign Affairs, January 16, 1997, http://bit.ly/14OS6fT.

10. Khaled Abu Toameh, "Kaddoumi: PLO Charter Was Never Changed," *Jerusalem Post*, April 22, 2004.

11. Shlomo Sharan, "Israel and the Jews in the Schoolbooks of the Palestinian Authority," *Israel Resource Review*, May 16, 2001, http://bit.ly/16jxeda; and Andrea Levin, "Palestinian Textbooks Teach Anti-Israel Hate," CAMERA: Committee on Middle East Reporting in America, June 1, 1999, http://bit.ly/16ScvDi.

12. "Palestinian Incitement to Violence Since Oslo: A Four-Year Compendium," Israel Ministry of Foreign Affairs, August 10, 1997, http://bit.ly/1cQfui0.

13. Karin Laub, "Barak's American Advisors React," Associated Press, May 19, 1999, at http://bit.ly/14OSWJy.

14. Ari Shavit, "End of a Journey—Interview with Shlomo Ben-Ami," *Haaretz*, September 14, 2001, http://bit.ly/19PmkE4.

15. Terry M. Neal, "Bush Backs into Nation Building," *Washington Post*, February 26, 2003.

16. David Barnett, "The Mounting Problem of Temple Denial," GLORIA Center: Global Research in International Affairs, August 29, 2011, http://bit.ly/sz7mQY.

17. Bill Clinton, *My Life* (New York: Vintage, 2005), pp. 865–69.

18. Shavit, "End of a Journey."

19. Ibid.

20. Clinton, p. 866.

21. Matthew Kalman, "Mideast Training Program Backfires, Palestinian Security Officers Schooled by U.S. Later Used Tactics Against Israel," *San Francisco Chronicle*, February 14, 2005.

CHAPTER 3: HAJ AMIN EL-HUSSEINI AND THE FORGOTTEN LESSONS OF THE BRITISH MANDATE FOR PALESTINE, 1917–1948

1. Eli Hertz, "'Mandate for Palestine': Legal Aspects of Jewish Rights," *Myths and Facts*, http://bit.ly/Ii6vb0. Reprinted with permission.

2. Denis Brian, *The Seven Lives of Colonel Patterson: How an Irish Lion Fighter Led the Jewish Legion to Victory* (Syracuse, N.Y.: Syracuse University Press, 2008), passim; J. H. Patterson, *With the Judaeans in the Palestine Campaign* (London: Hutchinson & Co., 1922), passim.

3. "The Balfour Declaration," November 2, 1917, at http://avalon.law.yale.edu/20th_century/balfour.asp.

4. Patterson, *With the Judaeans*, passim.

5. Brian, *Seven Lives*, pp. 150–51; Jacqueline Shields, "Pre-State Israel: Arab Riots of the 1920s," Jewish Virtual Library, http://bit.ly/176LZ5s.

6. Brian, *Seven Lives*, p. 151.

7. Ibid., pp. 151–57.

8. Ibid.

9. David G. Dalin and John F. Rothmann, *Icon of Evil: Hitler's Mufti and the Rise of Radical Islam* (New York: Random House, 2008), pp. 36–38.

10. Ibid., pp. 7–8. While in Cairo, Husseini studied at the same Al-Azhar University that President Barack Obama hailed during his speech in Cairo on June 4, 2009.

11. Ibid., pp. 39–40.

12. Jerold S. Auerbach, *Hebron Jews: Memory and Conflict in the Land of Israel* (Lanthan, Md.: Rowman and Littlefield, 2009), pp. 65–78; and Shields, "Pre-State Israel," p. 4.

13. Shields, "Pre-State Israel," p. 4.

14. "The Passfield White Paper" (1930), Jewish Virtual Library, http://bit.ly/153tVx4.

15. Christopher Sykes, *Crossroads to Israel: 1917–1948* (Bloomington: Indiana University Press, 1965), pp. 118, 172. Sykes's widely regarded account of the history of the British Mandate for Palestine is sympathetic to the British, Jews, and Arabs alike. Due to its concern with how events affected Britain first and foremost, it appears to me to be relevant for U.S. policy makers today; the British were, in many important regards, their predecessors in the region. Consequently, I use Sykes's history as my main source for the British Mandatory period, although the literature regarding this period is massive.

16. Ibid., p. 114.

17. Ibid., p. 142.

18. Ibid., pp. 145–46.

19. By the time the revolt petered out, Arab terror gangs had murdered five hundred Arabs. Jonathan Schanzer, "Palestinian Uprisings Compared," *Middle East Quarterly* 9, no. 3 (Summer 2002), pp. 27–37, http://bit.ly/aYnWyx; and Benny Morris, *Righteous Victims: A History of the Zionist-Arab Conflict 1881–1999* (New York: Alfred A. Knopf, 2000), p. 155; Klaus-Michael Mallmann and Martin Cuppers, *Nazi Palestine: The Plans for the Extermination of the Jews in Palestine* (New York: Enigma Books, 2005), pp. 22–23.

20. Ibid., pp. 25–26

21. Sykes, *Crossroads to Israel*, p. 150.

22. Ibid., p. 163.

23. Sykes, *Crossroads to Israel*, p. 176.

24. Ibid., p. 177.

25. One such step was the formation of the Woodhead Commission in early 1938, which called for establishing a Jewish state that, as Sykes notes, "reserved for the Jews the smallest pale of settlement that anyone had yet devised for them." Sykes, *Crossroads to Israel*, p. 190. It also called for another round of negotiations between the Jews and the Arabs in London; the Jews agreed to participate, but the Arabs refused. At the unilateral negotiations in London, the British demanded that the Jews "modify their [nationalist] ambitions in the hope that Arab nationalist resentment would be appeased" (pp. 191, 193).

26. Reprinted with permission from the National Library of Israel.

27. "British White Paper of 1939," at http://avalon.law.yale.edu/20th_century/brwh1939.asp.

28. Ibid., pp. 933, 934.

29. Reprinted with permission from the National Library of Israel.

30. Sykes, *Crossroads to Israel*, p. 198.

31. James Dunnigan, "The Last Time (1941) Iraq was Invaded," *Strategy*, November 26, 2002, http://bit.ly/1bXR8zP.

32. Dalin and Rothmann, *Icon of Evil*, p. 42.

33. Sykes, *Crossroads to Israel*, pp. 123–124.

34. Norman Cohn, *Warrant for Genocide: The Myth of the Jewish World Conspiracy and the Protocols of the Elders of Zion* (London: Serif, 2006).

35. Dalin and Rothmann, *Icon of Evil*, pp. 25, 31, 111. *The Protocols of the Elders of Zion* has been a mainstay on the best-seller lists in the Arab world. In 2004 Egyptian television produced a forty-part miniseries of the *Protocols* that was broadcast during prime time in Ramadan, the holiest month of the Islamic year. See "*The Protocols of the Elders of Zion*: The Renaissance of Anti-Semitic Hate Literature in the Arab and Islamic World," Anti-Defamation League, undated, http://bit.ly/15OJYF7.

36. Dalin and Rothmann, *Icon of Evil*, p. 40.

37. Mallmann and Cuppers, *Nazi Palestine*, pp. 44–50.

38. Matthias Kuntzel, *Jihad and Jew Hatred: Islamism, Nazism and the Roots of 9/11* (New York: Telos Press, 2007), p. 24.

39. Mallman and Cuppers, *Nazi Palestine*, pp. 29–43.

40. Dalin and Rothmann, *Icon of Evil*, pp. 43–44.

41. Mallman and Cuppers, *Nazi Palestine*, pp. 63, 66.

42. Dalin and Rothmann, *Icon of Evil*, p. 41.

43. Edwin Black, *The Farhud: Roots of the Arab-Nazi Alliance in the Holocaust* (New York: Dialog Press, 2010), passim.

44. Dalin and Rothmann, *Icon of Evil*, pp. 44–45.

45. Ibid., pp. 45–46.

46. Quoted in Ami Isseroff and Peter FitzGerald-Morris "The Iraq Coup of 1941, the Mufti, and the Farhud," *MidEastWeb*, 2005, http://bit.ly/186FdM9.

47. Ibid., p. 8.

48. Dalin and Rothmann, *Icon of Evil*, pp. 52–54.

49. Ibid., p. 57.

50. Ibid., pp. 58–59.

51. Quoted in Isseroff and FitzGerald-Morris, "Iraqi Coup," p. 70.

52. Dalin and Rothmann, *Icon of Evil*, pp. 62–65.

53. Despite British hostility, 67,000 Jews from the Palestine Mandate voluntarily served in the British armed forces in World War II. The total Jewish population there was 450,000, so their participation rate was among the highest in the Allied forces, as a percentage of overall population. See Colonel Benny Michaelson, "Palestine Jewish Volunteer Movement During World War II," Museum of the Jewish Soldier in World War II, http://bit.ly/1f7HURx.

54. Sykes, *Crossroads to Israel*, p. 251.

55. Ibid., p. 314.

56. Ibid., p. 325.

57. Ibid., p. 331.

58. Sykes, pp. 333, 337–38.

59. Eli Hertz, "'Mandate for Palestine': Legal Aspects of Jewish Rights," *Myths and Facts*, http://bit.ly/14pWH8Q. Reprinted with permission.

CHAPTER 4: YASSIR ARAFAT: THE WORLD'S FAVORITE TERRORIST

1. Barry Rubin and Judith Colp Rubin, "Who Is Yassir Arafat?" Foreign Policy Research Council, December 2003, http://bit.ly/12wuI64.
2. Arafat's Johannesburg Speech, March 10, 1994, Information Regarding Israel's Security, http://bit.ly/14pWWRj.
3. Efraim Karsh, *Arafat's War: The Man and His Battle for Israeli Conquest* (New York: Grove Press, 2003), pp. 60–62.
4. In 1996 Arafat visited Stockholm, where he was honored with a peace prize that he shared with the Israeli leftist group Peace Now. Speaking to a Muslim audience there, Arafat said, "I have no use for Jews. They are and remain Jews." Ibid., p. 58.
5. Christopher Sykes, *Crossroads to Israel: 1917–1948* (Bloomington: Indiana University Press, 1965), p. 163.
6. David G. Dalin and John F. Rothmann, *Icon of Evil: Hitler's Mufti and the Rise of Radical Islam* (New York: Random House, 2008), p. 82.
7. Barry Rubin and Judith Colp Rubin, *Yasir Arafat: A Political Biography* (Oxford: Oxford University Press, 2003), pp. 12, 14.
8. Dalin and Rothmann, *Icon of Evil*, p. 105.
9. "Nazi Ally Hajj Amin el Husseini Is Arafat's 'Hero,'" *Al Sharq al Awsat* (London), August 1, 2002, at http://bit.ly/16p4H5X.
10. Dalin and Rothmann, *Icon of Evil*, pp. 103–5, 138–39.
11. Ion Mihai Pacepa, "The Arafat I Knew," *Wall Street Journal*, January 10, 2002.
12. Christopher Andrew and Vasili Mitrokhin, *The World War Going Our Way: The KGB and the Battle for the Third World* (New York: Basic Books, 2005), pp. 1–26.
13. Jonathan Brent, "Doctors' Plot," YIVO Encyclopedia of Jews in Eastern Europe, August 4, 2010, http://www.yivoencyclopedia.org/article.aspx/Doctors_Plot.
14. Joel Fishman, "'A Disaster of Another Kind,' Zionism=Racism, Its Beginning, and the War of Delegitimization Against Israel," *Israel Journal of Foreign Affairs* V, no. 3 (2011), Israel Council on Foreign Relations, http://israelcfr.com/documents/5-3/5-3-6-JoelFishman.pdf.
15. "Introduction to the Fateh Constitution: The Essential Principles of the Constitution," at http://bit.ly/16WvuNa.
16. Rubin and Rubin, *Yasir Arafat*, p. 42.
17. Sean Gannon, "IRA-PLO Cooperation: A Long, Cozy Relationship," *Jeru-*

salem Post, April 8, 2009; Bruce Hoffman, "The PLO and Israel in Central America: The Geopolitical Dimension," Rand Corporation: Santa Monica, Calif., 1988, http://bit.ly/14M4A4U; Stefan Aust, *Baader-Meinhof: The Inside Story of the R.A.F.* (New York: Oxford University Press, 2009), p. 65; and Rubin and Rubin, *Yasir Arafat*, p. 97.

18. Michael Ledeen, *Accomplice to Evil: Iran and the War Against the West* (New York: St. Martin's Press, 2009), p. 52.

19. Rubin and Rubin, *Yasir Arafat*, p. 80.

20. Ibid., p. 91.

21. Ibid., pp. 88–97.

22. Ibid., p. 41.

23. "Chronology of Aviation Terrorism," Skyjack: Aviation Terrorism Research, undated, http://bit.ly/lzG8FL.

24. Rubin and Rubin, *Yasir Arafat*, p. 66.

25. Ariel Merari and Shlomo Elad, *The International Dimension of Palestinian Terrorism* (Boulder, Colo.: Westview Press, 1986), p. 5, cited in Rubin and Rubin, *Yasir Arafat*, pp. 40–41.

26. Ibid., pp. 97–98.

27. Ibid., p. 97.

28. Ibid., pp. 74–75.

29. Menachem Ganz, "We Sold You Out" (Hebrew), interview with former Italian president Francesco Cossiga, *Yediot Ahronot*, October 2, 2008. Cossiga revealed that the 1980 bombing of the Bologna train station, in which eighty people were murdered, was the work not (as the Italian government claimed at the time) of a fascist terrorist cell but of the PLO's Popular Front for the Liberation of Palestine. The Italian government hid the PFLP's role in order to maintain its relationship with the PLO. So too the Italians directly collaborated with the PLO in its 1982 bombing of a synagogue in Rome, in which a two-year-old boy was murdered. Before the terrorists set the bomb, the Italian police detail assigned to guard the synagogue during worship services was recalled to the station.

30. Joshua Muravchik, "Misreporting Lebanon," *Policy Review*, Winter 1983, pp. 11–66.

31. "The PLO's 'Phased Plan,'" at http://bit.ly/bwNc6f; and C. Sterling, *The Terror Network* (New York: Holt, Rinehart & Winston, 1981), passim.

32. Rubin and Rubin, pp. 72–73.

33. Bat Ye'or, *Eurabia: The Euro Arab Axis* (Madison and Teaneck, N.J.: Fairleigh Dickinson University Press, 2005), pp. 47–48.

34. Uzi Amit-Kohn et al., *Israel, the "Intifada" and the Rule of Law* (Tel Aviv: Israel Ministry of Defense Publications, 1993), pp. 27–30.

35. Ibid., pp. 27–30.

36. Ibid., p. 31.

37. Ibid., p. 32.

38. Ibid. In the decade before the Gulf War, Saudi assistance alone had come to more than $1 billion.

39. Clyde Haberman, "Palestinian Says His Delegation Will Assert P.L.O. Ties at Talks," *New York Times*, October 22, 1991.

40. Hugh Orgel, "PLO and Hamas Reach Agreement as They Continue to Vie for Support," Jewish Telegraphic Agency, November 21, 1994, http://bit .ly/16E2bwl.

41. "Fatal Terrorist Attacks Against Israel Since the DOP," Israel Ministry of Foreign Affairs, September 24, 2000, http://bit.ly/19nR5jt; "Terrorism Against Israel: Number of Fatalities (1920–2012)," Jewish Virtual Library, undated, http://bit.ly/6ZkbkE.

42. "Interview with Prime Minister Benjamin Netanyahu on PBS's *NewsHour with Jim Lehrer*, November 3, 1997," Israel Ministry of Foreign Affairs, http://bit.ly/17PYj93.

43. Roni Shaked, "Expose: Hamas Murderers Under Arafat's Aegis," *Yediot Ahronot*, October 15, 1997, pp. 2–5, at http://bit.ly/19kLNBJ.

44. Itamar Marcus and Nan Jacques Zilberdik, *Deception, Betraying the Peace Process* (Israel: Palestinian Media Watch, 2011), pp. 84–86.

45. Yaakov Katz, "Arafat Used Aid to Buy Weapons: Ex-PA Paymaster Says PA, Iran, Hizbullah Coordinated Attempted Import of Weapons," *Jerusalem Post*, May 17, 2006.

46. Ari Shavit, "End of a Journey—an Interview with Shlomo Ben-Ami," *Haaretz*, September 13, 2001, http://bit.ly/19PmkE4.

CHAPTER 5: PHONY REFORMERS AND TOTALITARIAN DEMOCRATS

1. "Abu Daoud, the Palestinian terrorist leader who died . . ." *Telegraph*, July 4, 2010, http://bit.ly/1axg3aw.

2. Itamar Marcus and Nan Jacques Zilberdik, "Abbas on Mastermind of Munich Olympics Massacre," *PMW Bulletins*, Palestinian Media Watch, July 6, 2010, http://bit.ly/13X4UxE.

3. Alexander Wolff, "The Mastermind: Thirty Years After He Helped Plan the Terror Strike, Abu Daoud Remains in Hiding—And Unrepentant," *Sports Illustrated*, August 26. 2002.

4. Harriet Sherwood, "U.S.-backed Palestinian Prime Minister Salam Fayyad Resigns," *Guardian*, April 14, 2013; Khaled Abu Toameh, "Rami Hamdallah: A Yes Man for Fatah," *Jerusalem Post*, June 4, 2013.

5. Rafael Medoff, "A Holocaust-Denier as Prime Minister of 'Palestine'?" David Wyman Institute for Holocaust Studies, March 2003, http://bit.ly/19Cu6Ok.

6. "Bush Administration Condemns Iran for Holocaust Skeptics Conference," Associated Press, December 12, 2006.

7. Hillel Fendel, "Report: Abbas' Holocaust-Denial Dissertation Widely Taught in PA," *Israel National News*, April 28, 2011, http://bit.ly/14BIwQ1.

8. The first agreement was signed in March 2007. It was scuttled three months later, when Hamas ejected Fatah personnel from the Gaza Strip. The second agreement was signed in May 2011. Neither it nor the third agreement, signed in February 2012, was implemented. "Abbas Swears in Hamas-Fatah Unity Government; Abbas: PA Extends Hand to Israel, Rejects Violence; Haniyeh: Resistance Is 'Legitimate Right' of Palestinians," Associated Press, in *Haaretz*, March 17, 2007; "Behind the Headlines: Doha Agreement Between Hamas and Fatah—A Barrier to Peace," Israel Ministry of Foreign Affairs, February 8, 2012, http://bit.ly/16S74SZ.

9. Elior Levy, "Abbas Meets Freed Palestinian Prisoners in Ankara ..." *Ynet News*, December 21, 2011, http://bit.ly/sEWFzb.

10. Greg Sheridan, "Ehud Olmert Still Dreams of Peace," *Australian*, November 29, 2009.

11. Ibid.; and "Olmert: Abbas Never Responded to My Peace Offer," *Haaretz*, February 14, 2010.

12. Khaled Abu Toameh, "Palestinians Accuse Peace Negotiators of Treason," Gatestone Institute International Policy Council, August 19, 2013, http://www.gatestoneinstitute.org/3939/palestinians-peace-negotiators.

13. Elior Levy, "IDF, PA Collaboration in West Bank Faltering," *Ynet News*, December 18, 2012, http://bit.ly/SMtS2d.

14. Ben Birnbaum, "The End of the Two-State Solution: Why the Window Is Closing on Middle East Peace," *New Republic*, March 11, 2013.

15. "Palestinian Statehood: Text of Mahmud Abbas's Letter to the UN," *Telegraph*, September 23, 2011.

16. Julius Stone, *Israel and Palestine: Assault on the Law of Nations* (Baltimore: Johns Hopkins University Press, 1981), cited in Eli E. Hertz, *This Land is My Land, "Mandate for Palestine," Legal Aspects of Jewish Rights* (Forest Hills, N.Y.: Myths and Facts, 2008).

17. Itamar Marcus and Nan Jacques Zilberdik, "What Is Abbas's True Ideology?" *PMW Bulletins*, Palestinian Media Watch, October 18, 2012, http://bit.ly/WEprWg.

18. Barak Ravid, "Erekat: Palestinians Will Not Accept Israel as 'Jewish State,'" *Haaretz*, November 12, 2007.

19. In 1997, $323 million, or 40 percent of the PA's budget, went missing. Stacey Lakind and Yigal Carmon, "The PA Economy (II)," Inquiry and Analysis Report No. 11, January 8, 1999, Middle East Media Research Institute, http://bit.ly/16KKl7m.

20. Issam Abu Issa, "Arafat's Swiss Bank Accounts," *Middle East Quarterly* 11, no. 4 (Fall 2004), pp. 15–23, http://bit.ly/a2TkQk.

21. Jim Zanotti, "U.S. Foreign Aid to the Palestinians," Congressional Research Service, June 15, 2012, http://bit.ly/9TvY4j.

22. Ibid., p. 27, citing International Monetary Fund, "Recent Experience and Prospects of the Economic of the West Bank and Gaza: Staff Report Prepared for the Meeting of the Ad Hoc Liaison Committee," March 31, 2012.

23. Bojan Pancevski, "£1.95bn EU Aid Lost in Palestine," Sunday Times, October 13, 2010, http://thetim.es/19CsAg3.

24. As Abu Issa notes, "Diplomats downplayed flagrant corruption. In August 2001, Israel seized close to a half million documents from Palestinian offices in Jerusalem and elsewhere. Subsequent State Department reports on Palestinian governance and terrorism made little use or even mention of these documents. European and US policymakers assumed Arafat's critics to be against the Oslo accord." For them, maintaining the peace process was all that mattered. The fact that the Palestinian Authority had developed into an authoritarian, terroristic kleptocracy was of no importance. Abu Issa, "Arafat's Swiss Bank Accounts."

25. "Palestinians Question Massive Security Budget," Nuqudy, January 10, 2013, http://bit.ly/14M72rX.

26. Steven Stotsky, "Does Foreign Aid Fuel Palestinian Violence?" Middle East Quarterly 15, no. 3 (Summer 2008), pp. 23–30, http://bit.ly/bGeJlM.

27. Ilan Ben Zion, "PA Spends 6% of Its Budget Paying Palestinians in Israeli Jails, Families of Suicide Bombers," Times of Israel, September 3, 2012.

28. Khaled Abu Toameh, "Fayyad Calls for Economic Boycott of Israeli Goods," Jerusalem Post, December 16, 2012.

29. "Palestinian Settlement Boycott Highlights," Settlement Report 20, no. 4 (July–August 2010), http://bit.ly/13MoL7N.

30. Khaled Abu Toameh, "Bethlehem Man Indicted for Buying from Settlement," Jerusalem Post, May 11, 2010.

31. Khaled Abu Toameh, "The Palestinians: Who's Afraid of Elections," Gatestone Institute International Policy Council, June 15, 2010, http://bit.ly/18G9G5S.

32. "Hamas Covenant 1988: The Covenant of the Islamic Resistance Movement," August 18, 1988, at http://bit.ly/Vyfc.

33. "Hamas Leader Khaled Mashaal: We Will Not Relinquish One Inch of Palestine from the River to the Sea," Al Aksa TV, December 7, 2012, at Middle East Media Research Institute, http://bit.ly/15jrwwI.

34. Steven R. Weisman, "Rice Admits U.S. Underestimated Hamas's Strength," New York Times, January 30, 2006.

35. "Rice on Palestinian Elections," Voice of America, January 17, 2006, http://1.usa.gov/13MpaXT.

36. Joel Fishman, "Did Condi Go on a Rampage?" Israel Resource News Agency, November 25, 2005, at http://bit.ly/188VXT0.

37 Weisman, "Rice Admits."

38. A poll in December 2005 found that support for Hamas had risen 55 percent over the previous year. Eighty-three percent viewed the Israeli withdrawal from Gaza as a victory for armed struggle. Palestinian Center for Policy and Survey Research, "With Optimism Fading . . ." Public Opinion Poll No. 18, December 10, 2005, http://bit.ly/1dAC792.

39 Itamar Marcus and Barbara Crook, "Fatah Boast About Lynch Murder," *PMW Bulletins*, Palestinian Media Watch, June 25, 2009, http://bit.ly/16paBnr.

40. In a survey of possible vice presidential candidates to serve under Arafat taken in March 2004, Abbas received only one percent of support. Palestinian Center for Policy and Survey Research, "While Three Quarters of the Palestinians . . ." Public Opinion Poll No. 11, March 14–17, 2004, http://bit.ly/179bllk.

41. Weisman, "Rice Admits."

42. "Kerry Calls Abbas, Urges Him to Mend Ties with Fayyad," Agence France-Presse, April 13, 2013, at http://bit.ly/YShSNR.

43. Jonathan Schanzer, "Chronic Kleptocracy: Corruption Within the Palestinian Political Establishment," testimony for the Committee on Foreign Affairs, Subcommittee on the Middle East and South Asia, U.S. House of Representatives, July 10, 2012, http://www.gpo.gov/fdsys/pkg/CHRG-112hhrg74960/html/CHRG-112hhrg74960.htm.

44 Meyrav Wurmser, "The Iran-Hamas Alliance," *Focus Quarterly* (Fall 2007), http://www.jewishpolicycenter.org/57/the-iran-hamas-alliance.

45. Khaled Abu Toameh, "Iran Enters the Peace Process," Gatestone Institute International Policy Council, July 29, 2013, http://bit.ly/1c5w7G3.

46 "Rep. Wants Hamas Payment Explained," Jewish Telegraphic Agency, August 13, 2007, http://bit.ly/15hSpjG.

47. Khaled Abu Toameh, "The Palestinian Authority's Inconvenient Truths," Gatestone Institute International Policy Council, January 3, 2012, http://bit.ly/X2A2cx.

48. Chico Menashe, "Four EU Members Tried to Block Condemnation of Hamas," Israel Radio, December 12, 2012, translated by Independent Media Review Analysis, http://bit.ly/179bzc6.

CHAPTER 6: DUMBING DOWN U.S. FOREIGN POLICY

1. Matthew Levitt, "Injustice in Gaza," *Baltimore Sun*, October 18, 2004.

2. Quoted in John Burns and Greg Myre, "U.S. Diplomatic Convoy in Gaza is Attacked, Killing at Least 3," *New York Times*, October 15, 2003.

3. "Justice Elusive for Americans Killed in Gaza," Investigative Project on Terrorism, August 1, 2011, http://bit.ly/14q23AY.

4. Ibid.

5. Rick Richman, "October 15, 2003 to October 15, 2007," *Jewish Current Issues,* October 15, 2007, http://bit.ly/14M9Rt2.

6. Ibid.

7. "Justice Elusive," Investigative Project on Terrorism.

8. "PA Investigator of Gaza Bombing Is Its Likely Perpetrator," Shurat Hadin—Israel Law Center, December 18, 2003, http://bit.ly/19CvOPu.

9. Abraham Rabinovich, "Escape from Cherbourg," *Jerusalem Post,* December 24, 2009; "West Germany Refuses to Sell Transport Planes to Israel, Observing the Arms Embargo," Jewish Telegraphic Agency, May 23, 1968, http://bit.ly/1dADyEl.

10. Contrary to popular belief, as we saw in Chapter 4, the "Zionism Is Racism" canard was not invented after the Six Day War. As Joel Fishman chronicles, the first attempt to malign the Jewish national liberation movement as a form of racism was undertaken by the Soviet delegation at the UN in 1965. Joel Fishman, " 'A Disaster of Another Kind': Zionism=Racism and the War of Delegitimization against Israel," *Israel Journal of Foreign Affairs* 5, no. 3 (2011).

11. George W. Bush, address to joint session of Congress, September 20, 2001, http://1.usa.gov/bTCM2J, emphasis added.

12. Based on casualty figures in "Victims of Palestinian Violence and Terrorism Since September 2000," Israel Ministry of Foreign Affairs, undated, http://bit.ly/13u79a8

13. Joel Fishman, "The Relegitimization of Israel and the Battle for the Mainstream Consensus," *Israel Journal of Foreign Affairs* 6, no. 2 (2012).

14. Raymond Aron, *De Gaulle, Israel and the Jews* (New York, 1969), pp. 24–25, quoted ibid.

15. Lieutenant General Ion Mihai Pacepa, *Red Horizons: The True Story of Nicolae and Elena Ceauşescus' Crimes, Lifestyle, and Corruption* (Washington, D.C.: Regnery Gateway, 1987), p. 25.

16. Bat Ye'or, *Eurabia: The Euro-Arab Axis* (Madison and Teaneck, N.J.: Fairleigh Dickinson University Press, 2004), pp. 39–62.

17. Ibid., pp. 47–48.

18. Ibid., p. 48.

19. Manfred Gerstenfeld, "Experiencing European Anti-Americanism and Anti-Israelism: An Interview with Jeffrey Gedmin," December 1, 2004, Jerusalem Center for Public Affairs, http://jcpa.org/phas/phas-27.htm. For general information on European anti-Americanism, see Russell A. Berman, *Anti-Americanism in Europe: A Cultural Problem* (Stanford, Calif.: Hoover Institution Press, 2004), passim.

20. Ye'or, *Eurabia,* pp. 225–48; and Gerstenfeld, "Experiencing European Anti-Americanism."

21. Richard Cohen, "Israel's Hostile Neighborhood," *Washington Post*, September 12, 2012.

22. Steven J. Rosen, "Kuwait Expels Thousands of Palestinians," *Middle East Quarterly* 19, no. 4 (Fall 2012), pp. 75–83, http://bit.ly/VycJq2.

23. Lamis Andoni, "PLO Maintains Strong Presence Behind the Scenes in Madrid Talks," *Christian Science Monitor*, October 31, 1991.

24. Khaled Abu Toameh, "Arab World Fed Up with Hizbullah," *Jerusalem Post*, July 17, 2006.

25. George W. Bush, *Decision Points* (New York: Random House, 2010), p. 414.

26. Mark Landler and Jodi Rudoren, "Chaos in Middle East Grows as U.S. Focuses on Israel," *New York Times*, July 1, 2013.

27. UN Security Council Resolution 508, June 6, 1982, http://bit.ly/19PpI1Q; UN Security Council Resolution 516, August 1, 1982, http://bit.ly/1541I2y.

28. Jeremy M. Sharp, "U.S. Foreign Aid to Israel," Congressional Research Service, March 12, 2012, p. 16, http://bit.ly/8Tf2FE.

29. Barry Rubin and Judith Colp Rubin, *Yasir Arafat: A Political Biography* (Oxford: Oxford University Press, 2003), pp. 97–98.

30. Donald Rumsfeld, *Known and Unknown: A Memoir* (New York: Sentinel, 2011), p. 31.

31. Michael Petit, *Peacekeepers at War: A Marine's Account of the Beirut Catastrophe* (Boston: Faber and Faber, 1986), pp. 115, 135, 137, 144–45.

32. Ibid., passim.

33. Douglas Feith, *War and Decision: Inside the Pentagon at the Dawn of the War on Terrorism* (New York: HarperCollins, 2008), pp. 207–8.

34. Caroline B. Glick, "One Minute to Zero Hour," *Jerusalem Post*, March 21, 2003.

35. Rumsfeld, *Known and Unknown*, p. 382.

36. Dick Cheney, with Liz Cheney, *In My Time: A Personal and Political Memoir* (New York: Threshold, 2011), p. 227.

37. Ibid., p. 472.

38. "Operation Opera: The Israeli Raid on the Osirak Nuclear Reactor, June 7, 1981," Jewish Virtual Library, undated, http://bit.ly/AAwcpE.

39. "Saudis, Emirates Push Nuclear Power Plans," UPI, July 26, 2012, http://bit.ly/QfdjEV.

40. Daniel Siryoti, "Egypt May Resume Civilian Nuclear Program, Morsi Says," *Israel Hayom*, August 30, 2012, http://bit.ly/N1hQOR; "King Abdullah: Israel Disrupting Jordan's Nuclear Program," *Ynet News*, September 12, 2012, http://bit.ly/SDDTP0.

41. George Gilder, *The Israel Test* (Minneapolis, Minn.: Richard Vigilante Books, 2009), passim.

CHAPTER 7: INTRODUCING THE PLAN

1. "Deciding the Fate of the Territories Occupied During the Six-Day War: An Ongoing Debate: The Government of Israel Discusses Israel's Peace Plan, 18–19 June 1967," Israel State Archives, declassified June 2012, http://bit .ly/17uE2be.

2. Ibid.

3. Ibid.

4. Ibid.

5. Ibid.

6. Ibid.

7. Khartoum Resolutions, September 1, 1967, at http://bit.ly/17uDZw1.

8. Revised and updated, July 21, 2008, at Jerusalem Center for Public Affairs, http://bit.ly/17eSFRc. Reprinted with permission from the Jerusalem Center for Public Affairs.

9. David Bedein, "Abba Eban: The June 1967 Map Represented Israel's 'Auschwitz' Borders," Israel Behind the News, November 17, 2002, http://bit.ly/ lNPVOm.

10. UN Security Council Resolution 242, November 22, 1967, http://bit.ly/ T9THrb.

11. Joint Chiefs of Staff to secretary of defense, memorandum JCSM-373-67, http://1.usa.gov/15cOw41; enhanced image in Arieh Stav, ed., *Israel and a Palestinian State: A Zero Sum Game?* (Tel Aviv: Zmorra Bitan, 2001), p. 361. Reprinted with permission from the Ariel Center for Policy Research.

12. "ID Cards for Residents of East Jerusalem" (Hebrew), Israel Government Archives, Prime Minister's Bureau, Office of the Arab Affairs Advisor, East Jerusalem, June 12, 1968, at http://bit.ly/1281tGt; English summary "ID Cards for Arabs in East Jerusalem (1967–1970)," January 29, 2013, *Israel's Documented Story: The English-language Blog of the Israel State Archives (ISA)*, http://bit.ly/17sz9OW.

13. Rachel Ehrenfeld and Alyssa A. Lappen, "U.S. Rewarding Arab Terrorism," FrontPageMag.com, March 24, 2008, http://bit.ly/1aImHQv; Hebrew version at http://bit.ly/1aImWec. Palestinian GDP numbers appear only in the Hebrew version. See also Efraim Karsh, *Arafat's War: The Man and his Battle for Israeli Conquest* (New York: Grove Press, 2003), pp. 43–45.

14. Yaakov Faitelson, "The Demographic Trends of the Arab Population of Judea, Samaria and the Gaza Strip" (Hebrew), January 2013, Institute for Zionist Strategies; based on data from Israel Central Bureau of Statistics reports.

15. *Developing the Occupied Territories, An Investment in Peace*, vol. 6, *Human Resources and Social Policy* (Washington, D.C.: World Bank, 1993), pp. 34–36, http://bit.ly/1cQmL1q.

16. UN Department of Economic and Social Affairs, *World Urbanization Prospects: The 2011 Revision* (New York: United Nations, 2012), http://bit.ly/Uv179q.

17. Karsh, *Arafat's War,* p. 44.

18. "The Health Services in the Areas of Judea-Samaria and Gaza Since 1967: A Review and Comparative Data," Israel Ministry of Foreign Affairs, April 1, 1992, http://bit.ly/1cQmX0F.

19. "The Activities of the Civil Administration in the Territories: Statistical Fact Sheet," Israel Ministry of Foreign Affairs, June 16, 1994, http://bit.ly/15JQcJB.

20. Karsh, *Arafat's War,* p. 44.

21. "Censorship and Freedom of the Press Under Changing Political Regimes: Palestinian Media from Israeli Occupation to the Palestinian Authority," *International Communication Gazette,* April 3, 2003, pp. 183–202.

22. Esco Foundation for Palestine, *Palestine: A Study of Jewish, Arab and British Policies* (New Haven, Conn.: Yale University Press, 1947), p. 2:934.

23. Alexander Safian, "Can Arabs Buy Land in Israel?" *Middle East Quarterly,* 4, no. 4 (December 1997), pp. 11–16, http://bit.ly/wG9Vm.

24. Ibid.

25. Boaz Haetzni (of the Samaria Regional Council), interview by author, January 22, 2013.

26. League of Nations Mandate for Palestine, Article 6.

27. "Israeli-Palestinian Interim Agreement on the West Bank and the Gaza Strip," September 28, 1995, at http://bit.ly/iPJ6vG.

28. Barry Rubin and Judith Colp Rubin, *Yasir Arafat: A Political Biography* (New York: Oxford University Press, 2005), p. 112; and "Stateless Again: Palestinian-Origin Jordanians Deprived of the Nationality," Human Rights Watch, February 2010, p. 2, http://bit.ly/1dIEQgC.

29. Ali Younes, "Revoking Citizenships: The Future of Palestinians in Jordan," *Al Arabiya News,* September 10, 2012, http://bit.ly/1aIoCVe.

30. "Stateless Again" Human Rights Watch.

CHAPTER 8: THE DEMOGRAPHIC TIME BOMB IS A DUD

1. Joel Greenberg, "Palestinian Census Ignites Controversy over Jerusalem," *New York Times,* December 11, 1997.

2. Moshe Gil, *A History of Palestine 634–1099* (Cambridge, U.K.: Cambridge University Press, 1992), pp. 1–3.

3. Israel Central Bureau of Statistics, "CBS Statistical Abstract of Israel, Population by Religion 1948–2011," http://bit.ly/12ElcOc. The ICBS distinguishes between Jews by religion and Jews by ethnicity. Jews by ethnic-

ity include citizens who immigrated to Israel due to their Jewish ancestry but who do not have a Jewish mother, as required by Jewish religious law. When this group, which is fully integrated into Israeli Jewish society, is added to the Jewish population, the percentage of Jews in Israel has not gone below 79 percent of the overall population. See for instance, ICBS, "CBS Statistical Abstract of Israel by Population Group," http://bit.ly/ 18fFo7V.

4. Bennett Zimmerman, Roberta Seid, and Michael L. Wise, "The Million Person Gap: The Arab Population in the West Bank and Gaza," Begin-Sadat Center for Strategic Studies, no. 65, Bar-Ilan University, February 2006, p. 4, http://bit.ly/14Ie6Wy.

5. Israel Central Bureau of Statistics; "Statistical Abstract of Israel—Population by Population Group," 2010, http://bit.ly/18xRFqn.

6. Israel Central Bureau of Statistics, "Press Release: On the Eve of Israel's 64th Independence Day," April 25, 2012, http://bit.ly/16LgVJz.

7. ICBS, "CBS Statistical Abstract ."

8. ICBS "Press Release."

9. Barak Ravid et al., "Olmert to *Haaretz:* Two-State Solution, or Israel Is Done For," *Haaretz*, November 29, 2007.

10. "Livni: In Order to Safeguard Israel as a Jewish State We Must Divide It," *Haaretz*, January 8, 2013.

11. "Text: Obama's AIPAC Speech," May 22, 2011, *National Journal*, http://bit .ly/mIN5lC.

12. Bennett Zimmerman, conversation with author, January 10, 2005.

13. The group's findings were first formally presented to an elite Israeli audience at Israel's annual Herzliya Conference in January 2006. There Eberstadt said that the group "caught the demographic professionals asleep at the switch."

14. The full findings of the 2005 study were published in February 2006. Zimmerman, Seid, and Wise, "Million Person Gap," http://bit.ly/14Ie6Wy.

15. Ibid., pp. 1–2.

16. Ibid., p. 13.

17. Israeli Cabinet Communiqué, Proceedings of Government Meeting, May 12, 2002, http://bit.ly/19F1e7t.

18. Zimmerman, Seid, and Wise, "Million Person Gap," p. 9.

19. Nicholas Eberstadt and Apoorva Shah, "Fertility Decline in the Muslim World," *Policy Review* 173 (June 1, 2012), emphasis added.

20. Zimmerman, Seid, and Wise, "Million Person Gap," p. 24.

21. Ibid., p. 25.

22. Ibid., p. 2.

23. Khaled Abu Toameh, "80,000 Palestinians Emigrated from the Territories

Since Beginning of the Year," *Jerusalem Post*, August 27, 2002; and Uriya Shavit and Jalal Bana, "The Secret Exodus: Palestinian Emigration," *Haaretz* (magazine section), October 5, 2001.

24. Khaled Abu Toameh, "Keep Out the PA," *Jerusalem Post*, September 11, 2004.

25. Zimmerman, Seid, and Wise, "Million Person Gap," p. 35.

26. Yakov Faitelson, "Demographic Trends in the Land of Israel" (Hebrew), Institute for Zionist Strategies, August 2013. In October 2013, the *Middle East Quarterly* published an English version of Faitelson's findings. See Yakov Faitelson, "A Jewish Majority in the Land of Israel: The Resilient Jewish State," *Middle East Quarterly* 20, no. 4 (Fall 2013), pp. 15–27, http://bit .ly/1bKjWzt.

27. Ibid., p. 31.

28. Zimmerman, Seid, and Wise, "The Million Person Gap," p. 4. Reprinted with permission.

29. Yakov Faitelson, "The Politics of Palestinian Demography," *Middle East Quarterly* 16, no. 2 (Spring 2009), pp. 51–59, http://bit.ly/6FiTaW.

30. Ibid. Between 2005 and 2012, the Palestinians changed their forecast of when they would become the majority west of the Jordan River four times; each time the projected Arab population rose or decreased by hundreds of thousands with no explanation.

31. Faitelson, "Demographic Trends in the Land of Israel." Unless otherwise noted, data regarding Arab and Jewish fertility rates and Palestinian emigration rates come from this article, which was based on data from the Israel Central Bureau of Statistics (ICBS), the Palestinian Central Bureau of Statistics (PCBS), the U.S. Census Bureau, various UN agencies, and the Norwegian statistical NGO FAFO.

32. Israel Central Bureau of Statistics, "Fertility Rates by Age and Religion," *Statistical Abstract of Israel 2012*, http://bit.ly/17YxqkC.

33. Jon Pedersen, Sara Randall, and Marwan Khawaja, "Growing Fast, the Palestinian Population in the West Bank and Gaza Strip," FAFO Report No. 353, FAFO Institute for Applied Social Science, 2001, cited in Faitelson, "Demographic Trends in the Land of Israel."

34. The other AIDRG members were Michael L. Wise and Yoram Ettinger.

35. *Arutz 7*, July 2, 2007, cited in Faitelson, "Demographic Trends in the Land of Israel."

36. Mark MacKinnon, "Heavy-Hearted Palestinians Taking Their Chances Abroad," *Globe and Mail*, November 20, 2006, at http://bit.ly/15c4CJw.

37. Zvi Yehezkeli, "The Young Are Fleeing Gaza" (Hebrew), Israel Television Channel 10, June 17, 2007, http://bit.ly/13KlmUI.

38. Faitelson, "Demographic Trends in the Land of Israel."

39. Israel Central Bureau of Statistics, "Table 1—Immigrants, by Period of Immigration (1948–2011)," http://bit.ly/16LjwmZ.

40. See data compiled by the Coordination Forum for Countering Antisemitism, http://antisemitism.org.il.

41. Yoram Ettinger, "Jewish-Arab Demography Defies Conventional 'Wisdom,'" *Yisrael Hayom*, October 19, 2012, http://bit.ly/RcqV6M.

42. Elizabeth Samson, "Is Gaza Occupied? Redefining the Legal Status of Gaza," Begin-Sadat Center for Strategic Studies No. 83, Bar-Ilan University, January 2010, http://bit.ly/12VRRhE.

43. Khaled Abu Toameh, "The Hamas-Egyptian Alliance," Gatestone Institute International Policy Council, February 8, 2013, http://bit.ly/WHxnVS.

44. In a study published in January 2013 in the Hamas's *Al Quds* newspaper, engineer Mustafa al-Farra recommended solving Gaza's overcrowding by expanding the enclave into Sinai. Farra raised the possibility of leasing lands in Sinai from Egypt for ninety-nine years. Khaled Abu Toameh, "Study: Allow Gaza Population to Expand into Sinai," *Jerusalem Post*, January 22, 2013.

45. Nicolas Pelham, *Sinai: The Buffer Erodes* (London: Chatham House, 2012), http://bit.ly/POAyHf.

46. "North Sinai Violence Flares Again," CNN, August 10, 2012, http://bit.ly/1dhDGdw.

47. Roi Kais, "Egypt's Brotherhood: Mossad Behind Sinai attack," *Ynet News*, August 6, 2012, http://bit.ly/MoJmRm.

48. Yaakov Lappin, "Analysis: Sinai's Growing Terrorism Problem," *Jerusalem Post*, July 8, 2013; "Rafah Crossing Closed for Second Day, Sources Say," *Egypt Independent*, July 6, 2013, http://bit.ly/1d2cWcj.

49. Khaled Abu Toameh, "Fatah wants Egypt to Overthrow Hamas," Gatestone Institute International Policy Council, September 6, 2013, http://bit.ly/154lOhI.

50. Mitch Ginsburg, "Defense Minister Ridicules Notion of Democracy in Mideast," *Times of Israel*, September 8, 2013, http://bit.ly/16cSbL2.

CHAPTER 9: A RECORD OF SUCCESS

1. Yehuda Avner, *The Prime Ministers: An Intimate Narrative of Israeli Leadership* (Jerusalem: Toby Press, 2010), p. 578.

2. Ibid., p. 580.

3. Ibid., p. 582.

4. Golan Heights Law, December 14, 1981, Israel Ministry of Foreign Affairs, http://bit.ly/1eXwjUN.

5. Zeidan Atashe, *Druze and Jews in Israel: A Shared Destiny?* (Brighton, U.K.: Sussex Academic Press, 1995), p. 6.

6. Zeidan Atashe, "The Druze in Israel and the Question of Compulsory Military Service," Jerusalem Center for Public Affairs, October 15, 2001, http://jcpa.org/jl/vp464.htm.

7. Phil Sands and Racha Makarem, "Who are Syria's Druze?" *National* (UAE), February 22, 2012, http://bit.ly/wpVA5H; Babk Dehghanpisheh, "Syria's Druze Minority Is Shifting Its Support to the Opposition," *Washington Post,* February 8, 2013.

8. Atashe, *Druze and Jews in Israel,* pp. 135–43.

9. Ibid.

10. Adi Hashmonai, "The Golan Druse want Israeli Citizenship" (Hebrew), *Maariv,* October 5, 2012, http://bit.ly/16eNwr6.

11. Ibid.

12. UN Security Council Resolution 497, December 17, 1981, at http://bit.ly/1aIvQIO.

13. Gil Sedan and Hugh Orgel, "Egypt Assures Israel that its Move on the Golan Will Not Affect Relations Between the Two Countries," Jewish Telegraphic Agency, December 28, 1981, http://bit.ly/16eNCPi.

14. Gil Sedan and Hugh Orgel, "U.S. Would Veto Sanctions Resolution," Jewish Telegraphic Agency, December 29, 1981, http://bit.ly/14gIPtu.

15. Efraim Inbar, "Israeli Control of the Golan Heights: High Strategic and Moral Ground," Begin-Sadat Center for Strategic Studies, no. 90, Bar-Ilan University, September 2011, pp. 1–2.

16. John Yemma, "Israelis Seek to Justify Annexing Golan Heights," *Christian Science Monitor,* December 22, 1981.

17. Avner, *Prime Ministers,* p. 580.

18. Inbar, "Israeli Control of the Golan Heights," pp. 3–12.

19. Yitzhak Rabi, "Blum: Israel's Action on the Golan Was Needed to 'Regularize the Situation' There in the Face of Syria," Jewish Telegraphic Agency, December 17, 1981, http://bit.ly/142B1PP.

20. "Deciding the Fate of the Territories Occupied During the Six-Day War," Israel State Archives, declassified June 2012, http://bit.ly/17uE2be.

21. Law and Administration Ordinance No. 1 of 5708-1948 (Hebrew), at http://bit.ly/1bA2DNR. On June 28, 1967 the Knesset added paragraph 11(B) to the law, which stipulated, "The laws, jurisdiction and administration of the State will be applied in all territory in the Land of Israel that the government determines by order."

22. "ID Cards for residents of East Jerusalem" (Hebrew), Israel Government Archives, Prime Minister's Bureau, Office of the Arab Affairs Advisor, East Jerusalem, June 12, 1968, at http://bit.ly/1281tGt; English summary "ID Cards for Arabs in East Jerusalem (1967–1970)," January 29, 2013, *Israel's Documented Story: The English-language Blog of the Israel State Archives (ISA),* http://bit.ly/17sz9OW.

23. UN General Assembly Resolution 2253 (ES-V), July 4, 1967, at http://bit .ly/1a8QXUq; and UN General Assembly Resolution 2254 (ES-V), July 14, 1967, http://bit.ly/142BEsM.

24. Avner, *Prime Ministers*, p. 174.

25. Ibid., pp. 178–79.

26. Israel declared Jerusalem its capital city in 1949.

27. Basic Law—Jerusalem—Capital of Israel, http://bit.ly/kwnWar.

28. UN Security Council Resolution 478, August 20, 1980, http://bit.ly/ XhxOk4.

29. Avner, *Prime Ministers*, p. 535.

30. "Costa Rica Moving Embassy from Jerusalem to Tel Aviv," *Israel National News*, August 17, 2006, http://bit.ly/14CxVxw.

31. Naomi Ragen, "An American in Israel," *Jerusalem Post*, February 28, 2013. In 1995 the U.S. Congress passed the Jerusalem Embassy Act, and President Bill Clinton signed it into law; see http://1.usa.gov/14VDAzW. It required the State Department to move the U.S. Embassy in Israel from Tel Aviv to Jerusalem. The law includes a waiver that allows the president to postpone the move for six months if he deems doing so necessary for U.S. national security. Since the law was passed, every president has used his waiver authority every six months to prevent the transfer of the U.S. embassy to Israel's capital city.

32. Eli E. Hertz, *Jerusalem: One Nation's Capital Throughout History, the Legal Aspects of Jewish Rights* (Forest Hills, N.Y.: Myths and Facts, 2011), pp. 11–12.

33. Nir Hasson, "A Surprising Process of 'Israelization' Is Taking Place Among Palestinians in East Jerusalem," *Haaretz*, December 29, 2012.

CHAPTER 10: WELCOME TO PALESTINE

1. Khaled Abu Toameh, "Jericho Man Murdered Over Home Sale: Muhammed Abu al-Hawa Was Shot, Tortured, for Selling A-Tur home to Jews," *Jerusalem Post*, April 14, 2006, http://bit.ly/18Txnpp.

2. Eugene Cotran and Chibli Mallat, *The Arab-Israeli Accords: Legal Perspectives* (London: Kluwer Law International for CIMEL, 1996), p. 52.

3. Ibid., pp. 51–52. Article 7, paragraph 9 of the agreement stipulated, "Laws and military orders in effect in the Gaza Strip or the Jericho Area prior to the signing of this Agreement shall remain in force, unless amended or abrogated in accordance with this Agreement." See "Agreement on Gaza Strip and Jericho Area," May 4, 1994, accessed at: http://bit.ly/15QmzYv.

4. Alexander Safian, "Can Arabs Buy Land in Israel?" *Middle East Quarterly* 4, no. 4 (December 1997), pp. 11–16, http://bit.ly/wG9Vm.

5. Ibid.

6. Abu Toameh, "Jericho Man Murdered Over Home Sale."

7. Khaled Abu Toameh, conversation with author, January 20, 2013. In 1997,

Amnesty International reported, more than one hundred Palestinians were detained without trial for selling land to Jews:

> Torture of those accused of "collaboration" with Israel or selling land to Israelis appeared to be systematic. Muhammad Bakr, accused of "collaboration" with Israel and land-dealing, was arrested in June and beaten while hung by the wrists in detention centres in Qalqilya and Nablus. . . . Unlawful killings, including possible extrajudicial executions, continued to occur. Three land-dealers were found dead during May after the Minister of Justice, Freih Abu Meddein, announced that the Palestinian Authority would begin applying a Jordanian law which provided for the death penalty for those convicted of selling land to Jews. There were fears that statements by the Minister of Justice and the failure to condemn the killings appeared to constitute permission to security services to carry out extrajudicial executions with impunity.

"Amnesty International Report 1998: The Palestinian Authority," http://bit.ly/19HY57A.

8. Justus Reid Weiner, *Human Rights of Christians in Palestinian Society* (Jerusalem: Jerusalem Center for Public Affairs, 2005), p. 13, http://bit.ly/17f0VQU.
9. Edmund Sanders, "Mahmoud Abbas Foresees Palestinian State with No Israelis," *Los Angeles Times*, July 30, 2013, http://lat.ms/11sdeaj.
10. Charles M. Sennott, "Christians Anxious Under Palestinian Rule," *Boston Globe*, January 17, 1999.
11. Weiner, *Human Rights of Christians*.
12. Ibid.
13. Harriet Sherwood, "Bethlehem's Christians Feel the Squeeze as Israeli Settlements Spread," *Guardian*, December 23, 2012.
14. Aaron Klein, "Christian Bookstore Owner Was Tortured Before His Death," *New York Sun*, October 11, 2007.
15. Nidal al-Muhghrabi, "Christians Sense Pressure to Convert to Islam," Reuters, July 26, 2012.
16. Khaled Abu Toameh, "The Palestinian Authority's Inconvenient Truths," Gatestone Institute International Policy Council, January 3, 2013, http://bit.ly/X2A2cx.
17. Lela Gilbert, *Saturday People, Sunday People: Israel through the Eyes of a Christian Sojourner* (New York: Encounter Books, 2012), p. 226.
18. Julie Stahl, "Palestinian Christians Suffering 'Severe Blows' from Muslims, Muslim Says," *CNS News*, November 14, 2008, http://bit.ly/1fekCtf.
19. Gilbert, *Saturday People*.
20. Giulio Meotti, "Bethlehem's Last Christians?" *Ynet News*, April 28, 2012, http://bit.ly/IugWJL.

21. Weiner, *Human Rights of Christians*, p. 5.

22. Gilbert, *Saturday People*, p. 225.

23. Ibid.

24. Ibid., and Joseph Hobeika, "Arafat's Massacre of Damour," *Canada Free Press*, January 2, 2009, http://bit.ly/OAZ8PJ.

25. Jeremy Sharon/Reuters, "Central Bureau of Statistics Report: Christian Population in Israel Is Growing," *Jerusalem Post*, December 25, 2012.

26. Mehran Kamrava, "What Stands Between the Palestinians and Democracy?" *Middle East Quarterly* 6, no. 2 (June 1999), pp. 3–12, http://bit.ly/ecTOLS.

27. Ibid.

28. Ibid.

29. Ibid.

30. Ze'ev Chafets, *Double Vision: How the Press Distorts America's View of the Middle East* (New York: William Morrow, 1985), pp. 224–25.

31. Peter Hirschberg, "The Dark Side of Arafat's Regime," *Jerusalem Report*, August 21, 1997, p. 20.

32. Nadav Haetzni, "In Arafat's Kingdom," *Commentary*, October 1996; reprinted in Neal Kozodoy, ed., *The Mideast Peace Process: An Autopsy* (New York: Encounter Books, 2002), p. 65.

33. Editorial, "Arafat's Course Is Risky and Wrong," *Montreal Gazette*, August 9, 1994, p. B2.

34. Haetzni, "In Arafat's Kingdom."

35. Julia Pitner, "Palestinian Media: A Reflection of Internal and Regional Political Fractures," *Perspectives* (Layalina Productions) 4, no. 1 (January 2012), http://bit.ly/143oKqP.

36. Robert Blum, "Telling the Truth About the Palestinians: A Briefing with Khaled Abu Toameh," *MEF Wires*, April 27, 2004, http://bit.ly/9tCzc5.

37. Jillian Kestler-D'Amours, "Dozens of Journalists, Activists Arrested as PA Cracks Down on Dissent," *Electronic Intifada*, May 1, 2012, http://bit.ly/Ir2m3t; and Khaled Abu Toameh, "After 36 Days, Palestinian Blogger Freed from Jail," *Jerusalem Post*, May 19, 2012.

38. "No News Is Good News: Abuses Against Journalists by Palestinian Security Services," Human Rights Watch, April 2011, http://bit.ly/i2u3wD.

39. Haetzni, "Arafat's Kingdom," pp. 62–63.

40. Khaled Abu Toameh, conversation with author, February 14, 2013; and Isabel Kershner, "Financial Strains Said to Threaten the Stability of Palestinian Authority," *New York Times*, September 17, 2012.

41. Abu Toameh, conversation with author.

42. "Palestinians Question Massive Security Budget," *Nuqudy*, January 10, 2013, http://bit.ly/14M72rX.

43. Editorial, "Palestinian Authority's Woes Are a Problem for U.S., Israel," *Boston Globe*, October 1, 2012.

44. Stacey Lakind and Yigal Carmon, "The PA Economy (I)," Inquiry and Analysis Report No. 10, January 7, 1999, Middle East Media Research Institute, http://bit.ly/17ha0a6.
45. Issam Abu Issa, "Arafat's Swiss Bank Account," *Middle East Quarterly* 11, no. 4 (Fall 2004), pp. 15–23, http://bit.ly/a2TkQk.
46. Mitchell Bard, "The Palestinian Money Trail," Fact Sheet No. 27, Jewish Virtual Library, October 13, 2003, http://bit.ly/13n18mw.
47. Kenneth C. W. Leiter, "Life Under the Palestinian Authority," *Middle East Quarterly* 5, no. 3 (September 1998), pp. 41–49, http://bit.ly/dkgiuX.
48. Gershom Gorenberg, "The Collaborator," *New York Times Magazine,* August 18, 2002.
49. Israeli-Palestinian Interim Agreement on the West Bank and Gaza Strip, September 28, 1995, http://bit.ly/iPJ6vG.
50. Gorenberg, "Collaborator," and Haetzni, "Arafat's Kingdom."
51. Gorenberg, "Collaborator."
52. Ibid.
53. Ibid.
54. Israel Central Bureau of Statistics, "Gross Domestic Product in Judea and Samaria by Main Economic Branches 1968–1993"; Israel Central Bureau of Statistics, "Gross Domestic Product in Gaza Area by Main Economic Branches, 1968–1993."
55. Rachel Ehrenfeld and Alyssa A. Lappen, "U.S. Rewarding Arab Terrorism," FrontPageMag.com, March 24, 2008, http://bit.ly/1aImHQv; Hebrew version at http://bit.ly/1aImWec. Palestinian GDP numbers appear only in the Hebrew version.
56. Khaled Abu Toameh, "Palestinian Authority Approves $3.8bn Budget," *Jerusalem Post,* March 29, 2013. Israel provides approximately 45 percent of the PA budget through the transfer of indirect taxes that it collects on goods imported into the areas. See Amira Hass, "PA's Budget Reflects Its Dependence on Israel, U.S.," *Haaretz,* March 31, 2013.
57. Elliott Abrams, "Chronic Kleptocracy: Corruption Within the Palestinian Political Establishment," testimony before the Committee on Foreign Affairs, Subcommittee on Middle East and South Asia, U.S. House of Representatives, 112th Cong., 2nd sess., July 10, 2012.
58. Douglas Jehl, "Frustrated Gaza Increasingly Faults its Rulers," *New York Times,* February 2, 1997.
59. Jillian C. York, "Make Fun of Mahmoud Abbas at Your Peril," *Al Jazeera,* February 13, 2013, http://aje.me/XzEUUm.
60. Palestinian Center for Policy and Survey Research, Public Opinion Poll No. 44, Joint Israeli-Palestinian Poll, June 17–23, 2012, http://bit.ly/LJUJCi.
61. Palestinian Center for Policy and Survey Research, "While Sharply Divided Over the Ceasefire . . ." Public Opinion Poll No. 5, August 18–21,

2002, http://bit.ly/1aIFBGY; Palestinian Center for Policy and Survey Research, Public Opinion Poll No. 38, December 29, 2010, http://bit.ly/18xUCXO.

62. "On Palestinian Attitudes to Democracy," Poll No. 6, part 1, May 1995, Jerusalem Media and Communication Centre, http://bit.ly/17he627.

63. CPRS Survey Research Unit, "Armed Attacks, PNA Performance," Public Opinion Poll No. 25, December 1996, http://bit.ly/13TrMTN.

CHAPTER II: WELCOME TO ISRAEL

1. Hen Kutz-Bar, "Introducing Eleanor Joseph: A Female Arab Combat Soldier in the IDF" (Hebrew) *Maariv*, February 6, 2010, http://bit.ly/acv96x.

2. "Not a Matter of Religion," Israel Defense Forces blog, June 20, 2013, http://bit.ly/11q4TnY.

3. Nir Hasson, "A Surprising Process of 'Israelization' Is Taking Place Among Palestinians in East Jerusalem," *Haaretz*, December 29, 2012.

4. "Arab Israelis," Israel Ministry of Foreign Affairs, August 20, 2001, http://bit.ly/16X3MvO.

5. Ibid.

6. Ben Sales, "Despite Hardships, Some Bedouins Still Feel Obligation to Serve Israel," Jewish Telegraphic Agency, August 20, 2012, http://bit.ly/RwtK66.

7. Elhanan Miller, "In Arab Israel, a Battle Over Christian Conscription," *Times of Israel*, June 27, 2013.

8. Ramon Marjiah, "Supported Military Service and Was Banned from the Church of the Annunciation" (Hebrew), *Maariv*, November 1, 2012, http://bit.ly/16DTkwQ.

9. Efraim Karsh, "Israel's Arabs: Deprived or Radicalized?" *Israel Affairs*, January 2013, pp. 1–19, http://bit.ly/TUTVBy.

10. Radio Monte Carlo in Arabic, July 1, 1994; al-Nahar, July 3, 1994; quoted ibid.

11. Ibid.

12. Karsh, "Israel's Arabs."

13. Roee Nahmias, "Arab MKs in Lebanon for a Solidarity Visit," *Ynet News*, September 14, 2006, http://bit.ly/1bXM92k; Rebecca Anna Stoil, "Arab MKs Visit Libya's Gaddafi," *Jerusalem Post*, April 26, 2010; Eliezer Yaari, "Syrian Crisis Reveals Hypocrisy of Israeli Arab MKs," *Haaretz*, February 6, 2012.

14. Isabel Kershner, "Israel Reveals New Details of Allegations Against Ex-lawmaker," *New York Times*, May 3, 2007.

15. Nachman Tal, "The Islamic Movement in Israel," *Strategic Assessment* 2, no. 4 (February 2000), http://bit.ly/15qfFMt.

16. Marjiah, "Supported Military Service"; and Yishai Friedman, "The Priest

Who Supports Military Service Has Become the Enemy of the City of Nazareth" (Hebrew), *Maariv*, December 22, 2012, http://bit.ly/1bNvkqB.

17. Khaled Abu Toameh, "Why Palestinians Want Israeli Citizenship," Gatestone Institute International Policy Council, October 23, 2012, http://bit.ly/Ri2fd4.

18. Nir Hasson, "3,374 East Jerusalem Residents Received Full Israeli Citizenship in the Past Decade," *Haaretz*, October 21, 2012.

19. Abu Toameh, "Why Palestinians Want Israeli Citizenship."

20. David Pollock, "What Do the Arabs of East Jerusalem Really Want?" Jerusalem Center for Public Affairs, September 7, 2011, http://bit.ly/1c9YgsY.

21. Ryan Mauro, "Anet Haskia: Israel Is My Homeland," RadicalIslam.org, December 12, 2012, http://bit.ly/UamfP5.

22. Philippe Assouline, "A Would-Be New Leader of Israel's Arabs Urges Full Integration with Israel," *Times of Israel*, October 30, 2012.

23. Daniel Siryoti, "Arab Christians Demand Equal Rights, and Equal Duties," *Israel Hayom*, June 28, 2013, http://bit.ly/1feuJy4

24. An April 2001 survey found that 74 percent of Palestinians supported suicide bombings and 80 percent supported continuing the terror campaign. "On Palestinian Attitudes Towards Politics including the Current Intifada," Poll No. 40, April 2001, Jerusalem Media and Communication Centre, http://bit.ly/14ydQx4.

25. "Involvement of Israeli Arabs in Terrorism," Special Information Bulletin, March 28, 2005, Intelligence and Terrorism Information Center, http://bit.ly/15cmFPx.

26. Exact figures regarding the number of Palestinians from Judea and Samaria who have been involved in terrorism are not publicly available. However, it is possible to extrapolate data pointing to the general size of the terrorist population. For instance, between April 2002 and August 2004, Israel took 6,964 terrorists out of action by killing 959 and arresting 6,005. The overwhelming majority of them were in Judea and Samaria. "Four Years of Conflict: Israel's War Against Terrorism," October 3, 2004, Israel Ministry of Foreign Affairs, p. 5, http://bit.ly/18FOJYL.

27. Michael Lerner, "Building a Jewish and Democratic State: A Conversation with Peter Beinart," *Tikkun*, May 11, 2012, http://bit.ly/KZHOSy; and Rebecca Steinfeld, "Liberal Zionism: A Contradiction in Terms?" *Jewish Quarterly*, March 2012, http://bit.ly/GTNmbs.

28. "Freedom in the World 2012: Israel," Freedom House, http://bit.ly/15qkYvc.

29. Yoram Hazony, "Judaism and the Modern State," *Azure* 21 (Summer 5765/2005), pp. 33–51, http://bit.ly/18W5e2X; and Fania Oz-Salzberger, "The Jewish Roots of Western Freedom," *Azure* 13 (Summer 5762/2002), pp. 88–132, http://bit.ly/19I7AU1.

30. Ibid., p. 96.

CHAPTER 12: THE LEGITIMATE SOVEREIGN, NOT AN OCCUPYING POWER

1. Marcus Dysch, "Israel's Deputy Ambassador Forced to Flee Essex University Lecture," *Jewish Chronicle* (U.K.), February 21, 2013, http://bit.ly/XmJtp2.

2. Bethany Mandel, "Israel's Bad Week on UK Campuses," *Commentary*, February 22, 2013, http://bit.ly/1dJ4vWs.

3. "British MP Ditches Debate Because Rival Is Israeli," *Times of Israel*, February 21, 2013.

4. Joel Fishman, "'A Disaster of Another Kind': Zionism=Racism, Its Beginning, and the War of Delegitimization Against Israel," *Israel Journal of Foreign Affairs* 5, no. 3 (2011), pp. 75–92, http://bit.ly/onaMHl.

5. Ibid., p. 76.

6. Ibid., p. 77.

7. Jonathan D. Halevi, "The Palestinian Authority's Responsibility for the Outbreak of the Second Intifada: Its Own Damning Testimony," Jerusalem Center for Public Affairs, February 20, 2013, http://bit.ly/13cJIXE.

8. "Victims of Palestinian Violence and Terrorism Since September 2000," Israel Ministry of Foreign Affairs, undated, http://bit.ly/fyqm.

9. Gerald Steinberg, "The Centrality of NGOs in the Durban Strategy," *Yale Israel Journal*, July 11, 2006, p. 2, at http://bit.ly/19URuKt.

10. Ibid.

11. Ibid.

12. See Lassa Oppenheim, *International Law: A Treatise*, vol. 1, *Peace* (London: Longmans, Green, 1905), pp. 2–10.

13. Charter of the United Nations and Statute of the International Court of Justice, San Francisco, 1945, http://bit.ly/fA2pq6.

14. Covenant of the League of Nations 1919 (Including Amendments adopted to December, 1924), at http://bit.ly/vncUZi.

15. American Law Institute, "Third Restatement on the Foreign Relations Law of the United States," 1987, Article 102.

16. "Convention Respecting the Laws and Customs of War on Land and Its Annex; Regulations Concerning the Laws and Customs of War on Land," The Hague, October 18, 1907, http://bit.ly/19I8LmE.

17. Covenant of the League of Nations.

18. Ibid., Article 22.

19. Ibid.

20. The Mandate for Palestine, July 24, 1922, Article 2, at http://bit.ly/1akYiAj.

21. Ibid.

22. Howard Grief, "Legal Rights and Title of Sovereignty of the Jewish People to the Land of Israel and Palestine Under International Law," *Nativ Online: A Journal of Politics and the Arts* 2 (2004), http://bit.ly/huobHJ.

23. Eli Hertz, "'Mandate for Palestine': Legal Aspects of Jewish Rights," *Myths and Facts*, http://bit.ly/14pWH8Q. Reprinted with permission.

24. Hertz, *Myths and Facts*. Reprinted with permission.

25. Mandate for Palestine.

26. Frank Jacobs, "The Elephant in the Map Room," *New York Times*, August 7, 2012.

27. Ibid.

28. Hertz, *Myths and Facts*.

29. Eli E. Hertz, *Jerusalem: One Nation's Capital Throughout History: The Legal Aspects of Jewish Rights* (Forest Hills, N.Y.: Myths and Facts, 2011), pp. 40–41.

30. UN Charter. Article 80 states: "Nothing in this Charter shall be construed in or of itself to alter in any manner the rights whatsoever of any states or any people or the terms of existing instruments to which Members of the United Nations may respectively be parties."

31. Judge Sir Elihu Lauterpacht, *Jerusalem and the Holy Places* (London: Anglo-Israel Association, 1968), quoted in Hertz, *Jerusalem*, p. 40.

32. Julius Stone, *Israel and Palestine, Assault on the Law of Nations* (Baltimore: Johns Hopkins University Press, 1981), quoted in Hertz, *Jerusalem*, p. 41.

33. Avi Bell, conversation with author, December 20, 2012.

34. "Uti Possidetis Juris," Legal Information Institute, Cornell University Law School, http://bit.ly/1feyO5q.

35. Avi Bell, conversation with author.

36. "Report of Judgments, Advisory Opinions and Orders, Case Concerning the Frontier Dispute (Burkina Faso and the Republic of Mali), Judgment of 22 December 1986," International Court of Justice, http://bit.ly/17845ba.

37. Ibid., p. 565 (15).

38. See "Israel's War of Independence: 1947–1949," Israel Ministry of Foreign Affairs, http://bit.ly/gyMsBZ; and Mitchell Bard, "Israeli War of Independence: Background and Overview, 1948–1949," Jewish Virtual Library, http://bit.ly/cQES50.

39. Ibid (both sources).

40. Stephen M. Schwebel, "What Weight Conquest?" *American Journal of International Law* 64, no. 2 (April 1970), pp. 344–47. As Schwebel explains, "The facts of the 1948 hostilities between the Arab invaders of Palestine and the nascent state of Israel further demonstrate that Egypt's seizure of the Gaza Strip, and Jordan's seizure and subsequent annexation of the West Bank and the old city of Jerusalem, were unlawful" (p. 346).

41. Yehuda Z. Blum, "The Missing Reversioner: Reflections on the Status of Judea and Samaria," *Israel Law Review* 3 (1968), pp. 279–301, at 279.

42. Schwebel, "What Weight Contest?," p. 346.

43. Ibid.

44. Blum, "Missing Reversioner."

45. Ibid., p. 294.

46. Ibid., p. 295.

47. See Dan Diker, "The Palestinians' Unilateral 'Kosovo Strategy': Implications for the PA and Israel," January 12, 2010, Jerusalem Center for Public Affairs, http://bit.ly/1djTRrs; and Dan Diker, "Israel's Return to Security-Based Diplomacy," November 12, 2011, http://bit.ly/15dgofH.

48. Lauterpacht, *Jerusalem*, and Stone, *Israel*, both cited in Hertz, *Jerusalem*, pp. 41–42.

49. Bell, conversation with author; United Nations, "Non-Self-Governing Territories," undated, http://bit.ly/JMcP7L.

50. Christopher J. Borgen, "Kosovo's Declaration of Independence: Self-Determination, Secession and Recognition," *ASIL Insights* (American Society for International Law) 12, no. 2 (February 29, 2008), http://bit.ly/14W2akb.

51. Antonio Cassese, "The Israel-PLO Agreement and Self-Determination," *European Journal of International Law* 4, no. 1 (1993), http://bit.ly/17feoZ5.

52. Ibid.

53. "Regarding the Secession of Quebec," Judgments of the Supreme Court of Canada, August 20, 1998, http://bit.ly/U1hegQ.

CHAPTER 13: THE INDIGENOUS PEOPLE, NOT COLONIAL USURPERS

1. Isabel Kershner, "Battir Journal: A Palestinian Village Tries to Protect a Territorial Ancient Wonder of Agriculture," *New York Times*, June 25, 2012.

2. Yigal Yadin, *Bar-Kochba: The Rediscovery of the Legendary Hero of the Last Jewish Revolt Against Imperial Rome* (London: Littlehampton Book Services, 1971).

3. Yisrael Medad, "Mutual Historic Heritage Recognition," *My Right Word*, May 30, 2012, http://bit.ly/16LGF8X; and Jonathan Tobin, "Heritage Site Is Jewish, Not Just Palestinian," *Commentary*, June 27, 2012.

4. Josephus, *The Jewish War* (New York: Penguin Books, 1981), p. 371.

5. Elli Fischer, "NYT Misses a Big Part of Battir's Cultural Heritage," *Times of Israel*, June 27, 2012.

6. "PM Slams UNESCO for Calling Rachel's Tomb a Mosque," *Jerusalem Post*, October 29, 2010.

7. Steven Erlanger and Scott Sayare, "UNESCO Approves Full Membership for the Palestinians," *New York Times*, October 31, 2011.

8. Guilio Meotti, "UNESCO Against the Jews," *Ynet News*, July 19, 2011, http://bit.ly/nJacfE.

9. David Meir-Levi, *Stolen History: How the Palestinians and Their Allies Attack*

Israel's Right to Exist by Erasing Its Past (Sherman Oaks, Calif.: David Horowitz Freedom Center, 2012).

10. "'Rachel's Tomb Was Never Jewish,'" *Jerusalem Post*, March 7, 2010.

11. The Palestinian National Charter, Resolutions of the Palestine National Council, July 1–17, 1968, http://bit.ly/eEK4G2.

12. Palestinian Media Watch has documented Palestinian historical fabrication in "Jewish History Rewritten," http://bit.ly/mcIrWt; "Palestinian History Fabricated," http://bit.ly/1bjN3UB; and "Jesus Misrepresented as 'Muslim Palestinian,'" http://bit.ly/u3GIst.

13. Quoted in "Jewish History Rewritten," Palestinian Media Watch.

14. Dore Gold, "Abbas's Temple Denial," *Israel Hayom*, March 2, 2012, http://bit.ly/wYc3wn.

15. Ibid., and Meir-Levi, *Stolen History*, p. 25.

16. Herb Keinon, "Abbas Denies the Jewish Connection to Jerusalem," *Jerusalem Post*, August 22, 2012.

17. Meir-Levi, *Stolen History*, pp. 36–37.

18. Ibid., p. 1.

19. Eli Hertz, *Jerusalem: One Nation's Capital Throughout History: The Legal Aspects of Jewish Rights* (Forest Hills, N.Y.: Myths and Facts, 2011).

20. Palestinian Negotiations Support Unit, "Strategy and Talking Points for Responding to the Precondition of Recognizing Israel as a 'Jewish State,' Memorandum to Palestinian Drafting Team," November 16, 2007, http://bit.ly/17NQL89, emphasis in the original.

21. "History of Politics and Continuity of Settlement," Research Department of the Council of Jewish Communities in Judea, Samaria and the Gaza District, October 2, 2011, http://bit.ly/1dxc3vt.

22. Ann Killebrew, *Biblical People and Ethnicity: An Archaeological Study of Egyptians, Canaanites, Philistines, and Early Israel 1300–1100 BCE* (Atlanta, Ga.: Society of Biblical Literature, 2005). Killebrew dates the disappearance of the Philistines as a separate political entity to between the tenth and seventh centuries BCE.

23. UN General Assembly Resolution 181, November 29, 1947, http://bit.ly/114DpCO.

24. Ibid.

25. Ibid.

26. Eli E. Hertz, *This Land is My Land: "Mandate for Palestine," The Legal Aspects of Jewish Rights* (New York: Myths and Facts, 2008), pp. 9–11.

27. Joshua 18:10.

28. Joshua 18:7.

29. Joshua 22:12.

30. Joshua 18:1.

31. I Samuel 1:24.

32. Israel Finkelstein and Eliazer Piasetzky, "The Iron I-IIA in the Highlands and Beyond: 14C Anchors, Pottery Phases and the Shoshenq I Campaign," *Levant* 38 (2006), pp. 45–61, http://bit.ly/1f5tpgW.

33. Ibid.

34. I Samuel 4:4–12.

35. Meredith Bennett-Smith, "Tel Shiloh Archaeological Dig Pitcher Suggests Biblical City in Israel Burned to the Ground," *Huffington Post*, January 17, 2013.

36. Jeremiah 41:5.

37. Yisrael Ben-Aryeh, "Ancient Shilo: Historical Survey," http://bit.ly/14yoHak.

38. Ibid.

39. Aryeh Savir, "Rare Artifact Stolen from Tel Shiloh Archaeological Site," *Jewish Press*, January 17, 2013, http://bit.ly/U3i7Da.

40. "Remembering Joseph's Tomb, and Madhat Yusuf," *Israel National News*, November 28, 2001, http://bit.ly/1fYxVOP.

41. "Mosque Construction Underway Atop Joseph's Tomb," *Israel Wire*, October 10, 2000, at http://bit.ly/18WdsIi.

42. Elad Benari, "Expert Warns of Waqf's Dangerous Plan for Temple Mount," *Israel National News*, February 24, 2012, http://bit.ly/19UWPkY.

43. "The Temple Mount History," Public Committee Against the Destruction of Antiquities on the Temple Mount, http://bit.ly/1dJeY4n.

44. "Destruction of Antiquities," Public Committee Against the Destruction of Antiquities on the Temple Mount, http://bit.ly/15qwZRh.

45. Ibid.

46. Etgar Lefkovits, "Temple Mount Relics Saved from Garbage," *Jerusalem Post*, April 14, 2005.

47. Nadav Shragai, "First Temple Artifacts found in dirt removed from Temple Mount," *Haaretz*, October 19, 2006.

48. "Cultural Landscape and Archaeological Remains of the Bamiyan Valley," UNESCO, http://bit.ly/kD0qi.

49. David Lee Miller, "Exclusive New Evidence About Historic Site," Fox News, January 24, 2011, http://bit.ly/LPphFO.

50. Author site visit, January 2011.

51. "History of Politics and Continuity of Settlement."

52. Josephus, *Jewish War.*

53. Michael Avi-Yonah, *The Jews of Palestine: A Political History from Bar Kokhba to the Arab Conquest* (Oxford: Basil Blackwell, 1976), pp. 18–19.

54. Ibid., p. 241.

55. Joshua Prawer, ed., *The History of the Land of Israel* (Hebrew) (Jerusalem: Yad Ben Zvi, 1981), pp. 6:72, 77.

56. Moshe Gil, *A History of Palestine 634–1099* (Cambridge: Cambridge University Press, 1997), p. 837.

57. "History of Politics and Continuity of Settlement."

58. Menashe Harel, *Historical Geography of the Land of Israel* (Hebrew) (Tel Aviv, 2002), p. 725.

59. David Farhi, "Ottoman Attitudes Towards Jewish Settlement," in Moshe Ma'oz, ed., *Studies on Palestine During the Ottoman Period* (Jerusalem: Magnes Press, 1975), p. 175.

60. Israel Kolatt, "The Organization of the Jewish Population of Palestine and the Development of Its Political Consciousness Before World War I," in Ma'oz, *Studies on Palestine*, p. 211.

61. Harel, *Historical Geography*, p. 735.

CHAPTER 14: LIKELY PALESTINIAN RESPONSES

1. Barak Ravid, "Abbas: If Stalemate Continues After Elections, Netanyahu Can Take Back the Keys to the West Bank," *Haaretz*, December 27, 2012.

2. Emily Hauser, "Abbas Threatens to Dismantle PA—Again," *Daily Beast*, December 28, 2012.

3. Khaled Abu Toameh, "What Do Abbas's Latest Threats Really Mean?" Gatestone Institute International Policy Council, December 31, 2012, http://bit.ly/VT6dI4.

4. Bret Stephens, "The Boring Palestinians," *Wall Street Journal*, July 16, 2013.

5. Ibid.

6. Palestinian Center for Policy and Survey Research, Joint Israeli-Palestinian Poll, June 17–23, 2012, http://bit.ly/LJUJCi; Palestinian Center for Policy and Survey Research, "While Sharply Divided over the Ceasefire . . . ," Public Opinion Poll No. 5, August 18–21, 2002, http://bit.ly/1aIFBGY; Palestinian Center for Policy and Survey Research, Public Opinion Poll No. 38, December 29, 2010, http://bit.ly/18xUCXO; "On Palestinian Attitudes to Democracy," Poll No. 6, part 1, May 1995, Jerusalem Media and Communication Centre, http://bit.ly/17he627; and Palestinian Center for Policy and Survey Research, "Armed Attacks, PNA Performance . . ." Public Opinion Poll No. 25, December 1996, http://bit.ly/13TrMTN.

7. Matthew Kalman, "Mideast Training Program Backfires: Palestinian Security Officers Schooled in U.S. Later Used Tactics Against Israel," *San Francisco Chronicle*, February 14, 2005.

8. Jim Zanotti, "U.S. Foreign Aid to the Palestinians," Congressional Research Service, January 18, 2013, p. 13, http://bit.ly/9TvY4j.

9. Caroline B. Glick, "Column One: Israel's American-Made Foes," *Jerusalem Post*, June 8, 2010.

10. Jim Zanotti, "U.S. Foreign Aid to the Palestinians," Congressional Research Service, June 15, 2012, p. 15, http://bit.ly/15VrQgu.

11. Robert Dreyfuss, "U.S. General Builds a Palestinian Army," *Nation*, May 10, 2009.

12. Kalman, "Mideast Training Backfires."

13. Marc Provisor (head of Security Projects for the One Israel Fund), interview by author, January 10, 2013; author site visits to Samaria regional council and communities, April 2012; and to Binyamin and Gush Etzion region communities, September 2012, January 2013, and March 2013.

14. Louise Bagshawe, "A Family Slaughtered in Israel—Doesn't the BBC Care?" *Telegraph*, March 24, 2011.

15. Brooke Goldstein, "Lawfare: The Use of the Law as a Weapon of War," Lawfare Project, http://bit.ly/tWl4bP.

16. Rome Statute of the International Criminal Court, at http://bit.ly/qqoeW6.

17. "ICC Prosecutor Rejects Palestinian Recognition," BBC, April 4, 2012, http://bbc.in/HifAOs.

18. "Tribunal in Palestine," *Global Post*, March 17, 2012, http://bit.ly/WQbYhk.

19. Yonah Jeremy Bob, "Analysis: Palestinian ICC Threat Is Overblown," *Jerusalem Post*, November 30, 2012.

20. "International Criminal Court to Consider Implications of UN vote on Palestine," *Times of Israel*, November 30, 2012.

21. Ibid.

22. Eugene Kontorovich, "Abbas's Bogus ICC Concession," *National Review Online*, April 24, 2013, http://bit.ly/12eiWvs.

23. Zach Pontz, "New Numbers Show UK-Israel Trade Is Booming," *Algemeiner*, March 15, 2013, http://bit.ly/XdDdNF; and Candace Kreiger, "Boycott, What Boycott? UK-Israel Trade Is Booming," *Jewish Chronicle* (U.K.), March 15, 2012, http://bit.ly/yWMfmd.

CHAPTER 15: LIKELY REGIONAL RESPONSES

1. Secretary-general of the League of Arab States to the secretary general, cablegram, May 15, 1948, UN Security Council S/745, May 16, 1948, http://bit.ly/bPhIp4.

2. "Muslim-Western Tensions Persist," Pew Research Global Attitudes Project, Pew Research Center, July 21, 2011, http://bit.ly/yhSmIc.

3. Ahmad Hashemi, "Anti-Semitism Is Why the Arab Spring Failed," *Times of Israel*, April 9, 2013.

4. Rania Abouzeid, "Bouazizi: The Man Who Set Himself and Tunisia on Fire," *Time*, January 21, 2011, http://ti.me/mZBzPA.

5. Elspeth Reeve, "What the Inside of Egypt's Biggest Protest in History Looks Like at Night," *Atlantic Wire*, July 1, 2013, http://bit.ly/11ZoZ5q.

6. David Goldman, "The Economic Blunders Behind the Arab Revolutions," *Wall Street Journal*, July 12, 2013.

7. David Goldman, "Egypt 'On the Verge of Bankruptcy,'" Jewish Institute for National Security Affairs, December 31, 2012, http://bit.ly/17fnV2l.

8. Sarah McFarlane, "Egypt's Wheat Problem: How Mursi Jeopardized the Bread Supply," Reuters, July 25, 2013, http://reut.rs/16LS9Jv.

9. David Goldman, "Egypt's Looming Economic Ruin," *MEF Wires*, May 30, 2013, http://bit.ly/1bjznsy.

10. Ben Hubbard and David Kirkpatrick, "Sudden Improvements in Egypt Suggest a Campaign to Undermine Morsi," *New York Times*, July 10, 2013.

11. David Kirkpatrick and Mayy el Sheikh, "Citing Deadlock, Egypt's Leader Seizes New Power and Plans Mubarak Retrial," *New York Times*, November 22, 2012.

12. Richard Engel, "Egyptians Fear Decades of Muslim Brotherhood Rule, Warn Morsi Is No Friend of the U.S.," *NBC News*, December 1, 2012, http://nbcnews.to/Qx0Gdv.

13. Lee Smith, "No More Morsi: A Coup in Ungovernable Egypt," *Weekly Standard*, July 22, 2013, http://bit.ly/18Rjehs; "Will Egypt Save Itself from Total Collapse by Going to War Against Israel?" *Tablet*, July 3, 2013, http://bit.ly/17Z7bL4.

14. Abigail Hauslohner, "Scores Killed as Egyptian Security Forces Fire on Demonstrators at Morsi Rally," *Washington Post*, July 27, 2013.

15. Jeffrey Fleishman and Ingy Hassieb, "Militants in Egypt's Sinai Peninsula Grow Stronger," *Los Angeles Times*, July 25, 2013.

16. Maggie Michael, "Egypt Destroys Homes for Possible Gaza Buffer Zone, Associated Press, September 1, 2013, http://yhoo.it/14iqWuI.

17. Ian Black and Patrick Kingsley, "Egypt: Mosque Is Stormed as Generals Plan to Outlaw Muslim Brotherhood," *The Guardian*, August 17, 2013, http://bit.ly/15T2ejK.

18. Reuters, "Suez Canal Authority Says Attack Attempted on Container Ship," *Jerusalem Post*, September 2, 2013, http://bit.ly/15JW0He.

19. "Muslim-Western Tensions Persist," Pew Research Center.

20. Moshe Phillips, "The Future of Egyptian Jew-Hatred Is Now," *NewsReal Blog*, February 6, 2011, http://bit.ly/e0gqW7.

21. Eldad Beck, "Egyptians Believe Morsi in Cahoots with US, Israel," *Ynet News*, July 6, 2013, http://bit.ly/1aLKGOv.

22. Max Fisher, "Muslim Brotherhood Site Says Egypt's New President Is Secretly Jewish," *Washington Post*, July 5, 2013.

23. Avi Bar-Eli and Reuters, "Egypt Cancels Natural Gas Deal with Israel," *Haaretz*, April 12, 2012; and Lee Smith, "How to Kill an Economy: Egypt Sours on Its (Lucrative) Gas Deal with Israel," *Weekly Standard*, March 12, 2012, http://bit.ly/wl9D5N.

24. Richard Behar, "News Flash: Jews Are 'Apes And Pigs.' So Why Is Egypt's Morsi the Elephant in America's Newsrooms?" *Forbes*, January 11, 2013.

25. Josh Rogin, "Exclusive: Morsi Implies Jews Control American Media," *Foreign Policy*, January 23, 2013.

26. Lee Smith, "Will Egypt Save Itself from Total Collapse by Going to War Against Israel?" *Tablet*, July 3, 2013, http://bit.ly/17Z7bL4.

27. "Egypt Accuses Ousted President of Murder, Conspiracy," Associated Press, July 26, 2013, at http://fxn.ws/14yyYTL.

28. Khaled Abu Toameh, "Fatah Wants Egypt to Overthrow Hamas," Gatestone International Policy Council, September 6, 2013, http://bit.ly/154lOhI.

29. Tony G. Gabriel, "Egyptian Authorities Detain Suspected 'spy bird,'" Associated Press, August 31, 2013, http://bit.ly/18t0XlF.

30. Elhanan Miller, "Jordanian Tribe Mourns Appointment of Clansman as Ambassador to Israel," *Times of Israel*, October 18, 2013.

31. Elhanan Miller, "Jordan's New Ambassador to Israel Warned by Tribe Not to Take the Job," *Times of Israel*, October 2, 2012.

32. Mudar Zahran, "A Plan B for Jordan?" Gatestone Institute International Policy Council, September 16, 2011, http://bit.ly/GRpaaM.

33. Robin Wright and Peter Baker, "Iraq, Jordan See Threat to Election from Iran," *Washington Post*, December 8, 2004.

34. Jeffrey Goldberg, "The Modern King and the Arab Spring," *Atlantic*, March 18, 2013.

35. "Stateless Again: Palestinian-Origin Jordanians Deprived of Their Nationality," Human Rights Watch, February 2010, http://bit.ly/1dIEQgC.

36. Khaled Abu Toameh, "Anti-Palestinian Discrimination in Jordan: Now It's Official," Gatestone Institute International Policy Council, August 6, 2012, http://bit.ly/OTJfkR.

37. Mudar Zahran, "A Plan B for Jordan?"

38. David Hale, cable to secretary of state, "The Right of Return: What It Means for Jordan," February 6, 2008, http://bit.ly/nTeCGo.

39. CIA World Factbook, "Jordan: Economy": "Jordan's economy is among the smallest in the Middle East, with insufficient supplies of water, oil, and other natural resources, underlying the government's heavy reliance on foreign assistance." Jordan's estimated budget deficit in 2012 was 11.4 percent of its GDP. Also see Nayla Razzouk, "Jordan Public Debt Rises to $20.2 Billion, Finance Ministry Says," *Bloomberg*, April 29, 2012, http://bloom.bg/JJFopy.

40. "As Beleaguered as Ever: King Abdullah Must Make Swift and Drastic Reforms to Resolve His Latest Political and Economic Crises," *Economist*, October, 13, 2012.

41. Michael Weiss, "Breaking: Syrian State Documents 'Show Assad Orchestrated Nakba Day Raid on Golan Heights,'" *Telegraph*, June 13, 2011.

42. Ibid.

43. Hanan Greenberg, "Syrian Death Toll Climbs; Majdal Shams Joins Riots," *Ynet News*, June 5, 2011, http://bit.ly/iCrzdL.

44. Roula Hajjar, "Violence at Palestinian Camp Funerals in Syria Leaves 20 Dead," *Los Angeles Times*, June 8, 2011.

45. Ibid.

46. Reuters, "Syrian Jets Bomb Palestinian Camp, Killing 25," *Jerusalem Post*, December 16, 2012.

47. Gavriel Fiske and AP, "Syria Accused of Gassing Palestinian Refugee Camp," *Times of Israel*, July 22, 2013.

48. "Report: 1036 Palestinians Killed in Syria Since March 2011," International Middle East Media Center, March 5, 2013, http://bit.ly/1dJpGrz.

49. "Palestinian Refugees Flee War in Syria," Associated Press, in *Haaretz*, January 28, 2013.

50. Dominiq Evans, "UN Curbs Golan Patrols After Peacekeepers Seized— Diplomats," Reuters, in *Daily Star Lebanon*, March 14, 2013, http://bit.ly/17hAM22.

51. Roi Kais, "Syrian Rebels Fire Shots at Golan Border," *Ynet News*, March 9, 2013, http://bit.ly/YM10qg.

52. Phoebe Greenwood et al., "Syrian Rebels Seize Territory North of Golan Heights," *Telegraph*, November 13, 2012.

53. Aaron Kalman, "Al Qaida Gunmen Study IDF Patrols on Israeli-Syrian Border," *Times of Israel*, March 6, 2013.

54. Aaron Kalman, "Syria Rebels Capure Intel Base Near Israel Border," *Times of Israel*, March 17, 2013.

55. "Israel Will 'Bring Down Assad' If He Retaliates for Future Airstrikes," *Times of Israel*, May 15, 2013.

56. Nouri al-Maliki, "The U.S. Has a Foreign Policy Partner in Iraq," *Washington Post*, April 13, 2013.

57. "Breaking: Syrian Opposition Forces Reportedly Bomb Hezbollah Compounds, as Hezbollah Goes All-In on Syria," Israel Project, February 21, 2013, http://bit.ly/1aMeo6j.

58. Julian Borger, "Iran and Hezbollah Have Built 50,000-Strong Force to Help Syrian Regime," *Guardian*, March 14, 2013; and Hilal Khashan, "Will Syria's Strife Rip Lebanon Apart?" *Middle East Quarterly* 20, no. 1 (Winter 2013), pp. 75–80, http://bit.ly/Y4oa90.

59. Ilan Ben Zion and Elhanan Miller, "Syrian Rebels Take Fight to Hezbollah in Lebanon," *Times of Israel*, February 21, 2013.

60. Quoted in Khashan, "Will Syria's Strife."

CHAPTER 16: LIKELY EUROPEAN RESPONSES

1. Ed Payne, Greg Botelho, and Mohammed Tawfeeq, "Opposition Presses for Weapons as Syrian Death Toll Tops 100,000," CNN, July 26, 2013.

2. Andrew C. McCarthy, "Syria Fairy Tales," *National Review*, July 26, 2013.

3. Dana Hughes, "U.S. Confirms Syrian Government Used Chemical Weapons," ABC News, June 13, 2013, http://abcn.ws/17KtXK6.

4. Hilal Khashan, "Will Syria's Strife Rip Lebanon apart?" *Middle East Quarterly* 20, no. 1 (Winter 2013), pp. 75–80, http://bit.ly/Y4oa90.

5. Tim Arango, Anne Barnard, and Dureid Adnan, "As Syrians Fight, Sectarian Strife Infects Mideast," *New York Times,* June 1, 2013.

6. Yaakov Lappin, "New Iran Crisis Looming," Gatestone Institute International Policy Council, June 12, 2013, http://bit.ly/11vk0b1.

7. "Guidelines on the Eligibility of Israeli Entities and Their Activities ..." *Official Journal of the European Union,* C205/9, July 19, 2013, http://bit.ly/15OYQIO.

8. Stuart Winer, "Full Text of EU Foreign Policy Chief's Letter on Settlement Labeling," *Times of Israel,* July 23, 2013.

9. Herb Keinon and Steve Linde, "Lithuanian FM: Heed Settlement Goods Label Issue," *Jerusalem Post,* May 22, 2013.

10. Avi Bell, conversation with author, July 24, 2013.

11. Robin Shepherd, "In Europe, an Unhealthy Fixation on Israel," *Washington Post,* January 30, 2005.

12. Benjamin Weinthal, "47% of Germans Think Israel Exterminating Palestinians," *Jerusalem Post,* March 16, 2011.

13. The Palestinians are portrayed in the European media and religious institutions as Christ figures. For instance in 2002 Italy's leading newspaper, *La Stampa,* published a cartoon on page one with a tank emblazoned with a Jewish star pointing its gun at baby Jesus, with the caption, "Surely they don't want to kill me again." A church in Scotland placed a mural in its chapel depicting a crucified Jesus surrounded by Israeli soldiers. For these and other examples, see Mortimer B. Zuckerman, "A Shameful Contagion," *US News & World Report,* September 29, 2002, http://bit.ly/1dk5Owm. Manfred Gerstenfeld argues that demonization has replaced the charge of deicide in Europe's public mythology, and that the connection between Jew hatred and anti-Israel sentiments is deep, indisputable, and dangerous. See Gerstenfeld, "Experiencing European anti-Americanism and Anti-Israelism: An Interview with Jeffrey Gedmin," December 1, 2004, Jerusalem Center for Public Affairs, http://jcpa.org/phas/phas-27.htm; Raphael Ahren, "EU Foreign Policy Chief Wants Settlement Goods Labeled," *Times of Israel,* March 1, 2013, http://bit.ly/149mvls.

14. "Guidelines on the Eligibility of Israeli Entities."

15. Noah Pollak, "The B'Tselem Witch Trials," *Commentary,* May 2011.

16. "A/S Posner Discusses Goldstone Report with Israeli NGOs, ICRC, and Legal Experts," U.S. Embassy, Tel Aviv, January 27, 2010, WikiLeaks, http://bit.ly/1cdhe1V.

17. Abe Selig, "Im Tirzu: NIF NGOs Gave Bulk of Goldstone Testimonies," *Jerusalem Post,* February 1, 2010.

18. Pollak, "B'Tselem Witch Trials."

19. Richard Goldstone, "Reconsidering the Goldstone Report on Israel and War Crimes," *Washington Post*, April 1, 2011.

20. "A/S Posner Discusses Goldstone Report with Israeli NGOs,"

21. "Knesset Considers Controversial NGO Legislation to Register as Foreign Agents," U.S. Embassy Tel Aviv, February 25, 2010, WikiLeaks, http://bit .ly/n1SXxj.

22. Barak Ravid, "Secret EU Paper Aims to Tackle Israel's Treatment of Arab Minority," *Haaretz*, December 16, 2011.

23. A 2004 Knesset study found that out of 15,000 illegal structures built in open areas by Jews in 2000, only 1,000 remained standing in 2004. "Background Report on the Subject of Illegal Building" (Hebrew), Knesset Research and Information Department, November 15, 2004, http://bit .ly/17bZB3f.

24. Shimon Ifergen, "The State Destroyed the Home of a Bedouin IDF Tracker" (Hebrew), Israel Channel 2 News, October 23, 2012, http://bit.ly/145TNCv.

25. Akiva Bigman, "The Islamic Movement Builds the Negev," *Mida*, May 6, 2013, http://bit.ly/16NWJsv.

26. Jillian Kestler-D'Amours, "The End of the Bedouin," *Le Monde Diplomatique*, August 2012, http://bit.ly/Onk9Lq.

27. "Countries and Regions: Israel: Trade Picture," European Commission website report on bilateral trade with Israel, http://bit.ly/1913VTF; and "Israel: EU Bilateral Trade and Trade with the World," European Commission, November 29, 2012, http://bit.ly/uTYAuK.

28. Soeren Kern, "EU 'Upgrades' Relations with Israel, Strangling Strings Attached," Gatestone Institute International Policy Council, August 3, 2012, http://bit.ly/QI0k1R.

29. "Barroso Hails EU-Israel Cooperation in Innovations and Research," European Jewish Congress, July 13, 2012, http://bit.ly/17c15dP.

30. In 2007 EU member states exported $263 million in arms to Israel. In 2012 total Israeli arms exports stood at $7 billion worldwide. In 2012 Israel agreed to purchase Italian trainer aircraft for its air force for $1 billion. In exchange, Italy agreed to purchase Israeli aviation equipment and logistical support valued at $750 million. Israel has in recent years signed multiple contracts with the Polish military totaling in excess of $1 billion. In 2013 Germany opted to purchase Israel's Heron drones over the U.S.-made Predator drones. See Leigh Phillips, "Arms Exports to Israel Worth 200 Million Euro," *EU Observer*, January 7, 2009, http://bit.ly/1cdiWAB; Amos Harel, "Israel's Arms Exports Increased by 20 Percent in 2012," *Haaretz*, January 10, 2013; "IAI Expects Another Large-Scale Italian Deal," *Israel Defense*, April 22, 2013, http://bit.ly/145UMCF; "Israeli Arms Firm to Invest Over $400 Million in Poland," February 17, 2004, Agence France-Presse,

at http://bit.ly/145UXhs; "Press Release: Polish Army Selects Aeronautics as Supplier of Mini UAV Systems," *Aeronautics*, July 27, 2007, http://bit.ly/19WJ313; "Germany 'May Buy Weaponised Drones from Israel,'" April 14, 2013, Agence France-Presse, http://bit.ly/19WJhW3.

31. Quoted in David Shamah, "No Longer 'That Sh**ty Country': Europeans Vie for Israel's High-Tech Affections," *Times of Israel*, November 2, 2012, http://bit.ly/Sx9spx.

32. Abigail Klein Leichman, "The Man Who Sells Europe on Israel," *Israel 21C*, December 5, 2012, http://bit.ly/VjsMGr.

33. Israel Chamber of Commerce in China, http://bit.ly/17jGPTO.

34. "Israel-China Signed Historic Cooperation Agreements to Build Eilat Railway," Port2port News Service, July 17, 2012, at Israel Port Development and Assets Co., http://bit.ly/16KoKvI.

35. Ibid.

36. "10bn Business: How Israel Became India's Most Important Partner in Arms Bazaar," *Economic Times* (India), September 23, 2012, http://bit.ly/YMOE4E.

37. "India-Israel Bilateral Relations," Embassy of India, Tel-Aviv, http://bit.ly/HZXGyS.

38. "India-Israel Trade Rises to $6 Billion in 2012–2013," *Hindu Business Line*, July 7, 2013, http://bit.ly/11sQKbm.

39. "Indo-Israel FTA Likely by Mid-2013," *Hindu*, July 30, 2012, http://bit.ly/OD6Xl6.

40. Ibid.; Anupama Airy, "India, Israel Set to Triple Trade," *Hindustan Times*, November 27, 2012, http://bit.ly/U16QP0.

41. David Wurmser, "The Geopolitics of Israel's Offshore Gas Reserves," Jerusalem Center for Public Affairs, April 4, 2013, http://bit.ly/14LlR24.

42. Avital Lahav, "Natural Gas Begins to Flow from Tamar Gas Field," *Ynet News*, March 30, 2013, http://bit.ly/14vYDNp.

43. Amiran Barkat and Hillel Koren, "Leviathan Gas Reserves Raised Again," *Globes*, May 1, 2013, http://bit.ly/16PojWm.

44. Wurmser, "Geopolitics of Gas Reserves."

45. Ibid.

46. Ibid.

47. Ibid.

48. Ibid.

49. Karl Vick, "Tapping the Promised Land: Can Israel Be an Energy Giant?" *Time*, April 30, 2013, http://ti.me/15Xc0XW.

50. Ian Dunt, "British-Israeli Relations Hit New Low After Settlement Proposal," *Politics*, December 3, 2012, http://bit.ly/1fgTDgx.

51. "Conversations with History," Institute of International Studies, University of California at Berkeley, 2002, at http://bit.ly/ieSNJ0.

52. In a 2012 poll Gallup asked a sample of Americans, "In the Middle East situation, are your sympathies more with the Israelis or more with the Palestinians?" Sixty-four percent of respondents said Israelis, 12 percent said Palestinians, and 23 percent expressed no preference. Lydia Saad, "Americans' Sympathies for Israel Match All-Time High," Gallup, March 15, 2013, http://bit.ly/WtkeRR.

53. "Gates: Prospects for U.S.-NATO Alliance Dim," CBS News, June 10, 2011, http://cbsn.ws/jMccCa.

54. Phillip Carter, "The French Connection: Why Is the United States Paying for Its Ally's Adventure in Africa?" Foreign Policy, January 24, 2013.

55. Carter, "The French Connection."

CHAPTER 17: DOES THE ISRAELI ONE-STATE PLAN MAKE SENSE FOR ISRAEL?

1. While opinions vary widely on the issue depending on the questions asked, two polls taken at almost exactly the same time, ahead of Israel's parliamentary elections, indicate the basic trend. In one, 53.5 percent of Israelis said they support the two-state model in theory, and 54 percent said it wasn't realistic. Mati Tuchfeld, "Israelis Want Two-State Solution, But Don't Believe It Will Happen," Israel Hayom, January 4, 2013, http://bit.ly/15tThBD.

   In the second, 45.4 percent of Israelis opposed the view that "two states for two peoples is the desired solution for a peace agreement with the Palestinians," while only 40.6 percent said they favored it. Daniel Tauber, "Poll: More Israelis Against the Two-State Solution Than For It," Jewish Press, January 3, 2013, http://bit.ly/X2LUv2. What these polls and multiple other surveys show is that the majority of Israelis believe that the Palestinians are unwilling to accept Israel's minimal demands for a peaceful resolution of the conflict on the basis of partition. These demands include Israeli insistence on defensible borders, Palestinian abandonment of their demand for unlimited Arab immigration to Israel under the "right of return," the retention of Israeli control of Jewish neighborhoods built outside of the 1949 partition lines in Jerusalem, and major Israeli population centers in Judea and Samaria, Palestinian recognition of Israel's right to exist as a Jewish state and abrogation of further territorial claim against Israel.

2. The poll was taken of Jewish Israelis. Avi Dagani and Dr. Rina Dagani, "The Public's Positions and Views Regarding Israeli Control of Judea and Samaria" (Hebrew), Geocartographia Information, Ariel University, April 2013.

3. Khaled Abu Toameh and Gil Hoffman, "Netanyahu on Prisoner Release: Sometimes PMs Have to Make Unpopular Choices for Good of Country," Jerusalem Post, July 27, 2013.

4. "Terrorists' Murder Victims (Partial List)—2013," Almagor Terror Victims Association, July 27, 2013, http://bit.ly/15WaAJT.

5. "Poll: 84% of Israeli Jews Against Palestinian Prisoner Release," *Israel Hayom*, July 26, 2013, http://bit.ly/12sVDBM.

6. Abu Toameh and Hoffman, "Netanyahu on Prisoner Release."

7. "Attacks by Terrorists Released 'Without Blood on Their Hands,'" Almagor Terror Victims Association, undated, http://bit.ly/1dnkXxX.

8. Elhanan Miller, "Top PA Official: We Haven't Agreed to Negotiate Yet," *Times of Israel*, July 21, 2013.

9. Atilla Somfalvi, "U.S. Confirms: Peace Talks to Begin Monday," *Ynet News*, July 28, 2013, http://bit.ly/15Xi8Mt.

10. Khaled Abu Toomeh, "PLO Official: Palestinians 'Seriously Considering' Declaring Failure of Peace Talks," *Jerusalem Post*, October 9, 2013.

11. Daniel Pipes, "Thoughts on the Release of 104 Palestinian Murderers," *National Review*, July 27, 2013.

12. In July 2013 Israelis opposed a deal with the Palestinians by 61 percent to 26 percent. Israeli Jews opposed a prospective deal by 71 percent to 18 percent. Aaron Lerner, "Poll: 61%:26% Israelis Oppose Expected Deal with Palestinians," July 23, 2013, http://bit.ly/12IemYe.

13. Yoram Ettinger, "Defying Demographic Projections," *Israel Hayom*, April 5, 2013, http://bit.ly/16BnlKH.

14. "The Israeli Economy: International Perspective, A Comparison of Recent Economic Developments in Israel and the Developed World 2009–2012," Israel Ministry of Finance, January 2013, at http://bit.ly/12jMOYI.

15. Zeev Klein and *Israel Hayom* staff, "Israel Has 5th Highest Life Expectancy Among OECD Countries," *Israel Hayom*, April 5, 2012, http://bit.ly/I2ijNW.

16. "OECD Better Life Index—Israel," April 2013, http://bit.ly/1aRpx7.

17. "Poll: Overwhelming 92% of Israelis Proud of Their Country," Zionist Organization of America, April 18, 2013, http://bit.ly/1fgVPEN.

18. Ilan Ben Zion, "Terrorist Attacks in West Bank, Jerusalem on the Rise," *Times of Israel*, January 7, 2013.

19. On April 30, 2013, Eviatar Borovsky, an Israeli actor, was stabbed to death at a bus stop in Samaria by a terrorist from Fatah's Al Aksa Martyrs' Brigades. The terror group said on its website that it had "received a green light to carry out military actions against Israeli targets." The only group that could have given such a green light was the Fatah leadership. And indeed, Fatah leaders praised the attack while criticizing their one colleague who sought to distance the movement from responsibility. See "Criticism of Fatah Official Who Expressed Reservations Regarding Tapuach Junction Terrorist Attack," Middle East Media Research Institute, May 2, 2013, http://bit.ly/18GZ8Sr.

20. According to the Congressional Research Service, spending on the security services constituted 31 percent of the PA's GDP in 2011. With more than

64,000 security personnel on its books, the Palestinians' ratio of security forces to citizenry is more than ten times higher than the U.S. ratio. The number of Palestinian security personnel was greater than the number of Palestinian education, health, and social services personnel combined. See Jim Zanotti, "U.S. Foreign Aid to the Palestinians," Congressional Research Service, January 18, 2013, http://bit.ly/9TvY4j.

21. Andrea Levin, "The Media's Tunnel Vision," *Middle East Quarterly* 3, no. 4 (December 1996), pp. 3–9, http://bit.ly/9x9FpY; Akiva Eldar, "Jerusalem Demolitions May Spark Repeat of 1996 riots," *Haaretz*, March 10, 1996.

22. Gal Luft, "Reforming the Palestinian Security Services," *Policy Watch* 382, Washington Institute for NearEast Policy Research, May 15, 2002, http://bit.ly/14EC1vB..

23. Robert Dreyfuss, "U.S. General Builds a Palestinian Army," *Nation*, May 10, 2009.

24. Aaron Kalman, "Third Intifadah Has Already Started, IDF Officer Says," *Times of Israel*, January 6, 2013.

25. Khaled Abu Toameh, "Iran Enters the Peace Process," Gatestone Institute International Policy Council, July 29, 2013, http://bit.ly/1c5w7G3.

26. Avi Bell, conversation with author, April 15, 2013.

CHAPTER 18: AMERICA, ISRAEL, AND THE ONE-STATE PLAN

1. John Kerry, "Remarks to Special Program on Breaking the Impasse," World Economic Forum, May 26, 2013, http://1.usa.gov/18kyoLD.

2. Ibid.

3. Ibid.

4. Tovah Lazaroff and Khaled Abu Toameh, "Kerry Holds Meetings with Abbas, Livni in Amman," *Jerusalem Post*, May 25, 2013.

5. Khaled Abu Toameh, "Palestinians Threaten Their Own Businessmen," Gatestone Institute International Policy Council, May 31, 2013, http://bit.ly/16v8MMB.

6. Khaled Abu Toameh, "Palestinians: Why Abbas Chose This Prime Minister," Gatestone Institute International Policy Council, June 2, 2013, http://bit.ly/1aVQYa2.

7. Evelyn Gordon, "Abbas: PLO Charter Reflects What Palestinians Want," *Commentary*, June 3, 2013.

8. Aaron David Miller, "Wooing the Gods of the Peace Process," *Foreign Policy*, December 20, 2010.

9. Daniel Pipes, "Don't Deal with Terrorists," *USA Today*, January 25, 2006, http://www.danielpipes.org/3309/dont-deal-with-terrorists.

10. Andrew C. McCarthy, *The Grand Jihad: How Islam and the Left Sabotage America* (New York: Encounter, 2010), pp. 25–26.

11. See "Obama Tells Al Arabiya Peace Talks Should Resume," *Al Arabiya News*, January 27, 2009, http://bit.ly/j1tBV; and "Full Text: President Barack Obama's speech to the Muslim World," June 4, 2009, at http://ti.me/IbB7Q.

12. David Spillius, "Barack Obama Criticized for 'Bowing' to King Abdullah of Saudi Arabia," *Telegraph*, April 8, 2009.

13. "Remarks by President Obama to the Turkish Parliament," White House, April 6, 2009, http://1.usa.gov/Ey7xD

14. Acting on advice he received from American Jewish supporters, during his visit to Israel in March 2013, Obama gave strong voice to the Jewish people's historic bonds to the land of Israel. But the four years between those remarks and his initial speech in Egypt, and the fact that he made that statement to Israelis—who already know about those ties—rather than to Muslims, who deny their existence, rendered his remarks insignificant from the perspective of Islamists. They likely viewed his statement as a move forced upon him by a Jewish conspiracy. Full text of the speech found at "Full text of Obama's Jerusalem speech," *Jerusalem Post*, March 21, 2013, http://www.jpost.com/Diplomacy-and-Politics/Full-text-of-Obamas-Jerusalem-speech-307327.

15. After Israel agreed to release 104 Palestinian terrorists from its prisons, and after Kerry succeeded in securing Abbas's agreement to send negotiators to Washington to meet with Israeli representatives, Abbas and his advisers insisted they would negotiate nothing. Israel could accept or reject their terms, but they would speak only about technical issues. See Noah Browning, "Abbas Wants 'Not a Single Israeli' in a Future Palestinian State," Reuters, July 29, 2013, http://reut.rs/13qs5jf.

16. Michael Gordon, Eric Schmitt, and Tim Arango, "Flow of Arms to Syria Through Iraq Persists, to U.S. Dismay," *New York Times*, December 1, 2012.

17. Matt Bradley, "Morsi Promises to Free 'Blind Sheik' from U.S. Prison," *Wall Street Journal*, June 29, 2012, http://on.wsj.com/OIKIeP.

18. Adam Kredo, "Left Out in the Cold: U.S. Aid Worker in Egypt Sentenced to Two Years in Prison," *Washington Free Beacon*, June 4, 2013, http://bit.ly/15xNQjn.

19. Ariel Cohen and Charles Rollet, "Egyptian Opposition Slams Obama, U.S. Ambassador," *Daily Caller*, July 1, 2013, http://bit.ly/19Q1MLr.

20. The day before the Egyptian military ousted Mubarak from power and so paved the way for the Muslim Brotherhood to run and win Egypt's first open elections, James Clapper, the director of national intelligence, told the House Select Committee on Intelligence that the Muslim Brotherhood is a "largely secular" movement that devotes itself to social work. Z. Byron Wolf, "Director of National Intelligence James Clapper: Muslim Brotherhood 'Largely Secular,'" ABC News, February 10, 2011, http://abcn.ws/zrEDqz.

21. Mark Thiessen, "Obama Blew It in Egypt—Again," *Washington Post*, July 8, 2013.

22. Adam Entous, "Crackdown in Egypt Fans U.S. Fears," *Wall Street Journal,* July 29, 2013.

23. "Israel: Kerry's Efforts Yield 'Hardcore' Palestinian Prisoners Release," Associated Press, July 20, 2013.

24. Jonathan Tobin, "Would Americans Release Terrorist Killers?" *Commentary,* July 28, 2013.

25. Jamie Weinstein, "Israel's Troubling Release of Palestinian Prisoners," *Daily Caller,* July 28, 2013.

26. Jim Zanotti, "U.S. Foreign Aid to the Palestinians," Congressional Research Service, January 18, 2013, pp. 6–7, http://bit.ly/9TvY4j.

27. Jonathan Schanzer, "The Brothers Abbas," *Foreign Policy,* June 5, 2012.

28. Zanotti, "U.S. Foreign Aid."

29. Caroline B. Glick, "Column One: Israel's American-Made Foes," *Jerusalem Post,* June 8, 2010; Robert Dreyfuss, "U.S. General Builds a Palestinian Army," *Nation,* May 10, 2009.

INDEX

Abbas, Mahmoud, xv
  authoritarian practices, 153
  denying Jewish history, 181–183
  Hamas and, 71
  Holocaust denial, 69–71
  Munich Olympics massacre and,
    67
  PA prime minister, 68–69
  on PLO goals, 248–249
  policies, 72–73
  rejecting statehood and peace,
    72–74
  resignation threat, 195–196
  terrorism and, 71–72
  on terrorist release, 247
  U.S. embracing, 68
  Zionism and, 70
Abdel-Rahman, Omar, 254
Abdullah II, 118, 212–213
Abu al-Hawa, Muhammad, 144
Abu Bakr, Mohammed, 214
Abu Harabish, Mahmoud Salam
    Saliman, 257
Abu Issa, Issam, 75
Abu Libdeh, Hasan, 122
Abu Meddein, Freih, 115, 145
Abu Rihan, Jamal, 150
AEI (American Enterprise Institute),
    126
Ahmadinejad, Mahmoud, 70, 253

AIPAC (American-Israel Public
    Affairs Committee), 125
AIRDG (American-Israel
    Demographic Research Group),
    125, 127, 129, 132
Allenby, Edmund, 26
Allon, Yigal, 111–112
Almagor Terror Victims Association,
    236
Alzamili, Yussuf, 181
American Enterprise Institute (AEI),
    126
American-Israel Demographic
    Research Group (AIRDG), 125,
    127, 129, 132
American-Israel Public Affairs
    Committee (AIPAC), 125
Annapolis Peace Summit, 9, 74
Anti-Americanism, 90
Anti-Semitism, 52
  of Morsi, 209
  political force in Europe, 89
  of Sadat, 93
  worldwide surge, 133
Anti-Zionism, 52–53
Arab League, 45, 46, 56, 93, 110
Arabs
  Arafat as bane of, 56–57
  Arafat inciting, 157–158
  hatred of Israel, 92–96

Arabs (*cont'd.*)
  Israel attraction, 159–161
  of Mandatory Palestine, 29, 31
  modern politics, 39–40
  Soviet-Arab narrative against
    Israel, 90–92
Arab Spring, 206, 241
Arab Terror War of 1936
  British Mandate and, 33–35
  Husseini and, 32–33
  Peel Commission Report and,
    33–35
  White Paper of 1939 and, 34–39
Arafat, Yassir, xv, xvi, 48, 124
  bane of Arabs, hope of West,
    56–57
  at Camp David peace summit,
    2000, 19, 166, 199
  Clinton and, 15, 21, 64
  death of, 65, 82
  denying Jewish history, 181
  diplomatic convoy attack, 2003,
    and, 85–86
  Fatah founded by, 4, 53–54
  Gulf War of 1991 and, 94
  Hamas and, 65
  Husseini as mentor, 50–51
  inciting Israeli Arabs, 157–158
  international terrorism architect,
    57–60
  intifada against Israel, 61–63
  Iran and, 59
  Israel-Soviet political war and,
    52–53
  media and, 149–150
  modern Palestinian movement and,
    53–55
  Nasser and, 55
  PLO leader, 49
  Saddam Hussein and, 63
  terrorism, 7, 49–66
  U.S. rescue, 63–66

  world statesman, 60–61
Ark of the Covenant, 186
Aron, Raymond, 89
Ashton, Catherine, 222–223
Assad, Bashar, 95, 215–218, 220
al-Assad, Hafez, 136
Atatürk, Mustafa Kemal, 39
Atrash, Milad, 155, 161
Atrash, Muhammad, 155, 161
Avner, Yehuda, 136, 141
Azzam, Abdul Rahman, 46

Baker, Alan, 222–223
Balfour, Arthur, 24
Balfour Declaration, 26, 30
al-Banna, Hassan, 39
Barak, Ehud, 16, 17, 18–19, 72, 98, 124
Begin, Menachem, 136, 139–140
Bell, Avi, 174–175, 177, 244–245
Ben-Ami, Shlomo, 19, 21–22
bin Laden, Osama, 58
Bishara, Azmi, 157–158
Biton, Sharon, 132
Blum, Yehuda, 140, 176
Bols, Louis, 26
Bolton, Nathan, 164
Bourguiba, Habib, 94
Brezhnev, Leonid, 55
British Mandate, xv. *See also* Mandate
    for Palestine
  Arab Terror War of 1936 and,
    33–34
  end of, 46–47
  establishment, 248
  Great Britain betraying, 30–32
  Husseini, Nazis and, 40–44
  Husseini shaping modern Arab
    politics and, 39–40
  Peel Commission Report, 33–35
  postwar period, 1945-1948,
    44–48
  uniqueness of, 170

White Paper of 1939, 34–39
World War I and, 24–28
Buck, Xavier, 229
Bush, George H. W., 63–64, 93
Bush, George W.
  demands erosion, 9
  on diplomatic convoy attack, 2003,
    85
  Hezbollah and, 95
  on Israeli occupation, 12
  one-state plan and, 250–254
  PA and, 75
  on Palestinian reform, 5–8, 11,
    67–68
  Sharansky on, 8–9
  on terrorists, 88

Camp David peace summit, 2000,
    xxiii, 19, 124, 166, 199, 251
Carter, Jimmy, 91
Ceauşescu, Nicolae, 89
Cheney, Dick, 5, 101
China, 230
Christians
  in IDF, 156
  PA land sale law against, 146–148
  PLO persecution, 147–148
Clinton, Bill, 10, 47–48
  Arafat and, 15, 21, 64
  backing Barak campaign, 18–19
  Israel and PLO peace process,
    15–16
  legacy of blind faith, 15–23, 249–
    250
  parameters for final peace, 20–23
Cohn, Norman, 40
Communism, 52
Crossroads to Israel, 1917–1948 (Sykes),
    30–31

Dalin, David, 29
Damour, Lebanon, 147

David, Assaf, 212
Dayton, Keith, 199, 240–241
Dead Sea Scrolls, 182
Declaration of Principles, 16, 64
Defensible borders, 111–112, 113
De Gaulle, Charles, 87, 89
De Gaulle, Israel and the Jews (Aron),
    89
Demographic fraud, 125–130
Druze, 97, 123
  conscription, 156
  in Golan Heights, 136–138, 140, 197

Eban, Abba, 112
Eberstadt, Nicholas, 126–127
EEC (European Economic
    Community), 90
Egypt
  meaning of revolutionary for Israel,
    208–209
  Muslim Brotherhood and, 207–
    208, 210, 241, 254–255
  one-state plan response, 206–211
  strategic value, 206
Eichmann, Adolf, 44
Elad, Shlomo, 58–59
Erdogan, Recep Tayyip, 95, 180
Erekat, Saeb, 74, 247
Eshkol, Levi, 141
Eurabia: The Euro-Arab Axis (Ye'or), 90
Eurobarometer poll, 224
Europe. See also One-state plan,
    European responses
  European Court of Auditors, 76
  Israel policies, 222–225
  limitations of leverage over Israel,
    229
  obsession with Jewish state, 225–
    228
European Economic Community
    (EEC), 90
Extremism, ix, 69

Faitelson, Yakov, 130, 132

Fatah
  Al Aksa Martyrs Brigades,
    240
  Arafat founding, 4, 53–54
  constitution, 54
  corruption, 82
  Hamas agreement, 11
  Judea, Samaria and, 83
  outdoing Hamas, 197
  PLO and, 4
  terrorism, 59

Fatwa, 33, 145

Fayyad, Salam, 68–69
  denying Jewish history, 181–182
  economic warrior, 77–78
  man of war, 76–77
  PA prime minister, 74–75
  U.S. favorite reformer, 74–76

Finkelstein, Israel, 186

Fogel, Ehud, 200–201

Fogel, Elad, 201

Fogel, Hadas, 201

Fogel, Ruth, 200–201

Fogel, Tamar, 201

Fogel, Yishai, 201

Fogel, Yoav, 201

Foreign policy, U.S.
  cost of denying Israel's importance,
    96–99
  false assumptions about Middle
    East, 99–100
  Iraq and, 98–99
  Israel alliance, 101–105
  Israel and Palestinians, 87–92
  Lebanon and, 96–98
  misunderstanding Arab hatred of
    Israel, 92–96
  overview, 85–87
  PLO dialogue, 91
  Western Europe influencing,
    87–92

Gaddafi, Muammar, 94

Galloway, George, 164

Gates, Robert, 233

al-Gaylani, Rashid Ali, 41–42

Gaza, xviii, xxi
  emigration, 132–133
  excluded from one-state plan,
    133–135
  Gaza-Jericho Agreement, 49–50
  Hamas in, 134–135
  Israel policy, 62
  Israel withdrawal, 83–84, 124

Geneva Conventions, 168–169, 223

George, David Lloyd, 24, 26, 30

Gil, Moshe, 190

Gingrich, Newt, xii

Ginsburg, Yitzhak, 3

Golan Heights, xviii
  control significance, 139–140
  Druze in, 136–138, 140, 197
  Golan Heights Law, 136–140

Goldstone, Richard, 226–227

Gorenberg, Gershom, 152

Great Britain. See also British
    Mandate
  British Mandate betrayal, 30–32
  failures, 23
  Palestine Mandate and, 26

Grobba, Fritz, 41

Gulf War of 1991, 63–64, 91
  Arab League during, 93
  Arafat and, 94

Gunther, John, 38

Hagel, Chuck, 84

Halul, Shady, 161

Hamas, 51. See also Muslim
    Brotherhood
  Abbas and, 71
  Arafat and, 65
  budget, xxi
  covenant, 79

electoral victory, 82–83
extremism, 69
Fatah agreement, 11
founding and ideology, 78–80
gaining ground, 63–64
in Gaza, 134–135
international fortunes, 84
Iran and, 82–83
jihad against Jews, 79
Muslim Brotherhood and, 79, 134
Obama and, 83–84
outdoing Fatah, 197
overview, 78–80
PLO and, xxii
Rice on, 80–81
roots of popularity, 80–84
terrorism, 4
totalitarianism, 79
Hamdallah, Rami, 69
Hariri, Saad, 219
Haskia, Anet, 160, 161
Hazony, Yoram, 163
Hezbollah, xi, 83, 238
    George W. Bush and, 95
    one-state plan response, 218–220
    Rice and, 95
    threats, 217–218
Himmler, Heinrich, 44
Hitler, Adolf, 38, 40–41
    Husseini and, 42–43
    Jewish annihilation, 43–44
Hobbes, Thomas, 163
Ho Chi Minh, 57
Holocaust
    Abbas denial, 69–71
    aftermath, 53
    survivors, 45–46
Hope-Simpson report, 30
Human Rights Watch (HRW),
    150–151
Hussein, King, 56, 62, 94, 117–118
Hussein, Saddam, 51, 63, 94

Husseini, Haj Amin, xv–xvi
    Arab Terror.War of 1936 and, 32–33
    Arafat mentor, 50–51
    destruction of Zionism and, 33
    genocidal hatred of Jews, 29
    geopolitical environment and, 53
    grand mufti appointment, 28, 33
    Hitler and, 42–43
    leadership role, 28–30
    as Nazi agent, 38, 40–44
    Passover riots and, 27
    Protocols of the Elders of Zion and, 40
    shaping modern Arab politics,
        39–40
    terrorism, 29–30

ICBS (Israel Central Bureau of
    Statistics), 130–131
ICC (International Criminal Court),
    202–203
IDF. *See* Israel Defense Force (IDF)
IMF, 68, 76–77
Inbar, Efraim, 139
India, 230
Indigenous people. *See also* Jewish
    history
    overview, 179–184
    Palestinian theft of artifacts,
        187–189
    rights to Judea and Samaria,
        184–187
    settlement history, 189–191
International Criminal Court (ICC),
    202–203
International law
    definition, 167–169
    Land of Israel and, 170–174
    modern Middle East and, 169–170
Iran. *See also* Hezbollah
    aggression, xi
    Hamas and, 82–83
    nuclear weapons, xi, xx, 103, 220

Iraq, x
  nuclear reactor, 101–102
  U.S. foreign policy and, 98–99
Ir David Foundation, 188
Islamism, 28, 255–256
Israel. *See also* Land of Israel
  anti-Israel forces, 161–162
  Arab hatred of, 92–96
  Arafat incitement of Israeli Arabs,
    157–158
  attraction for Arabs, 159–161
  Citizenship Law, 119
  defensible borders, xiv
  economy, 204
  energy exporter, 231–232
  European policies toward, 222–225
  Gaza policy, 62
  Gaza withdrawal, 83–84, 124
  integrationist impulse, 158–161
  international position, xxi
  intifada against, 61–63
  Israel Jordan war, xiii
  Jewish democracy, 162–163
  Judea and Samaria policy, 62
  Obama policy, 10–11
  as occupiers, xxv
  Operation Defense Shield, 6
  overview, 155–157
  PA incitement against, 8
  peace treaties, xiii
  PLO destruction of, 18
  PLO peace process, 15–16
  revolutionary Egypt and, 208–209
  Rice on, 9
  sovereign rights, 244–245
  Soviet-Arab narrative against,
    90–92
  Soviet political war and, 52–53
  strategic vulnerabilities, 13
  supporting one-state plan, 235–237
  terror attacks against, 3–4
  U.S. ally, xxv, 101–105, 256–259
  U.S. policy toward, 10, 87–92
Israel Central Bureau of Statistics
  (ICBS), 130–131
Israel Defense Force (IDF), xxii, 6
  Christians in, 156
  counterterror operations, 73
  forces, 98
  Golani Infantry Brigade, 155
  operations, 226
  as restraining force, 97
  Syria and, 94
Israeli sovereignty, xiii, xviii, 243
  defining international law, 167–169
  international law and Land of
    Israel, 170–174
  international law and modern
    Middle East, 169–170
  overview, 164–167
  Palestinians claims to sovereign
    rights, 177–178
  rights and, 174–177
  uti possidetis juris principle, 174–175
Ivry, David, 101

Jabotinsky, Zev, 27
Jerusalem, xiv, xxiii, 142
Jewish people. *See also* Indigenous
  people
  Abbas denying, 181–183
  Arafat denying, 181
  Fayyad denying, 181–182
  fertility rates, 131
  Hamas Jihad against, 79
  Husseini's genocidal hatred of, 29
  Jewish democracy, 162–163
  Jewish National Home, 25
  Jewish property rights, xvi
  Jihad against, 39–40
  PA education on, 18
  PA land sale law against, 146–148
  in Palestine Mandate, 33–35, 37–39
Jihad, 4, 33

of Hamas, 79
against Jews, 39–40
Johnson, Lyndon, 140–141
Jordan
  Hashemite regime, 105
  illegal occupations, 175–176
  Israel Jordan war, xiii
  Jordanian Law, 145
  one-state plan response, 212–215
  in Six Day War, 1967, 114, 141
Joseph, Eleanor, 155, 161
Josephus, 190
Judea and Samaria, xiii–xv, xix,
    109–111, 258. *See also* Israeli
    sovereignty; West Bank
  applying sovereignty in, 178, 243
  demographic trends, xvii
  Fatah and, 83
  under Israeli rule, 112–117
  Israel policy, 62
  Israel rights in, xix, 114
  military control, 200
  Palestinians in, xvii, xix, 260
  rights to, 184–187
  terrorist infrastructure, 6

Kader, Hatem Abdul, 159
Kadima Party, 124
Kamrava, Mehran, 148–149, 154
Karinaoui, Attef, 160–161
Karsh, Efraim, 157, 162
Kerry, John, 95, 224, 237
  Netanyahu and, 257
  one-state plan and, 246–249
  on Palestinian economy, 246–247
KGB, 89
Khaddam, Abdul Halim, 136
Khartoum Declaration of Three No's,
    110
Khomeini, Ayatollah, 56
Knesset, 221
  elections, 119–120, 158, 160

Knesset Law, 136, 140–142, 162
  members, 156–157
Kokhba, Simon Bar, 179
Kosygin, Aleksei, 55
Kupper, Beate, 224
Kuttab, Douad, 150

Labor Party, 16
Land of Israel
  identity in, 184–185
  international law and, 170–174
  national history, 181
Lauterpacht, Elihu, 173–174
League of Nations, xiii, 26. *See also*
    Mandate for Palestine
  end of existence, 172
  general mandates, 169
  Permanent Mandates Commission,
    36
Lebanon, 56–57
  one-state plan response, 218–220
  in U.S. foreign policy, 96–98
Likud Party, 221
Linkevicius, Linas, 222
Livni, Tzipi, 124

MacDonald, Ramsay, 30
Madrid Peace Conference of 1992, 94
Makor Rishon, xxiii
al-Maliki, Nouri, 218
Mandate for Palestine, xiv, 26, 102,
    140, 170–172, 185–186. *See also*
    British Mandate
  Arabs, 34, 41
  close Jewish settlement in, 223
  Jews in, 33–35, 37–39
  United Nations and, 46
Mansour, Adly, 208
Mashaal, Khaled, 80, 84
Masri, Zafir, 62
Meinertzhagen, Richard, 27
Meir-Levi, David, 182

Merari, Ariel, 58–59

Middle East
international law and, 169–170
Obama on instability, 13–14
security, 258
U.S. false assumptions, 99–100

Middle East Quartet, 7

Mizrahi, Avi, 198–200

Moeller, Michael, 198

Montell, Jessica, 227

Morsi, Muhammad, 134, 206–207
on Abdel-Rahman, 254
anti-Semitism, 209
overthrow, 209–210, 241

Mubarak, Hosni, 100, 134, 206, 208,
211, 230

Mughiyeh, Imad, 97

Muslim Brotherhood, xi, 11, 93, 95
Egypt and, 207–208, 210, 241,
254–255
formation, 39
Hamas and, 79, 134
Obama and, 83, 255–256
popularity, 100

Muslim world, ix–x, 44, 51, 127,
252–254

Nasser, Gamal Abdel, 51, 55, 141

National Socialism, 28, 51

NATO, 233

Nazis, 31–32, 38, 40–44

Negotiations Support Unit (NSU),
183–184

Netanyahu, Benjamin, xiii, xxii, 10,
72, 180, 183, 221
concessions, 18
Kerry and, 257
land transfers and, 17–18
U.S. pressuring, 236

NGOs, 149, 181, 226–227

Nixon, Richard, 59

Noel, Cleo, 59

NSU (Negotiations Support Unit),
183–184

Nuremberg Laws, 40

Obama, Barack, x–xi
Hamas and, 83–84
Israel policy, 10–11
on Middle East instability, 13–14
Muslim Brotherhood and, 83,
255–256
Muslim world speech, 252–254
one-state plan and, 250–254
PA and, 75
on Palestinians, 125
on two-state solution, 12

OECD, 238–239

Oil embargo, 1973, xx, 61, 88

Olmert, Ehud, 72, 124

Olympic team massacre, 1972, 58, 67

One-state plan. *See also* Indigenous
people; Israeli sovereignty; Judea
and Samaria; Two-state solution;
*specific responses to (immediately
below)*
advantages, 240–243
background, xii–xiii
dangers of implementing, 238–239
demographic fraud and, 125–130
emigration and, 131–133
fertility hysteria and, 130–131
Gaza exclusion, 133–135
implementation, xvii
international actors, xix–xx
Israel-Palestine differences and,
xvii–xviii
Israeli support, 235–237
Israel's sovereign rights and,
244–245
principles, xv
real demographic threat, 243–244
statistical terror war and, 122–125
success record, 136–143

United States and. *See* One-state
plan, United States and
One-state plan, European responses
China and India and, 230
Israel as energy exporter and,
231–232
limitations of Europe leverage, 229
military option, 233–234
obsession with Jewish state, 225–
228
overview, 221–222
possibilities, 229, 231–232
roots of policies toward Israel,
222–225
summary, 234
One-state plan, introduction, 117–119
Israeli solution, 119–121
Judea and Samaria under Israeli
rule, 112–117
overview, 109–110
search for defensible borders,
111–112, 113
One-state plan, Palestinian responses
diplomatic option, 200–204
overview, 195–198
terrorism option, 198–200
One-state plan, regional responses
Egypt, 206–211
Jordan, 212–215
Lebanon-Hezbollah, 218–220
overview, 203
Syria, 215–218
One-state plan, United States and,
xxi
Clinton legacy, 249–250
embracing plan, 259–260
George W. Bush and, 250–254
Israel as U.S. ally, 256–259
Kerry and, 246–249
Obama and, 250–254
Operation Defensive Shield, 6, 153,
199–200

Operation Desert Storm, 101
*Other Side: Secret Relationship Between
Nazism and Zionism* (Abbas), 70
Oudeh, Mohammed Daoud, 67
Oz-Salzberger, Fania, 163

PA. *See* Palestinian Authority (PA)
Pacepa, Ion, 51, 89–90
Palestine Liberation Organization
(PLO), xiv–xv
Abbas on, 248–249
Arab League and, 56
Arafat as leader, 49
as architects of modern terrorism,
237
demand for Temple Mount in
Jerusalem, 20–21
destruction of Israel and, 18
Fatah and, 4
Hamas and, xxii
on historical claims, 180–181
Israel peace process, 15–16
journalists and, 60
King Hussein and, 62, 94, 117–118
in Lebanon, 56–57
Nasser founding, 55
phased plan, 61
release of terrorists demand, 236
right of return, 214
terrorism, 58–59
U.S. dialogue, 63, 91
war terror, 19–20
Palestinian Authority (PA), xiv–xv
Abbas, Mahmoud, 68–69
budget, 151
Christians persecuted by, 147–148
corruption, 82
creation, 16
destruction of economy, 153–154
anti-Jewish indoctrination, 18
establishment, 116, 144
Fayyad as prime minister, 74–75

Palestinian Authority (*cont'd.*)
  George W. Bush and, 75
  household confiscations, 77
  incitement against Israel, 8
  land sale law against Jews and
    Christians, 146–148
  legal jungle, 144–146
  massacre of collaborators, 152–153
  media and, 149–151
  NGOs and, 149
  Obama and, 75
  terrorism, xxi, xxiii–xxiv, 76–77
  tyranny of, 148–152
  U.S. supporting, 259
Palestinian Central Bureau of
    Statistics (PCBS), 122–123,
    126–130
Palestinian Central Elections
    Commission (PCEC), 126
Palestinian Media Watch (PMW),
    181
Palestinian National Council (PNC),
    62
Palestinians. *See also* One-state plan,
    Palestinian responses
  breaching commitments, xxii
  Bush on reform, 5–8, 11, 67–68
  claims to sovereign rights, 177–178
  denied freedoms, xviii–xix
  fertility hysteria, 130–131
  Judea and Samaria, xvii, xix
  in Judea and Samaria, 260
  nature of, 84
  Obama on, 125
  refugee camps, 244
  refugees, 16–17
  theft of artifacts, 187–189
  U.S. policy, 87–92
Passfield White Paper, 30
Passover riots, 1920, 26–28
PCBS (Palestinian Central Bureau of
    Statistics), 122–123, 126–130

PCEC (Palestinian Central Elections
    Commission), 126
Peel, William, 33–34, 177
Peel Commission Report, 33–35, 37
Peri, Yaakov, 49
Petit, Michael, 97–98
Pi Gelilot explosion, 3–4
PLO. *See* Palestine Liberation
    Organization (PLO)
PMW (Palestinian Media Watch),
    181
PNC (Palestinian National Council),
    62
Politics
  Arab modern, 39–40
  Soviet political war, 52–53
  zero-sum game, ix
Pollock, David, 159
Popular Front for the Liberation of
    Palestine, 4
Popular Resistance Committees, 86
Posner, Michael, 227
Powell, Colin, 5, 85
Power, Samantha, 233
Protocols of the Elders of Zion, 40, *79*,
    157

Al-Qaeda, 51, 58, 88, 217–218
  blocking, 233–234
  forces, 221–222
al-Qidra, Khalid, 115
Qutb, Sayyid, 39

Rabin, Yitzhak, 49
Reagan, Ronald, 59, 97
Red Horizons (Pacepa), 89–90
Reich, Roni, 189
Reza Pahlavi, 42
Rice, Condoleezza, 12–13, 74
  on diplomatic convoy attack, 2003,
    86
  on Hamas, 80–81

Hezbollah and, 95
Iraq nuclear reactor and, 102
on Israel, 9
Rosenne, Meir, 165
Ross, Dennis, 10
Rothmann, John, 29
Roth-Snir, Alon, 164
Rubin, Barry, 59
Rubin, Judith Colp, 59
Rumsfeld, Donald, 100
Rusk, Dean, 141

Sabri, Ikremah, 145
Sadat, Anwar, 93
Safian, Alex, 115
as-Said, Nuri, 41
Salem, Paul, 219–220
Samaria. *See* Judea and Samaria
Samuel, Herbert, 27–28
Schwebel, Steven, 176
Selden, John, 163
September 11, 2001 terrorist attacks, 58
Settlement freeze, xvi
Shabo, Avishai, 4
Shabo, Neria, 4
Shabo, Rachel, 4
Shabo, Zvika, 4
Shah, Apoorvah, 127
Shalit, Gilad, 71
Shamir, Yitzhak, 63
Sharansky, Natan, 8–9
Sharon, Ariel, xiii, 81, 124, 138
Shaw Commission, 30–31
Shi'ites, x, 56, 83, 96–99, 213, 222
Shubaki, Fuad, 65
Six Day War, 1967, xvi, 10
aftermath, 91, 140
Jordan defeat, 114, 141
results, 87–88
Shilo reconstitution, 187
Smith, Lee, 209

Soviet-Arab narrative against Israel, 90–92
Soviet political war, 52–53
Sudan ambassador assassination, 1973, 58
Sunnis, x, 56, 95, 137, 222, 238
Supreme Muslim Council, 28
Sykes, Christopher, 30–31
Syria, xi
civil war, 219
IDF and, 94
one-state plan response, 215–218

Tabernacle, 186–187
Taliban, x–xi, 189
Taylor, Waters, 27
Temple Mount, Jerusalem, 20–21
historical significance, 187–188
sovereignty transfer, 72
Terrorism
Abbas and, 71–72
Almagor Terror Victims Association, 236
Arafat, 7, 49–66
Fatah, 59
Hamas, 4
Husseini, Haj Amin, 29–30
international, 57–60
against Israel, 3–4
Judea and Samaria infrastructure, 6
PA, xxi, xxiii–xxiv, 76–77
as Palestinian response to one-state plan, 198–200
PLO, 58–59, 237
September 11, 2001 terrorist attacks, 58
statistical terror war, 122–125
U.S. counterterror strategy, xxiii
Trans-Jordan, 171–172
Truman, Harry, 45
Two-state solution, ix–xi, 68, 242.
See also One-state plan

Two-state solution (*cont'd.*)
  basis of, xxiv
  embracing, xix
  failure, xv–xvi, xxii
  mythology, 260
  Obama on, 12
  roadmap, 7–8
  tyranny of, xxvi
  U.S. and, xvi–xvii, xxv–xxvi

UN Educational, Scientific
    and Cultural Organization
    (UNESCO), 179–180, 189
United Nations
  Palestine Mandate and, 46
  partition plan, 47, 172–173, 177
  Resolution 67/19, 203
  Resolution 181, 173–174
  Resolution 242, 91
  Resolution 252, 140
  Resolution 478, 142
  Resolution 497, 138
  Resolution 2254, 140
  Resolution 3379, 53, 61, 165–166
  Resolution A/67/L.28, 73
  World Conference against
    Racism, Racial Discrimination,
    Xenophobia, and Related
    Intolerance, 166
United States. *See also* Foreign policy,
    U.S.; One-state plan, United
    States and
  Abbas embraced by, 68
  Arafat rescue, 63–66
  counterterror strategy, xxiii
  Fayyad as favorite reformer, 74–76
  Israel policy, 10
  Israel supported by, xxv
  as liberators, xxv
  Middle East position, x, xii

Netanyahu pressured by, 236
  one-state plan and, xxi
  Palestinian army and, xxiv
  PLO dialogue, 63
  supporting PA, 259
  two-state solution and, xvi–xvii,
    xxv–xxvi
Universal Declaration on Human
    Rights, 145
UN Special Commission on Palestine
    (UNSCOP), 46
U.S.-Israel Strategic Cooperation
    Agreement, 138–139
Uti possidetis juris principle, 174–175

Waqf, 188
Wauchope, Arthur, 32
Weinberger, Caspar, 138
Weiss, Michael, 215–216
West Bank, 176, 185
Wheeler, Earl, 112
White Paper of 1939, 34–39
World War I, 24–28
Wurmser, David, 231
Wye Plantation Accords, 18

Ye'or, Bat, 90
Yom Kippur War, 1973, 88
Yusuf, Madhat, 187

Zer, Moshe, 115
Zimmerman, Bennett, 125
Zionism, 25
  Abbas and, 70
  anti-Zionism, 52–53
  dawning of, 122, 191
  Husseini and, 33
  Palestine Administration and, 27
  racism and, 53, 165–167
Zion Mule Corps, 25